£22·60

AWN

High and Low Politics in Modern Britain

High and Low Politics in Modern Britain

Ten Studies

Edited by
Michael Bentley
and
John Stevenson

CLARENDON PRESS · OXFORD
1983

Oxford University Press, Walton Street, Oxford OX2 6DP

London Glasgow New York Toronto
Delhi Bombay Calcutta Madras Karachi
Kuala Lumpur Singapore Hong Kong Tokyo
Nairobi Dar es Salaam Cape Town
Melbourne Auckland
and associated companies in
Beirut Berlin Ibadan Mexico City Nicosia

Oxford is a trade mark of Oxford University Press

Published in the United States by
Oxford University Press, New York

British Library Cataloguing in Publication Data

High and low politics in modern Britain.
1. Great Britain—Politics and government—
19th century   2. Great Britain—Politics and
government—20th century
I. Bentley, Michael   II. Stevenson, John
320.941   JN216

ISBN 0-19-822652-7

Library of Congress Cataloging in Publication Data

Main entry under title:

High and low politics in modern Britain.

Includes index.
1. Great Britain—Politics and government—19th
century—Addresses, essays, lectures. 2. Great Britain—
Politics and government—20th century—Addresses,
essays, lectures. I. Bentley, Michael, 1948- .
II. Stevenson, John, 1946- .
JN 327.H53   1983   320.941   83-8224
ISBN 0-19-822652-7

Typeset by Joshua Associates, Oxford
Printed in Great Britain by
The Thetford Press Ltd.
Thetford, Norfolk

Contents

Introduction

This volume comprises ten essays intended to highlight various aspects of the British political environment over the past century and a half. It has grown out of an interest shared by the editors in a genre of historical writing concerning 'high politics' that has established itself, since the mid-1960s, as a major force in explanations of political practice in Britain. Few modern studies remain uncoloured by the view that a half-closed world peopled by senior politicians, civil servants, and publicists perpetuated in post-Reform Britain ground rules of party government of which the masses knew little and which the coming of 'democracy' did little to supplant. Yet although the literature to which this instinct has given rise is now voluminous, its character has proved uniformly forbidding and inaccessible to a broader audience: it has tended to congeal into monographs and articles in the learned journals as densely textured narratives of closely confined problems of government. In some degree this result followed naturally from the nature of the subject-matter confronted by historians interested in the working of politics 'at the top' and the forms of evidence which such activity typically deposited in the archives. On the other hand, there seems no logical impediment to adopting a more relaxed and synoptic approach when thinking about the nature of high politics; and it may be that the essay form better suits the freer treatment that might encourage students and workers in adjacent fields to discover interesting questions in high-political discussion to apply to their own areas of interest and periods of study. Certainly this ambition has presented one rationale for commissioning the writing of these studies.

Another arises from the lack of resolution emerging from a 'debate' over high-political methodology which was conducted with considerable ferocity in the first half of the 1970s but has since withered away. Many of the labels attached to writers on both sides of the argument have since become illegible or unstuck: proponents of high-political explanations have manifested ideological ambitions and those who once caricatured them sometimes now see sense where formerly they saw sin. A changing mood perhaps prescribes a taking of stock to discover the destinations to which the high-political argument has led and those it never reached. Asking historians who have written on all sides of the question to return to the problem in considering a topic of their own choice presents, we believe, a more attractive way of proceeding than by formulating an arid manual of method and criticism. Each author has, in the first place, written what he wanted to write rather than bent the tendency of his mind in some direction dictated from without. The essays therefore stand by themselves as individual perspectives and possess a validity independent of any 'school' or party line. A second recommendation lay in obviating the repetitive statements and hortatory tone that a volume directed singly at high politics as a historiographical phenomenon might have invited. By persuading our contributors to write on their own highly variegated areas of specialism it has been possible to produce a collection useful to readers for whom historiographical considerations remain a secondary interest.

Certain themes nevertheless supply an undertow of argument throughout the book. All the contributions are concerned with the problem of how influence, information, and ideology are dispersed within a hierarchic political structure. In some of them the question arises in a study of policy formation and the pressures—popular, administrative, intellectual, ministerial—which help determine governmental behaviour. Dr Harris, Dr Stevenson, Dr Pelling, and Professor Watt approach the interpretation of high politics in this way though the focus of their discussion ranges over most areas of policy. Other contributors demonstrate an interest in the fortunes and strategies of low-political organizations in a hostile environment. Professor MacDonagh's survey of O'Connell's Irish party in the 1840s and Dr Harrison's consideration of the politics of the women's movement illustrate one sub-plot in such a story; a rather different one is suggested by Dr Morgan's analysis of populist and élitist moods in the history of the Labour party. A third group of studies may be discerned which treat the relationship between 'ideas' and politics with one eye on the apparent erasure of ideology from the writings of students of high politics. Dr Hilton returns to the perennial difficulty of Gladstone's ideological complexion and Dr Clarke examines, from the other side of the fence as it were, the political content of Keynes's thought. Dr Bentley's essay, meanwhile, presents a more synoptic study of the relationship. Yet all these differences between the contributors amount to shifts of scope, emphasis, and tone rather than any fundamental denial or dismissal of the centrality of the issues. Penetrating all the studies is an interest in treating the history of political institutions in Britain as emblems of an occult society.

We have organized the book on chronological lines rather than broken up the subject-matter into sections. Students may need to move around the volume to discover the lines of enquiry that interest them but it has been thought worthwhile to arrange the essays so that they can be read seriatim like the chapters of a book. Authors have been left to decide whether they wished to offer a case-study or a more expansive treatment, and some blurring of boundaries between the contributions has been the inevitable (and not undesirable) result. It hardly needs saying that gaps none the less remain: a collection of this kind can expect neither to exhaust the field of enquiry nor even to present examples of all its forms of scholarship. But we believe that these studies go a considerable way towards providing undergraduates and a general historical readership with a range of perspectives to stimulate discussion among students of the modern party system and raise questions pertinent for historians of government, ideology, and popular politics.

A project of this kind draws heavily on the goodwill and patience of its contributors and we are pleased gratefully to acknowledge the co-operation of everyone involved in the writing of these essays. Some historians not represented here have been generous with their encouragement in correspondence, and again we are in their debt. We owe a special obligation to Mr Ivon Asquith of Oxford University Press for his interest in and support for this venture.

Sheffield, March 1983   MICHAEL BENTLEY
                                          JOHN STEVENSON

1

O'Connell and Repeal, 1840–1845
Oliver MacDonagh

I

The various issues of 'high' and 'low' politics are usually discussed in terms of the struggles for office, or for leadership or decisive influence in a major party, within the parliamentary system. But there is quite another range of pertinent questions—where the party is by its very nature excluded from cabinet participation (let alone the monopoly of office); where the leadership can be regarded as not only the *primum mobile* but even the creator and maintainer of the party; where the party itself is merely a tactical device in a mass movement, to be inflated or run down as circumstances may suggest; and where leader, party, movement, all, are dependent in part upon the level of national agitation and in part upon the expansion of activity into extra-political fields. Even a brief reflection on O'Connell's repeal campaign of the early 1840s may throw some lights upon these larger matters.

The editors of this volume have asked contributors to bear in mind throughout their pieces one particular question, 'how helpful is the "high politics" mode of political explanation in the understanding of the gestation of policy in modern British political history?' The gestation of the policy of repeal is not readily categorizable in such terms. At any rate, the present author can find no simple or single answer. But it may none the less be useful to review the leading forces which went into the making and reshaping of latter-day repeal, and in particular to do so by looking at the question, first, from above, through O'Connell's eyes and disposition, and then from below, as the exigencies of the undertaking altered its character and enlarged its elements.

II

No one should have known better than O'Connell that his demand for the 'simple repeal' of a British Act of Parliament passed in 1800 contradicted the entire trend of his political activity and agitation since that date.

The Union had ended a system of government in Ireland characterized by a Protestant monopoly of political power and a form of indirect rule by the British Cabinet. In so far as cabinet government existed in Ireland between 1782 and 1800, it was British. The key to the whole situation is that the rise of 'Grattan's Parliament' coincided almost exactly with the subjection, in essentials, of royal power to cabinet power in Great Britain. Essentially, the king of Ireland acted, or refused to act, on the advice and with the consent of his British ministers. Of course, so bald a statement oversimplifies the matter greatly. But it does state the main truth of the constitutional situation. In 1782, the Irish parliament had modified but not repealed Poynings's Act. The consent of the British privy council to Irish bills was no longer necessary, but the assent of the sovereign under the Great Seal, not of Ireland, but of England, had been expressly reserved. It was this which lent some colour to the Irish Unionist argument that Ireland possessed more real independence after the Act of Union than before, because she now enjoyed at least some influence over the selection of her rulers. It was this which explained Wolfe Tone's observation in 1791 that all Ireland was inferior in power to Yorkshire or even Birmingham.

Even when he first revived repeal as a definite political objective in 1840, O'Connell must have been aware that, literally interpreted, his demand was nonsensical. He could not have meant the reconstitution of three hundred Irish constituencies, the great majority of them controlled by the Crown, patrons, proprietors, or bribes, or the reimposition of those Roman Catholic disabilities, which had been removed statutorily or had disappeared by desuetude since 1800. Yet both these 'safeguards' had been pre-conditions of 'independence' for the great majority of Irish Protestants before 1800. In fact, the Union had come about, so far as they were concerned, because even these bulwarks had been felt to be too flimsy, in an increasingly dangerous world, for the maintenance of Protestant ascendancy, or even of Protestant security and possessions. The events of the 1830s—whether the test was police, local government, the magistracy, or the inviolability of the established church—had further weakened the Protestant 'securities'; and to say the least O'Connell could scarcely have contemplated reversing a series of changes which he himself had, indirectly, wrought. Further, as the repeal movement developed in the early 1840s, its leading 'practical objects' were declared to include the total abolition of the tithe charge, fixity of tenure, and fair rents;[1] and almost the entire programme of the People's Charter—manhood suffrage, vote by ballot, equal electoral districts, triennial parliaments, and the abolition of the property qualifications—was specified as 'ancillary to, and promotive of, the great cause of Repeal'. It was this which led Isaac Butt, then the rising star of the stern unbending Unionists, to contend, with some justice, in the Mansion House debate of 1843 that 'repeal was revolution . . . the proposition was not to return to any state of things which had previously existed in Ireland—not to adopt the constitution of any European state—but to enter on an untried and wild system of democracy'.[2]

Perhaps it would be unfair to hold O'Connell *au pied de la lettre*. His opponents had certainly not known clearly what they meant by union in 1800. Even such a vital matter as whether or not the Irish executive, under a lord-lieutenant and chief secretary, should be retained was not determined until after the event. Even then, it was apparently determined more by *vis inertiae* than by any course of deliberation or decision. Many of the significant political changes in Ireland since 1800 had been the work of British parties and opinion rather than Irish; and, as such, should have been, in logic, mandatory upon Irish Unionists. Again, O'Connell was a universal radical, as early nineteenth-century men construed the term. His incorporation of the body of the People's Charter in the repeal manifesto of 1842 may have derived from tactical considerations. But all the evidence indicates that O'Connell believed in such things as absolute political goods, for

[1] *Nation*, 26 Nov. 1842 and 7 Jan. 1843.
[2] Ibid., 4 Mar. 1843.

Great Britain or France or Belgium no less than Ireland. How could he have failed to ask, for a constitutionally separate Ireland, what he was asking for the United Kingdom, and for all mankind? When therefore O'Connell agitated for a simple repeal of the Act of Union, it may have been a nonsensical political demand, but it was also one whose nonsense might be much reduced by a liberal and rational allowance for forty years of Anglo-Irish history. Yet whatever allowance we may make, the fact remains that he campaigned for the annulment of a particular statute, and that this was in itself a meaningless demand.

Why, then, did he present the issue in such terms? Various types of answer may be proffered. First, repeal appeared to evidence extraordinary political consistency, given the great length and variety of O'Connell's public experience. 'It is a curious thing enough', he once observed, 'that all the principles of my subsequent political life are contained in my very first political speech.'[3] His emergence into public life was to protest against the Bill of Union in 1800, or more precisely to demonstrate that there was a body of educated Irish Catholics, however small, who refused to be accomplices in the 'crime'. With the extravagance which he commonly used to clarify his position, he spoke of the perpetuation of the Protestant ascendancy and even a return to the anti-Catholic penal laws as preferable to the loss of an 'independent' Irish parliament.[4] Throughout the long campaign for Catholic civil rights, he lost no opportunity of emphasizing its secondary nature: confessional liberation, he always said, was ultimately meaningful in the context of repeal. In the Whig years 1830–41, his abatement of Ireland's claim was ever presented as contingent, and was in fact apparent rather than real. If the fruits of repeal could be achieved without the formality of repeal, O'Connell argued, why surrender substances for shadows? But even this was spoken of as an unpromising hypothesis that must be tested. When towards the

---

[3] R. Dunlop, *Daniel O'Connell and the Revival of National Life in Ireland*, London, 1900, pp. 18–19. I can find no earlier reference to these words, although their substance is to be found in W. J. O'Neill Daunt, *Personal Recollections of the late Daniel O'Connell, M.P.*, London, 1848, i. 203.

[4] J. O'Connell, ed., *Select Speeches of Daniel O'Connell*, Dublin, 1868, i. 8–11; *Dublin Evening Post*, 14 Jan. 1800.

close of 1842 he committed all his energies at last, to a total assault upon the Union, the old man of sixty-seven may have looked back in imagination to the young of twenty-five, and told himself that in his beginning was his end. The very Act which he had opposed in 1800 he still opposed in 1842; all that he had ever sought was the restoration of the status quo. In his final years, he recalled his feelings of 1801 when he first heard the bells of St. Patrick's Cathedral pealing out in joy at the surrender: 'My blood boiled, and I vowed that morning that the foul dishonour should not last, if *I* could ever put an end to it.'[5]

Was O'Connell, in part, the victim of his own attitudinizing? A very young man may fall in love and, having loved and lost, insulate himself against much that is unpleasant and indulge himself in much that it is safely titillating, by professing devotion to the woman married to another. Then her husband dies, and the man has to determine what he really means. Of course, such a young man no longer exists, even—or perhaps particularly—within the covers of a novel. But in the nineteenth century he was not inconceivable to the patrons of Mudie; and even today, although sexual relations may be inappropriate, it is not difficult to envisage the same sort of situation in another field. Now, does this analogy help to expose part at least of O'Connell's motivation? Some portion of the stereotype seems to fit. Certainly, O'Connell lived for forty years in very tolerable political comfort without the woman. Certainly, if we take the husband to represent plausible reasons for not pursuing her, he really did expire once Peel's second administration had been established, with its majority secure and O'Connell's active years patently near their end. Certainly, the woman had aged almost out of recognition since 1800, and yet O'Connell was constrained by his previous behaviour to ignore the change. At this point the analogy clearly fails. For one thing, he could ask for her loudly with fair assurance of a brusque refusal; and for another, the fundamental questions—what his innermost vision of the woman was in 1842, and whether he really wanted that any longer—cannot be answered in such terms. He could not but have felt the force of the scepticism of his

[5] O'Neill Daunt, *Personal Recollections*, i. 203.

Catholic colleague, Denys Scully, 'They called it our Parliament; it was their clubhouse.' None the less it may be important to remember that repeal gave unity to O'Connell's long career. He could present himself, even to himself, as changeless from first to last, tacking perhaps to contrary winds, but unvarying in his destination, a Fabius among national liberators. Demagogues may live through a temporary failing in applause, but hardly disbelieving in themselves.

Secondly, O'Connell was not only an Irish nationalist but also a leading British radical, in certain senses at certain stages, the leading British radical of his day. In radicalism, he could reconcile his personal drives and ambitions and his early grounding in the ideology of the enlightenment. Resentment of and refusal to acquiesce in the condition of inferiority into which, as an Irish Catholic, he had been born, were constant urges in his life. In addressing the Clare electors in 1828, he broke out:

Standing here, I may be considered the representative of the sufferings of my country. Lord Manners, the very week before he left Ireland, put thirteen brother barristers over my head. I beg to state, that for the honesty of my right honourable candidate I have the highest respect; but I am the son of a gentleman—my mother was the daughter of a gentleman, and in rank and station I am quite on an equality with him. In hereditary property possibly I am his equal—probably I am not. My profession gives me a splendid income, and yet this man, in my native land—the land of my ancestors—where my forefathers were for centuries the Chieftains of the land, and the friends of her people, makes it a species of kindness that he honours me with his patronage. I treat with disdain and contempt the condescension of such patronage.[6]

This passion for parity was ideologically articulated in terms of civil equality. That O'Connell was the complete egalitarian, in the formal and legal senses in which contemporaries understood the word, there can be no reasonable doubt. One can find no measure of civil rights which came within his sphere of action or comment which he did not support. His rejection not only of slavery as an institution but even of all aid or approbation from slave-holding interests was, to all appearances, conscientious. Thus, O'Connell could speak of his drive for formal political equality for Irishmen and Catholics

---

[6] *Freeman's Journal*, 4 July 1828. For a slightly variant version of the same passage, see M. MacDonagh, *The Life of Daniel O'Connell*, London, 1903, p. 158.

within the United Kingdom (paradoxically but inevitably it took the form of destruction of that union which permanently denied them parity!) as a particular manifestation of a general and absolute principle. Repeal could be and was fitted into universalist radicalism. The demand for legislative independence was the apotheosis, the highest expression of egalitarianism. At the same time, it served as a burning glass for all the bitterness which racial and religious discrimination had engendered.

There was, however, another level at which O'Connell's radicalism helps to explain his emphasis on repeal. As a political technique, as distinct from a body of ideas, British radicalism for the first two-thirds of the nineteenth century centred upon the removal of a number of clearly specified abuses or restraints. The classic form of campaign, beginning with that against the slave trade, was to institute an agitation for abolition by parliamentary action. Each campaign was a separate undertaking with a separate target—happiest of all if the target were a particular statute or body of legislation. To present the constitutional rearrangement of the British Isles in the same sort of terms as the abolition of the slave trade, or church disestablishment, or the repeal of the Corn Laws, was therefore a natural action for O'Connell. It was also one underpinned by the solid advantages, for the purposes of mass agitation, of limpid simplicity and the clear identification of a visible enemy. That this enemy was a comparatively recent Act of Parliament, and one moreover of so large a sweep that almost every contemporary misfortune could be plausibly ascribed to it, were further heavy advantages for a popular movement. Thus, both the nature and the art of contemporary radicalism suggested the wisdom of a campaign for 'simple repeal', as the O'Connellites themselves named this particular choice of platform.

Thirdly, it should never be forgotten that O'Connell had to work in and through the political system of the United Kingdom. T. P. O'Connor well apostrophized this system, so far as Ireland was concerned, as the attempt to govern one country through the public opinion of another. It was a British ministry, a predominantly British House of Commons, British opinion (and behind them, requiring a still greater force to overcome, the Crown and House of Lords) which O'Connell had to move, by threats, blandishments, demonstrations, dangers, and discomfort—but with violence disavowed. In the best circumstances, it was a daunting journey. But had O'Connell announced in so many words that his objective was not really a return to any former state of things, but an advance to a novel state of things which, whatever its constitutional form, implied mass democracy, tenant right, and disestablishment, it would have been pointless for him to have ever moved one foot before the other.

Instead, 'simple repeal' conveyed, or was meant to convey, the ideas of restoration and of Protestant security, if not of actual Protestant domination. The repeated use of 'Grattan's Parliament' and 'College Green' in repeal oratory suggested no more than a revival of moderate colonial nationalism and even perhaps an acceptance of renewed ascendancy leadership, freed of its former sectarian oppression. The backward references also commonly included the comforting incantation of 'king, lords and commons'; and fervent expressions of adherence to the Crown were from first to last a leading feature of the O'Connellite campaign. The very title of the association began with 'Loyal'; 'The Queen' was the opening toast at every repeal banquet; and O'Connell incessantly called for Her Majesty with all the sentimental hyperbole of a two-bottle parson. Moreover, the chosen issue was well designed to counter the four main obstacles facing any Irish agitation directed at British opinion—the British fears of violence, revolution (political, social, or economic), popery, and separatism. The choice of 'simple repeal' with its implicit and explicit invocations of '1782', could scarcely have been bettered as a device for allaying the *furor Britannicus*. Not that British opinion was likely to be deceived, except perhaps in the direction of over-imputing machiavellianism to O'Connell. But to agitate merely for repeal at least transferred the onus of proof. On the surface, it was difficult to assail as unconstitutional at any point. Thus, it constituted the safest means of exerting mass extra-parliamentary pressure and represented the highest opening bid which, in O'Connell's view, an Irish agitation of the 1840s could securely make.

Fourthly, as this last point suggests, the truth would seem

to be that O'Connell did not intend to make a proposition or demand by launching his last movement for repeal. It was rather, in lawyer's language, an invitation to treat.[7] What he intended in 1840-5 was to elicit a proposition from the British Government. Repeal was only *apparently* a demand. Superficially, it resembled the call for Catholic emancipation. But even if 'Catholic emancipation' were a gross misnomer, the removal of specified disabilities was at least a meaningful and practicable legislative objective, recognizable and definable by friend and foe. Repeal was very different. Its true counterpart was not Catholic emancipation, tithe abolition, or Irish church disestablishment, but Parnell's 'home rule'. Parnell avoided, so far as possible, specification of his objective. His pressure was designed to force out a counter-offer, which might be accepted, rejected as insufficient, or used as a start for bargaining. The essential similarity of O'Connell's situation and leadership to Parnell's is apparent in this extraordinary passage towards the close of the Mansion House debate:

a Parliament inferior to the English Parliament I would accept as an instalment if I found the people ready to go with me, and if it were offered to me by competent authority. It must first be offered to me— mark that—I will never seek it. By this declaration I am bound thus far, that if the period should come when I am called upon practically to act upon it, I will do so; but I will not give up my exertions for the independent legislation until from some substantial quarter that offer is made. . . .
    Upon this subject I must not be mistaken, I will never ask for or look for any other, save an independent legislative, but if others offer me a subordinate parliament, I will close with any such authorized offer and accept that offer.[8]

Despite the initial hedges of 'an instalment' and 'the people ready', O'Connell was showing much more of his hand than Parnell would ever do. Still he worked within the same ambience. Each man sought to force a declaration from a British party, and to make none himself. Some apparently specific goal had to be announced; otherwise a movement could never have been set afoot. Parnell's devices were silence and an

---

[7] For an elaboration of this argument, see O. MacDonagh, 'Ambiguity in nationalism—the case of Ireland', *Historical Studies*, 19, No. 76 (Apr. 1981), 337-52.
    [8] J. Levy, ed., *A full and revised report of the three days' discussion in the corporation of Dublin on the repeal of the union* . . . , Dublin, 1843, pp. 191-2.

ambiguous and amorphous name and programme; O'Connell's, garrulity, inconsistency, and an impossible ostensible object. But this was a mere difference of mode and style. They were at one in being separatists, whose measure of separation was relative, to be determined ultimately in Great Britain, and who committed themselves to no abstraction or ideal form of state.

III

In one sense, the repeal association formed part of a continuum stretching back through a dozen evanescent organizations to the Catholic Association of 1823. The machinery had changed comparatively little in between. Although the names and ostensible primary objectives ranged widely, reflecting changes from collaboration to defiance and back again, each successive movement could be fitted into the same general classification. In much the same way, an orthodox political party is organically continuous despite changes in emphasis and platform from year to year.

The very Repeal Association of 1840 began as an attempt to muster Irish national opposition to Stanley's Registration Bill of 1840. On 15 April O'Connell launched the 'National Association of Ireland for Full Justice or Repeal' to counter the Bill, and proposed simultaneous mass meetings for petitioning parliament, and a parochial network of wardens and fund collectors, on the model of the Catholic Association of the 1820s.[9] The meetings and machinery, however, failed to reach or even approach the hoped-for scale. In order to attract Irish Liberal support, O'Connell had presented repeal as the mere alternative to achieving his political ends through 'Full Justice'. But as the Liberals ignored him and he was charged with lukewarmedness, or worse, towards repeal itself, he abandoned his first structure in July, substituting the 'Loyal National Repeal Association' as a title.[10]

[9] *Freeman's Journal*, 16 Apr. 1840. See generally, Reports, addresses, etc. of the Precursor Society of Ireland and of the National Association of Ireland for Repeal with draft constitutions of both, MS 3191, National Library of Ireland (hereafter NLI). I acknowledge gratefully the assistance of Dr P. Travers in elucidating the mechanics of the repeal association.
[10] *Freeman's Journal*, 14 July 1840. O'Connell argued that it was 'idle now to expect anything of the imperial Parliament'.

For more than two years the Repeal Association advanced little, and this slow progress was partly responsible for the development of something like a general programme. In his efforts to widen his appeal, O'Connell took aboard various popular demands, especially those appealing to the small tenant farmers. The abolition of the tithe charges was one obvious example. Another was the replacement of the new Irish Poor Law by a system financed by a tax on annual incomes of over £500, or, better still, a partly state-aided, partly voluntary scheme to aid the sick poor: the farmers were groaning loudly under the novel burden of the poor rate. But the most promising adoption was fixity of tenure.[11] This was rather a misnomer, as the association's proposal amounted to little more than compensation for tenant improvements and a minimum of twenty-one years for leases. None the less, it was a radical demand in the climate of the early 1840s.

Similarly, O'Connell set up committees of the association to sustain interest in and manufacture business for the weekly meetings. The committees, whose membership was identical and determined solely by O'Connell, the universal chairman, investigated and reported on such subjects as the passage of the Act of Union, financial relations with Great Britain, the progress of repeal, and the restoration of the Irish House of Commons.[12] The main consequence of the reports was to enlarge O'Connell's own oratorical armoury and to keep up the spirits of the faithful—even the report on the progress of repeal was much more an essay in propaganda than an attempt to remedy serious organizational failings. But they also, almost accidentally, led to the acquisition of policies at several points. Here too we reach the paradoxical conclusion that 'simple repeal' by its very failure to take off politically ended up with various shreds and patches of an extra-constitutional platform.

The critical change came in late 1842 when the inefficiency of the existing organization at last came under attention. The Dublin wardens were re-ordered; and inspectors of wardens, charged with the establishment and maintenance of a thorough-

[11] K. B. Nowlan, *The Politics of Repeal: a study of the relations between Great Britain and Ireland, 1842–50*, London, 1965, pp. 37–9.

[12] *Freeman's Journal*, 16 and 20 Apr., 5 May 1840; 5 and 9 Nov. 1842.

going system of propaganda, fund-collection, and communication with the centre, were appointed for the towns and groups of parishes, with chief inspectors for still larger regions.[13] Simultaneously, O'Connell began to emphasize much more strongly the importance of the wardens' work, and the need to recruit them widely. Leading members of the committee, notably O'Neill Daunt, Tom Steele, and Maurice O'Connell were dispatched on tours of the provinces to organize meetings, select officers, and generally establish a network for agitation. Rapidly, the parishes were supplied with one, two, three, or even four wardens; these in turn usually appointed collectors to gather in the repeal 'rent'; and they themselves were subject to the control and direction, immediately of the inspectors, and ultimately of Conciliation Hall.

Thus well before the great Mansion House debate of 28 February 1843 when O'Connell virtually proclaimed a crusade for 'simple repeal', the foundations of the mass movement of that year were being laid. The new stress on organization was not without some ideological implications. Total community mobilization was being attempted—O'Connell's aim of three million enrolments within three months[14] implied as much. This led to extensions of the notions of internal policing and internal legal adjudication, which had been vaguely adumbrated in the early years. Repeal police and a repeal arbitration system for land disputes pointed in the direction of alternative government from below and the supersession, in part, of the formal agencies of law and order. Again, the exigencies of agitation were adding new political dimensions to repeal.

Increasingly large and enthusiastic popular meetings had been held in several widely dispersed counties between November 1842 and February 1843. But when the campaign of monster meetings—vast successive Sunday rallies—was announced early in April 1843, fresh forces came into play. On the one hand, 1843 was declared to be repeal year. This implied a climax to the season of agitation. On the other, the movement was necessarily dynamic. It had to produce the impression of continuous growth, in both scale and intensity, if the strain on the British Government were to be maximized.

[13] *Freeman's Journal*, 5 Nov. 1842.   [14] *Nation*, 5 Jan. 1843.

These characteristics had two important consequences. First, an ultimate apparently practicable culmination to the campaign season had to be devised. At one of the earliest monster meetings, held in Sligo at the end of April, O'Connell proclaimed that once the three million members of the association had been enrolled—say, by July or August—each 'district' in Ireland would express 'confidence' in particular persons who would meet 'spontaneously' in Dublin as the Council of Three Hundred. He added that the council would at once draw up 'Bill no. 1' to repeal the Act of Union, and 'no. 2', to reinstitute the Irish House of Commons:[15] it seemed to be implied that further parts of the association programme would be taken up similarly, seriatim. Clearly, O'Connell was promising the unilateral establishment of a virtual parliament, but equally the 'expression of confidence' rather than polled votes, and the 'spontaneous' assemblage of individuals rather than the summoning of elected representatives were meant to keep the association within the borders of the law. There could be no doubt however that, under the pressure to formulate a climax, repeal had taken a further massive step in the direction of something very different from its original character, that is, towards becoming a prototype Sinn Fein.

Secondly, the nature of the enterprise of 1843, with the need to marshal and control many tens of thousands of people every week and to evoke and release sentiments of historic resentment and mass-attitudinizing, inevitably led the orators to the brink of the martial. As an English visitor described the Mullaghmast meeting, 'The men yelled and clawed with rage; the women screamed and clapped their hands. The vast multitude—I believe there were really 100,000 present—moved and moaned like a wild beast in agony.'[16] O'Connell guarded his language very carefully: bombast was one thing, words capable of being construed as seditious quite another. Perhaps deliberately, his speeches at the monster meetings were highly repetitive. But in practice it was not possible to resist all military or minatory flights in the charged emotional exchange between damagogue and people. At the Kilkenny

[15] *Nation*, 29 Apr. and 6 May 1843.
[16] J. B. Atkins, *The Life of Sir William Howard Russell*, London, 1911, i. 30.

monster meeting of 8 June for example O'Connell broke out,

> I stand today at the head of a group of men sufficient, if they underwent military discipline, to conquer Europe. (Cheers). Wellington never had such an army. (Cheers). There was not at Waterloo at both sides as many brave and determined men as I see before me today. . . . They are as well able to be submissive to the Repeal wardens, or anyone else told to take care of them, as if their leaders were called captains or sergeants.[17]

Three days later, having been inflamed by a vast public meeting (reported as 400,000 strong!) at Mallow, O'Connell at the evening banquet was led on by the thunders of applause and the presence of a ladies' gallery to the fiery topic of Cromwell's massacre of the women of Wexford.

> Three hundred of the grace, the beauty, and the virtue of Wexford were slaughtered by these English ruffians. . . . Sacred Heaven! (Cries of 'Oh, oh, oh! and tremendous sensation, many of the ladies screaming in terror). I am not at all imaginative when I talk of the possibility of such occurrences now. But yet, I assert there is no danger to the women of Ireland. . . . We were a paltry remnant in Cromwell's time; we are nine millions now!

A few minutes earlier, he had cried, 'I say, they may trample on me; but it will be my dead body they will trample on, not the living man.'[18]

The collapse of the repeal movement, with the proclamation of the final monster meeting scheduled at Clontarf on 5 October, is commonly ascribed to an unfortunate accident: the phrase 'repeal cavalry' was employed in the notice without O'Connell's knowledge.[19] But, as we have seen, some such 'accident' was bound to happen, sooner or later, given the rhetoric necessary for the campaign; and indeed the very meeting site, Clontarf, was chosen, like several of the other sites, because it represented a scene of heroic resistance to, or slaughter by, the invader. Correspondingly, the records make it clear that had O'Connell attempted practical steps towards selecting and summoning the Council of Three Hundred, Graham, the Home Secretary, would have called on the armed forces to suppress it:[20] this too was a collision course.

---

[17] MacDonagh, *O'Connell*, pp. 313–14.   [18] *Nation*, 17 June 1843.
[19] Ibid., 7 Oct. 1843. See also *Hansard*, 3rd, lxxi, cols. 1005–10.
[20] Nowlan, *Politics of Repeal*, p. 55.

In short, the very scale and pace of the agitation of 1843 helped to reshape 'repeal'; and the equivalent is of course true of the groups whom O'Connell had to recruit as sub-managers and organizers. We have seen already how the programme was developed to appeal to the tenant farmers; and attempts were also made to involve both shopkeepers and tradesmen by the establishment of repeal boards of trade in Dublin and provincial cities such as Limerick.[21] But much more important—indispensable, in fact—was active participation of the bulk of the Catholic clergy. The support, or at the very least neutralization, of the bishops was a prerequisite, as they effectively controlled the lower clergy. This had been substantially secured by the beginning of 1843. Almost two-thirds of the episcopate had joined the association, and none of the remainder was publicly opposed.[22] But it was the ordinary parish priests, and to a lesser extent their curates, who carried the movement on their shoulders.

When the association was reconstructed in the late autumn and winter of 1842, it was almost invariably the parish priest (as often as not O'Connell knew him personally) whom the organizers from Dublin first approached. He would arrange the initial meeting, nominate likely men for wardenships, supervise the repeal rooms once they were established, and largely plan the monster meeting if one were to be held later in his district. A typical case was that of the Revd Mr McEvoy, parish priest of Kells. The repeal organizer stayed with him on his first visit, and through him arranged the initial meeting. It was McEvoy who selected the repeal wardens, and who acted as general organizer of the later mass meeting (an attendance of 150,000 was claimed) which O'Connell addressed. He also acted as host to O'Connell on the occasion, and from first to last was the channel of communication between Kells and Conciliation Hall.[23] Many of the priests became repeal wardens, though they by no means constituted a majority of the corps. Almost always, outside the cities, they filled the critical office of inspector. Even where they were not officially

[21] T. Steele to O'Connell, Jan. 1841, Steele correspondence, MS 13648, NLI.

[22] O. MacDonagh, 'The politicization of the Irish catholic bishops, 1800–1850', *Historical Journal*, 18, no. 1 (1975), 46–8.

[23] N. McEvoy to T. M. Ray, 20 Apr. 1843; Misc. letters, MS 13646, NLI; *Freeman's Journal*, 25 Apr. and 3 May 1843.

inspectors, most of the dealings with the wardens took place through them, and it was they who distributed the association's circulars. The chief speakers at the monster meetings stayed at the local parochial houses; and clergy constituted a high percentage of the platform party at both the meetings and the evening banquets where one of the inevitable toasts was that drunk to 'The clergy of Ireland'.

This is not to say that the repeal movement of 1843 was overtly or even substantially sectarian. Its difference in this regard from the emancipation agitation of the 1820s was continually stressed in speeches and publications. Every Protestant recruit (especially if he were a clergyman) was fêted as a lost sheep found; and there were not a few lost-found sheep. None the less, the Catholic priests and bishops were accorded the full deference which their indispensability to the organization and agitation deserved. After investigating one dispute at Waterford, for instance, O'Connell censured all 'language of a disrespectful nature' to the Catholic clergy, and threatened any member of the association who used such language with expulsion.[24] As it happened, no religious issue arose during 1843, and O'Connell was required to go no further in respecting clerical susceptibilities or serving clerical interests than public flattery of the grossest kind. But when Peel and Graham attempted a counter-offensive in 1844–5 in the hope of dividing the Irish Church by concessions to Catholicism, a more practical quid pro quo was necessary.

Late in 1843, after O'Connell's arrest, the Conservative Government determined, if possible, to weaken his Irish support. Land and other economic reforms were considered, but the main thrust was to be religious. The Irish episcopate was already divided. Although a considerable majority of the bishops were open repealers, of varying degrees of enthusiasm, the rest were surreptitious opponents or political neutrals. It was this latter group whom Peel and Graham hoped to conciliate by concessions, thereby erecting 'a barrier—a line of Churchmen—behind which the well-thinking part of the Roman Catholic laity will conscientiously rally'.[25] Two of

---

[24] O'Connell to T. M. Ray, n.d., Loyal National Repeal Association correspondence, MS 3143, NLI.

[25] C. S. Parker, *Sir Robert Peel, from his private papers*, London, 1899, iii. 133.

the four practical measures which they devised were ineffec-
tual in fomenting Irish discord. In 1844, the papacy was
prevailed upon, not without difficulty, to condemn publicly
all clerical involvement in the repeal movement.[26] But this
was simply, though respectfully, dismissed by the recalcitrant
bishops as either based on ignorance of Irish circumstances or
applicable only to *excesses* of behaviour, which of course
never occurred.[27] The Maynooth Act of 1845, increasing the
recurrent grant to the Catholic seminary and providing it
with £30,000 of capital for building, did arouse fierce opposition—but only among British Protestants. The Irish Catholics,
of every camp, took without weeping.

The Charitable Donations and Bequests Bill of 1844 did,
however, achieve something of the government's objective.
The Bill certainly advanced Catholic interests. But the bishops
had not been consulted beforehand; the Catholic members of
the proposed board would be in a permanent minority; and
a clause voiding religious bequests made within three months
of death was commonly taken as a slur on the honesty of
purpose of the Irish clergy. The 'moderate' bishops (practically identical with the anti- or non-repeal faction) hesitantly
accepted and eventually co-operated with the measure. But
the majority led by Archbishop MacHale of Tuam violently
resented both its imparity of treatment and the supposed
reflection upon Catholic integrity. O'Connell's initial reaction
had been mild and sensible. As a lawyer, he pointed to the
practical advantages of simply rendering the Catholic clergy
so many corporations solely for administering the charitable
trusts, in place of the cumbersome and sect-divided board.[28]
But once the repeal prelates had condemned the Bill outright, he followed them in their denunciations, which the
assocation formally endorsed. This marked the beginning of
the division with the association between the main body,
headed by O'Connell, and the Young Ireland section, who,

[26] J. F. Broderick, *The Holy See and the Irish Movement for the Repeal of the
Union with England*, Rome, 1951, pp. 185-8; C. S. Parker, *Life and Letters of Sir
James Graham*, London, 1907, i. 401-2.

[27] MacDonagh, 'Politicization of the Irish catholic bishops', pp. 49-50.

[28] Nowlan, *Politics of Repeal*, p. 67. See generally, W. J. Walsh, *O'Connell,
Archbishop Murray and the Board of Charitable Bequests*, Dublin, 1916, pp. 1-
17.

as Davis put it, were determined that it should not become a 'priests' party'.[29]

The fourth Peel–Graham tactic, the provision of tertiary educational opportunities for Catholics (and incidentally also for Presbyterians), had still more serious consequences.[30] The Academical Institutions (Ireland) Bill, introduced in May 1845, had ended, after protracted ministerial discussion, as a proposal for non-denominational university colleges, with a considerable degree of governmental control over their conduct. The Irish prelates divided on almost exactly the same lines as before. The 'moderates' were willing to give the scheme a fair trial, especially after Graham had conceded residential halls managed by religious. Once again, O'Connell's initial reaction was comparatively mild. He accepted mixed education in literature and science as proper, although in religion and theology 'each denomination ... should be educated by their respective religious instructors'.[31] But as the MacHale party's opposition hardened—by September 1845 it reached the point where they publicly denounced the proposed colleges as dangerous to faith and morals[32]—O'Connell also became a firm opponent, taking up and using as his own Inglis's description of the scheme as 'Godless education'.[33] As a body, the Repeal Association followed his lead, but on this occasion only at the expense of open schism. The Davis party warmly approved the Bill's principle as a step towards national enlightenment and a blow against religious division in Irish society; and Smith O'Brien refused to follow O'Connell's line. Probably as a diversion O'Connell induced the association to declare specifically for the secret ballot and household suffrage.[34]

Thus in the long run the organization's dependence on the church gave new shades to the meaning of 'repeal'. It would be too much to say that the association became sectarian.

[29] T. Davis to W. S. O'Brien, n.d., Smith O'Brien papers, vol. 432, no. 895, quoted in Nowlan, p. 88. See generally, D. Gwynn, *O'Connell, Davis and the Colleges Bill*, Cork, 1948.

[30] See generally, J. C. Beckett and T. W. Moody, *Queen's, Belfast, 1849–1949: the history of a university*, London, 1959, i. 1–80; Nowlan, *Politics of Repeal*, pp. 83–9.

[31] *Hansard*, 3rd, lxxxi, cols. 1089–98.

[32] *Nation*, 27 Sept. 1845.   [33] Ibid., 19 July 1845.

[34] Nowlan, *Politics of Repeal*, p. 89.

But under pressure, it did take on a more confessional air, and develop a more confessional ethos. No specifically Catholic policy was adopted. But where a choice of attitude was enforced, as with the bequests and colleges bills, it had to follow the direction of the repeal bishops and below them of the lower clergy, who were almost exclusively repealers. At the same time, this alienated the *Nation* group, the young intellectuals or clerisy, who had carried much of the burden of propaganda and 'consciousness-raising' particularly for the middle and artisan classes of the towns. The conflict spread into the area of nationalism itself, and was ultimately fatal to 'repeal'. Meanwhile, the necessities of the campaign had altered the meaning or at least the emphasis of its objective yet again.

IV

Thus, 'simple repeal' ended as rather complex repeal, without much coherence in its accretions or clear direction in its development. It began as an attempt to prevent nationalist votes from being dis-registered, and always retained an element of 'pure' political radicalism. The repeal manifesto of 1842 adopted *inter alia* manhood suffrage, vote by ballot, and equal electoral districts, and the association re-endorsed these, in milder form, in 1845. The explanation is simple. Not merely was O'Connell himself a lifelong constitutional radical, but even household suffrage, together with the other two reforms, would probably have given him a fairly well-disciplined party of 110 or 120 in the House of Commons instead of a ragged 'tail' of twenty-five or thirty.

The need to appeal to the small farmers led the association into a primitive tenant-right programme, as well as a vague state-paternalistic alternative to the Chadwickian type of poor law. Similarly, a hazy form of protectionism for native manufacture and crafts followed the wooing of merchants and artisans. The committees, whose evident purpose was propagandist, sometimes incidentally added to the programme. That on financial relations prefigured in a rough and ready way the Irish claims *vis-à-vis* imperial taxation which were to be pressed successfully in the 1890s, while that on the post-repeal Irish House of Commons committed the association to the strictest representation according to population without much alteration of the electoral units—even though this made Cork county a twelve-seat and Dublin city an eight-seat constituency.[35]

The move to popular organization and agitation upon a massive and ever-mounting scale inevitably changed the tone and emphasis of repeal. Bellicosity and extra-constitutionality, which O'Connell had been almost obsessively careful to avoid from the beginning, could no longer be altogether restrained, and the latter even took on the form of a threat–promise of an independent 'spontaneous' assembly. But still more important was the organizational dependence on the church which was implicit in such a mass movement, as well as a lesser but still very heavy dependence upon the young intellectuals for inspiriting popular literature, patriotic—not to say, chauvinistic—ideology, bridges across the generational gaps, and the enlistment of the educated classes. Without both of these recruitments the titanic campaign and the great national front of 1843 would never have been possible. But they brought with them such fresh glosses upon 'repeal' and such irreconcilable visions of the future that their employment was ultimately fatal to the cause.

It is important to bear in mind that O'Connell was already a man of sixty-five in 1840, and that his political experience, however wide and varied, was confined to agitation and, latterly, back-bench membership of the House of Commons. His outlook was never modified by either serious rivals for leadership or ministerial responsibility. For all his inventiveness in political mechanics, he was never called upon to change his fundamental ends or means. Hence his late eighteenth-century social and political formation, which 'repeal' epitomized, is crucial in explaining his attitudes and conduct.

Much more than any other leading figure in modern Irish history was he the product of and attuned to Gaelic culture. More—perhaps even as much more—than any leading figure in modern Irish history except de Valera did he reflect and respond to traditional native Catholicism. Yet he consistently refused to regard nationality as rooted either in culture—as

[35] *Freeman's Journal*, 5 May 1840.

the current orthodoxy of southern Ireland would have it—or in religion—as the current orthodoxy in the north would say. He practically ignored, throughout a long life, the Gaelic element in Irish life, and wished and (by inactivity at least) worked to eradicate it from the political scene. Quite as deep-rooted and persistent, I believe, was his repugnance and resistance to religion as the definer of the political group. It is true that this is much more disputable. In 1843–5 Davis increasingly detected sectarianism in O'Connell's conduct, and after Davis's death similar charges became more frequent and violent amongst the Young Irelanders. It seems unquestionable that O'Connell followed the lead of his episcopal faction on two of the issues of 1844–5; and from 1845 onwards, he certainly tended to identify repeal and Catholicism more and more. In my view, however, all this fails to constitute a serious deviation from primitive liberalism. By and large, and even still, the Young Irelanders have had the advantage of being their own historians. For the years 1843–5, the evidence suggests that the sectarian division derived less from O'Connell's actions or inaction than from Davis's suspicions of popery. In any event, tactical considerations would seem to account sufficiently for the variations. In the great political complex which he built and managed, the repeal priests and bishops were an indispensable constituent—immediately, much more important than Young Ireland—and as with every national party composed of sections with independent bases, certain prices had to be paid to retain support. This was a far cry from adopting religion as the core of separatism. Such a course would have violated both O'Connell's invariable strategy and his professed creed.

For the key to his type of separatism, we must look, not to categories of nineteenth-century nationalist theory, groups defined by race, religion, or culture, still less to twentieth-century groups defined by economic class or relationship, but to the eighteenth-century radicals and philosophers. O'Connell spoke Tone's language, but not Davis's. Tone defined Irish nationalism in essentially the same terms as the framers of the Declaration of Independence had defined American. But Davis spoke 'spiritually', like Mazzini. O'Connell—it need hardly be said—would have parted company with Tone, where the turnings to revolution or secularity appeared. But for a long way he travelled the same road. For each, particular societies were essentially agglomerations of individuals; and as an individual realized himself by the assertion of his independence and the pursuit of his isolated good, so also did a collective individual, or nation. Nationality was a means of actualizing one's dignity and freedom as a human person, and a necessary means to adopt where the group with which one was associated was inferior either in law or in the estimation of the world at large. Thus the solution of the puzzle whereby the assumptions that all men were essentially separate and essentially similar, and possessed essentially the same rights and worth, could end in assertions of the right of national self-determination, would seem to lie in enlightenment concepts of equality. These did not necessarily—or in fact often—imply proposals for social levelling. O'Connell certainly accepted the continuance of a hierarchical and teleological organization of his group. But it was none the less crucial that the hierarchical structure to which he belonged should be equal to any corresponding structure.

This form of nationalism was assailed, ultimately with considerable success, by the forces which O'Connell nurtured and exploited in his campaign of 1840-5. The substantial identification of Catholicism and Irish nationality was not openly avowed in the mid-nineteenth century or in any later epoch. But in the immediate aftermath, and as a direct consequence of O'Connell's last repeal campaign, it appeared in its most provocative form: the priest (or more precisely the bishop) in politics. The 1850s were remarkable for the degree—as well as the incoherence—of Irish ecclesiastical intervention in elections and policy formation alike.[36] Conversely, the repeal movement had given the journalists and littérateurs both a national platform and the stimulus to clarify their ideology and compact themselves as a group. Indirectly but essentially O'Connell had made possible the development of a Young Ireland party; and this party moved steadily towards the articulation of a nationalism antithetical to O'Connell's. The new model was a derivative of German romanticism, sharing its assumptions that national culture,

[36] MacDonagh, 'Politicization of the Irish catholic bishops', pp. 51-3.

national history, and national language were integral to national identity. Liberation was conceived of as something far beyond a mere change in the management of the political and economic systems. The new emphasis was on *cultural* division and hostility; on feeling rather than rationality; on group rights rather than individual. This second child of repeal was, like the first, soon destined to devour its parent.

V

To return to the specific question of the gestation of policy, we find that repeal was the product of factors both high and low, in so far as the terms can be applied to an extra-parliamentary phenomenon. In one minor respect, the conventional categories may be applicable. The Peel–Graham initiatives of 1844–5 certainly produced some change in the character of repeal by forcing divisions, which had hitherto been restrained, upon the association; and such a result had been intended. Whether Peel and Graham sought this policy in order to attain, or retain, power, or sought power in order to realize such a policy, is a secondary question in terms of this essay. Their wedge was but one of many forces that shaped and re-shaped repeal. Of course, their imperial-strategic concept of repeal belonged to a thought-world quite alien to the Irish. Even O'Connell and his lieutenants were engrossed by considerations which bore little or no relation to the ministers'. The formation and maintenance of a national front was their essential concern. Cashing it in for concessions was always a remote and unknowable affair. As for the energized multitudes, and the clerical sergeants and lay corporals of the movement, the mere labours and excitements gave their own rewards and provided their own narcotics for waking misery.

If, however, we do try to apply the tests of 'high' and 'low' political behaviour to a national mass movement which was without hope of significant parliamentary representation, the first observation must be that repeal was clearly one of O'Connell's means, his final means, of mobilizing power. But it was also his *idée fixe*, a set of images and symbols, a mode of expressing deep urges and ambitions, peculiar to himself and to his intellectual maturation in 1785–98. We can safely say that without him 'simple repeal' would never have dominated Irish politics, let alone have produced the massive convulsion of 1843. All this may be classified in a rough and ready way as 'high' explanation, even if with serious internal conflict between the elements. But as we have seen, O'Connell was the creature as well as the creator of his campaign. The very organization and sustaining of his type of politics forced changes of emphasis and direction continuously upon him, and in the end released counter-concepts and counter-agents who proved inimical—and indeed fatal—to the entire venture. This in turn suggests two simple propositions—doubtless mere truisms, when looked hard in the face—about repeal: first, that the process of gestation never ceased—before death; and secondly that not only did high and low factors contribute to the gestation, but that the one necessarily implied the other, in endless sequence.

This may seem an indeterminate conclusion. But there was a work, written in Dublin more than a century before, which seemed to see the high and low in politics as bound together —alternating, it is true, but with all the irrefragable connection of the diastole and systole.

It is alledged indeed, that the high Heels are most agreeable to our ancient Constitution: But however this be, his Majesty hath determined to make use of only low Heels in the Administration of the Government, and all Offices in the Gift of the Crown; as you cannot but observe; and particularly, that his Majesty's Imperial Heels are lower at least by a *Drurr* than any of his Court. . . . We apprehend his Imperial Highness, the Heir to the Crown to have some tendency towards the High-Heels; at least we can plainly discover one of his Heels higher than the other; which gives him a Hobble in his Gait.[37]

[37] J. Hayward, ed., *Selected Prose Works of Jonathan Swift*, London, 1949, p. 148.

2

Gladstone's Theological Politics

Boyd Hilton

I

Gladstone described himself in 1874 as 'a man, much . . . of whose life and strength has been spent in the endeavour to deliver himself, for the sake of Truth, from the sway of pre-conceived opinions'.[1] Taking this for its central theme, Morley's *Life* showed Gladstone's intrinsic Liberalism emerging triumphantly in the course of his gradual deliverance from the shackles of inherited bigotry and superstition. A more recent *Life* presents the shift from theocratic Toryism, through Peelism, to Liberalism as an intellectual exercise, 'more outward than inward', which left Gladstone's Tory instincts unchanged.[2] Whichever view is correct, a consensus has recently developed that Gladstone's emergence as a Liberal involved a fundamental change in his perceptions as to the normative basis of society. H. C. G. Matthew writes that Gladstone abandoned the ethical absolutes of political tractarianism, in favour of 'an alternative if less elevated synthesis', whose key features were administrative reform, colonial affairs, 'the morality of free trade and finance, and the morality of international affairs'. Following Matthew, D. M. Schreuder sees the rejection of Puseyism and the espousal of mass politics and reform as a switch 'from moral idealism to moral pragmatism'; Gladstone came to see that the nation's 'conscience' was located in 'the broad mass of respectable society', instead of in the state. Likewise, M. D. Stephen shows how Gladstone came to regard majority will as a surer guide to 'truth' than

I should like to thank the Master and Tutors of Ormond College, Melbourne, and the Librarian and staff of the Joint Theological Library, for their hospitality during the preparation of this essay.

[1] Gladstone to Herbert Spencer, 12 Jan. 1874, in *Correspondence on Church and Religion of William Ewart Gladstone*, ed. D. C. Lathbury, London, 1910, ii. 98.

[2] E. J. Feuchtwanger, *Gladstone*, London, 1975, p. 124.

Anglican dogma.[3] My purpose is not to challenge this consensus, but to explore it further by looking at Gladstone's own
writings on the subject of religion and political morality.
'Swimming for his life, a man does not see much of the
country through which the river winds.'[4] It may be misleading to place too much store by Gladstone's own rationaliza-
tions of events, especially when they were honed during the
final decade of his life. Yet he was a genuinely introspective
man, a model of the self-scrutinizing evangelical 'striving after
truth',[5] and perusal of his writings over seventy years—his
numerous diaries, letters, speeches, gleanings, memoranda,
articles, and pamphlets, as well as the elderly autobiographical fragments—reveals a remarkable consistency of thought
and even of phraseology. Some historians would insist that
the Christian sinner and the party politician 'are not to be
fused'[6] if either is to be understood properly. Two have even
gone so far as to suggest that Gladstone's 'greatness' consisted
in an 'ability to move rapidly from one world and atmosphere
to another and perhaps incompatible one, forgetting for the
time all the other contexts in which he operated'.[7] Indeed,
the separateness of 'politics' has often been seen as an important ingredient in Gladstone's brand of Liberalism. Stephen
believes that, in order to become a Liberal, Gladstone had to
effect a divorce between his religious and political selves (to
the benefit of both), and Perry Butler seems to agree that he
'put a gulf' between the two when he abandoned his High-
Tory, High-Anglican ideal.[8] I would suggest that the opposite

[3] H. C. G. Matthew in *The Gladstone Diaries*, ed. M. R. D. Foot and H. C. G.
Matthew, Oxford, 1968-, iii. *xxxiv* and *passim*. Deryck Schreuder, 'Gladstone and
the conscience of the state', in *The Conscience of the Victorian State*, ed. P. T.
Marsh, Hassocks, Sussex, 1979, pp. 101 and 119. M. D. Stephen, 'Liberty, church
and state: Gladstone's relations with Manning and Acton, 1832-70', *Journal of
Religious History*, 1 (1960), 217 and 226-7. Professor Schreuder's essay covers
similar ground to mine, but with different emphases. My obligation to Dr Matthew's
writings will be obvious, but I have also benefited greatly from personal discussion
with him.
[4] *The Gladstone Diaries* (31 Dec. 1868), vi. 655.
[5] M. R. D. Foot in *The Gladstone Diaries*, i. *xx*.
[6] A. Jones, 'Where "Governing is the use of words" ', *Historical Journal*, 19
(1976), 256.
[7] A. B. Cooke and J. Vincent, *The Governing Passion: Cabinet Government
and Party Politics in Britain, 1885-6*, Brighton, 1974, p. 53.
[8] Stephen, p. 227; P. Butler, *Gladstone: Church, State and Tractarianism—
a study of his religious ideas and attitudes 1809-59*, Oxford, 1982, pp. 234-5.

is the case; that politics ceased to be merely an instrument for implementing dogmatic truths, derived from religious authority, and became instead the main arena in which to trace the operational workings of divine providence. It would have cost him 'a tremendous tussle'[9] to have admitted it, but Gladstone became, in effect, a Lockeian, as he turned gradually towards 'liberty' for the only means whereby men may discover God's natural laws, or Truth. As political liberty can provide ordinary citizens with an understanding of how society works, so, for Gladstone the Liberal statesman, the 'machinations of high politics', no less than 'working the institutions of government' (his other passion), became an indispensable element in the elucidation of God's intentions for mankind.

Certainly, the impression given by Gladstone's own writings is that he had a most uncompartmentalized mind, one that could never forget 'all the other contexts in which it operated'. Despite successive 'missions', his thoughts usually moved laterally, binding and blending, and, as Schreuder says, he 'saw politics whole'. Like all public men he could sometimes drive extraneous thoughts from the head, 'but not out of my nerves'.[10] At all events, and through all his public metamorphoses, politics remained subordinate to his duties as a Christian, and, as a child of the early nineteenth century, his Christianity cannot be understood without reference to that powerful and amorphous movement of thought and feeling known as the 'evangelical revival'.

Like the future papists William Ward and Henry Manning, and many other sons of evangelical business men who came of age around 1830, Gladstone emphatically rejected the religion of his youth in favour of the high church. Partly they were alienated by the growing pentecostal and millenarian wings of evangelicalism, Irvingites, Recordites, Watchers, and so forth, whose emotional extremes diverged sharply from the 'natural theology' tradition of moderate Anglican evangelicalism centred on Clapham. In particular, Gladstone was at first fascinated but then repelled by the Calvinist evangelicalism of Bulteel and the St. Ebbes set during his undergraduate days

---

[9] J. Morley, *The Life of William Ewart Gladstone*, 3 vols., London, 1903, iii. 476–7.
[10] *The Gladstone Diaries* (3 July 1864), vi. 287.

at Oxford.[11] Moreover the 'evangelical school', being 'beyond all others . . . the school of private judgement',[12] seemed to conservative youths like Gladstone too 'individualising' and therefore anarchical for a period of revolutionary alarms like the early 1830s. Gladstone habitually counterpoised 'authority' and 'will', and he accordingly abandoned the spiritual wilfulness of evangelicalism for the authoritarian comforts of a historic and corporate church. However, in saying this, it is necessary to distinguish between the institutional and doctrinal aspects of evangelicalism. Institutionally he rejected it totally and for ever, but he clung fervently to the central doctrines of moderate and Arminian evangelicals: providence, sin, conversion, conscience, atonement, salvation, and judgement. All were integral to his conception of politics.

Admittedly, with respect to conscience, Gladstone does seem to have abandoned true evangelical doctrine temporarily, an incidental victim perhaps of his assault on utilitarian individualism. In that Coleridgean extravaganza *The State in its Relations with the Church* (1838), he virtually denied the existence of personal conscience. The 'system of individual morality' was a 'degraded' and 'injurious legacy of Locke'. Citizens should be considered, 'not as individuals, but only as constituents of the active power of the life of the state', who were able to acquire moral sensibilities by merging into an organic national conscience. The state, which was 'the self-governing energy of the nation made objective', had a duty to direct the lives of its citizens, to rescue them from the temptations of mammonism and infidelity; the established clergy's function was to interpret God's will for the nation, and then to influence the policies of the state.[13]

It is not clear how seriously Gladstone ever believed his own theocratic ideas.[14] He may have been led further than he

---

[11] Butler, pp. 9-37 and 52-4. Butler discusses many aspects of Gladstone's religious development comprehensively, but has little to say about the evangelical and Butlerian elements discussed in this essay.

[12] Gladstone to R. H. Hutton, 6 Oct. 1890, in *Correspondence on Church and Religion*, i. 406.

[13] W. E. Gladstone, *The State in its Relations with the Church*, London, 1838; 4th edn., London, 1841, i. 73-8, 88, 124, 149, and 296-7; see Matthew in *The Gladstone Diaries*, iii. *xxv-xxviii*; A. R. Vidler, *The Orb and the Cross*, London, 1945, pp. 26-47.

[14] For examples of what Dr Matthew calls his 'lifelines to utilitarianism and

really intended by his disappointment with Thomas Chalmers, from whose celebrated *Lectures in Defence of Religious Establishments* (1838) he had expected so much, and who contented himself with strictly utilitarian and prudential arguments in his case against disestablishment. At all events, Gladstone's rediscovery of 'conscience' went *pari-passu* with his emergence as a Peelite-Liberal. Within a few years of 1838 he had engaged on a 'process of lowering the religious tone of the state, letting it down, demoralizing it—i.e. stripping it of its ethical character, and assisting its transition into one which is mechanical'.[15] The Maynooth crisis left him reflecting that 'the state cannot be said now to have a conscience . . . inasmuch as I think it acts . . . as no conscience—that is, no personal conscience (*which is the only real form of one*) —can endure'.[16] The subsequent collapse of the Oxford Movement completed his disillusion. If Dr Matthew's brilliant analysis of the 1853 budget scheme for an income tax-paying franchise is correct, Gladstone had by then already reversed his former view that the state should impose moral standards on its subjects. Now, if anything, the citizenry was to impose morality on the state, by refusing to pay for corrupt, inefficient, or bellicose governments. This carried the implication that 'if the electorate would not force on parliament the retrenchment necessary to create the conditions in which income tax could be repealed, then the electorate would have to be reformed'.[17] And when Gladstone took up parliamentary reform after 1864, the notion of 'personal conscience' as 'the only real form of one', and confidence in the potential for development of conscience in conditions of civil liberty, was a hallmark of his liberal rhetoric, a key to his alliance with the aspiring artisans in their progress 'onwards and upwards'.

consequently secularism when the [tractarian] ship sank', see *The State in its Relations with the Church*, i. 109, 123, and 301, and ii. 46. See also M. J. Lynch, 'Was Gladstone a tractarian? W. E. Gladstone and the Oxford Movement, 1833–45', *Journal of Religious History*, 8 (1974-5), 364-89.

[15] Gladstone to Manning, 19 Apr. 1846, in *Correspondence on Church and Religion*, ii. 272.

[16] Gladstone to Newman, 19 Apr. 1845, ibid. i. 72.

[17] H. C. G. Matthew, 'Disraeli, Gladstone, and the politics of mid-Victorian budgets', *Historical Journal*, 22 (1979), 626-30.

Maynooth was significant,[18] but the most important theoretical influence on this rediscovery of 'conscience' was Bishop Butler. Gladstone had absorbed the *Analogy of Religion* (1736) at Oxford in 1830-1, but was at first revolted by the ethical psychology of the *Rolls Sermons* (1726). In fact, Butler's 'teaching in the sermons on our moral nature was not integrated, so to speak, until several years later by larger perusal of the works of Saint Augustine'.[19] This must have been about 1835. Then in the aftermath of Maynooth, in June and July 1845, he set about re-reading Butler systematically, and quickly became obsessed with his own indebtedness to the philosopher–divine whose works he was later to edit and annotate at great length. Butler became 'a guide of life', 'as much in *practical* as in speculative things'; 'I never take a step in life without thinking how Butler would have advised me.'[20] And, of course, the central tenet of Butler's moral philosophy was that, notwithstanding the sensationalist ideas of Locke, man possesses a supreme or 'superintending faculty' called 'conscience'.

But if Butler led Gladstone back to the idea of 'conscience', and 'conscience' was central to evangelical theology, what did Gladstone mean by observing, more than once, that Butler had 'helped to emancipate me from the narrow evangelicalism of my boyhood'?[21] There are two possible explanations. In the first place, Butler's emphasis on the importance of external forms in religion led him, like Gladstone, to be accused of crypto-Romanism by nineteenth-century critics; evangelicals, on the other hand, had a dismally 'negative' attitude to sacraments and liturgy. More importantly, Butler—together with Hooker and Palmer—helped Gladstone to overcome certain other evangelical 'negatives'. The majority of Anglican evangelicals were probably not Calvinists, but they did tend to think

---

[18] See Stephen, pp. 223-6.

[19] Gladstone memorandum, 'Early religious opinions' [26 July 1894] in Historical Manuscripts Commission, *The Prime Ministers' Papers: W. E. Gladstone*, ed. J. Brooke and M. Sorensen, London, 1971-81, i. 150; see also, ibid. i. 140-1, and Gladstone to the Revd C. Beard, 23 Aug. 1884, in *Correspondence on Church and Religion*, ii. 325: 'Augustine's . . . doctrine of human nature is substantially that of Bishop Butler.'

[20] Gladstone to his son Willy, 1 Aug. 1860, ibid. ii. 164.

[21] Gladstone's 'Autobiographical retrospect', 22 June 1894, in *The Prime Ministers' Papers: Gladstone*, i. 38 and 150-2.

that, since faith was essential to salvation, by implication God must have condemned to eternal perdition millions of souls that had never even heard of him. This belief was what gave them their missionary fervour, but it seemed to Gladstone to be spiritually 'narrow'. Like his evangelically inclined political mentors, Canning and Peel,[22] like the philosopher of mid-Victorian liberalism, J. S. Mill, Gladstone disliked the 'damnatory clauses' of the Athanasian Creed. As he wrote much later, about his 'redaction' of opinions,

> At this moment I am as closely an adherent to the doctrines of grace generally, and to the general sense of Saint Augustine [as in 1828]. I hope that my mind has dropped nothing affirmative. But I hope also that there has been dropped from it all the damnatory part of the opinions taught by the evangelical school; not only as regards the Roman Catholic religion, but also as to heretics and heathens; nonconformists and presbyterians I think that I always let off pretty easily.[23]

It is clear that the 'affirmatives' not dropped were precisely those elements of the evangelical (and Augustinian) gospel scheme listed above—providence, sin, salvation, and so forth. And indeed, it would be the opposite of the truth to suppose that Butler's theology was in any way opposed to orthodox early nineteenth-century evangelicalism. William Wilberforce, Daniel Wilson, John Bird Sumner, and Thomas Chalmers, to name only four prominent publicists for the movement, were all acknowledged Butlerians. In *Studies subsidiary to the works of Bishop Butler* (1896) Gladstone argued at length that, however they might be lacking in 'evangelical flavour, or unction',[24] Butler's writings were based on and inseparable from an evangelical gospel scheme. Assuredly, Butler provided the statesman with a 'lifeline' back to an evangelical moral philosophy as the idealist ship sank.

The doctrine of conscience rested on that of original sin. No reader of Gladstone's private diaries can doubt his conviction of personal depravity, his belief 'in a degeneracy of man, in the Fall—in *sin*—in the intensity and virulence of

---

[22] Canning to Dr Philpotts, 11 May 1825, in *Some Official Correspondence of George Canning*, ed. Edward Stapleton, London, 1887, i. 363; J. Morley, i. 150.

[23] Gladstone in *The Prime Ministers' Papers: Gladstone*, i. 152.

[24] Gladstone's *Studies subsidiary to the works of Bishop Butler: companion volume to the works of Joseph Butler*, ed. W. E. Gladstone, London, 1896, p. 112.

sin'.[25] This too was taken from Augustine and—less obviously—from Butler. The *Studies subsidiary to Butler* include an assault on those critics who found the lapsarian and soteriological aspects of Christianity insufficiently emphasized by Butler. The *Analogy* was not primarily concerned with such matters, but it contained sufficient incidental references to render its position——for Gladstone at any rate——unambiguous.

In truth, if there be any one topic on which repetition may plausibly be made a charge against Butler, it is the sad and solemn topic of the misery, debasement, and corruption which virulent, and inveterate sin has brought about in the world.[26]

Gladstone maintained to the end that sin, righteousness, and judgement made up a 'code of moral regeneration for mankind',[27] and the key to that code, or what evangelicals called 'the hinge of christian truth', was of course the Atonement. During Gladstone's lifetime, more and more Christians turned against the orthodox literal interpretation of the Crucifixion, much to his regret. He blamed this on the increasing 'tenderness' of the times, something which in its other manifestations, such as abolition of bear-baiting, discouragement of duelling, promotion of public health, he applauded. As men grew more squeamish, they found the idea repellent that God should have inflicted pain on an innocent whipping-boy, Christ. Gladstone countered that to think like this was to 'presuppose . . . that *pain is essentially or at least universally an evil. . . .* But this, it seems to me, ought to be denied. Pain is not in its nature an evil in the proper sense, nor is it invariably attended with evil as a consequence.' After all, the most common effect of pain was to 'energise . . . feelings of self-mortification and self sacrifice',[28] which both evangelicals and tractarians regarded

[25] Gladstone speaking to Mrs Humphry Ward, 8 Apr. 1888, as reported in *The Life of Mrs. Humphry Ward*, by Janet Penrose Trevelyan, London, 1923, p. 59.

[26] Gladstone, *Studies subsidiary to Butler*, p. 113.

[27] Gladstone to B. M. Malabari, 20 July 1889, in *Correspondence on Church and Religion*, ii. 117-19.

[28] Gladstone, 'On the mediation of Christ', written in 1830 and printed as an appendix to *Studies subsidiary to Butler*, pp. 327-33. See Gladstone to Manning, 16 Nov. 1869, in *Life of Cardinal Manning*, by Edmund Sheridan Purcell, London, 1895, ii. 407: 'It was in the year 1830, I think, that I began to be powerfully acted upon by the writings of Bishop Butler (one of my four great teachers), and I then wrote a paper on his chapter concerning Mediation, the matter of which

as the surest harbingers of virtue, in nations as well as individuals. Moreover, the doctrine of the Cross

alone had given full meaning to life, and had given the firmest control over the springs of human action, by incorporating it in a person, and making it, liable to love. . . . In this scheme, the doctrine of free pardon (through Christ) is not a passport for sin, nor a derogation from the moral order *which carefully adapts reward and retribution to desert*, but stands in the closest harmony with the component laws of our moral nature.[29]

This conception of a 'moral order which carefully adapts reward and retribution to desert' introduces us to Gladstone's powerful sense of providence. Is God, he asked rhetorically, a 'Divine Governing Power, which will some day call all of us to account for every thought we conceive, and for every word we utter', or is he 'a mere abstract idea dwelling in the air, and in the clouds'?[30] The evangelical doctrine of providence was inherited from eighteenth-century natural theology, but adapted to suit nineteenth-century pessimism. When the universe had seemed to operate harmoniously, like a perfect machine, and it had been assumed that (if left to their own devices) men might co-operate happily, natural theologians had deduced the existence of a loving and powerful God from the evidences of design in his world. Such Paleyan complacency became impossible to sustain after the events of 1792-4, the Napoleonic wars, the rise of a proletariat, Malthus's ecological predictions, and other evidences of unhappiness in the world. Evangelicals therefore depicted God as governing, not *naturally* so that all might receive pleasure, but *morally* that all might receive justice. The point was made succinctly by Wilberforce in the *Christian Observer* of 1803.

The goodness of God is the only moral attribute which is apprehended by Dr. Paley to be manifest from the appearances of the natural world. No observation occurs . . . concerning the holiness or justice of the

I still view with interest in no way abated. The tendency to rationalise in this sense has continued, and I wish to encourage it, believing it to be truly Evangelical, Apostolical, and Catholic.'

[29] Gladstone, 'True and false conceptions of the Atonement', in *The Nineteenth Century*, xxxvi (1894), 317-31, and reprinted in Gladstone, *Later Gleanings: theological and ecclesiastical*, London, 1897, pp. 312-37 [italics added].

[30] Gladstone in House of Commons, 26 Apr. 1883, *Parliamentary Debates*, third series, cclxxviii, 1193.

Deity; nothing of those tendencies of virtue to produce happiness, and of vice to produce misery, which are so judiciously and so unanswerably enforced by Bishop Butler, and analogically applied as proofs that the world is not now in that state in which it originally appeared from the hands of the Creator, but that it is evidently in a state of degradation and ruin—that the Creator is a *moral* governor.[31]

This transcendental idea of God was central to the Anglican evangelical world-view in the first half of the nineteenth century, and became quickly unfashionable thereafter. But Gladstone clung to it ferociously. Writing in 1877, for example, he conceived of God

as standing in certain relations to us; as carrying on a moral government of the world. He is held to prescribe and favour what is right; to forbid and regard with displeasure what is wrong; and to dispose the course of events in such a way that, in general and upon the whole, there is a tendency of virtue to bring satisfaction and happiness, and of vice to entail the reverse of these, even when appearances, and external advantages, might not convey such an indication.[32]

And in the *Studies subsidiary to Butler* he virtually repeated Wilberforce's point about the incompleteness of Paley's natural philosophy: 'although the argument of design took its rise within the precincts of the physical order, it did not end there. And Butler has here laid down for us the cardinal principle on which is founded its extension to the moral universe.'[33] Like most evangelicals, Gladstone moved from here to the consolatory reflection that, since vice is punished *either* in this world *or* the next, terrestrial misfortunes were really marks of divine favour, encouraging the reformation of the sinner and so insuring him against condign punishment eternally. His response to bankruptcy and to his daughter's dangerous illness was, typically, not self-pity, but the reflection that he had 'never seen the workings of the prudential and moral laws of God's providence so signally exhibited'.[34]

[31] Wilberforce in *The Christian Observer*, ii (1803), 369–74. The authorship has been adduced from internal evidence.

[32] Gladstone, 'On the influence of authority in matters of opinion', in *The Nineteenth Century*, i (1877), 10, wrongly cited by Schreuder, p. 80, as appearing in the *Edinburgh Review*.

[33] Gladstone, *Studies subsidiary to Butler*, p. 292.

[34] Gladstone to Manning, 12 Mar. 1848, in *Correspondence on Church and Religion*, ii. 278–82.

Clearly, one was meant to respond positively to the 'admonitions' of providence, in other words, to react. Gladstone vested enormous significance in the word 'action'.

Our Almighty Father is continually, aye day and hour, calling upon us, almost compelling us, to act. Now acting is not the mere discharge of an outward function. It is a continuing process, in which we are responsible throughout. What is meant by being responsible? It is meant that we expose ourselves to consequences flowing from our actions. These are (say) of two kinds. First, there is alteration of environment; which implies that in the future actings, which cannot be escaped, we shall have to cast our account anew with circumstances. The second cuts deeper still. It is that our action modifies, that is to say progressively but silently alters, from time to time, and eventually shapes, our own mind and character.[35]

Gladstone often explained such imperceptible character development with reference to Butler's doctrine of habit. By acting virtuously, men acquire a habitude for virtue, and so improve themselves as well as their environment. It was thus that 'in those little tutored but yet reflective minds' of the Lancashire operatives, lauded by Gladstone for stoically supporting the Northern States against their own supposed economic interests, 'by a process of quiet instillation, opinions and sentiments gradually form themselves of which we for a long time remain unaware, but which, when at last they make their appearance, are found to be deep-rooted, mature, and ineradicable'.[36] Moreover, if action was a key to the good life, politics, once thought sordid,[37] came to be seen as an arena for the grandest actions. 'The vital principle of the Liberal Party,' Gladstone told Granville, 'like that of Greek art, is *action*.'[38] As Schreuder puts it, mature Gladstonian politics were 'practical experiments in truth . . . a series of evolving

[35] Gladstone, *Studies subsidiary to Butler*, p. 9. See Joseph Butler, *The Analogy of Religion, Natural and Revealed, to the Constitution and Course of Nature*, ed. Samuel Halifax, London, 1834, p. 133 [Book One, Chapter Five]: 'There is a third thing, which may seem implied in the present world's being a state of probation; that it is a theatre of action, for the manifestation of personal characters, with respect to a future one.'

[36] Gladstone in House of Commons, 27 Apr. 1866, *Parliamentary Debates*, third series, clxxxiii, 148-9.

[37] Gladstone to Manning, 2 Apr. 1837, in *Correspondence on Church and Religion*, i. 31-2.

[38] Gladstone to Granville, 19 May 1877, in *The Political Correspondence of Mr. Gladstone and Lord Granville 1876-1886*, ed. Agatha Ramm, Oxford, 1962, i. 40.

strategies, policies, postures, enthusiasms, missions, and tactical forays',[39] endless attempts to evoke such 'responses as his nature craved'.

The problem of course is to know *how* to act, and here Gladstone was unpardonably obscure. He was no metaphysician—'his intellect would not bite' on philosophy, as a friend conceded[40]—and grandiloquent references to 'the mode of Providential government as interpreted by Butler',[41] do not help much. Even the celebrated analysis of his own political 'opportunism', his understanding of when and how to act, is largely obscure. He said that providence had provided him with one 'striking gift', which was, 'at certain political junctures . . . appreciation of the general situation and its result'. This was *not* a 'simple acceptance of public opinion', but 'an insight into the facts of particular eras, and their relations one to another, which generates in the mind a conviction that the materials exist for forming a public opinion, and for directing it to a particular end'.[42] It was Butler, more than any other writer, who provided Gladstone with his 'moral insight' into the facts of an era, who showed him where to look for evidence, or at least 'probable evidence', since partial information is the most we can expect God to vouchsafe us, given the 'very limited nature of our faculties'.[43] Butler's doctrine that 'probability is the guide of life' provided the theme of all Gladstone's political analysis.[44] (It also provided scope for ambiguities, through which all sorts of ulterior motives might, consciously or otherwise, enter his calculations.)

[39] Schreuder, p. 85.

[40] Henry Scott Holland, *Personal Studies*, London, 1905, p. 41.

[41] Gladstone to Maud Stanley, 27 Jan. 1856, in *Correspondence on Church and Religion*, ii. 30.

[42] Gladstone, 'General retrospect', in *The Prime Minister's Papers: Gladstone*, i. 136. There are several analyses of this famous passage, of which perhaps the most interesting are in Philip Magnus, *Gladstone. A biography*, London, 1968, pp. 190-1, 440-2.

[43] Gladstone to B. M. Malabari, 20 July 1889, loc. cit.

[44] Gladstone, 'The law of probable evidence, and its application to conduct', written in 1845 but published in *The Nineteenth Century*, v (1879), 908-34, and reprinted in *Gleanings of past years*, London, 1879, vii. 153-99, and also in *Studies subsidiary to Butler*, 334 et seq. See Gladstone to the earl of Pembroke, 29 Sept. 1873, in *Correspondence on Church and Religion*, ii. 92-6: 'Probable knowledge, or, to speak more accurately, probable evidence, may entail the obligation of action, the obligation of belief, as truly as knowledge which is demonstrative, and this probable knowledge is the "guide of life".'

Having tried and failed to knit himself a complete and 'systematic philosophy' in 1838, Gladstone subsequently made a virtue of incompleteness and uncertainty. Hence his criticism of that avowed, but 'thoroughly unsound',[45] Butlerian, J. H. Newman (elsewhere referred to as 'no Butlerian at all, though a warm admirer of Butler'):[46]

I think there is nothing more characteristic of the unphilosophic mind than impatience of doubt and premature avidity for system. That seems to me . . . to have been Newman's snare all along. No man can grasp truth entire. Butler took it in fragments, but his wise instinct enabled him so to lay each stone that it would fit in with every stone that might be well and truly laid in the double light of thought and experience. . . . Newman also laid his stones; but at every period of his life he seems to have been driven by a fatal necessity to piece them all together, to make a building of them, and he has made half a dozen; and when the winds blew and the floods beat they gave way.[47]

Clearly, Gladstone derived from Butler more of a method than a system. His 'four teachers' (Augustine, Aristotle, and Dante were the other three) all possessed an architectonic sense of measure and function, an understanding of the relationship of parts to wholes, of the adaptation of means to ends—quite simply, of the fitness of things. They helped to give Gladstone his acute sense of propriety, seen for example in his exaggerated concern, even while advocating radical constitutional change, for procedural precedent. Thus it saddened him that, of all European nations, the British most signally lacked any sense of visual propriety. Where else would they select the leading Gothic architect to design an Italianate Foreign Office, and the leading *palazzo* architect for a perpendicular House of Parliament? This reflection led him predictably to an analogous moral paradox. 'In what country

[45] Gladstone to R. H. Hutton, 6 Oct. 1890, in *Correspondence on Church and Religion*, i. 407.

[46] Gladstone to Acton, 1 Sept. 1890, ibid. i. 405.

[47] Gladstone to Sir F. Rogers, 25 Feb. 1866, ibid. ii. 301. Newman's 'reply', made originally in response to some remarks of Gladstone's political mentor, Peel, at the opening of the Tamworth Reading Room, was reprinted in J. H. Newman, *An Essay in Aid of a Grammar of Assent*, London, 1870 (new impression, 1901), pp. 94–5: 'Life is not long enough for a religion of inferences; we shall never have done beginning, if we determine to begin with proof. We shall ever be laying our foundations; we shall turn theology into evidences, and divines into textuaries. I would rather be bound to defend the reasonableness of assuming that Christianity is true, than to demonstrate a moral governance from the physical world.'

except ours could . . . a parish ball have been got up in order to supply funds for procuring a parish hearse?'[48] Such solecisms aroused his evangelical abhorrence of levity, his fear of seeming to mock God, his conviction (which he would have called Butlerian) that means were indistinguishable from ends, as manners were from men. 'Right action' demanded prodigious self-scrutiny and self-consciousness if it was to perform its main function of shaping 'our own minds and character'.

Butler provided statesmen with one other clue to the 'facts of particular eras'—a belief in what might loosely be called the Manichean or dialectical workings of providence, and in 'the laws of action and reaction in human thought'.[49] His Deity was a supremely moral one 'because He takes sides in that conflict between virtue and vice, which necessarily prevails in the world'.[50] 'In the battle of good and evil, Providence, though it may seem to be fighting in disguise,[51] chooses its side and makes known its choice.'[52] Possibly Gladstone derived such notions from an important review of his own first book by another Butlerian, Keble. The latter applauded the intentions of the author of *The State in its Relations with the Church*, but opposed his establishmentarian message. As Keble saw it, the church and the world were locked in mortal combat, and the only hope for the former was for it to break away from the world, that is from the state, if need be violently. Gladstone's vision of a revitalized church dominating the state from within was absurdly utopian, since in practice the state would gain an upper hand over 'heretical pastors', secularized bishops, and jack-in-office clergy. And even if that were not to happen, Gladstone's proposals for the Church 'excluded persecution', whereas what Keble wanted, the 'violent separation of church and state, seems almost to invite it'. 'There is no blood of martyrs in Gladstone's prospect' —and it was only such blood that could sow 'the seed of

---

[48] Gladstone, 'Ritualism and ritual', in *The Contemporary Review*, xxiv (1874), 668 (reprinted in *Gleanings*, vi. 117–18). He ascribed such behaviour to a national 'incapacity of detecting discord, and . . . tendency to solecism'.

[49] Gladstone, 'The evangelical movement: its parentage, progress, and issue', *The British Quarterly Review*, lxx (1879), 14 (reprinted in *Gleanings*, vii. 221).

[50] Gladstone, *Studies subsidiary to Butler*, pp. 14–15.

[51] i.e. evil sometimes appears to prosper in the temporal world.

[52] Gladstone, *Studies subsidiary to Butler*, pp. 293–310.

future diffusion and victory'.[53] Gladstone considered Keble's review 'elevated, and most interesting'.[54] He may also have been influenced by an idiosyncratic book which he read several times, Lord Lindsay's *Progression by Antagonism* (1846).[55] This work, which also drew on Butler, was intended as a theoretical key to Lindsay's *magnum opus* on the historical development of Christian art. It defined the three life-forces in artistic endeavour as sense, mind, and spirit, respectively associated with Greek, Roman, and Hebraic cultures. Progress in Christian art then occurred dialectically, through the antagonism of half-truths, towards true spiritual awareness, though it required some great artist in each era to inspire his contemporaries with the necessary vision, and to direct aesthetic opinion towards a particular end. Gladstone held a similar view of the statesman's duty, which was to interpret providence to his contemporaries, and to make them 'feel the issue of the moment as part of the eternal duel between good and evil'.

II

Gladstone's first experience of dialectical moral politics came with the corn law crisis of 1845-6. If Gladstone embraced 'the morality of free trade and finance', as Matthew puts it, it must be remembered that for 'liberal' or 'Peelite' Tories like him, free trade and 'sound' (non-interventionist) finance were less matters of *enrichissez-vous* and social progress (though there were elements of these) than of leaving providence to its own devices, the better to display God's handiwork, his wise and moral economy of the world.[56] Thus Gladstone, applying

[53] [J. Keble] in *The British Critic and Theological Quarterly Review*, xxvi (1839), 395-6.

[54] *The Gladstone Diaries* [8 Oct. 1839], ii. 631. It seemed to Gladstone that Keble must have 'the gift of prophecy in its larger sense, so accurately does he interpret many hidden meanings that are in my mind rather than in my book'. *Correspondence on Church and Religion*, i. 18.

[55] Lord Lindsay, *Progression by Antagonism. Theory, Involving considerations touching the present position, duties, and destiny of Great Britain*, London, 1846, *passim*. Lindsay and Gladstone later conducted parallel researches into Olympian mythology and the theology of the Homeric Age. See Gladstone to Lindsay (Earl Crawford), 14 and 16 Feb. 1874, and Lindsay to Gladstone, 15 and 27 Feb. 1874: British Library, Gladstone MSS, 44442 fos. 230, 252-3, 264, and 272-3.

[56] See Boyd Hilton, *Corn, Cash, Commerce. The economic policies of the tory*

natural theology to monetary economics, wrote of God's providential 'counterpoises, both physical and social, for the advantage of his creatures', such as 'the wonderful monetary system of civilized countries, which exhibits its balance of forces in a manner more curious and striking than any mere physical [i.e. human] ponderation can do it'.[57] But if he was a theoretical free trader for some years before 1845, it was not until then that he felt free trade to be the 'issue of the moment'. As he later told his father, he had been accustomed to speak 'of protection, not as a thing good in principle, but to be dealt with as tenderly and cautiously as might be according to circumstances, always moving in the direction of free trade'. It was the Irish famine that 'materially altered' the situation and ruled out such a 'cautious course', demanding instead an immediate commitment to principle.

A great struggle was imminent, in which it was plain that two parties only could really find place, on the one side for repeal, on the other side for *permanent* maintenance of a corn law and a protective system generally and on principle.[58]

Now there is no sublunary reason why the famine should have banished pragmatism in favour of war *à outrance*; but then the famine was not, in Gladstone's eyes, a sublunary phenomenon.

Here is a calamity most legibly Divine; there is a total absence of such second causes as might tempt us to explain it away; it is the greatest horror of modern times, that in the richest age of the world, and in the richest country of that age, the people should be dying of famine by hundreds, and we, the English community, have scarcely as yet got even the feeblest notion of this horror in its aspect to us. No mere giving of money will do, it can only be met by national and personal humiliation.[59]

Where other politicians, such as Trevelyan, were inclined to see the hand of God directed against the Irish themselves for

governments 1815–1830, Oxford, 1977, pp. 303–14; also Boyd Hilton, 'Peel: a reappraisal', *Historical Journal*, 22 (1979), 606–14.

[57] Gladstone, *Studies subsidiary to Butler*, pp. 14–15.
[58] Gladstone to his father, 30 June 1849, quoted by Matthew in *The Gladstone Diaries*, iii. xxxviii–xxxix, and by Hilton, 'Peel: a reappraisal', loc. cit., p. 612.
[59] Gladstone to Manning, 9 Mar. 1847, in *Correspondence on Church and Religion*, ii. 275–6.

their profligacy and sloth, Gladstone saw at once 'its aspect to *us*', its judgement on 'our usual tone of thoughtless joyous or ambitious life'. Ireland was not the object but 'the *minister* of God's retribution. . . . Ireland forces upon us these great social and great religious questions. God grant that we may have courage to look them in the face and to work through them.'[60] In this context, repeal of the Corn Laws could be seen as an atoning sacrifice of the wealth of the British ruling class, rather than as an attempt to galvanize commercial and manufacturing prosperity.

Unfortunately, Peel's defeat in the House of Commons on another Irish issue (which Gladstone regarded as a perfect example of 'Butler's doctrine of retribution in this world'[61]) impaired the clear-cut nature of the free traders' victory in 1846. Gladstone was disappointed by Peel's later refusal to reactivate the issue, and bring it to a decisive conclusion, by withdrawing support from Russell and letting in a Tory party still committed to the restoration of protection. Disraeli's acceptance of free trade in 1852, and his own tidying-up budgets, disposed of the question shortly afterwards, and it became necessary to find another issue on which to spill the 'blood of martyrs'. But the 1850s seemed sadly lacking in polarizing issues, and consequently incoherent and meaningless. Gladstone's diagnosis of the problem in an article of 1856 is extremely revealing of his approach to political engagement. As he saw it, Parliament was no longer functioning properly, no longer legislating in response to public initiatives, with the result that the organic union of government and nation, which could only be maintained by such 'responsible' dialogue, had been lost. Partly this was due to Palmerston's lassitude, but the main problem was that such initiatives were harder to sustain in the present age of equipoise. The heyday of Parliament had been 1832-46 when, according to Gladstone, two rigid parties had held the legislature in a tight grip. This had given rise to intense hatreds, admittedly, but also, and more importantly, to 'strong attachments', 'unswerving confidence', and 'warm devotion'. Though a man's politics

---

[60] Gladstone to his wife, 12 Oct. 1845, ibid. ii. 266 [italics added].

[61] Apparently because of Peel's equivocations on the subject of the sugar duties in 1841. *The Gladstone Diaries* [10 July 1846], iii. 557.

'were not profound, they were *intelligible*, and so were his companion's'. Moreover, such political polarization had only been possible because society was itself normatively divided after 1832.

Town and country, upon the whole, represent the respective preponderances in Great Britain of Church and Dissent, of Authority and Will, of Antiquity and Novelty, of Conservation and Reform; and Town and Country had received from the Reform Act each its separate organisation, acutely distinct and angular, while all the intermediate, nondescript, miscellaneous influences, that under the old system had darkened the dividing lines and softened the shock of the adverse powers, had been but too ruthlessly swept away.[62]

Historically this was nonsense. British society in the thirties and forties had not been divided neatly into two such cultural, religious, constitutional, and economic camps. But the analysis does reflect a perception, certainly Gladstone's own perception, of social conflict at that time. It made politics 'intelligible' and 'legible', and it made protection the obviously central issue.

Politics never recovered the dualistic simplicities of Gladstone's youth. And so, frustrated by the mid-Victorians' normative and economic consensus, Gladstone had to resurrect conflict—artificially, as it seemed to his opponents— by pitting visions of the future against the present. In this way the most Burkean of statesmen became the most *un*-Burkean, interfering with society gratuitously, not from the dictates of reason, but in the belief that societies which are not in turmoil will stagnate. 'The growth of the body politic renders stereotyped law intolerable.'[63] 'You cannot fight the future. Time is on our side.'[64]

Presumably Gladstone was only able to think like this because, living through the fifties, he naturally imbibed new notions concerning the passage of time, which accompanied geological, biological, and anthropological discoveries.[65] It

[62] [Gladstone], 'The declining efficiency of parliament', *Quarterly Review*, xcix (1856), 527–8 and 521–70 *passim*.

[63] Ibid.

[64] Gladstone in House of Commons, 27 Apr. 1866, *Parliamentary Debates*, third series, clxxxiii, 152.

[65] See J. W. Burrow, *Evolution and Society. A study in Victorian social theory*, Cambridge, 1968, pp. 98–100, 115–17, and *passim*.

was in this respect that he made his greatest, perhaps his only real, break with classical evangelicalism. The latter was based on an assumption that this world is but a place of moral trial, a prelude to eternity; its conception of the passage of time was static, or perhaps cyclical, and it envisaged a sharp break between this world and the next. 'Dispensations of providence' such as wars and famines were manifested in the 'here and now', and required an immediate, redemptive response from man. But as is well known, Darwinian and other evolutionary advances introduced a more linear conception of time, an idea of continuity between earth and eternity, a view of God as immanent rather than transcendent. Thus Gladstone, late in life, excusing his youthful opposition to an extension of the franchise in 1832, complained that because of his evangelicalism he had missed 'that greatest of historical facts', the fact that society was divine.[66] In the course of becoming a Liberal he came to see God as directing the progress of society as well as saving souls. His speeches came to be studded with such concepts as 'the great social forces which move onwards in their might and majesty', the 'silent changes in the earth's crust', 'the great subterranean movements of society', 'silent changes in the very bed and basis of modern society'. In other words, as Britain passed, as it seemed to Gladstone to do, 'from a stationary into a progressive period',[67] so the natural theologian in Gladstone stopped looking for evidences of God's omnipotence in the workings of the machine, and sought them instead in the moral improvement of society: 'When we contemplate many of the political societies, such as the Roman, the British, the American, their movement through successive stages is astonishing. But each of these stages is a new presentation of the argument of *design*.'[68]

So while many other fundamentalist Christians found Darwinian theory disturbing, Gladstone was untroubled. As he wrote to Jevons in 1874,

Indeed, I must say that the doctrine of Evolution, if it be true, enhances in my judgement the proper idea of the greatness of God, for it makes

[66] Gladstone's 'Autobiographical retrospect', 22 June 1894, in *The Prime Ministers' Papers: Gladstone*, i. 38.

[67] Gladstone, *A Chapter of Autobiography*, London, 1868, p. 11 (reprinted in *Gleanings*, vii. 101-2). [68] Gladstone, *Studies subsidiary to Butler*, p. 305.

every stage of creation a legible prophecy of all those which are to follow.[69]

Note the word 'legible'. The Irish famine had been a 'calamity legibly Divine'. Unfortunately, as critics of 'special' providences did not tire of pointing out, interpretation of such calamities is likely to be somewhat arbitrary. It had seemed providential at the time because of 'the total absence of such second causes as might tempt us to explain it away'. Now, in 1874, Gladstone was prepared to welcome second causes, or scientific laws, as a buttress of divine providence. In *Studies subsidiary to Butler* he quipped that 'evolution' might be better termed 'devolution', since it showed that God, rather than making a 'special creation', had—'still more admirably' —devolved the task on secondary or scientific laws.

The more we have of system and fixity in nature, the better. For, in the method of natural second causes, God as it were takes the map of His own counsels out of the recesses of His own idea and graciously lays it near our view; condescending, as it were, to make us partakers of His thought.[70]

Reflecting on Butler's view as to the evolution of conscience, and on his speculations about the possible immortality of brutes, Gladstone was able to reassure himself that 'the idea of evolution is without doubt deeply ingrained in Butler'.[71]

Gladstone's relations with what I have defined (for want of a better word) as evangelicalism may be elucidated by considering the similar relations that existed between J. S. Mill and utilitarianism. Mill's premises differed markedly from Gladstone's—truculent agnosticism and deep suspicion of Butler, for example—but he arrived at a similar vision of Liberalism. His dialectical conception of truth emerging gradually through the 'collision of adverse opinions',[72] and his vivid awareness that such collisions in themselves enhance

[69] Gladstone to Stanley Jevons, 10 May 1874, in *Correspondence on Church and Religion*, ii. 101.
[70] Gladstone, *Studies subsidiary to Butler*, 307-9. Most moderate, Anglican, evangelicals of the Clapham School and its satellites would have agreed with Gladstone's analysis.
[71] Gladstone to Argyll, 9 Dec. 1895, in Morley, *Life of Gladstone*, iii. 521. See Gladstone to Müller, 24 Dec. 1872, Bodleian Library, Max Müller MSS, d. 170.
[72] J. S. Mill, *On Liberty*, ed. M. G. Fawcett, London, 1960, p. 65 [Chapter II].

the minds and morals of the participants, was quintessentially Gladstonian. Mr Cowling aptly characterizes Mill's Liberalism as containing, not philosophical proofs, but 'commitments to action'; his object was to give workers a 'sense of participation', which in turn would involve them in 'active critical self-examination; energetic pursuit in every particular of the closest approximation to Truth. Mill's society is a society of seekers after Truth.'[73] It is widely accepted that what Mill did in effect was to introduce ideas of qualitative progression into the static and mechanical calculus of Bentham; or, as he put it, to envisage *utility* in its 'largest sense, grounded on the permanent interests of man as a progressive being'.[74] This parallels what Gladstone did with moderate Anglican evangelicalism, which had been a sort of spiritual counterpart of utilitarianism, in that it had been predominantly individualist, mechanicist, and consequentialist. Evangelicals held (with Butler) that God ruled the world by a system of rewards and punishments. This was his 'scheme of salvation', his 'divine economy', which encouraged individual sinners to seek out salvation through faith. In the same way, Bentham envisaged secular governments operating through rewards and punishments, with the hope of encompassing the *social* redemption of its citizens, saving them, as it were, from their selfish and anti-social dispositions. In both cases, the context of the operation was static and mechanical, and what Mill and Gladstone did was to introduce mid-century notions of development and qualitative progress into the respective schema, without discarding the basically empirical and anti-idealist structures of both systems, utilitarianism and evangelicalism.

III

In a penetrating discussion of mid-century ethical norms, Houghton has distinguished between the contrasting, but often compatible, modes of earnestness and enthusiasm. Earnestness, which derived from puritan and mercantile traditions, stressed the need to conquer the 'sinful desires of the ego' by exercise of 'moral will' or conscience; enthusiasm, a more

[73] Maurice Cowling, *Mill and Liberalism*, Cambridge, 1963, pp. 77 and 91-2.
[74] Mill, *On Liberty*, 16 [Chapter I].

romantic and aristocratic mode, looked rather to sweeping selfishness aside in a welter of high ideals, noble emotions, and elevated aims. Nearly all Victorians, according to Houghton, applauded both qualities, but nearly all also accorded primacy to one or the other. Most preferred to stress earnestness, but there was a minority group—Houghton cites Mill, Morley, Dickens, Browning, and Eliot—'who substituted "noble" for "earnest" as the term of highest praise for a man or a life'.[75] Houghton's analysis fits Gladstone neatly. He never gave up a puritan or evangelical stress on conscience, but he also came to lean more and more on enthusiasm, and might well have said of politics, as Thomas Arnold said of poetry, that it can 'put us above ourselves . . . awaken our devotion, our admiration, or our love'.[76] It was in such a spirit that Gladstone commended the fierce party strife of 1832–46 for its 'strong attachments', 'unswerving confidence', and 'warm devotion'.

However, this is not the place to consider how far Gladstone's political philosophy can explain his political actions, or to what extent it masked ulterior motives. The question continually troubled Gladstone himself, as his diaries show. There was in him what Schreuder calls an 'extraordinary complex symbiotic relationship between ethical principles and acute sense of the opportune, between the moral imperative of conscience and the hard Parliamentary realities of power pragmatically wielded'.[77] Cynics accused him of 'backing winners' at the eleventh hour, whether they were Italians, Yankees, Fenians, or Bulgars; Gladstone would have replied that, since 'winners' may be presumed to have God on their side, he was simply prophesying providence, or detecting those 'forces which will shape the future'. Other critics complained of the self-righteous conviction with which Gladstone would propound policies that he had previously, and equally self-righteously, opposed. Yet it was genuinely important to Gladstone to feel that he had had to battle against error before embarking on new enthusiasms. In the same way,

[75] Walter E. Houghton, *The Victorian Frame of Mind 1830–70*, New Haven and London, 1957, pp. 263–5.

[76] Thomas Arnold, 'Preface to poetry of common life' (1831), reprinted in *The miscellaneous works of Thomas Arnold*, London, 1845, p. 253.

[77] Schreuder, p. 84.

evangelicals needed to feel that they had been heinously sinful in their unregenerate days, if they were now to feel saved; because they held that salvation is by faith, and that faith needs to be heartfelt, so they craved something like a conversion experience. Gladstone too held that 'The idea of conversion requires and depends upon the idea of sin',[78] and so the fact that he had previously defended the Confederacy, for example, made him feel more, not less, justified in offering support to the Union. Again Gladstone's search for polarizing issues led him to some absurdly far-fetched 'analyses of the general situation'. Perhaps the silliest example of all is his response to the Commons division of 9 July 1864, when Palmerston's government survived Disraeli's motion of censure on its handling of the Schleswig-Holstein crisis by a paltry eighteen votes. 'This debate ought to be an epoch in foreign policy', he wrote in his diary, while, according to another diarist, in conversation 'G. expressed himself astonished at the strength and unanimity of the parliamentary declaration in favour of peace: said it marked a new era in our foreign policy.'[79] Since the vote was neither decisive nor specifically in favour of peace as against war, Gladstone's search for a 'Little Englander' type of mission was transparently false on this occasion. Finally, it has often been pointed out that Gladstone preferred his enthusiasms to divert attention away from 'bread and butter' questions of social policy, that he particularly liked missions which for one reason or another could never be accomplished (as was the case with Home Rule, perhaps), and that he sometimes seemed reluctant to allow his crusades to be brought to a successful resolution.[80]

[78] Gladstone to Argyll, 14 July 1865, in *Correspondence on Church and Religion*, ii. 87.

[79] *The Gladstone Diaries* [8 July 1864], vi. 288. Stanley's diary entry for 24 July 1864, reporting a conversation with Lord Enfield, in *Disraeli, Derby, and the Conservative Party. Journals and memoirs of Edward Henry, Lord Stanley 1849–1869*, ed. John Vincent, Hassocks, Sussex, 1978, p. 222.

[80] There is some evidence, for example, that he would have liked to prolong the Irish Church Disestablishment crisis, rather than allow a broadly successful resolution in July, 1869. (Ibid., pp. 341–2.) As for accusations of diversion, see the parallel in Mill, *On Liberty*, pp. 54–6 [Chapter II]. Mill believed that as experts resolved more and more of the seriously controversial issues, so the scope for public debate would narrow, in which case it behoved 'the teachers of mankind . . . to provide a substitute'—even, if necessary, by reviving Socratic and medieval disputations. The dichotomy which has frequently been noted between

All such criticisms are justified but beside the point, for Gladstone never pretended that he wanted to reconstruct society. The 'old man in a hurry' preferred his followers to run on the spot, as it were, in a flurry of mental and moral *activity*, rather than to create a heaven on earth.

IV

The tribulations that attended Gladstone from 1847 to 1852 were crushing: the deaths of his daughter, and of his father, and then of his political 'father', Peel; the antics of his sister Helen; the shame and worry of his wife's family bankruptcy; thwarted political ambition; persistent 'temptations to impurity', causing agonies of self-mortification which could only be assuaged by what he uncoyly called 'the blessings of discipline'; and, as a backdrop to all this, the gradual disintegration of the Oxford Movement, beginning with Newman's apostasy and culminating in the secessions to Rome, after the Gorham Judgement, of his devoted friends, Henry Manning and James Hope-Scott. Gladstone was devastated:

I have . . . a knowledge right in the very inmost parts of myself: that I am, even among guilty ones, the guiltiest. These two terrible years have really displaced and uprooted my heart from the Anglican Church, seen as a personal and *living* Church in the *body* of its Priests and members: and at the same time the two friends whom I might call the only supports for my intellect have been wrenched away from me, leaving me lacerated, and I may say barely conscious morally.[81]

Yet notwithstanding all this, sensitive critics have noted the heroic, redemptive aspects of those years. Morley wrote lyrically about 'the golden trumpet notes of a new time',[82] and G. M. Young, marvelling at the sudden relaxation of social tensions between 1848 and 1851, commented: 'It was in that Maytime of Youth recaptured that Gladstonian Liberalism was conceived. It was the only atmosphere in which it could

the two levels of Gladstone's first government (1868-74)—a high-flown but 'diversionary' moral politics on the one hand, and practical or expert administrative intervention on the other—may owe something to Mill's insights in the matter.

[81] *The Gladstone Diaries* [19 Aug. 1851], iv. 352-3.
[82] Morley, *Life of Gladstone*, i. 385.

have been conceived; an atmosphere composed in equal measure, of progress, confidence, and social union.'[83]

Juxtaposition of these contrasting modes, glad confidence and abject despair, characterizes Gladstone's Liberalism excellently. As early as 1843 he wondered to himself whether it had been 'sufficiently considered, how far pain may become the ground of enjoyment. How far satisfaction and even an action delighting in pain may be a true experimental phenomenon of the human mind.'[84] Historians from Morley onwards have well understood the rationalist, optimistic, and tolerant elements of Liberalism, but there was also this evangelical ingredient, which more than any other generated its 'visceral thrills' (to borrow Professor Vincent's happy phrase), its powers of redemptive expostulation. For what had made evangelical religion so vital was precisely its dual belief, on the one hand in man's natural depravity and spiritual danger, and on the other, in the joyful prospects of spiritual rescue and salvation.

This brings us back to the delicate relationship between Gladstone's Liberalism and evangelicalism, a movement he reviewed sympathetically but critically in 1879. He complained that too many evangelicals had fallen into the Lutheran fallacy of regarding grace as something wholly external and 'unconditional', able to enter the frailest of human vessels, even without holy endeavour on their part. Certain others had, by their careless terminology, helped to reduce the great doctrine of the Atonement to the status of a 'forensic' process or, worse still, a mere commercial transaction, a 'bargain in a shop' affair, whereby Christ merely *bought* our ransom with his blood in a morally neutral way. On the whole, however, Gladstone credited evangelicals with having nobly restored attention from the doctrine of justification to

[83] G. M. Young, *Today and yesterday. Collected essays and addresses*, London, 1848, p. 33.

[84] *The Gladstone Diaries* [4 Jan. 1843], iii. 250–1: 'May not such virtue often exist, as shall find when the lower faculty is punished or straightened, a joy in the justice and in the beneficial effects of that chastisement.' Ibid. See also Gladstone's reaction to being beaten up by Peckwater hearties during his undergraduate days: 'It is no disgrace to be beaten for Christ was buffeted and smitten.' He was consoled also by the thought that the incident gave him an opportunity, all too rare alas, to forgive his enemies, even as Christ had done. Ibid. [24 Mar. 1830], i. 290–1.

the person of Christ himself; by insisting that justification requires constant and active faith, they had presented the Atonement as a 'guarantee' of holiness, not a 'substitute' for it, and as serving 'the great end of sanctification'. He concluded that, although evangelicalism had had an inadequate appreciation of sacramental religion, 'all its other parts have been appropriated by the Church of England at large, and have been greatly and beneficially developed'.[85]

And yet, when a great moral challenge did confront the nation in the form of Beaconsfieldism, Gladstone was dismayed to find that it was nonconformist churchmen, not Anglicans, who mainly responded to his prophetic admonitions. As Schreuder points out, Midlothianism was 'the radicalism of the Evangelical conscience . . . not that of the Christian socialist or even the social gospeler',[86] and unsurprisingly, it made little impact on an established church[87] which was fast abandoning evangelical or retributive doctrines, in favour of a 'Broad', 'Maurician', or 'Christian Socialist' theology, centred on the doctrine of the Incarnation rather than the Atonement.[88] Gladstone attributed the Church's failure of response to the deadening effects of its function as an establishment. 'He judged that her moral will had lost spontaneity, had grown timid and callous through a situation which impregnated her with the poison of a worldly erastianism.'[89] At any rate, it seems clear that the sympathy, ostensibly incongruous, between the High-Church statesman and the nonconformists,

[85] Gladstone, 'The evangelical movement', in *British Quarterly Review*, lxx (1879), especially 14, and in *Gleanings*, vii. 221-2.

[86] Schreuder, p. 125.

[87] R. T. Shannon, *Gladstone and the Bulgarian Agitation 1876*, London, 1963, p. 171: 'The unsympathetic attitude of the great majority of the bishops and lesser clergy gave to the Church as a body a tone more or less hostile to the agitation.'

[88] See Geoffrey Rowell, *Hell and the Victorians. A study of the nineteenth-century theological controversies concerning eternal punishment and the future life*, Oxford, 1974, *passim*.

[89] Holland, *Personal Studies*, pp. 48-9. Holland, himself a Christian Socialist, claimed—quite wrongly in my view—that Gladstone kept abreast of these developments in the Church. 'If Mr. Gladstone had retained his original Evangelicalism, he might have contented himself with renouncing the facts or the work of the Devil. But he had read Bishop Butler. He had found the Fathers. He had absorbed the rich creed of the Incarnation, in all its fulness, in its hugeness of historical preparation, in its superb honour for flesh and blood.' Ibid., p. 44. See Stephen, p. 219.

was based on their common belief in a fundamentalist or evangelical theology, now eclipsed in the established church. As Gladstone saw it, nonconformists' vigour, moral energy, and vital commitment sprang from their essentially redemptionist and Manichaean view of the world. But, as he was also aware, such beliefs were rapidly waning, even among nonconformists,[90] during the last two decades of the century. He was acutely conscious of 'a decline', even among believers, 'in the sense of sin, which, instead of being, as under the Christian system it ought to be, piercing and profound, is passing with very many into a shallow, feeble, and vague abstraction'.[91] Equally perturbing was the relegation of the doctrine of eternal punishment 'to the far-off corners of the Christian mind . . . there to sleep in deep shadow as a thing needless in our enlightened and progressive age'.

A portion of Divine truth, which even if secondary is so needful, appears to be silently passing out of view, and . . . the danger of losing it ought at all costs to be averted. . . . It is not now sought to alarm men by magnifying the power of God, and by exhibiting the strictures and sovereignty of the law of righteousness. The anxiety now is to throw these subjects into the shade, lest the fastidiousness of human judgement and feeling should be so offended as to rise in rebellion against God for his harshness and austerity.[92]

Similarly, the softer interpretation of the Atonement, which shrank from the evangelical doctrine that God the Father had literally inflicted pain on an innocent party, his Son, was dulling our sensibility to 'corrective' or 'remedial' justice, and was making it harder for us to feel that 'kind of joy in salutory pain' that had so wonderfully galvanized Gladstone himself from time to time.[93]

All of which may provide a small clue to what befell the Liberal party in the First World War. When we talk about the 'decline of nonconformity' in the context of the Liberals'

[90] See the brilliant discussion of the decline of nonconformist fundamentalism in Richard J. Helmstadter, 'The nonconformist conscience', in *The Conscience of the Victorian State*, pp. 140-4.

[91] Gladstone to Malabari, 20 July 1889, in *Correspondence on Church and Religion*, ii. 117-19.

[92] Gladstone, *Studies subsidiary to Butler*, pp. 199-201 and 206.

[93] Gladstone, 'True and false conceptions of the Atonement', in *Nineteenth Century*, xxxvi (1894), 327.

eclipse, we refer less to a numerical reduction in personnel than to a loss of the sublime self-righteousness that had given Gladstone's Liberalism and Bright's radical nonconformity their common *élan*. At this level it may be that Lloyd George's politics remained truer to the Gladstonian creed than Asquith's. As Michael Bentley has reminded us, in his distinguished study of the liberal *mind*, 'exclusively to accord to the Asquithians the mantle of true Liberalism is a strong temptation, but it is one to be avoided. Both in parliament and in the country significant numbers of Liberals followed Lloyd George after 1916 without, in their own estimation, alienating their Liberalism.' Lloyd George too, avers Dr Bentley, 'had a spirituality to sell', and one which captivated men like Edward Grigg, who regarded him as a crusader. But when it comes to characterizing the Lloyd George crusade, Dr Bentley subscribes to the common view that its salient features were organization and efficiency, virtues that effectively cut him off from 'true' Liberalism. 'The cumulative impression is one in which empirical-minded Lloyd Georgians combat quasi-religious Asquithians.' Quoting one of the former, MacCallum Scott, to the effect that 'Liberalism is not a programme, a formula, a formal and dogmatic creed. It is a spirit, a motive, an attitude towards the world', Dr Bentley comments that Lloyd George himself would probably not have understood this.[94]

Perhaps so. There is obviously some validity in tracing the fissure within the Liberal party along the lines of 'efficiency' versus 'spirituality'. Even so, it must be remembered that during the Boer War it had been the Liberal Imperialists like Asquith and Grey who had aligned themselves with 'efficiency', the pro-Boers like Lloyd George with 'spirituality'. And anyway, it is not certain whether, in the First World War, Lloyd Georgites fought fiercely because they believed in 'efficiency', or whether they preached 'efficiency' because they had chosen to fight. Probably, the distinction between 'old' and 'new' liberalism misses the point to some extent. What really emasculated the Asquithians in 1914–18, as Bentley's elegiacs brilliantly reveal, was their inability to

[94] Michael Bentley, *The Liberal Mind 1914–1929*, Cambridge, 1977, pp. 71–3, 83, and 219.

respond emotionally to a providential national catastrophe. Their moral muscles, which is to say their very liberalism, had atrophied. As Asquith later plaintively observed, quoting the by now hopelessly antiquated Bishop Butler, 'it is as easy to close the eyes of the mind as of the body. But is it as easy to open them?'[95] Asquithian minds mostly remained closed in the First World War. The obvious response Liberals might have made was, of course, the Morley–Trevelyan, pacifist or 'Midlothian' one, but there was another option. For though Disraeli's Turkish policy had been morally wicked, supporting as it did a patently 'unjust war', Augustine had also preached the doctrine of a Just War. In such a context, the extent to which conscription, for example, or DORA, contradicted the 'old' Liberal tradition of *laissez-faire*, may have been less important than the simple fact that Lloyd George could, and Asquith could not, invoke the concept of a 'holy war' against the road hog of Europe. As the former put it in a famous speech, which reverberated in public opinion for many years after it was delivered in September 1914:

We have been living in a sheltered valley for generations. We have been too comfortable and indulgent—many, perhaps, too selfish—and the stern hand of fate has scourged us to an elevation where we can see the great everlasting things that matter for a nation—the great peaks we had forgotten, of Honour, Duty, Patriotism, and, clad in glittering white, the great pinnacle of Sacrifice pointing like a rugged finger to Heaven.[96]

As theology, this may have been the crudest pastiche, but it is evident that Lloyd George's rhetoric could awaken the 'old' Liberal conscience. Bentley quotes from an address by the Council of the Baptist Union to Lloyd George in November 1918: 'You believed, as we believed, that the good hand of God was upon us, that we were battling for the Kingdom of God and His righteousness against the forces of darkness which were destroying the conscience of the world.'[97]

    [95] Asquith to Murray, 19 Nov. 1926, quoted in Bentley, p. 207.
    [96] Lloyd George's speech at Queen's Hall, 19 Sept. 1914, quoted in Peter Rowland, *Lloyd George*, London, 1975, p. 288.
    [97] Bentley, op. cit., p. 200; D. W. Bebbington, *The Nonconformist Conscience, Chapel and Politics 1870–1914*, London, 1982, pp. 125-6; Clyde Binfield, *So Down to Prayers. Studies in English Nonconformity 1780–1920*, London, 1977, pp. 232-44.

Indeed, there is some evidence that, by shattering a national mood of complacency and security, the Great War temporarily revived, at many levels of society, a theology of redemption, an awareness (as William Temple was to put it later) that 'much in this evil world is irrational and strictly unintelligible'.[98] In this sense, the war 'did not so much challenge liberal principle as create it'[99]—or promise to. Liberals succumbed—not because theirs was a rational, articulate, compromising, and optimistic creed that could only survive in an orderly, harmonious, and tolerant society—but because they could no longer respond emotionally, in the 'old' Gladstonian way, to irrational forces of darkness in the world. They succumbed because they had completely outgrown their 'evangelical' roots.

[98] Alan Wilkinson, *The Church of England and the First World War*, London, 1978, pp. 161, 188-92, 234, and 241-9. See also Paul Fussell, *The Great War and Modern Memory*, London, 1975, *passim*. F. A. Iremonger, *William Temple, Archbishop of Canterbury. His life and letters*, London, 1948, p. 607.

[99] Bentley, p. 209.

3

The Transition to High Politics
in English Social Policy, 1880–1914

José Harris

'The question to what extent the State should intervene is one of high policy and in this my Department is not specially concerned'

(President of the Local Government Board 1903)[1]

I

Writers on social questions often refer to 'social policy' as though it were a peculiarity of modern or advanced or industrialized societies: but this view is misplaced. All political regimes have social policies of some kind, even if such policies consist simply in leaving the pursuit of welfare to the family or the local community or the corporation or the market. A social policy is none the less a social policy even when it is not mediated through a bureaucracy or does not pursue certain preconceived goals of subsistence or redistribution. *Laissez-faire* or riotous pluralism are just as much expressions of social policy as local authority social services or centralized planning. Like defence and public order, social policy (however implicit) is one of the defining characteristics of any organized political system: it was as inherent in the Aristotelian *polis* as in any modern welfare state.

Social policy of some kind is, therefore, one of the invariants of all eras of political history. What clearly does vary, however, is the substantive content of social policy and its underlying values, the goals it pursues, the interests it serves, its unintended consequences, its impact on social and economic structure. What also varies is the degree to which the content of social policy is seen as 'given', or, contrariwise, as part of the arena of political bargaining and conflict. At

[1] Public Record Office (PRO), CAB 37/67/79, Walter Long on 'Alien Immigration', 30 Nov. 1903.

one end of the theoretical spectrum is the view that social policies are part of a pre-ordained (theistic, natural, psychological) order: at the other end is the view that social policy is a product of acts of political will. Few people in real historical settings have held either of these views with pristine purity; individual belief and public debate have always oscillated between the two. In certain periods, however, the 'pre-ordained' approach has been predominant; such periods have often been characterized by attempts to take social policy 'out of politics', or at least to confine it to questions of detail rather than principle. At other times the content of social policy has been seen as controversial, contingent, and open-ended: it is at such times that social policy becomes a focus of 'high political' debate. By high politics I mean, not merely shadow-boxing within a carefully roped-off institutional arena, but anything which involves a real contest over the distribution of power and resources within the state.

The following essay will be concerned with a period in which these two alternative models of social policy were locked in contest with each other—Great Britain between 1880 and 1914—when the reified certainties inherited from the Peelite era were challenged by the more dynamic and existential social politics practised by Chamberlain, Churchill, and Lloyd George. At the beginning of this period many politicians believed that the fundamental principles of social policy had been fixed for all time by an earlier political generation. Social policy was believed to have been 'taken out of politics' by the Poor Law of 1834 in much the same way as monetary and commercial policy had supposedly been taken out of politics by the Bank Charter Act of 1844 and the repeal of the corn laws in 1846. All these measures were perceived, not merely as political triumphs, but as embodiments of certain supra-political behavioural laws. This did not mean that social policy had ceased to have a political dimension; but it was a dimension that was largely confined to questions of detail and to the sphere of local government. Where battles over the Poor Law *did* have wider political implications, they were largely based on resistance to decentralization and on manipulation of the franchise, rather than substantive questions of policy.[2] At the central level, social policy proposals rarely came before the Cabinet, and when they did so cabinet ministers saw their main role as being to 'neutralize the great inconvenience' that came from such demands.[3] Exceptions to this rule—mainly education and the Irish land question—penetrated the inner temple of high politics, not because of their social welfare implications, but because of their bearing on religion and the constitution. The various centralized social policy departments created or remodelled by the nineteenth-century revolution in government were all (with the exception of the Home Office) seen as 'low status' departments, far inferior to the Foreign Office, Colonial Office, and Treasury, and concerned merely with regulation and administration rather than issues of high policy. Questions about social problems were often asked in Parliament, and it was an established convention that in order to deal with them the President of the Local Government Board should always sit in the Commons; but parliamentary discussion rarely went beyond the scope of complaints about the local workhouse, problems of vagrancy, or what Cecil Rhodes contemptuously described as 'the questions raised by Mr. Tanner on the important matter of Mr. O'Brien's breeches'.[4] Such questions were rightly seen as the antithesis of high politics; and the unusually full programme of small-scale social legislation that was passed in 1886 has been ascribed to 'the virtual absence of high politics from the Commons for much of the session'.[5]

By 1914 this approach to social policy had profoundly changed, sometimes invisibly, sometimes in a highly spectacular way. By direct contrast with the vast bulk of nineteenth-century social legislation, only three of the twelve major social policy enactments introduced under the Liberal governments of 1906-14 were operated through local authorities;[6]

[2] Derek Fraser, 'The Poor Law as a Political Institution', in Derek Fraser (ed.), *The New Poor Law in the Nineteenth Century*, London, 1976, pp. 111-27.

[3] PRO, CAB 41/22/22, W. E. Gladstone to the Queen, 17 Dec. 1892.

[4] PRO, CAB 41/30/8, Arthur Balfour to the King, 11 Mar. 1905; Cecil Rhodes Papers, MSS Afr. t. 1, item 19, C. Rhodes to W. T. Stead, 19 Aug. 1891.

[5] A. B. Cooke and John Vincent, *The Governing Passion. Cabinet, Government and Party Politics in Britain 1885-6*, Brighton, 1974, p. 16.

[6] i.e. the Acts relating to school meals (1906), school medical inspection (1907), and smallholdings and allotments (1908). Moreover, the first two of these

the other nine were financed and directly or indirectly administered by central departments of state. At the same time social policy questions began to occupy far more of the time of the commanding heights of the political system: cabinet memoranda on social policy issues increased twelvefold in absolute terms between 1880-4 and 1905-9, and fourfold as a percentage of total cabinet business.[7] Among cabinet ministers, the heads of the humble social policy departments began to press their claims for full equality of status with the traditional high policy departments, on grounds of the 'great and growing' pressure of social questions and their 'first-rate political importance'.[8] In 1905 Gerald Balfour, as President of the Board of Trade, claimed that his own department and the Local Government Board were doing work just as important as that of the Foreign Office and Treasury, and he urged that social policy ministers should be raised to the rank of Secretary of State.[9] Even without this promotion, the social policy departments became increasingly attractive to talented and ambitious young politicians anxious to make a name for themselves in the public eye. Within the Treasury itself there was at the end of the period a determined attempt to 'expand the traditional functions of the budget from a purely accounting significance to a prime weapon of policy, and especially social policy'.[10] Among parties in opposition, detailed measures were the product of back-bench and 'expert' pressures, rather than of cabinet policy-making.

[7] Based on List of Cabinet Papers 1880-1914 (Public Record Office Handbooks, no. 4), a list that is not entirely complete, particularly for the 1880s. The calculation includes papers on Irish social issues, but does not include papers on fiscal questions, which only began to include an explicit 'social welfare' dimension in the mid-1900s. If the latter had been included both the absolute and proportional increase would appear much greater.

[8] Asquith Papers, vol. 19, fos. 188-9, Sir George Murray to H. H. Asquith, 12 Dec. 1907. The claims of the LGB and Board of Trade were considered in 1904 by a committee under Lord Jersey, who recommended that the latter but not the former should be given the status of a Secretariat of State (Cd. 2121/ 1904). Such advancement was strongly resisted by the Treasury on both financial and policy grounds. Board of Trade ministers and officials were eventually given the salaries, though not the rank, of a senior department in 1909; the LGB remained throughout a low status department.

[9] Asquith Papers, vol. 19, fos. 224-5, Gerald Balfour to Austen Chamberlain, 30 Jan. 1905.

[10] H. V. Emy, 'The Land Campaign: Lloyd George as a Social Reformer 1909-14', in A. J. P. Taylor (ed.), *Lloyd George: Twelve Essays*, London, 1971, p. 66.

planning on social policy issues, and careful calculation of their democratic significance, became an important part of the run-up to a general election—thereby flouting the Peelite tradition that 'Oppositions should not prescribe until called in'.[11] Perhaps the most dramatic change, however, occurred in the scope and content of socio-political rhetoric. The reformers of 1834 had viewed with horror the possibility that promises of state welfare might be used to bribe and debauch a democratic electorate; and the avoidance of 'promises' and 'programmes' was assiduously observed by the vast majority of mid-Victorian statesmen. The convention was infringed in the early 1870s by Disraeli; but Disraeli's promises, though theatrically exciting, were both transient and vague. The real breach in the dike came in 1885 with Joseph Chamberlain's Unauthorized Programme—a programme that sparked off twenty years of debate among party leaders about the ethics and constitutionality of binding ministerial hands with prior electoral commitments. Even as late as 1906 party leaders were nervous about encumbering themselves with overt social programmes; but a few years later, all such inhibitions had been cast aside, and ministers in office were unashamedly exploiting the style of social rhetoric pioneered by Chamberlain when in opposition. Churchill's Lancashire campaign of 1908 and Lloyd George's speeches at Limehouse, Newcastle, and Whitefield's Tabernacle in 1910–11 provide classic examples of the use of social welfare oratory in a mass democratic theatre.

All these changes—at cabinet, departmental, party, and mass politics level—suggest that perceptions of the political significance of social policy had fundamentally changed during the period under review. It had sprung out of the Pandora's Box of the 1834 Poor Law into the realm of political contingency. As Churchill wrote in an essay on 'The People's Welfare' in 1909, 'Nothing is settled either for or against us. . . . All is still in our hands for good or ill.'[12] And accompanying this politicization of social policy was a widespread sense

[11] British Library (BL) Add. MS 41217, correspondence between Sir Henry Campbell-Bannerman and Herbert Gladstone, 1903–5, *passim*; Add. MS 41214, H. Fowler to Sir Henry Campbell-Bannerman, 26 Dec. 1904.
[12] Winston Churchill, *The People's Rights*, London, 1910, p. 138.

that social issues were no longer marginal to the major concerns of high politics. Even among politicians whose primary concerns were defence, order, and expansion of the empire, social policy came to be seen not as separate from but as complementary to those functions. Among those whose main interest was in social questions, social policy was increasingly viewed as central to the effectiveness, the stability, and even the legitimacy of the state.[13]

Why and how did this transition from low to high politics come about? For the rest of this paper I shall consider what were the pressures behind this change: was it a transient response to specific and peculiar historical circumstance? Or was it part of a wider and largely irreversible process of political 'modernization'? Some historians have attempted to explain the change in terms of a buttressing of state and upper-class power and of the reinforcement of social control over a potentially conflict-ridden society.[14] Such an explanation is not difficult to support with documentary evidence; but it has the disadvantage either of being tautologically true or of begging the question it is designed to answer (i.e. why was state power more in need of buttressing and society more in need of control in this than in other periods?). I shall, therefore, approach the problem by reviewing a range of contextual factors, and by trying to weigh their relative importance and interrelationship.

II

The first and perhaps most obvious factor to be considered is how far social policy was constrained by a quasi-democratic electorate. Was there any truth in the oft-quoted view of Sidney Webb that the intrusion of social welfare into high

[13] Geoffrey Searle, *The Quest for National Efficiency*, Oxford 1971, pp. 65–7; Winston Churchill, op. cit., pp. 48–9; J. A. Hobson, *The Crisis of Liberalism*, London, 1909, pp. 77–8, 159–75.

[14] Roger Davidson, 'The Board of Trade and Industrial Relations 1896–1914', *Historical Journal*, 21 (1978), 590–1. For the problems entailed in 'social control' models, see Roy Hay, 'Employers' Attitudes to Social Policy and the Concept of "Social Control", 1900–1920', in Pat Thane (ed.), *The Origins of British Social Policy*, London, 1978, pp. 107–25.

politics was simply the 'economic obverse of democracy'?[15]
Recent historians have pointed out that the British electorate
between the franchise acts of 1884 and 1918 (under eight
million male voters in 1910, including half a million plural
votes) fell far short of the mass democracy proclaimed by Edwardian constitutional theory; and others have suggested
that, far from being bribed by social welfare, the English
working class was on the whole indifferent or hostile to state
intervention and social legislation.[16] For the purposes of this
discussion, however, these factors are less important than the
questions of how far politicians *thought* that they were operating in a democratic context and how far they *thought* that
social policy was electorally significant when they imported
social issues into the arena of high politics. One thing that
seems clear is that politicians increasingly believed that
voters *were* motivated by social welfare issues. Chamberlain's
land campaign of 1885 and tariff reform campaign of 1903
specifically aimed to appeal to voters over the heads of parliament on property, employment, and fiscal questions.[17] Within
the Local Government Board ministers, officials, and inspectors regarded the period after 1884 as the 'political epoch' of
the Poor Law, when expansion of both central and local franchise transferred control over the Poor Law into the hands of
a class virtually indistinguishable from the recipients of poor
relief.[18] Plans laid by the Liberals for recapturing power from
the Conservatives in 1903-5 specifically centred on social
policy questions and, although the 1906 election was fought
primarily on Free Trade, the main thrust of Liberal propaganda was not on the business advantages of Free Trade but
on its relevance to working-class living standards. By-election

[15] Bentley B. Gilbert, *The Evolution of National Insurance in Great Britain.
The Origins of the Welfare State*, London, 1966, pp. 25-6.

[16] N. Blewett, 'The Franchise in the United Kingdom 1885-1918', *Past and
Present*, 32 (1965), 27-56; H. C. G. Matthew, R. I. McKibbin, and J. A. Kay, 'The
Franchise Factor in the Rise of the Labour Party', *English Historical Review*, 91
(1976), 723-52; Henry Pelling, 'The Working Class and the Origins of the Welfare
State', in *Popular Politics and Society in Late Victorian Britain*, London, 1968,
pp. 1-36.

[17] Joseph Chamberlain, *The Radical Programme*, repr. from the *Fortnightly
Review* (1885); and *Imperial Union and Tariff Reform* (1903).

[18] Asquith MSS, vol. 78, fo. 89, typescript notes on reports of Royal Commission on the Poor Laws.

losses to Labour in 1907 and to the Conservatives in 1908–9 almost certainly reinforced Liberal commitment to social policy, and enabled the party's reformers to gain the upper hand over flagging or sceptical moderates.[19] In both major parties radical activists urged upon their colleagues the democratic indispensability of progressive social legislation. 'I think the country cares much more about these issues than about mere political change', wrote Winston Churchill in 1908, in support of his proposals for a massive social programme. 'They would not merely benefit the state but fortify the party.'[20] And the same point was made three years later by the Secretary of the Unionist Social Reform Committee when urging Conservatives to accept social reform as 'the essential counterpoint' to the theme of tariffs: 'Unless you put yourself straight with the people on social questions all your Tariff Reform, Home Rule, or Constitutional thunderbolts will be discharged in vain.'[21]

Social reform was, therefore, an important factor in the electoral calculations of at least some of the high politicians of the Edwardian period. This point must, however, be qualified in a number of ways. One qualification is that by no means all the social legislation of the period can be explained in terms of anticipation of electoral gain; the 1902 Education Act, for example, was pressed through against the sustained opposition of large numbers of potential Conservative voters; and the Liberal Trade Boards Act can scarcely have been an electoral bait, since it applied mainly to voteless, propertyless women. Not all leading politicians agreed that voters were more concerned with social welfare than with the Constitution.[22] Moreover, the belief that social policy was electorally advantageous did not necessarily lead politicians to act upon such a belief. Lord Salisbury in 1888 ascribed by-election losses to the adverse votes of the homeless unemployed: but this did not induce him to frame a policy for homelessness

---

[19] Gilbert, op. cit., 209–10; Bruce Murray, 'The Politics of the People's Budget', *Historical Journal*, 16. 3 (1973), 556.
[20] Asquith MSS, vol. 11, fos. 239–44 and 249–53, W. S. Churchill to H. H. Asquith, 26 and 29 Dec. 1908.
[21] John Ramsden, *The Age of Balfour and Baldwin*, London, 1978, p. 76.
[22] Asquith MSS, vol. 23, fos. 64–6, memo by Sir Edward Grey, 31 Jan. 1910.

or unemployment.[23] On both sides of parliament throughout the period there were politicians who took pride in resisting the idea that measures of social welfare should be put up to public auction. Another important factor was that not all zealous reformers were equally zealous democrats, often quite the reverse. In spite of the comment of Sidney Webb cited above, Webb himself believed in 'the superiority in social value of "administration" over House of Commons "politics" '. 'Nothing in England is done', he claimed, 'without the consent of a small intellectual yet practical class in London not 2000 in number.'[24] Supporters of the 'national efficiency' movement frequently deplored the constraints of parliamentary democracy and its continued attachment to muddled, outworn, sentimental liberal freedoms: no elected House of Commons, it was complained, would ever countenance such desirable social policy measures as making habitual poverty a crime or subjecting the unemployed to compulsory detention.[25] A more muted variant of the same theme was the often expressed view that social reform was a democratic imperative, not so much to satisfy the wishes of the electors as to tame and civilize and educate them to be worthy of their democratic responsibilities.[26] A third factor was that even politicians who *were* both reformers and democrats were well aware that the composition and the desires of the electorate were far from simple. Although voters might demand 'social reform' there was no uniform conception of what social reform entailed. In certain circumstances it was just as likely to mean public retrenchment or subsidies for sectional groups as general relief of poverty. There was no automatic equation between enlargement of the franchise and downwards redistribution.

Democratic constraints therefore offer only a partial

[23] PRO, CAB 41/21/3, Lord Salisbury to the Queen, 12 Feb. 1888.

[24] Sidney Webb, *Grants in Aid: a Criticism and a Proposal*, London, 1911, p. 9; *The Letters of Sidney and Beatrice Webb*, ed. Norman Mackenzie, Cambridge, 1978, i. 101.

[25] 'National efficiency' proposals were viewed in the Local Government Board with profound scepticism, as totally incompatible with parliamentary democracy (PRO, HLG 29/65, item 3, minute by Mr Russell, 31 May 1897; and *LGB Annual Report* (1906-7), p. 285).

[26] 'The Liberal Cabinet—an Intercepted Letter', *National Review* (Jan. 1905), 789-802.

explanation of the politicization of social policy and its intrusion into high politics. A problem of a related but slightly different kind is the question of how far social policy was a response to the growth of class-stratification. Historians of widely differing viewpoints have identified this as a period in which the gulf between middle class and working class solidified, and class loyalties replaced earlier religious, regional, and personal ties as the basis of political commitment. Bread-and-butter questions concerning resources and living standards, so it is argued, replaced the ethical and constitutional concerns of mid-Victorian middle-class liberalism. Assessments of the historical significance of the Liberal social programme have largely turned on whether or not it satisfied the rising material aspirations of an increasingly organized working class.[27] Social policies of the period have been variously interpreted as concessions to the demands of the working-class movement and as attempts to subject it to middle-class modes of regulation. Reformist ministers have been seen by some historians as fomenting, by others as stifling, class antagonism.[28] That social policies involved a complex of class-relationships is impossible to deny, and the language of politicians when discussing welfare issues constantly referred to the need to elevate, discipline, appease, or assist different sections of the working-class population. Socialists in the Social Democratic Federation, in the ILP, or later in the Labour party constantly reiterated the essential link between getting poverty accepted as a political question and advancing the claims of the working class. Nevertheless, the class dimension in social policy was more elusive and more elastic than historians have sometimes supposed. One complicating factor is that the fiercest class battle of the period, both in social policy and in 'high politics' generally, was that fought between the upper classes and certain sections of the middle classes over progressive taxation and land. Another is that many of the rules with which Liberal politicians sought to 'regulate' the working class were derived from the rules with

[27] Peter Clarke, *Lancashire and the New Liberalism*, Cambridge, 1971, pp. 393–407.

[28] Maurice Cowling, *The Impact of Labour 1920–1924*, Cambridge, 1970, p. 24; Roger Davidson, loc. cit., p. 591.

which certain sections of the working class had long regulated themselves, via friendly societies and trade unions.[29] Moreover, factors cutting across social class divisions resolutely refused to cast themselves into the dustbin of history. The very fact that 'new Liberalism' won over working men in Lancashire, but singularly failed to do so in London or Birmingham, suggests that local political culture and tradition were still of major importance. When examined in detail, many of the major social policies of the period seem to have been directed towards, or at least largely conditioned by, sectional interest-groups rather than social classes. Anglican, Roman Catholic, and nonconformist churches; trade unions, friendly societies, insurance companies; doctors, business men, Poor Law officials; ratepayers' associations, and philanthropic societies—all these groups seem to have been more directly influential in shaping the substance and structure of welfare legislation than any group who can be categorically identified with the middle or working classes. A reassertion of the legitimacy of 'interests'— after nearly a century in which many Englishmen had viewed interest-groups as by definition 'sinister' and part of Old Corruption—seems to be at least as important a feature of Edwardian social policy as the crystallization of social class.[30] What most severely blunts the edge of a purely class analysis, however, is the continuing, and possibly even increasing, significance of classes *within* classes. At no time during the period was there anything remotely approaching a unanimous perception of either middle- or working-class interests and needs. A majority of middle-class people (certainly in England, as opposed to Wales and Scotland) appear to have disliked the 1909 Budget, even though most of them were, or were intended to be, its main direct beneficiaries.[31] So far as the

---

[29] e.g. the rules governing unemployment benefit under the 1911 National Insurance Act were directly derived, sometimes verbatim, from the rules of Trade Union benefit funds (Cd. 5073, 1911, *Tables Showing the Rules and Expenditure of Trade Unions*).

[30] e.g. PRO, CAB 41/22/15, W. E. Gladstone to the Queen, 31 Oct. 1892. An enthusiastic sponsor of interest-group politics was Winston Churchill, who in 1910 pressed for the formal integration of interest groups in government social administration, on the German model of Paritätisch (Asquith MSS, vol. 22, fos. 89–92, W. S. Churchill to H. H. Asquith, 12 Jan. 1909).

[31] For the beneficent effect of Lloyd George finance on middle income groups, see Bruce Murray, *The People's Budget*, Oxford, 1978, p. 294.

working class was concerned, one of the very reasons why
social questions began to loom so large in the minds of politicians was the wide gulf between the 'very poor' and the rest
of the working classes—a gulf that had been continually increasing since the 1870s and was only very slightly narrowed
by the downturn of real wages in the 1900s. There was no
necessary sense of identity between the 'very poor' and the
affluent working class—even though many working people
migrated at various times in their lives between the two.[32]
Statistics of London pauperism suggest that some at least of
the working-class Poor Law unions were meaner to paupers
than lower-middle-class unions—and much more likely to
put them in public institutions.[33] The 'submerged tenth' was
smaller than the membership (plus dependants) of the trade
union movement, but the number of working men who were
ratepayers was considerably larger than either.[34] Whether
trade-unionists and working-class ratepayers would identify
with the middle classes or would throw in their lot with the
'very poor' was one of the great unstated political questions
of the period, and has indeed continued to be so for the rest
of the twentieth century.

What weight should be attached to less overtly political
factors, such as movements of ideas? Political ideas are sometimes seen by historians of high politics as the antithesis of
political action and therefore of no relevance to their subject of enquiry. This approach seems to me profoundly misconceived, since mastery over men's minds is one of the most

[32] B. Seebohn Rowntree, *Poverty: a Study of Town Life*, London, 1901,
pp. 136-7.

[33] 'Ratio of outdoor to total paupers', compiled by C. N. Nicholson, *Charity
Organisation Review*, xi (Mar. 1895).

[34] Norman McCord, 'Ratepayers and Social Policy', in Thane (ed.), *The Origins of British Social Policy*, pp. 21-35. The actual number of ratepayers and their
class distribution are extraordinarily elusive figures. Though there is an immense
mass of data on rateable value and rate income, no figures for national or local
ratepayers are given in LGB reports or local taxation returns, nor in the works of
any of the classic Edwardian authorities on rating, such as Josef Redlich, Sidney
Webb, or Edwin Cannan. Since rates in rented properties were paid by tenants
(either directly or through 'compounding') it seems reasonable to equate the number of domestic ratepayers with the number of separate households, for which the
most significant global estimate is the Census category of 'tenements in the occupation of private families'. Just under 8 million such tenements were recorded in
1911. This figure does not of course include commercial and agricultural ratepayers.

subtle and effective modes of wielding real political power. However, for the purpose of analysing real politics, it is clearly important to discriminate between ideas which bit into the imagination of the political nation and those which did not. Theories about eugenics, for example, received an immense amount of attention from Edwardian social commentators and have received even more from historians; but, with the sole exception of mental deficiency legislation, their impact on politics and social policy was remarkably slight. There was never the remotest possibility in Edwardian England that selective breeding-out of the socially unfit would become a serious political question. Among ideas which *were* acceptable it is important to distinguish between those which explain the specific content of policy and those which were merely part of the universal currency of fashionably political discussion. From the 1880s through to the First World War social and political thought in England were dominated by a mixture of philosophical idealism, sociological empiricism, and ideas about social evolution—three strands of thought that have often been used to explain the growth of political commitment to interventionist social policies.[35] This interpretation is, however, slightly out of focus, since the language and concepts of all three schools were shared equally by interventionists and non-interventionists, by diehard individualists and by the prophets of a new moral economy.[36] They help to explain why social problems became a flash-point of political conflict, and therefore an issue of high politics—but not why social policy developed in the specific direction of increased state intervention. Another line of thought that is often emphasized is the loss of faith in classical political economy that gradually gathered momentum from the mid-1870s.[37] This loss of faith seems to me of some importance

[35] Michael Freeden, *The New Liberalism: an Ideology of Social Reform*, Oxford, 1978.

[36] See, e.g. Stefan Collini, 'Hobhouse, Bosanquet and the State: Philosophical Idealism and Political Argument in England 1880-1918', *Past and Present*, 72 (Aug. 1976), 86-111; Bernard Bosanquet, 'Idealism in Social Work', *Charity Organisation Review*, iii (Jan.-July 1898), 122-33; and Helen Bosanquet, review of Rowntree's *Poverty*, ibid., xi (Jan.-June 1902), 260-6.

[37] T. W. Hutchinson, *A Review of Economic Doctrines 1870-1929*, Oxford, 1953, pp. 1-31; Reba Soffer, *Ethics and Society in England*, Berkeley, 1978, chs. 3 and 4.

in explaining why distribution came to be seen as a question
of politics rather than of nature and in eroding belief in a full-
employment equilibrium. Both these heresies—that redistribution was possible and unemployment a genuine problem—
were increasingly accepted by senior Liberal politicians of the
post-1906 period, as political speeches and cabinet papers of
the time make clear.[38] But too much emphasis should not be
placed on the decline of classical economics, since the mar-
ginalism that replaced it was even more inclined than Ricar-
dianism to reduce social welfare to private calculations of
personal utility.

A perhaps more fruitful area to consider than the realm of
abstract theory is the development of practical social thought
at the more humdrum level of day-to-day social administration. Here some unpretentious but quite fundamental changes
in social and political attitudes were taking place in the last
three decades of the nineteenth century. On a pessimistic
note, there was a marked decline in that confident belief in
universal human rationality that had been such a hallmark of
the Chadwick era. Whereas Chadwick had believed that the
poorest of the poor could help themselves if given incentives
to do so, in the 1880s there was a growing belief that at the
bottom of the social heap lay a class of people who were
powerless to help themselves however hard they tried and
whatever inducements were offered.[39] The existence of such
a class (in itself a challenge to the basic premises of liberal
political thought) became an important part of the Edwardian social policy debate: what to do with this class became
one of the great unsolved problems of the period. On a more
positive level, the goals and principles which guided the New
Poor Law in the late nineteenth and early twentieth centuries
were very far from being as chaotic and repressive as much
reformist propaganda suggested. As several recent historians
have shown, Poor Law schools, hospitals, child care, and
medical treatment could stand comparison in many areas

[38] *The Times*, 29 Apr. 1909 (report of Lloyd George's budget speech); Asquith
MSS, vol. 77, fos. 139-69, typescript notes on reports of the Royal Commission
on the Poor Laws.
[39] e.g. Mansion House Conference on the Condition of the Unemployed,
1887-8; 'How to Organise Relief in a Parish in a Time of Exceptional Distress',
Charity Organisation Review, ix (1895), 520.

with services provided by voluntary bodies or with what the
middle classes could buy for themselves through the private
market. By the 1900s middle-class patients were willing to
pay for the privilege of treatment in Poor Law hospitals; and
even the much despised workhouse was by no means as universally unpopular as later generations believed.[40] Socialist
critics of the Poor Law in the 1890s saw it as a system that
was full of flaws and injustice, but capable of conversion into
a community-based welfare service under popular control. At
the higher levels of Poor Law administration a new spirit was
slowly emerging in the last decade of the nineteenth century.
Great, if somewhat grudging, efforts were being made to lay
down decent standards for Poor Law services, and the principle that paupers must always be worse off than 'the lowest
paid independent labourer' was increasingly regarded as obso-
lete and impracticable. In the early 1900s the Local Government Board introduced a system of 'statutory disregards',
which allowed people to claim poor relief without forfeiting
small private savings—a concession which conservative critics
interpreted (quite correctly) as 'the small end of the wedge'
in breaking down status barriers between paupers and the
wider community.[41] However, greater humanity in Poor Law
administration, combined with less visible factors like profound demographic change, meant that Poor Law costs were
zooming. Both aggregate Poor Law expenditure and the
amount per head spent on individual paupers doubled between
1870-1 and 1905-6; and by the early 1900s the greatest restraint upon more constructive treatment was not so much the
harshness of the workhouse as the growing cost-consciousness
of local ratepayers.[42] The great problem of Poor Law administration in the 1900s, and one grossly underrated by both
reports of the Royal Commission on the Poor Laws, was not

[40] Jean Brand, *Doctors and the State*; Derek Fraser, 'The English Poor Law
and the British Welfare State', in Wolfgang Mommsen (ed.), *The Emergence of the
Welfare State in Britain and Germany*, London, 1981, pp. 9-31; M. A. Crowther,
The Workhouse System 1834-1929, esp. ch. 3, and 'The Later Years of the
Workhouse 1890-1929', in Thane (ed.), *The Origins of British Social Policy*,
pp. 36-55.

[41] PRO, HLG 29/84, vol. 76, fos. 141-50, J. S. Davy to Sir Samuel Provis, 10
June 1903, *The Times*, 13 Aug. 1904.

[42] *LGB Annual Report* (1899-1900), pp. 432-5; *LGB Annual Report* (1911-
12), pp. 180-4; Norman McCord, loc. cit., pp. 21-35.

the deterrent principles of 1834 but the infinitely more complicated problem of the structure of local finance.[43]

III

This brings me to what was perhaps the most crucial factor in forcing social policy into the arena of high politics at the end of the nineteenth century—the question of who was to pay for it. Distribution of resources had become a negotiable issue, not merely at the point of demand but at the point of supply. The resource problem should not be confused with the more fundamental constraint of basic economic scarcity that had overshadowed the social policies of the 1830s. The growth of national income between 1870 and 1914 does not suggest that social policy was severely inhibited by economic stagnation: on the contrary, it was almost certainly the first time in English history in which subsistence-level poverty became at least notionally curable by political means.[44] The problem was not lack of resources, but the mobilization of resources through the medium of public finance. The financial problem must be considered at two levels: the distribution of burdens among local authorities (a problem that dated back to the 1860s) and the emergence in the 1890s of a fiscal crisis in central government.

Local responsibility for the provision and financing of social welfare needs had always been based on certain unresolved ambiguities. Since the sixteenth century local authorities had been statutory creations of Parliament; and yet political discussion of local responsibilities often referred to local communities as though they were moral persons, with autonomous rights and duties. The Poor Law was rooted in the idea that entitlements to welfare derived from the local

[43] José Harris, *Unemployment and Politics. A study in English Social Policy 1886–1914*, Oxford, 1972, pp. 78–9, and Appendix A on 'Social Policy and the Problem of Local Taxation'; Avner Offer, *Property and Politics 1870–1914*, Cambridge, 1982, pp. 283–313.

[44] Real net national income trebled between 1870 and 1914, while real income per head doubled. Real income per head in 1870 was 25 per cent above the Rowntree poverty line; by 1913 it was 150 per cent above (calculated from A. R. Prest, 'National Income of the United Kingdom', *Economic Journal* (Mar. 1948), 58–9, and B. R. Mitchell, *Abstract of British Historical Statistics*, Cambridge, 1962, pp. 366–8).

rather than the national community—though the existence of the settlement laws suggested that, even in the pre-industrial period, localism had not always accorded with functional reality. The rooting of social administration in the locality did not mean that before the end of the nineteenth century social questions had never erupted into high politics; but such eruptions had nearly always taken the form of central intervention to enforce or re-define local obligations.[45] The balance of central versus local power had been politically contested in the 1830s and 1840s, when local communities, backed up by the vast majority of parliamentarians, had fought successfully to maintain local autonomy against encroaching Benthamites. The 1850s had been the golden age of *esprit de clocher* in English social administration—central government involvement being more or less confined to general policy guidelines and annual grants-in-aid to agricultural areas.

This retention of local control had generally been regarded as a triumph for local democracy; but even as early as the 1860s there were signs that local democracy had taken on rather more than it had bargained for. Uneven economic development, migration of population, the segregation of towns into rich and poor communities and into 'business' and 'residential' areas—all meant that there was no necessary correlation between local rating resources and local needs; and this imbalance constantly tended to intensify with overall economic progress. The problem was reinforced by the prolonged agricultural depression that began in the 1870s, by the growth of personal at the expense of landed wealth, and by the decline in both fertility and mortality (which meant a rising ratio of dependants to working population). The full dimensions of the problem were rarely understood at the time, and from the 1880s onwards there was a widespread tendency to ascribe financial difficulties to the importunate demands of a working-class electorate[46]—even though,

[45] e.g. Paul Slack, 'Book of Orders: the Making of English Social Policy 1577–1631', *Transactions of the Royal Historical Society*, 5th s. 30 (1980), 1–22.

[46] W. A. B(ailward), 'Local Government and Popular Election', *Charity Organisation Review*, xviii, no. 108 (Oct. 1905), 183–94; J. P. D. Dunbabin, 'The Politics of the Establishment of County Councils', *Historical Journal*, 6. 2 (1963), 241.

as has already been pointed out, many working men were themselves ratepayers and showed little inclination to be more extravagant than their middle-class counterparts. Other more realistic complaints were that rates ought to fall on personal as well as real property and that rating burdens ought to be pooled to take account of the growing scale of social organization.[47] Between the 1860s and 1890s ratepayers' grievances were met by a series of piecemeal concessions—enlarging the rateable unit of the Poor Law, pooling certain kinds of Poor Law expenditure, increasing government subsidies to local authorities—all of which left the basic structure of the problem virtually untouched.[48] The creation of county councils in 1888, which should in theory have relieved the problem by enlarging the local administrative unit, served rather to enhance it by locking local issues much more closely into the straitjacket of national party politics.[49] By the 1890s two radically different strategies towards the rating problem had emerged within the Conservative and Liberal parties—Conservatives favouring the de-rating of agricultural land and extension of grants-in-aid, Liberals a combination of taxation of site-values and redistribution of rate income between rich and poor local authorities.[50] A Royal Commission on Local Taxation sitting between 1896 and 1901 failed to solve any of these problems and served mainly to uncover the hornets' nest of interests and opinions involved. Moreover, expert witnesses disagreed drastically about the most equitable basis of the rates, the 'real incidence' of taxation and whether working-class ratepayers preferred economy or extravagance. By the 1900s rate-levels and public expenditure had become the flashpoint of local politics in virtually every area of the country; and in 1909 the vast majority of county councils reacted with horror when the Royal Commission on the Poor Laws proposed to confer on them vast new powers over social services without first solving the problem of local rates.[51] Out of the cockpit of conflicting interests

[47] Harris, pp. 369-70.   [48] Sidney Webb, *Grants in Aid, passim.*
[49] E. P. Hennock, 'Finance and Politics in Urban Local Government in England 1835-1900', *Historical Journal*, 6. 2 (1963), 224.
[50] Offer, esp. chs. 14 and 16.
[51] See particularly the conflicting opinions of Sir Edward Hamilton, assistant Secretary to the Treasury, and Thomas Mackay (C. 9528/1899, *Classification and*

came a curious alliance—between socialist and progressive social reformers on the one hand and aggrieved ratepayers on the other—to shift social policy on to the shoulders of national government. Liberal ministers came to power in 1905 cautiously sceptical about the demands of their radical followers that such issues as unemployment should be seen as a national problem and that local responsibility was 'logically' indistinguishable from state-responsibility.[52] But they found the problem of rates no more easy to solve than their predecessors—and no less pressing, in view of the large number of Liberal voters who were owners or occupiers of small-scale property. Officials in the Local Government Board were charged with preparing a radical reconstruction of the rating system; but the task proved too much for them and was transferred to a Treasury committee which did not report till just before the outbreak of war in 1914. In the event it proved simply easier to evade the issues of both Poor Law and rating reform, and to take on pensions, unemployment, and health reform as responsibilities of national government.[53]

Social legislation did not pay for itself, however, and if ratepayers were to be let off the hook who was to be put on it? At this point, the politics of social policy became enmeshed with the other major financial problem of the time —the fiscal crisis in central government. In the 1890s the fiscal policy of central government was still shrouded by the conventions laid down in Gladstone's early career as Chancellor of the Exchequer: in practice, if not in principle, mid-Victorian budgets and patterns of taxation had been 'taken out of politics' no less than the Poor Law or Free Trade.[54] The Treasury was firmly committed to the view that the most effective allocation of resources was pre-ordained by the very nature of economic activity, and that taxation should be levied purely for revenue and not for redistribution. Beyond

Incidence of Imperial and Local Taxes). On the work and significance of the Commission, see Offer, pp. 242–5.

[52] BL Add. MS 41238, fos. 8–11, Sydney Buxton to Campbell Bannerman, 16 Jan. 1905.
[53] Harris, pp. 233, 268–9; *Report of the Departmental Committee on Local Taxation* (Cd. 7315/1914).
[54] H. C. G. Matthew, 'Disraeli, Gladstone, and the Politics of Mid-Victorian Budgets', *Historical Journal*, 22. 3 (1979), 616.

that, it was believed that revenue should be roughly shared between 'direct' and 'indirect' taxation, that there should be no taxation of necessities, and no disproportionate taxation of higher incomes.[55] Against radical complaints about the unfairness of taxing the working classes, Goschen in the 1880s had strongly defended the levying of taxes on all classes as a buttress of social solidarity and community feeling.[56] In the 1890s, however, rising national expenditure together with rising scepticism about the 'natural' distribution of resources combined to undermine these beliefs. The central relief to local taxation granted in 1888 coincided with rising naval expenditure to produce in the early 1890s the first signs of a fiscal crisis. Both parties began to look for new sources of taxation, though within high political circles the discussion was initially focused purely on devices to raise revenue and not on taxation as a tool of social welfare. Harcourt's budget of 1894, which introduced graduated death duties, passed with surprisingly little comment (except from Lady Bracknell) on its social implications. But what began as a fiscal expedient proved in the long run to be a trail of gunpowder. The next eight years saw a doubling of central government expenditure, caused initially by the rising cost of subsidies to local government but greatly exacerbated by the Boer war. In 1901 and 1902 the Conservative government breached the Peelite concensus by putting tariffs on coal and corn; and in 1903 Joseph Chamberlain set the trail alight by demanding a complete reconstruction of the fiscal system on the basis of tariff reform. Moreover, Chamberlain more clearly than any previous politician identified taxation as an issue of social welfare: the disutilities incurred by taxes on food were to be far outweighed by using tariffs to create employment and to pay for old-age pensions.[57] Finding an alternative to Chamberlain forced Liberal leaders to commit themselves far more firmly than before to direct taxation and its progressive

[55] PRO, T 168/152, memo by E. W. Hamilton, 13 Dec. 1901; T 168/57, memo by E. W. Hamilton, 22 July 1902.
[56] PRO, HLG 29/42, fo. 192, copy of letter from George Goschen to Mr Paget, 5 Jan. 1870.
[57] Joseph Chamberlain, *Imperial Union and Tariff Reform*, London, 1903, pp. 163, 171-2, 201.

graduation.[58] Progressive income tax had the multiple advantages from the Liberal point of view of buttressing free trade, curing the fiscal crisis, reducing the National Debt, paying for both defence and social reform, and—perhaps most important of all—shifting the burden of existing social expenditure away from 8 million ratepayers on to the 200,000 who paid income tax at or above the standard rate.[59] The budgets of 1907-9 and 1914 are famous for their reconstruction of the income tax and of taxes on landed estates. Behind this reconstruction lay the intention that at least half of the revenue from the new taxes should be earmarked from the start for the 'performance by the State of . . . services (education, pauper or lunatic relief, main roads, etc.) at present performed at the expense of the local authorities', together with 'many items which fall under the general head of public health'.[60]

Social policy therefore became increasingly politicized during this period, partly because of democratic pressures, partly because of structural change, partly because of the resurgence of organized interest groups, and partly because of certain movements of ideas; but the catalyst that transformed these pressures and precipitated social policy into the theatre of high politics was public finance. If, *per impossibile*, parishes and philanthropists had been able to cope with the expanding social needs of an advanced industrial society, then the Poor Law might have stayed within its box—or, more probably, would have climbed out of it slowly by a less dramatic process of organic evolution. The question remains of whether this injection of high politics was temporary or irreversible. Throughout the twentieth century there have been spasmodic attempts to restore social policy to an apolitical context— either by corporatism, or by a revival of the parochial model of 1834, or by the inelegantly termed process of 'recommodi-

[58] PRO, CAB 41/31/13, Campbell-Bannerman to the King, 13 Apr. 1907; H. H. Asquith to St. Loe Strachey, 9 May 1908 (quoted in A. M. Gollin, *Proconsul in Politics. A study of Lord Milner in opposition and in power, 1854-1905*, London, 1964, p. 152).

[59] There were just over one million income tax payers in 1910, but of these over 800,000 (with incomes between £160 and £700 p.a.) received 'abatements'.

[60] PRO, CAB 41/32/22 and 41/45/11, H. H. Asquith to the King, 23 June 1909 and 2 May 1914. Liberal relief to ratepayers, financed out of progressive income tax, was designed to equal an annual rate of 9*d*. in the pound.

fication'. In Britain such attempts have always ended in at least partial failure, but the success of such schemes in certain other countries suggests that 'politicized' social welfare is by no means a necessary feature of all modern societies. The history of the 1890s and 1900s helps to pinpoint the factors that determine whether social policy plays an active or passive role within a political system. Where there is no general agreement about what constitutes 'the community', where patterns of distribution are seen as inherently debatable, and where competing interest groups are active in society but not integrated in the state—then 'social policy' will tend to constitute a major part of 'high policy'. It was these factors that made social welfare a crucial aspect of the Edwardian high-politics debate.

4

Women's Suffrage at Westminster
1866–1928[1]

Brian Harrison

I

Like any other political innovation, the advent of the suffragettes entailed a revision of attitudes to the recent past. Organized in Mrs Pankhurst's Women's Social and Political Union (WSPU), they were a militant outcrop of the suffragist movement,[2] and their view of British suffragist history between the 1860s and the 1920s, energetically propagated (with minor variants) by all three leading Pankhursts, divides the period into three phases.

In the first, non-militant campaigning over forty years to pledge MPs to women's suffrage somehow fails to bring votes for women any closer. Indeed, in some ways women's situation worsens after the 1860s because the ballot frees male voters after 1872 from being openly responsible to women, and the enlargement of the male franchise in 1884 increases the educated woman's resentment at her political subordination, while at the same time downgrading the priority of further electoral reform on the political agenda; women's opportunities for employment are therefore increasingly vulnerable to governments influenced by pressure from male-dominated trade unions. Suffragists also dislike the way Woodall's woman suffrage amendment to the Reform Bill is treated in 1884, when Gladstone engages in what Sylvia Pankhurst later described as the 'autocratic buffoonery' involved in staking the government's survival on its rejection.[3]

[1] Much of the research for this essay was completed while I was in receipt of a Personal Research Grant from the Social Science Research Council, whose timely help I gratefully acknowledge here.
[2] The term 'suffragist' will therefore be used to denote any participant in the movement for women's suffrage, whereas the term 'suffragette' will denote only those suffragists who used militant methods.
[3] E. S. Pankhurst, *The Suffragette Movement*, London, 1931, p. 70.

Suffragettes were particularly scathing, both at the time and later, about the non-militants' 'narrow and trivial' political tactics before 1906.[4] The annual non-militant deputations to MPs before 1906, writes Mrs Pankhurst, would engage in mutual politenesses, and then depart 'a trifle sad but entirely tranquil', and MPs would resume 'the real business of life, which was support of their party's policies'. By contrast, suffragette heroines march through taunt and difficulty towards the dawn, united in hope, with banners resolutely pointing towards 'a wider morrow'.[5] Sylvia Pankhurst recalled the non-militant National Union of Women's Suffrage Societies (NUWSS) as being 'so staid, so willing to wait, so incorrigibly leisurely'; its Queen's Hall meeting of 1905 seemed tame by comparison with socialist meetings in the North. She credits militancy with injecting 'a thrill of life' into a suffrage movement which 'had sunk into an almost moribund coma of hopelessness'.[6]

The second phase in suffragette historiography runs from 1906 to 1914, and sees male obstinacy, partisan loyalty, and even trickery, as driving suffragists into accelerating militancy, which is all the more justifiable because women lack the male's constitutional outlets. 'What is the good of the constitutional policy to those who have no constitutional weapon?', Christabel Pankhurst asks, at a suffragette meeting in 1911.[7] Politicians ignore suffragists' questions at public meetings, goad them with inflammatory speeches into simulating the violence of earlier male franchise campaigns, and implicitly depreciate non-militant forms of pressure by ignoring them. Fred Pethick-Lawrence thought G. M. Trevelyan took 'the wrong slant' on women's suffrage in a conversation over dinner in 1949; when prolonged peaceful agitation fails to get results, he wrote, 'extraordinary and extralegal methods' are necessary.[8] Like Christabel Pankhurst, he thought these

[4] E. S. Pankhurst, *The Suffragette Movement*, p. 92.

[5] E. Pankhurst, *My Own Story*, London, 1914, p. 39; 'The March of the Women', printed in *The Vote*, 17 June 1911, p. 97.

[6] E. S. Pankhurst, op. cit., p. 485; see also pp. 182, 399; E. S. Pankhurst, *The Life of Emmeline Pankhurst*, London, 1935, p. 50.

[7] *Votes for Women*, 31 Mar. 1911, p. 421.

[8] Trinity College, Cambridge, Pethick-Lawrence MSS: F. Pethick-Lawrence to G. M. Trevelyan, 3 Oct. 1949 [Box 6, fos. 280(1–2)], quoted by permission of the Master and Fellows of Trinity College.

methods won public support and alarmed the government before 1914.

Phase three runs from 1914 to 1928; it sees militancy suspended during the war, but credits the politicians' recollection of it with a major role in getting the women the vote. It cites Lord Crewe's speech of January 1918, in which he urges settlement of the question during a 'political backwater in which it is possible to take a far calmer view', whereas delay may cause militancy to revive.[9] From 1918 the journey to equal franchise in 1928 is seen as smooth, inevitable, and hardly worth discussion, but there is an epilogue to the suffragette view which is of wider significance. Suffragettes tend to blame Asquith personally for their setbacks. For Christabel in 1921 there was 'no more flagrant breach of statesmanship . . . on record';[10] nor has George Dangerfield been alone in viewing Asquith's conduct in terms of trickery and craft. Asquith's anti-suffragism is used by former suffragettes to help explain Liberal decline; the Liberal party's impending doom permeates the suffragette view quite as continuously as it permeates *The Strange Death of Liberal England*. Pethick-Lawrence in 1925, for instance, thought the beginning of the party's decay was 'largely attributable to the fast-and-loose method that they adopted in dealing with . . . woman suffrage'. And when Christabel's posthumously published memoirs elaborate on Liberal leaders' failure to assert 'their principles' by rejecting women's suffrage as a policy option in December 1905, she directs one final blow at the old enemy.[11]

The suffragette view cannot be lightly dismissed, if only because parts of it have gained currency among professional historians. Of the seventeen parliamentary divisions on women's suffrage between 1867 and 1907, five produced majorities for women's suffrage, yet politicians failed to act; and on five occasions—1877, 1905, 1906 (twice), and 1907 —a parliamentary division was prevented because opponents

[9] *H.L. Deb.* 9 Jan. 1918, c. 448. See also Trinity College, Cambridge, Pethick-Lawrence MSS: Christabel Pankhurst to F. Pethick-Lawrence, 25 May 1957 [Box 9, fo. 45(3)].

[10] *Weekly Dispatch*, 17 Apr. 1921.

[11] *H.C. Deb.* 20 Feb. 1925, c. 1531; C. Pankhurst, *Unshackled. The Story of how We Won the Vote*, London, 1959, p. 59.

talked out the Bill.[12] Even Mrs Fawcett felt in 1909 that parliament had 'not been honest on the subject'.[13] Smoking-room tactics of obstruction were particularly rife among parliament's anti-suffragist lawyers and bachelors, whereas suffragists who —like the Pankhursts—lived by Dr Pankhurst's dictum that 'life is nothing without enthusiasms', felt comfortable only when discussing the substantive issue in the open. Anti-suffragism, well entrenched within the party machines, attracted 'some of the ablest men in the house', who could effectively obstruct any private member's bill. Loulou Harcourt, a prominent Anti, was reported as saying in 1911 that 'he . . . would not hesitate at *anything*' to stop women's suffrage, and later told Curzon, when refusing to address a public meeting, that 'the intricate nature of my negotiations . . . demand [*sic*] that I should appear as little as possible in public'.[14]

All this seemed insulting to suffragists who were eager to get on with their many other interests and causes. 'Why is it there has to be such a fight, such a struggle to win a just cause', Annie Kenney naïvely asked Balfour in 1909; 'there seems to be such hypocracy [*sic*], such insincerety [*sic*], such lying and such a lot of humbug'.[15] MPs often failed to attend parliamentary divisions on the question, or voted in contradiction to earlier promises. According to the anti-suffragist W. R. Cremer, in the debate of 1904, 'to show what a hollow mockery it . . . was, some of the Members who voted in favour of the Motion came to him after the division and thanked him for his opposition, and said he had expressed the opinions which they entertained'.[16]

[12] See my *Separate Spheres. The Opposition to Women's Suffrage in Britain*, London, 1978, pp. 28-9.

[13] Lambeth Palace Library, Randall Davidson Papers: Mrs Fawcett to Randall Davidson, 6 Mar. [1909] (1909 File W. 7, Women's Suffrage).

[14] Sir Richard Temple, *Report of Speech on the present Aspect of Women's Suffrage on March 16th, 1895* (London, n.d.), p. 7 (copy in John Rylands Library, Manchester, Women's Suffrage Collection Box 3); London School of Economics, Frederick Harrison MSS, 1/113: Mary Ward to Frederic Harrison, 27 Dec. 1911; India Office Library, MSS Eur F 112/35 (Curzon MSS): Harcourt to Curzon, 27 Dec. 1912.

[15] B[ritish] L[ibrary] Add[itional] MSS 49793 (Balfour Papers), fo. 117: Annie Kenney to Balfour, 18 Dec. 1909; cf. E. Sharp, *Hertha Ayrton 1854-1923. A Memoir* (1926), p. 218.

[16] *H.C. Deb.* 8 Mar. 1907, c. 1148, cf. *H.C. Deb.* 11 July 1910, c. 53 (F. E. Smith).

Still worse, since the presentation of the first woman suffrage petition in 1832, MPs had treated the subject as an excuse for facetiousness and even for insulting comments about women. Labouchere was a major culprit here, but speeches of this kind were still being made in 1912. The politicians' failure to take women seriously seemed but a symptom of the wider problem the feminists faced. Suffragettes undoubtedly resented such treatment; the WSPU's first militant act originated with the talking-out of the 1905 bill, and a similar attempt in 1906 provoked interruption from the ladies' gallery. When there was laughter during parliament's discussion of forcible feeding in 1909, *Votes for Women* said that it 'will not be forgotten . . . when the history of this movement comes to be written it will serve to explain to an incredulous generation the nature of the opposition which women had to face'.[17]

Nor did politicians encourage pressure to take non-violent directions; Asquith's dismissive response to the suffragists' huge Hyde Park demonstration in 1908, for instance, caused militancy to be resumed in that year. The politicians were giving no guidance to the extra-parliamentary movement. Suffragettes were as good as anyone at organizing peaceful public meetings, said Christabel Pankhurst in 1911, but these seemed to have no impact: 'what, then, does count? They refuse to tell us.' It was with some justice, in a deputation of 1913, that the non-militant Mrs Rackham asked Asquith 'do you not think that . . . something is actually owing to us?'[18] Catherine Marshall, the non-militants' parliamentary secretary, took a similar line when corresponding with Lloyd George in the same year. Politicians apparently required from the women tests of public support more stringent than they imposed on male reformers. The Liberal government was quite ready to promote reforms which evoked little enthusiasm in the country—to enfranchise more men, for example, or to abolish plural voting.

Women also lacked the constitutional outlets available to

[17] *Votes for Women*, 1 Oct. 1909, p. 2.
[18] *Votes for Women*, 31 Mar. 1911, p. 421; *Common Cause*, 15 Aug. 1913, p. 322. See also *Votes for Women*, 25 June 1908, p. 265; A. Rosen, *Rise Up Women! The Militant Campaign of the Women's Social and Political Union 1903–1914*, London, 1974, p. 106.

male reforming movements; for example, nonconformists, Irishmen, and (after 1874) working men had enjoyed direct representation at Westminster. Furthermore, sixty years after women gained entry there, the House of Commons still seemed 'a deeply masculine place', not unlike a boys' boarding-school in mood, and welcoming only women who acquiesced in male procedures.[19] And in contrast to Australia and the United States, the British political system offered no chance of advancing piecemeal through a federal structure. It is hardly surprising that suffragists carried to an extreme that anti-party, anti-political mood which lies near the surface of many other reforming movements.

Sympathetic suffragist male politicians shared suffragette disquiet at parliament's conduct. Snowden thought that in its handling of the Conciliation Bill in 1910, parliament was 'mocking and exasperating the women'; similar sentiments were expressed by Edward Grey and Lord Robert Cecil.[20] Arthur Henderson even insisted on applying the word 'tricks' to the obstructive methods employed.[21] Asquith and McKenna, aloof from popular passions and pedantic in public statement, did all too little to remove these suspicions, and even non-militant suffragists repeatedly found themselves pleading with Liberal ministers for guidance. This was not the customary role of Whig and Liberal leaders when faced by popular move-ments, and Asquith's government added to its offence by mishandling the suffragists at several crucial junctures.

The trouble began at the beginning, when leading Liberals ignored suffragist questions at public meetings. Then there was the mishandling by Herbert Gladstone, as Home Secre-tary, of suffragette prisoners, and Lloyd George's somewhat childish delight at 'torpedoing' the Conciliation Bill in 1910, despite Mrs Swanwick's effort to dissuade him from describ-ing his conduct so provocatively.[22] Asquith deeply offended even Mrs Fawcett by failing to take her into consultation

[19] Shirley Williams, in BBC Radio 3 broadcast, 10 Apr. 1980 on 'Women in Parliament'.
[20] Snowden, *H.C. Deb.* 29 July 1910, c. 2592; Grey, *H.C. Deb.* 27 Jan. 1913, c. 1059; Cecil, *H.C. Deb.* 27 Jan. 1913, cc. 1037–8.
[21] *H.C. Deb.* 27 Jan. 1913, c. 1033, cf. Bodleian Library, Oxford: MS Sel-borne 102, fo. 35, Selborne to his wife Maud, 19 Nov. 1911.
[22] H. M. Swanwick, *I Have Been Young*, London, 1935, p. 216.

about future policy after the Speaker had unexpectedly ruled against women's suffrage amendments to the Government's franchise bill in January 1913.[23] On at least two occasions Liberal ministers—Herbert Gladstone in 1908 and Sir Charles Hobhouse in 1912—virtually incited the militancy they later condemned by noting the absence from the women's suffrage movement of that violent pressure which had occurred in 1831-2 and 1866-7.[24]

All this constitutes a formidable indictment, and it has entered into the folk-memory of government's critics ever since. Discussing the tactics of the campaign for Nuclear Disarmament with Peggy Duff in 1959, Bertrand Russell said that he was 'constantly reminded of the agitation in favour of votes for women in which I was active fifty years ago. I disliked the unconstitutional methods of the Suffragettes, but in the end one had to confess that it was they who had secured votes for women. Recollections of that campaign make me hesitate to condemn direct action.'[25] Yet it would be simplistic to leave matters there, if only because this would impute an implausible response to the politician. It is a testimony to the under-worked state of British women's history that even in this, its most heavily researched area, many major questions remain to be asked.

II

The suffragette view must first be juxtaposed with the view of the women's suffrage question taken at Westminster. Unfortunately Asquith's memoirs give little help towards recreating this because he sees suffragettes purely in terms of public order, and contents himself with describing A. E. Metcalfe's *Woman's Effort* as 'a curious book', though he admits that some suffragettes 'showed the temper of the confessors and martyrs of a persecuted faith'.[26] In his declining years

[23] *Common Cause*, 24 May 1918, p. 63.
[24] Gladstone, *H.C. Deb.* 28 Feb. 1908, c. 244; Hobhouse, *Votes for Women*, 23 Feb. 1912, p. 326.
[25] R. W. Clark, *The Life of Bertrand Russell*, London, 1975, p. 574; cf. Tariq Ali in *New Statesman*, 11 Dec. 1981, p. 6.
[26] H. H. Asquith, *Memories and Reflections 1852-1927*, 1928, i. 220-1; *Fifty Years of Parliament*, London, 1926, ii. 126.

during the 1920s, any sustained attempt at self-vindication probably did not seem sufficiently lucrative or worth the effort. There is a particular need here for the reconciling role of the historian—for his insistence that posterity should understand both sides in a controversy better than they understood themselves; Herbert Butterfield thought this the historian's special responsibility.[27]

The Westminster perspective modifies the suffragette view in several respects. It first contests the suffragettes' threefold periodization. The local and national funding pattern of women's suffrage organizations for the period clearly reveals instead a fourfold periodization (see graphs 1 and 2). Plotting their annual income on a semi-logarithmic scale makes it possible to include in the same graph organizations of contrasting size, and to compare their growth-patterns. These patterns would of course alter in shape if changing purchasing power were allowed for; figures would be somewhat depressed up to 1892, slightly raised from then until 1906, depressed slightly from then to 1914, substantially depressed from 1914 to 1921, and to a diminishing extent thereafter; but the mutual relationship between the growth-patterns of different organizations would remain unchanged.

The growth-pattern of feminist organizations (graph 1) shows that, after initial success between 1866 and 1871, a long period of decline sets in; this is slow at first, but rapid after the major setback of Gladstone's Reform Bill. Revival begins about 1900 and peaks between 1910 and 1913; thereafter the long period of decline continues up to the Second World War. This undulating pattern contrasts markedly with the much smoother growth-pattern for non-feminist women's organizations (graph 2), seven of which have been analysed for the same period. The strength of the feminist undulation would be even more apparent if feminist funds were aggregated, for a boom period like the years 1906–14 is accompanied by schism, whereas trough periods like the 1890s or the years after 1914 are accompanied by organizations' amalgamation or demise. The contrasting fortunes of feminist and non-feminist organizations in the 1930s emerge clearly from comparing the fate of, on the one hand the feminist National

[27] H. Butterfield, *The Whig Interpretation of History*, London, 1931, p. 2.

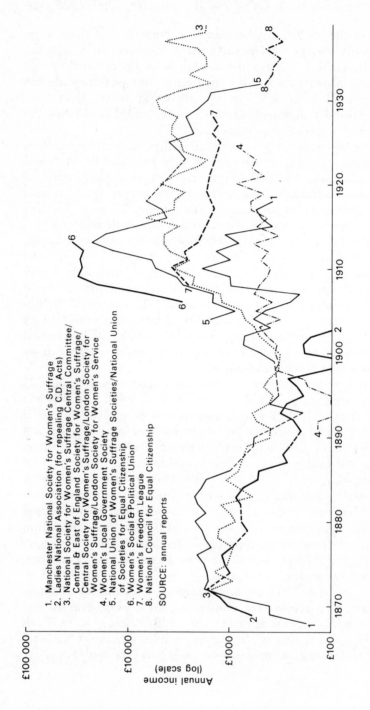

1. Manchester National Society for Women's Suffrage
2. Ladies National Association (for repealing C.D. Acts)
3. National Society for Women's Suffrage Central Committee/
   Central & East of England Society for Women's Suffrage/
   Central Society for Women's Suffrage/London Society for
   Women's Suffrage/London Society for Women's Service
4. Women's Local Government Society
5. National Union of Women's Suffrage Societies/National Union
   of Societies for Equal Citizenship
6. Women's Social & Political Union
7. Women's Freedom League
8. National Council for Equal Citizenship

SOURCE: annual reports

Graph 1. Annual Income of prominent feminist British women's organizations, 1866–1939

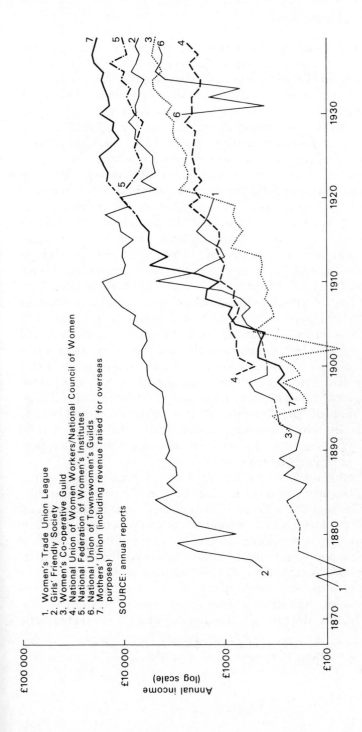

1. Women's Trade Union League
2. Girls' Friendly Society
3. Women's Co-operative Guild
4. National Union of Women Workers/National Council of Women
5. National Federation of Women's Institutes
6. National Union of Townswomen's Guilds
7. Mothers' Union (including revenue raised for overseas purposes)

SOURCE: annual reports

Annual income (log scale)

£100 000

£10 000

£1000

£100

1870   1880   1890   1900   1910   1920   1930

Graph 2. Annual Income of prominent non-feminist British women's organizations, 1866–1939

Union of Societies for Equal Citizenship (NUSEC) and the National Council for Equal Citizenship (NCEC), and on the other hand the self-consciously non-feminist National Union of Townswomen's Guilds and National Federation of Women's Institutes. Not that the distinction between these two types of women's organization should be drawn too firmly: a non-feminist or even anti-feminist organization may well develop the self-confidence of women, despite its beliefs.

Two criticisms of the suffragette view emerge from the pattern thus revealed. The first is to emphasize the brevity of the suffragette moment, the long history of the non-militant activity which preceded it, and the abundance of women's organizations, feminist and non-feminist, active at the time. The non-militant achievement before 1906 was prodigious, if only because early suffragist perspectives were so broad. Through school board elections and local government and poor law reforms, late Victorian women made major advances in political participation. And so substantial were late Victorian reforms of married women's property, divorce and guardianship law, so great was the late Victorian expansion in women's educational and professional opportunity—that anti-suffragists adduced these reforms to support their claim that women had no need of the vote.[28] Indeed, it is difficult to think of any feminist reform that was at all widely demanded which was not eventually conceded between 1866 and 1906, and it is only with articulated grievances that politicians can fairly be expected to deal.

These reforms were not always overtly promoted by suffragists, but here, as so often elsewhere in the period, franchise reform 'was the residual beneficiary of most pressure group activity'. There was a circular relationship between late Victorian feminist reforms whereby non-political campaigns simultaneously recruited feminist self-confidence and suffragist ranks. Already by 1876 the suffrage movement could be seen as 'a nucleus round which all who desire justice done to women may gather, and draw from more or less direct association, the strength which comes of union with sympathetic

[28] e.g. A. V. Dicey, *Letters to a Friend on Votes for Women*, London, 1909, p. 26; Heber Hart, *Woman Suffrage: A National Danger*, London, 1912, p. 151.

minds'.[29] Furthermore a parliamentary majority for women's suffrage was being built up after 1897 which the militants subsequently helped to destroy, and a powerful intellectual case was being prepared which Edwardian anti-suffragists had difficulty in refuting, and from which suffragette militancy later provided (for anti-suffragists) a welcome distraction.

The vote was of course an important question of status, but the Edwardian preoccupation with it diverted attention from wider feminist reforms. Edwardian suffragist periodicals narrowed in scope, and in the militants' *Votes for Women* and *The Suffragette* the suffragist apologia degenerates into recurrent attempts at justifying militant tactics. There was in the Edwardian suffragist movement, as Mrs Billington-Greig pointed out at the time, a 'sudden loss of breadth'.[30] Inter-war feminists saw the post-war burst of feminist reforms as a consequence of women's emancipation in 1918, but some of these might well have occurred earlier if all Edwardian eyes had not been so firmly directed towards the suffrage.

The growth-pattern of women's organizations (graph 1) also brings out the suffragists' entanglement with the fluctuating fortunes of political parties. It provides a basis for a second critique of suffragist tactics which suffragettes never articulated, and which can be directed at both militants and non-militants. Suffragism prospers as a political issue during years of Liberal optimism: between 1866 and 1871 and between about 1901 and 1911. It wanes during those periods of overseas distraction which so often coincide with Conservative government, especially during the 1880s and 1890s and after 1914. In these circumstances, it would have been wiser for suffragists to cease operating like non-feminist women's organizations (graph 2) and instead to work closely with the grain of party. Such partisan commitment would of course have been only a temporary expedient; once the vote had been won, feminists would be free to join any party, and feminist organizations could then become less volatile in their

---

[29] Quotations from P. Hollis (ed.), *Pressure from Without in Early Victorian England*, London, 1974, p. 9; *Englishwoman's Review*, 15 Apr. 1876, p. 149.

[30] T. Billington-Greig, *The Militant Suffrage Movement. Emancipation in a Hurry* (Frank Palmer, London, n.d.), p. 75.

patterns of growth. Why, then, did suffragists retain their
non-party strategy?

Here it is necessary to recognize the scale of their psychological and even their Manchester-based geographical distance
from the leading politicians. Likening their movement to the
Anti-Corn Law League and the other successful earlier emanci-
patory agitations, in which they had themselves often participated, they assumed that it was only a matter of time and
effort before their obviously just cause would prevail. The
political process was but a tedious interval made necessary by
parliament's undemocratic and even corrupt mood; extra-
parliamentary idealists must purge it. References to political
'scoundrels' and 'trickery' abound in suffragette oratory, inspired as it often was by that black-and-white view of the
political process which—as Orwell once wrote—'belongs to
the nursery'. By 1912 even Mrs Fawcett was privately referring to the tricks politicians were playing on her movement.[31]

Distance from Westminster entailed distance from the political parties which originated and were directed from there.
Contempt for party loyalty was widespread among late Victorian reforming movements, but the historical parallels were
misleading. In early Victorian conditions, the campaigns
against slavery and the Corn Laws might prevail over party,
but after the 1860s—when political parties adapted themselves to cater for an expanded electorate—this was dimin-
ishingly possible. Yet suffragists continued to assume that it
was the reforming movement, not the political party, which
embodied democratic principles. A non-party outlook was
continuously peddled in the *Women's Suffrage Journal* of
the 1870s and 1880s, and remained with Mrs Fawcett to the
end: 'my work has been wholly outside party lines', she
wrote in 1924, '—to endeavour to influence public opinion,
and therefore all parties, not by force, but by reason, experience, and common sense'.[32] Suffragist non-party attitudes
were reinforced by the gains suffragists made from the

[31] B. Crick, *George Orwell. A Life*, London, 1980, p. 374; City of London
Polytechnic, Fawcett Library Autograph Collection, 7013: Mrs Fawcett to Lady
F. Balfour, 11 Feb. 1912. See also Fred Pethick-Lawrence, *The Man's Share. Mr.
Pethick Lawrence's Defence of Militancy* (Woman's Press, n.d.), p. 11.

[32] *Woman's Leader*, 22 Feb. 1924, p. 26; cf. City of London Polytechnic,
89/149: Mrs Fawcett to Sir John Simon, 9 Dec. 1918.

wartime coalition—an experience that was once again a misleading precedent for feminists after party alignments had revived in the early 1920s. The inter-war political career of Eleanor Rathbone illustrates the tendency, as does feminist prominence among signatories to the Next Five Years Group's *Essay in Political Agreement* of 1935. We can now see that a closer involvement with a political party would not only have been the best route to women's suffrage, but also the best way for women to gain long-term political influence. After the 1860s the political parties had themselves become the vehicles of popular participation, the instruments of an aroused public opinion; their democratized structure henceforward relegated the non-party pressure group to a subordinate role; feminists failed to see that it was now too weak as an instrument for realizing their objectives.

Their non-party outlook led suffragists naturally on to the private member's bill as a political device, and to the pledging of MPs from all parties to support it. Yet this was less appropriate in a House of Commons whose mounting pressure of business made it necessary to entrust governments with control over its timetable. At first suffragists thought they could overcome the difficulty by making their bill short and simple, and therefore capable of rapid and unobtrusive enactment. So they emphasized the smallness of their reform, which would render 'what is theoretically a great change practically a very small measure'; only one-seventh of the representation would be enjoyed by the female half of the nation.[33] The idea of simply removing the sex discrimination from the existing franchise had a quadruple attraction: it gave suffragists a simple objective to guide them through a political process they distrusted; it provided a readily intelligible demand to unite and inspire the extra-parliamentary movement; it deprived anti-suffragists at Westminster of opportunities for amendment; and it was compatible with cultivating support from within both major political parties.

By the 1880s the shrewder suffragists, especially Sir Charles Dilke, perceived the drawbacks of this non-party strategy, yet suffragists remained wedded to it. The suffragettes showed some insight when they jettisoned the private member's bill

[33] *Women's Suffrage Journal*, 2 May 1870, p. 18, cf. p. 17.

and held the government directly responsible for initiating reform. Shortly before she died, Christabel Pankhurst took pride in the fact that it was the militants who 'were really the *constitutional* suffragists', not 'the old-fashioned section'.[34] At the time she had buttressed her changed strategy with citations from Anson's *Law and Custom of the Constitution* and Sidney Low's *Governance of England*; like several Edwardian suffragists and experts on the constitution, suffragettes emphasized the extent of the executive's control over the modern legislature.[35] 'It is the Government alone that we regard as our enemy', Mrs Pankhurst declared at her trial in 1912, 'and the whole of our agitation is directed to bringing just as much pressure as necessary upon those people who can deal with our grievance.'[36]

Yet here is a typically Pankhurstian combination of irreverent tactical insight and over-confident political iconoclasm, for if it was right to abandon the private member's bill, the associated non-party outlook should have been jettisoned too. Instead, the suffragettes resorted to militancy as a way of coercing governments. Three major errors lie behind this: the constitutional impropriety involved in failing to see that party power was increasing only because politicians had to find ways of facilitating increased political participation, and that coercion of parliament could not therefore be convincingly presented as democratic; the psychological implausibility of assuming that a male-elected, male-recruited parliament could be intimidated by women using a physical force which in effect undermined the very profession of politics, and that the public would support politicians who allowed themselves to be thus coerced; and the political misjudgement involved in seeking to supplant a potentially suffragist Liberal government by a government whose Conservatism was instinctively anti-suffragist, and three-quarters of whose parliamentary following (according to Curzon in 1911)

[34] Pethick-Lawrence MSS, Box 9, fo. 40(2): Christabel Pankhurst to Fred Pethick-Lawrence, 10 Mar. 1957.

[35] C. Pankhurst in *Votes for Women*, 13 Aug. 1908, p. 377; cf. F. Pethick-Lawrence, ibid., 6 May 1910, p. 512; 21 Apr. 1911, p. 474; E. Pethick-Lawrence, ibid., 13 Jan. 1911, p. 244.

[36] *Votes for Women*, 24 May 1912, p. 533, cf. Christabel Pankhurst, *Suffragette*, 10 Oct. 1913, p. 904; 6 Mar. 1914, p. 459.

opposed the change.[37] Christabel might argue that the Liberals in opposition would respond more readily to suffragist pressure;[38] but such sympathy need not necessarily involve plumping for the equal franchise, nor do oppositions enjoy the initiative in legislation. These were not mistakes that the WSPU's authoritarian structure and reverential mood towards its leaders were calculated to remove.

The Home Rule parallel was particularly misleading here, for although Parnell's irreverence towards political party did perhaps encourage Gladstone to take up the question in 1885, Home Rule's subsequent fortunes surely illustrated both how seriously militancy could damage a cause, and (in Redmond's hands) how helpful it might be to harness a political party. By 1911 several of Christabel's suffragist critics held up Redmond to her as an alternative model,[39] and even Mrs Pankhurst had to confess in 1913 that the parallel between suffragism and Home Rule was not complete; suffragists, she said, lacked direct parliamentary representation, 'so we are obliged to take to other methods, similar to those which, added to Parliamentary obstruction, led to the passing of the Irish Land Acts'.[40] Yet Parnell had never directly promoted militancy: on the contrary, he had tried to contain it. Two other influences, besides the false historical parallel, help to explain Christabel's mistake. The first is the feminist's natural reluctance to work with organizations as firmly dominated by male methods and objectives as the Edwardian political parties; Christabel's feminism would at least have been diluted by holding to the WSPU's initial Lib–Lab connection, quite apart from the split within suffragist ranks that such a party connection would entail. The second influence is simply the personal difficulty involved for the spoilt child whose adult confrontation with Asquith was seen in exaggeratedly personal terms, and whose militancy can to some

---

[37] House of Lords Record Office, Bonar Law MSS, 18/7/162: Curzon to Bonar Law, 3 Mar. 1911, cf. Cumbria County Record Office, Carlisle, Catherine Marshall MSS, Box 9: Robert Cecil to Catherine Marshall, 19 Nov. 1913.

[38] *Suffragette*, 3 Oct. 1913, p. 884; 6 Mar. 1914, p. 459.

[39] e.g. *Freewoman*, 23 Nov. 1911, p. 4; BL Add. MSS 58226 (H. D. Harben MSS), fo. 33: typescript from Christabel Pankhurst's private secretary to Annie Kenney.

[40] *Suffragette*, 28 Feb. 1913, p. 309.

extent be seen as the petulant stamping of an institutional foot.

What, then, would have been the best party strategy for suffragists? There was a case for getting the Conservative party committed to the equal franchise. Salisbury in the 1880s more than once hinted at the possibility,[41] and the declaration against women's suffrage published by *The Nineteenth Century* in 1889 originated partly in an anti-suffragist attempt to head it off.[42] Both religious and class factors rendered the equal franchise attractive to Conservatives. 'A good deal of the political battle of the future will be a conflict between religion and unbelief,' Salisbury told Lady Janetta Manners in June 1884, 'and the women will in that controversy be on the right side.'[43] And in a decade of mounting socialist propaganda, Conservatives might profit from enfranchising the relatively small number of property-holding women who would qualify if women acquired a property-based franchise originally designed for men.

Yet the Conservative party could not easily be united behind a reform whose social implications were so radical. And whereas experience in 1867 and 1884–5 showed that party interest could drive Conservatives into supporting democratic reforms, and therefore in this case towards adult suffrage (the Liberal route to women's suffrage), Liberals could scarcely be driven towards the type of conservative reform which equal franchise had become by the late Victorian period. The party for late Victorian suffragism was therefore the Liberal party, and the strategy for women's suffrage (as Sir Charles Dilke early realized) was adult suffrage.

Liberals had no reason in principle to oppose adult suffrage, which was fully in accord with their values and traditions, and had often been championed at early nineteenth-century radical meetings. J. S. Mill's commitment to the equal franchise in the 1860s had stemmed only from the tactical consideration that 'women's suffrage has quite enemies enough, without adding to the number all the enemies of universal

[41] e.g. *Women's Suffrage Journal*, 1 Jan. 1885, p. 5; 1 Jan. 1889, p. 3.

[42] Frederic Harrison MSS, 1/68: F. Harrison to John Morley, 27 May 1889.

[43] Hatfield House MSS, Third Marquess, D28, fo. 235: Salisbury to Lady John Manners, 14 June 1884 (typescript copy); cf. Lord John Manners, quoted in *Women's Suffrage Journal*, 1 July 1885, p. 113.

suffrage'; furthermore he feared that feminists who espoused adult suffrage would be dropped from the bill at the point of legislation, and 'we should start again in a more disadvantageous position than we are in at present'.[44] Mill's objective in the 1860s was feminist, but feminism was as yet too weak to suffice as a sole basis for agitation: feminists therefore had to summon in aid the prestige of the household franchise and the prevailing valuation of a link between voting and property ownership. His strategy envisaged the household suffrage principle of 1867 being extended to include female heads of household—that is, widows and spinsters with the requisite property qualification. Yet he told suffragists in 1870 that women's suffrage had its own special justification, and that there was no necessary link between feminism and the campaign for equal franchise; the suffrage, he said, 'is a thing apart'.[45]

Unfortunately suffragists made little headway in converting Liberals to their reform, and in 1884 Gladstone was therefore free to enfranchise more men without including any women; he told Dilke that women's suffrage was 'a vast social question, which is surely entitled to be considered as such', and insisted on the clarity of the distinction 'between supporting a thing in its right place and thrusting it into its wrong place'.[46] Gladstone later declared against women's suffrage as such, and so became a villain for the feminists. '*Women* have every reason to hate and despise Gladstone's memory,' wrote Mrs Elmy, who saw him as 'the main cause of the long delay of our Suffrage victory.' Suffragists in 1912 were still claiming that he had 'thrown overboard' the women to 'lighten the ship' in 1884;[47] in reality, the women had never even embarked, for, as Labouchere rightly pointed out at the time, 'we are here by a distinct mandate of the country;

[44] J. S. Mill, *Later Letters* (ed. F. E. Mineka and D. N. Lindley), iv, Toronto, 1972, p. 1728 (Mill to Dilke, 28 May 1870).

[45] *Report of a Meeting of the London National Society for Women's Suffrage, held at the Hanover Square Rooms, on . . . March 26th, 1870*, p. 3.

[46] BL Add. MSS 43875 (Dilke MSS), fo. 165: Gladstone to Dilke, 13 May 1884.

[47] BL Add. MSS 47453 (Elmy MSS), fo. 155: Mrs Elmy to Mrs McIlquham, 14 Aug. 1903; Add. MSS 47451 (Elmy MSS), fo. 214: Mrs Elmy to Mrs McIlquham, 29 May 1898; Catherine Marshall MSS, Box 8: printed article headed 'The Election Fighting Fund', endorsed 'not printed'.

one of the reasons why we were elected [in 1880] was that we pledged ourselves to vote in favour of the franchise being given to agricultural labourers'.[48] Mid-Victorian suffragists never converted enough Liberals to the equal franchise for any other course to be feasible for Gladstone in 1884; it must therefore be questioned whether this really was one of the two major pre-war lost opportunities for getting women the vote.[49]

The defeat of Woodall's equal franchise amendment in 1884 accentuated the suffragist decline (graph 1); it provoked bitterness among suffragists, but not strategic re-thinking. In retrospect we can now see that a strictly feminist approach to franchise reform was possible for Liberals only during the brief first phase of suffragist success between 1866 and 1884; thereafter the party must in the end prefer democracy to equality. A change of suffragist strategy was therefore required after 1884: the acceptance of a Liberal connection and there-fore of adult suffrage as the means to the suffragist end. In principle this should not have been too difficult. The campaign for women's suffrage had, after all, been launched primarily by Liberals. J. S. Mill had begun it; Courtney, Jacob Bright, Dilke, and Henry Fawcett had been its leading parliamentary pioneers; Mrs Fawcett, who began as a Liberal, became its leading extra-parliamentary spokesman. In only three of the seventeen divisions on women's suffrage between 1867 and 1904 did Conservatives and Unionists contribute a higher per-centage of the total suffragist vote than Liberals and radicals.[50]

In the event, suffragists persisted with their non-party strategy, and were therefore prevented from either having their cake or eating it. After 1884 they offered sustained under-cover resistance to Dilke's adult suffragist strategy (reinforced by distaste after 1886 for his marital life), held even more tightly to the equal franchise strategy, and insisted even more firmly that women must get the vote before any further extension of the male franchise took place. Sylvia Pankhurst later recalled that in 1905, when Mrs Pankhurst

[48] *H.C. Deb.* 12 June 1884, c. 174.
[49] C. Rover, *Women's Suffrage and Party Politics in Britain 1866–1914*, London, 1967, pp. 191–2.
[50] See my *Separate Spheres*, p. 29.

told her how important it was to get women the vote before it was extended to more men, 'she appeared so greatly to distress herself that I feared for her health and her reason'.[51] Again in 1911–13 it is the memory of 1884 that makes suffragists, whether militant or non-militant, so wary of Asquith's proposal to allow feminist amendments to the Government's Franchise Bill. Suffragists' tactical conservatism helps to explain why the initial dalliance with suffragism by several significant mid-Victorian radicals—Herbert Spencer, John Bright, Dicey, Goldwin Smith, Chamberlain, Labouchere, Morley—did not persist in later life.

Suffragists did not always object to adult suffrage as such. Indeed, the militant and non-militant formula seeking votes for women 'as it is or may be granted to men' aimed at attaching their reform to any type of male franchise. Conservative suffragists like Maud Selborne, Lady Frances Balfour, or Emily Davies might dislike adult suffrage, and might even see the equal franchise as a useful barrier against it—but by no means all suffragists thought this. Mrs Pankhurst thought the Conciliation Bill's variant of women's suffrage too limited in 1910. Brailsford in 1911 thought the suffragettes ready for womanhood suffrage if they could only be sure that manhood suffrage would not in practice be substituted for it. Christabel Pankhurst in January 1912 claimed that a Labour party that was really in earnest could push Asquith into adult suffrage by threatening him with parliamentary defeat unless he introduced it.[52] As for the non-militants, although they publicly opposed Geoffrey Howard's adult suffrage measure of 1909, they were privately divided on the matter, and in her correspondence with Lloyd George in 1913 Catherine Marshall, their parliamentary secretary, urged him to 'start a really effective demand for Adult Suffrage (which there has never been yet) at the same time as your Land campaign'; she saw it as potentially 'a grand programme on which to go to the country'.[53]

---

[51] E. S. Pankhurst, *Suffragette Movement*, p. 181.

[52] For Mrs Pankhurst, see A. Rosen, op. cit., p. 135; Manchester University Library, C. P. Scott MSS, 332/13: Brailsford to Scott, n.d. (before Nov. 1911); Public Record Office, H.O. 45/219337: police report of WSPU meeting at Pavilion Theatre on 22 Jan. 1912, p. 2.

[53] House of Lords Record Office, Lloyd George MSS, C/9/5/20: Catherine

Why, then, did suffragists repudiate the adult suffrage strategy? They knew that at a time of intense party feeling this would virtually entail abandoning political feminism as an integrated movement. An adult suffrage programme would alienate Conservative suffragists, and did not yet seem certain to capture the Liberal party, whose anti-suffragists helped to produce after 1884 what Dilke later described as 'the silent conflict between the friends of manhood suffrage and those who desire a greater change'.[54] Furthermore feminist impact would be seriously diluted if suffragists campaigned simultaneously to enfranchise more men. As Christabel Pankhurst later recalled, 'our main concern was not with the *numbers* of women to be enfranchised but with the removal of a stigma upon womanhood as such'.[55] Suffragists thought it important to advertise feminist principle, and not submerge it into a generalized radical reform.

Nor was adult suffrage widely demanded. Woodall pointed out in 1884 that women's suffrage meetings were 'generally larger and more influential than those held on behalf of the agricultural labourers',[56] and the same was said of the miscellaneous group of men who still lacked the vote in the Edwardian period. In 1909 Snowden described the attempt to mobilize adult suffragists as 'a ludicrous failure', and many adult suffragists were accused of being anti-feminists cloaking their views in democratic disguise.[57] For reformers who thought there should be an almost one-to-one relationship between extra-parliamentary agitation and political outcome, this was unsatisfactory. Why saddle feminism with an adult suffrage cause so weakly demanded and so dubious in motive? Snowden therefore confidently spoke (though he did not vote) as advocate for the suffragist societies against Geoffrey Howard's Adult Suffrage Bill of 1909; the Bill had 'no more chance of becoming law in this Parliament than the new

Marshall to Lloyd George, 29 Aug. 1913; see also Manchester City Library, Fawcett MSS, M50/2/1/280: Walter McLaren to Mrs Fawcett, 15 Mar. 1909.

[54] Sir Charles Dilke, *Woman Suffrage and Electoral Reform* (People's Suffrage Federation, n.d., shelved in BL at 08415 df 61/1), p. 4.
[55] C. Pankhurst, *Unshackled*, p. 186.
[56] *H.C. Deb.* 10 June 1884, c. 1953.
[57] *Christian Commonwealth*, 31 Mar. 1909.

aeroplane has of making a trip to Mars'. *Votes for Women* even saw Howard's Bill as 'a trick dictated by Mr. Asquith, with a view to postpone indefinitely the question of Woman Suffrage'.[58] For all these reasons, suffragist leaders both militant and non-militant took up public positions which could be somewhat misleadingly described as hostile to adult suffrage.

By 1904, however, at least one shrewd female labour activist had begun to move on. Margaret Llewellyn-Davies of the Women's Co-operative Guild had come to see that the 'equality' involved in the equal franchise was specious: no reform which subjected women to a special electoral disability on marriage, or which enfranchised only those women unusual enough to qualify for a predominantly male franchise, could plausibly be described as equal between the sexes. Nor could any nominal equality in electoral law produce a genuine political equality between sexes whose social situation so markedly diverged.[59] Could not Britain follow New Zealand and Australia by introducing women's suffrage on the basis of an adult franchise? This was surely the progressive route to women's suffrage; no Conservative voted for Howard's Adult Suffrage Bill in 1909, whereas at the second reading of equal franchise bills between 1867 and 1908, Conservative votes never fell below 12.5 per cent of the total votes in favour, and on Woodall's amendment in 1884 they had risen as high as 69.3 per cent.[60] Labour party surveys might show that many working women would vote under an equal franchise, but adult suffragists could effectively reply that their own reform would enfranchise still more.

To Liberal ministers like Lloyd George and Churchill, aware that Liberal vitality depended on continued alignment with the left, adult suffrage seemed the only possible strategy. Care for the deprived of both sexes must take priority over a sex disability whose simple removal might actually strengthen

---

[58] Snowden, ibid.; *Votes for Women*, 12 Mar. 1909, cf. Christabel Pankhurst, in *Daily News*, 18 Mar. 1909, p. 4.

[59] Women's Co-operative Guild, Walthamstow: Scrapbook on the WCG and Women's Suffrage entitled 'News Cuttings', undated, unsigned MS, pasted with pamphlets dated 1904; cf. Rosalind Nash's letter dated 22 Nov. to *Manchester Guardian*, pasted in the same volume.

[60] See my *Separate Spheres*, pp. 28-9.

the forces of darkness by duplicating the anomalies of the existing franchise, including plural voting; 'two Liberals' writing in 1907 even thought it would 'seal the doom of the Liberal and Labour Parties for a generation, if not for ever'.[61] A democratic franchise could not rest on 'the more or less fortuitous relationship which exists between a man and his house or room'; it must attach to the human being rather than to the residence.[62] Churchill and Lloyd George therefore opposed the Conciliation Bill in 1910; Churchill was astonished at Liberal and Labour MPs who could support such 'an anti-democratic Bill', and even Henderson had qualms.[63] Labour MPs supported women's suffrage in any form, but they were still keener on adult suffrage, which more readily attracted the extra-parliamentary party. When it came to voting in parliament on adult suffrage in 1909, thirty MPs labelled 'Labour' were united in its support, and none opposed it.

Given the rise of party, then, it was through adult suffrage that an equal franchise could be most readily won, and the female labour leaders publicly or privately declaring their preference for it include Margaret Bondfield, Mary Macarthur, Margaret Llewellyn-Davies, Margaret MacDonald, Margaret Macmillan, Katherine Glasier, and Marion Phillips.[64] Margaret Llewellyn-Davies rightly pointed out that 'altho[ugh] the *subject* of Suff[rage] is non-party—the *form* in wh[ich] it may be given is very party—and party camps are becoming more and more inevitable'.[65] Whatever the short-term difficulties, adult suffrage was in the long term working 'in the line of least resistance',[66] and had the ancillary long-term

---

[61] 'Two Liberals', *The Difficulties of Women's Suffrage* (proof copy dated Feb. 1907), p. 5, in Greater London Council Record Office, W. H. Dickinson MSS, Box. 2.

[62] *H.C. Deb.* 19 Mar. 1909, c. 1410, cf. MS letter from W. H. Dickinson to Margaret Llewellyn-Davies, 27 Oct. 1907, pasted in scrapbook cited in fn. 59.

[63] Churchill, *H.C. Deb.* 12 July 1910, c. 224, cf. Asquith, ibid., c. 253; Henderson, *H.C. Deb.* 5 May 1911, c. 788.

[64] See *Verbatim Report of Debate on Dec. 3rd 1907: Sex Equality (Teresa Billington-Greig) versus Adult Suffrage (Margaret G. Bondfield)*, Manchester, 1908, pp. 14–16; *Daily News*, 15 Mar. 1909, p. 6; M. A. Hamilton, *Arthur Henderson. A Biography*, London, 1938, p. 78.

[65] Catherine Marshall MSS, Box 7: Margaret Llewellyn-Davies to Miss Marshall, n.d. [endorsed 'probably 26 Sept. 1910']; cf. Box 8: Eleanor Acland to K. Courtney, n.d. [posted 1 Apr. 1912].   [66] *Daily News*, 15 Mar. 1909, p. 6.

advantage of helping to entrench women within the political parties. The non-party strategy for women lingered on into the 1920s, but nothing ever came of the Women's Party, and Eleanor Rathbone's career as an independent MP did not furnish the model for future women politicians, who eventually made their careers through the Labour or Conservative parties. The Westminster view must therefore also challenge the epilogue to the suffragette view, which relishes the Liberal party's ineluctable doom. Liberal agents strongly opposed the Conciliation Bill's limited franchise of 1911, and F. D. Acland told Asquith that the equal franchise 'really means (except for owners and lodgers) *a middle and upper class landlord made vote*';[67] no wonder such a measure attracted a Conservative aristocrat like Lord Robert Cecil. In the parliamentary debate of 1913 Asquith therefore described adult suffrage as 'the only logical, the only rational, defensible proposal' and he told Sylvia Pankhurst's deputation of June 1914 that 'if a change is to come, it must be democratic in its basis'.[68] Already in 1912-14 he was preparing the ground for the change of position he eventually announced in 1916.

Can his anti-suffragism be seen, with P. F. Clarke, as 'the most serious criticism that can be made of his leadership'? Is John Grigg correct in labelling as 'a serious blemish' on the Liberal government's record the fact that it did not at an early stage introduce a proper women's suffrage measure? Did Asquith's myopia on electoral reform contribute (as David Morgan claims) 'to the failure of the "New Liberalism" and the rise of the Labour party'?[69] The verdict must distinguish between Asquith's anti-suffragism and his hostility to particular ways of introducing women's suffrage.

Asquith certainly misjudged the likely consequences of women's suffrage and was almost perversely blind to its importance as a status question. He was also insensitive in

---

[67] Bodleian Library, Oxford, MS Asquith 13: F. D. A[cland], memo endorsed 'probably Nov. 1912'; see also Nuffield College, Oxford, Gainford Papers, Box [112], cabinet paper dated Nov. 1911, submitted by the Chief Whip.

[68] *H.C. Deb.* 6 May 1913, c. 1909; *Suffragette*, 26 June 1914, p. 178.

[69] P. F. Clarke, *Lancashire and the New Liberalism*, Cambridge, 1971, p. 399; J. Grigg, 'Liberals on Trial', in A. Sked and C. Cook (eds.), *Crisis and Controversy. Essays in honour of A. J. P. Taylor*, London, 1976, p. 35; D. Morgan, *Suffragists and Liberals. The Politics of Woman Suffrage in England*, Oxford, 1975, p. 158.

handling a movement which badly needed political guidance, though there were several more significant Liberal pressure groups for him to reckon with in those difficult years between 1906 and 1914. But these are relatively peripheral matters. The central facts are that Asquith's resistance to women's suffrage was not absolute, as his attitude to franchise reform between 1911 and 1914 shows, and that in resisting a simple removal of the sex disability from the existing franchise, he was effectively promoting Liberal interests; he was thereby aligning himself behind some of his more progressive colleagues, most notably Lloyd George, and was aligning his party behind the more progressive among Liberal, Labour, and feminist groupings. No Liberal government with life in it could have taken any other course, least of all a Liberal government confronted by the militancy of an autocratically-led suffragette movement which sought to coerce the majority through tactical violence.

One member of the Pankhurst family did come to realize the mistake involved in the suffragists' long-standing non-party policy. In her *The Suffragette* (1911), Sylvia Pankhurst gives no hint of her subsequent adult suffragist, Labour-based critique of her mother and sister, but her move to the East End convinced her in 1913–14 how strong were the arguments for adult suffrage. Raising the slogan 'human suffrage' in 1915, she abandoned the old one-clause equal-franchise measure and sought to base women's suffrage once more on the mass support which had been envisaged by the WSPU in its earliest days. She now abandoned the middle-class, dog-in-the-manger, 'same terms' strategies of the old suffrage societies, whether militant or non-militant; in her *Suffragette Movement* she concludes that 'in the light of later events, it is now obvious that a grave mistake was made in leaving the field of adult suffrage—the true field of the Labour movement—to those who were either hostile or indifferent to the inclusion of women'.[70]

This new alignment performed a personal service for her too, because she reached the conclusion that a Manchester-

[70] E. S. Pankhurst, *Suffragette Movement*, p. 203. See also *Woman's Dreadnought*, 27 Nov. 1915, p. 368; 18 Dec. 1915, p. 384; 29 Jan. 1916, p. 414; 27 May 1916, p. 482.

based leadership would have held late Victorian suffragists on a more firmly democratic course.[71] In thus rebelling against her mother and her sister Christabel during 1913-14, she was reuniting with the radicalism of her father, and repairing the breach with her substitute-father Keir Hardie which her mother had created by shifting the WSPU away from its early Lib-Lab connections. Christabel had always criticized her father for being 'advanced' all round instead of focusing on a single reform, but this was not a criticism of her father that the later Sylvia was likely to echo.[72]

It was the suffragist clash with party loyalties, then, that held the suffragette and Westminster views so firmly apart, and party conflict between the 1860s and 1920s was intensifying. For Edwardian Liberals it seemed urgent to uphold free trade, social justice, parliamentary democracy, and religious freedom in the face of an imperialist, property-based, House-of-Lords-entrenched and aggressively anti-socialist Unionism which might exploit the equal franchise issue to promote its own class interest. In this context, the compromises involved in the Conciliation Bill seemed to partisans on both sides merely dishonest, for the bill was attracting support on contradictory grounds from politicians whose philosophies diverged. Some anti-suffragists even saw it as a device for keeping women's suffrage out of electoral debate; anti-suffragists thought that 'conciliation' was being engineered behind the backs of the public, not between suffragists and anti-suffragists, but between different types of suffragist.[73] It was inevitable also that the issue would be exploited for party advantage. Lord Hugh Cecil privately admitted that he supported the bill in the House 'both ostensibly and really in order to embarrass the present government'. Conversely, it was inevitable that Lloyd George would 'torpedo' a bill which threatened his successful waging of 'the battle of the poor and of the oppressed'.[74]

---

[71] E. S. Pankhurst, *Suffragette Movement*, p. 34.

[72] Bodleian Library, Oxford, MS Eng. Misc. e. 618/4: Nevinson Diary, 17 Apr. 1915.

[73] *The Times*, 14 June 1910, p. 10; House of Lords Record Office, St. Loe Strachey MSS, S5/5/19: A. V. Dicey to Strachey, 30 May 1910.

[74] Bodleian Library, Oxford, MS Eng. Lett. d 429 (Countess of Selborne MSS), fo. 69a: Lord Hugh Cecil to Maud Selborne, 26 Oct. 1910; Lytton MSS, Knebworth: typescript copy of deputation to Lloyd George, 28 Sept. [1910].

Party warfare was even more intense in 1912 when women's suffrage seemed likely to arrive through a feminist amendment to the Government's Franchise Bill. Asquith's public anti-suffragism had been so uncompromising and recent that his position was bound to be undermined if his government had to enact the reform, and both Loreburn and Churchill privately feared this would be the issue that broke up the Government.[75] Ardent Conservatives such as F. E. Smith relished the prospect,[76] and Bonar Law thought the party must avoid helping the Liberals overcome their difficulties: 'it seems to me . . . that from our point of view—which is naturally the desire to defeat the Government—the less part we take in this question the better'.[77] In such a situation, MPs' pledges to support women's suffrage readily dissolved. Some had always thought it important to retain freedom of judgement on public policy; others may well have weakly responded to whichever pressure was strongest at the time. But some sincerely accepted the general principle of women's suffrage when legislation was far off, while feeling free to oppose specific measures if unsatisfactory in their details. The closer the reform, the more prominent the details and mechanisms became.

In 1912, G. R. Lane-Fox drew attention to the peculiar circumstances in which private members' bills and resolutions were debated: 'everybody knows the House of Commons on those occasions resolves itself for the time being practically into a debating society, and to lay stress on the votes given on those occasions is to give them a value and an effect which they certainly do not deserve'.[78] He might have added that an MP's pledge is always made in particular circumstances, that in politics circumstances rapidly change, that no politician can make pledges which are binding in all circumstances, and that only when legislation draws near is

[75] India Office Library, Curzon MSS, MSS Eur F 112/19: Loreburn to Curzon, 31 Jan. 1912. For Churchill, see R. S. Churchill, *Winston S. Churchill*, ii, London, 1967, 403, 405; Bodleian Library, Oxford, MS Eng. Misc. c. 686 (Countess of Selborne MSS), fo. 3: Lord Lytton to Lady Selborne, 19 Nov. 1912.

[76] House of Lords Record Office, Bonar Law MSS, 24/5/157: F. E. Smith to Bonar Law, 27 Dec. 1911.

[77] Bonar Law MSS, 33/4/1: Bonar Law to Arnold Ward, 15 Jan. 1912 (carbon copy); cf. 30/1/6: George Cave to Bonar Law, 4 Aug. 1913.

[78] *H.C. Deb.* 28 Mar. 1912, c. 678.

the enemy's full strength called out; anti-suffragists between 1866 and 1908 had felt no need to mobilize except at the parliamentary level. All this was easily misunderstood from without, and an accusing suffragette finger was pointed at politicians who repeatedly voted for women's suffrage without advancing it further. Politicians (with the notable exception of Lloyd George, who did not allow militant provocation to deter him from providing suffragists with numerous shrewdly instructive speeches and deputations) did all too little to clarify the suffragist mind.

III

The Westminster view erodes not only the suffragettes' periodization and analysis of tactics; it is restive under the suffragettes' harsh analysis of the politician's personality and motive. For the delays and diversions which so infuriated the suffragettes stemmed from factors other than deviousness, obscurantism, and immorality. To begin with, the politicians were unsure about the real state of public opinion. They were wary of a suffrage movement so firmly based on the middle class. It was the middle-class women—the Garretts, Pankhursts, Brights and McLarens, the Cobden sisters, and the Pethick-Lawrences—who provided the suffragist leadership and much of the early rank and file. 'A *great lady* or a *factory woman* are independent persons—personages,' Lydia Becker once pointed out, but 'the women of the middle classes are *nobodies*.'[79] If the aristocratic woman had fewer grievances and more opportunities for rectifying them, the working woman had more grievances but lacked the capacity to organize. Politicians were therefore faced with a double dilemma: the contented upper-class woman was most likely to bring her views to their attention, especially to Conservative politicians, whereas it was the working woman whom the Liberal MP hoped primarily to benefit. Given the increasing permeation of Edwardian politics by class attitudes, the political difficulties facing a feminist movement based on the middle class were acute.

[79] Quoted H. Blackburn, *Women's Suffrage. A Record of the Women's Suffrage Movement in the British Isles*, London, 1902, p. 42.

Public opinion was confused further, for the politician, by recurrent suffragist schism. First there were disputes on affiliation: the non-militants divided in 1871 on whether Josephine Butler should be openly supported, in 1888 on whether the Women's Liberal Federation should be free to join, and in 1915 on whether suffragism should align itself with the peace movement. On tactics, suffragists diverged (in 1886–7, 1874–5, and 1889) about whether wives should be explicitly excluded from suffrage bills, in 1889 on whether suffragists should confine their feminist crusading to the vote alone, and during the Edwardian period on adult suffrage and militant methods. Personal and regional antagonisms lay beneath these disputes, and during the 1890s there was also continuous friction about party alignment. Such disputes delighted the anti-suffragists, especially when they produced a riot between suffragists in 1892; still more agreeable to them was the suffragist disarray of 1896, when two competing suffrage bills destroyed one another in parliament. Suffragist schism was compounded by the fact that Edwardian militancy required an authoritarian structure which generated schismatic splinter groups. By 1913 suffragists were trying to operate three distinct electoral strategies; as Sylvia Pankhurst later pointed out, such disputes involved 'a tragic waste of energy'.[80]

Politicians therefore came to doubt the accuracy of the women's suffrage movement as a guide to opinion; sympathetic politicians—such as Sir Richard Temple and R. B. Haldane in the 1890s or Lloyd George and Sir Edward Grey in the Edwardian period—repeatedly urged the movement to work up more vigorous and united public support. Furthermore, after 1908 suffragists had to reckon with organized anti-suffragism, and everyone knew that many women did not bother to exercise the local government franchise they already possessed. Nor could politicians allow policy to be entirely determined by the clash between organized groupings: unorganized opinion had at least to be guessed at, if only because organized opinion could easily be stage-managed. Petitions, for example, were viewed sceptically by this time, yet political parties refused to take the issue to the electorate. Out of 670 MPs elected in 1906, the addresses of only 48 favoured

[80] E. S. Pankhurst, *Suffragette Movement*, p. 436.

women's suffrage; the subject was more prominent in addresses
at the 1910 general elections, but no candidates gave electoral reform first priority; only 36 per cent of the addresses
even mentioned it in January, and only 27 per cent in December.[81] In the few places where suffragist candidates stood in
defiance of party they failed abysmally. Suffragists could
take refuge only in dismissing the mandate theory of policy-
formation, in denying the accuracy of elections as guides to
opinion, or in allegations of party tyranny.

The only other possibility, in the absence of systematic
opinion polls, was the referendum, but Curzon pointed out
that the suffragists 'shiver at the very idea'; Lady Strachey
thought it would be 'the ruin of our cause for an incalculable period of time'.[82] Suffragists thought the measurement
of opinion irrelevant for two reasons: some feared that the
referendum would lend influence to the least instructed,
whereas they knew that women's suffrage was at present
supported only by an élite, and that pressure from minorities had often secured social legislation in the past; 'personally, I do not attach special importance to the sanction of
numbers', Mrs Fawcett confessed.[83] Others echoed J. S. Mill
in thinking that public policy should not be determined by
electors' bashfulness; Lord Lytton in 1914 cited Gladstone's
statement of 1884 on the agricultural labourers: 'I am not
concerned whether they want it or not; the State wants it for
them.'[84] Still, these suffragist responses inevitably worried
the politician for whom legislation must bear some relation
to public opinion.

A further source of misunderstanding between suffragists
and politicians arose from the fact that, in a pluralistic system of representative government, the politician (but not his
critics) must respond to many simultaneous pressures. A
plurality of prior commitment, and a consequent need always

[81] *H.C. Deb.* 19 Mar. 1909, c. 1400; N. Blewett, *The Peers, the Parties and the People. The General Elections of 1910*, London, 1972, pp. 317, 326.

[82] *Anti-Suffrage Review*, Dec. 1912, p. 292 (speech at the Glasgow meeting of the Scottish National Anti-Suffrage League, 1 Nov. 1912); City of London Poly-technic, Letters of Lady Strachey, Box 92: Lady Strachey to Lady Selborne, 23 Jan. 1912 (draft).

[83] *The Times*, 17 Jan. 1907, p. 4.

[84] *H.L. Deb.* 6 May 1914, c. 122; cf. J. S. Mill, quoted by Isaac Foot, in *H.C. Deb.* 29 Feb. 1924, c. 894.

to assess the bearing of one issue upon another, introduces delays and difficulties within the political system which the idealist in his single-mindedness finds hard to endure. If the idealist happens to be female, and is grappling with an all-male parliament, she may be tempted to blame the male sex for difficulties that are inherent in political life. H. W. Massingham told suffragists in 1909 that 'Cobden gave up a good part of a lifetime to "agitating" Free Trade; nearly all the Chartists and the Radicals of the early nineteenth century died without coming into their kingdom, or after seeing but a very faint vision of it.'[85] There were many well-mobilized Edwardian long-standing Liberal causes more compatible with Liberal ideals and traditions than abolishing the sex-discrimination within the existing franchise.

One of these was Home Rule, which dispersed suffragists widely between the political parties in the 1880s. It was one of those Liberal causes which the Liberal leadership employed temporarily to subordinate all other issues; as the *Women's Suffrage Journal* complained in May 1886, it 'dwarfs by comparison all the Reform Bills that have at any time been introduced, and every other question that Parliament has had to settle in the whole course of its existence'.[86] Ireland obstructed women's suffrage still further in the Edwardian period. Equal franchise was impossible for Liberals because it would damage their electoral interests. But women's suffrage as part of an adult suffrage measure was also impossible because the House of Lords would delay it unless accompanied by the redistribution of seats desired by the Conservatives, who knew that this would produce a drastic reduction in the number of Irish seats; but Irish MPs would not accept this reduction till their reform had been won.[87]

Lloyd George was at least as interested in Welsh church disestablishment as in Home Rule; it had been agitated for sixty years by a nation whose MPs were almost united behind it. Social welfare and land reform followed close behind, and both had profound implications for women in all classes.

[85] *The Nation*, 25 Sept. 1909, p. 906.
[86] *Women's Suffrage Journal*, 1 May 1886, p. 60.
[87] H. Pelling, *Popular Politics and Society in Late Victorian Britain*, London, 1968, p. 163; cf. D. Morgan, *Suffragists and Liberals*, p. 148.

When Christabel Pankhurst urged him to resign solely on the question of women's suffrage, he pointed out that 'Cabinet and party exist not merely for the promotion of one question, but of several.'[88] The question of priorities was particularly acute for franchise reform, because parliament lost authority once a new register had been compiled; franchise reforms were therefore normally brought in only towards the end of a parliament after a government had enacted most of its other measures. Broadly speaking, the politician in a system of representative government shapes his conduct according to the balance of pressures within the community. The role of the extra-parliamentary reformer is to re-order the politicians' priorities, which are never abstractly prescribed. Unfortunately for the suffragists, their programme, tactics, and influence were never sufficiently formidable to alter the political agenda.

A pluralistic political system also creates difficulties for politicians by denying them total overall control at the highest levels. Asquith was no dictator within his Cabinet, nor was his Cabinet in undisputed control of parliament. Outsiders tend to collapse distant but distinct political institutions into a monolithic oppressive entity in rather the same way that insiders tend to weld protest movements into a globally integrated subversive conspiracy. A Liberal government facing a hostile House of Lords had to arrange its legislative timetable carefully. Liberal home secretaries— confronted by insurgent suffragette prisoners, facing an independent judiciary and operating within a libertarian tradition —had to tread carefully. The culmination of this institutional pluralism was perhaps the Speaker's ruling of January 1913, which disrupted all the Government's plans for enabling women's suffrage to be introduced as an amendment to its Franchise Bill; according to Asquith it 'was not in the least degree anticipated by His Majesty's Government or as I believe, by the great majority of the House'.[89] The politician's misjudgements are readily criticized by those who have never faced the complexities of his task, particularly when hindsight whisks aside all those unpredictable and uncontrollable

[88] *Common Cause*, 29 Feb. 1912, p. 800.
[89] *H.C. Deb.* 27 Jan. 1913, c. 1022.

factors which provide the politician with his most stringent test.

The politician also labours under the misfortune of being unable to predict the future. The years 1906–14 presented numerous difficult, sometimes dangerous, and often inter-related issues with which single-issue reformers did not need to concern themselves. To take only international relations, Asquith's biographers point out that, although for narrative purposes the history of domestic and foreign policy can be told separately, 'it must always be borne in mind that the most difficult and dangerous of the home and foreign crises either ran simultaneously or overlapped one another'.[90] The Pethick-Lawrences' periodical *Votes for Women* does not mention the international crisis until its number for 31 July 1914, and Christabel Pankhurst's *Suffragette* does not even hint at the impending catastrophe till after it has begun. Like other freelance domestic reformers, but unlike Cabinet Ministers, suffragists enjoyed the luxury of ignoring foreign affairs. In the light of subsequent events, many suffragists—including Emmeline and Christabel Pankhurst—would perhaps have shared *The Times* view of 2 June 1914 that 'among public affairs of the moment the question of woman suffrage is, comparatively, unimportant'.[91]

IV

If suffragettes underestimated the scale of the difficulties politicians faced, the growth-pattern of women's organizations shows that they also exaggerated their own contribution after 1906 to eventual suffragist success. Unlike the riot, tactical violence which is engineered by a minority cannot plausibly be portrayed as articulating mass opinion. Even suffragette claims to have revived the movement in 1906 beg several questions. The WSPU certainly expanded fast in 1906–7,[92] and Mrs Fawcett thought it had lent energy even to non-militants. Yet she was too modest: the non-militants had been

[90] J. A. Spender and C. Asquith, *Life of Herbert Henry Asquith*, vol. ii, London, 1932, p. 57.
[91] Quoted, A. Rosen, op. cit., p. 239.
[92] See figures in A. Rosen, op. cit., pp. 83–4, 88.

reviving well before 1906, as the annual income figures (graph 1) for both Manchester and London non-militant organizations show. Changes in organization and personnel within the North of England Society for Women's Suffrage between 1894 and 1902 had already stirred Lancashire mill-girls into suffragist action by 1902,[93] and even the secession of the WSPU in 1905-6 did not preclude the society's continued growth. Edwardian suffragist prosperity also owes much to the healing in 1897 and 1900 of the splits which had opened up in the 1880s, and the consequent creation in 1900 of the NUWSS, which in 1903 made the crucially important transition from mere co-ordinating body to organization directly receiving funds; between 1902 and 1904 the number of its affiliated societies rose from seventeen to twenty-five. In the 'momentous' year following its national convention of October 1903, a campaign fund helped to extend the movement by forming constituency committees; seventy-three of them were formed in 1903-4, sixty in 1904-5, and many later grew into fully fledged NUWSS branches.[94]

A change in the political context supplemented non-militant restructuring in reviving Edwardian suffragism: this was but one among several Liberal causes coming to the fore during the Liberal revival after 1900. As Ramsay MacDonald noted later, such causes 'were coming up before a single voice was raised in militant protest', and 'would have attained their present position in the political field had no militant organisation disturbed a meeting or held a riotous demonstration'.[95] Not only does the suffragette critique of the non-militants ignore their revival before 1906, it contains two mutually incompatible branches. The non-militants allegedly failed because insufficiently energetic in non-violent methods, yet at the same time non-violent methods could allegedly never succeed; suffragettes believed only in the

---

[93] Manchester National Society for Women's Suffrage, *Annual Report, 1894-5,* p. 8; North of England Society for Women's Suffrage, *Annual Report, 1899-1900,* p. 8; *Annual Report, 1900-1901,* p. 4; *Annual Report, 1904-5,* pp. 5-6; National Union of Women's Suffrage Societies, *Annual Report ... presented at the Annual Meeting ... May 2nd, 1902,* p. 4.

[94] NUWSS, *Annual Report, 1903-4,* pp. 9, 25; *Annual Report, 1904-5,* p. 19.

[95] J. R. MacDonald, *Margaret Ethel MacDonald,* London, 2nd edn., 1912, p. 202, cf. p. 204.

policy of attacking governments, and repudiated the pledging of MPs.

Even if the focus rests narrowly on the years 1906–14, the militant achievement seems small. Both wings of the movement can be criticized for narrowing their feminist range during this period and for confining their tactical options to a non-party standpoint. None the less the non-militants remained organizationally, numerically, and educationally superior throughout the period and maintained their growth-rate more successfully, as NUWSS figures for annual income (graph 1) display: the number of NUWSS branches rose from 33 in October 1907 to 70 in March 1910, and to 478 in February 1914. Membership grew accordingly—from 22,000 in January 1911 to 52,000 by February 1914. If local and national funds are aggregated, the non-militant total had reached about £45,000 by the financial year 1913/14. The militants raised £37,000 nationally in that year, and to this the funds raised by the branches should be added; but by 1913 WSPU branches had so declined in importance that publicity-conscious militants did not think their membership worth advertising, whereas NUWSS revenue rested on a much more extensive, participatory, and therefore relatively secure, structure. Although militant funds were mounting right up to 1914, the pace of their growth had slackened after 1909, and income attributable to new members declined after 1910.[96]

But even if the suffragettes did foster the suffragist revival after 1906, what next? Their tactics could hardly extract women's suffrage from a male parliament, if only because they could not mobilize physical force of an order that would intimidate the politician. Yet this did not prevent their methods from making enemies for women's suffrage, especially—as politicians saw it—the dishonesty of their leaders, which seems to have operated at more than one level. As Home Secretary, Herbert Gladstone was disgusted at what he saw as frequent but private lying from the WSPU's leaders, and was echoed in this by McKenna later.[97] But more

[96] Statistics from NUWSS and WSPU annual reports, and from A. Rosen, op. cit., pp. 211–12.
[97] C. P. Scott MSS, 128/133: Herbert Gladstone to Scott, 7 Jan. 1910; BL Add. MSS 46068 (Viscount Gladstone papers), fo. 195: Gladstone to 'Margaret', 9 Jan. 1910. McKenna, *H.C. Deb.* 2 Apr. 1913, c. 406; John Rylands Library,

damaging, perhaps, was the public deception involved in the suffragettes' 'double shuffle between revolution and injured innocence'. This implicitly capitalized on the chivalrous attitudes towards women that were more widespread among anti-suffragists; suffragettes courted punishment from government, refused to acquiesce in it with dignity, and forced the authorities into the appearance of brutality.[98] Not only did the suffragettes seem to flout politicians' codes of honour: they also disappointed suffragists who hoped that women would elevate moral standards in public life.[99] Such methods, said one non-militant, 'caricatured indignation and cheapened rebellion'.[100]

All this helped to insulate the militants still further from the general public, and therefore from the politicians; matters were made still worse by the 'utterly contemptible' intrusion of suffragette militancy into the private lives of opponents and even friends. Walter Long in 1913 praised Asquith's 'fine courage and unruffled dignity' during such incidents, and thought them 'a discredit and a disgrace to our country as a whole'.[101] Already by 1909 Mrs Fawcett was privately worried at the damage the militants were doing, and by 1912 the militants had become for her 'the chief obstacles in the way of the success of the suffrage movement in the House of Commons'.[102] She claimed to have supported the militants when they were right, but ceased to support them after stone-throwing began in July 1908, when she thought they were wrong. The year 1912 saw the first defeat of a women's suffrage Bill in a parliamentary division since 1892; this was blamed by MPs partly on militancy. By 1913-14 the anti-suffragists were publicly and privately rejoicing at the 'priceless

Manchester: Correspondence File of Manchester Men's League for Women's Suffrage, typescript copy of Snowden's letter dated 13 Sept. 1913 to J. Beanland.

[98] T. Billington-Greig, *Militant Suffrage Movement*, p. 4.
[99] e.g. Randall Davidson MSS, Box on 'Women's Suffrage 1908-14': Randall Davidson to A. W. Chapman, 19 Oct. 1910.
[100] C. P. Scott MSS, 332/137: Mrs Swanwick to Scott, 23 July 1912.
[101] *H.C. Deb.* 5 May 1913, c. 1954 (Harold Cawley); *H.C. Deb.* 6 May 1913, c. 1938.
[102] Mrs Fawcett quoted in *Irish Citizen*, 31 Aug. 1912, p. 115; cf. C. Marshall MSS, Box. 8, notes headed 'Political Situation', endorsed 9-10 Oct. 1912. See also Manchester City Library, M50/2/1/270: Mrs Fawcett to Alice Stone Blackwell, 22 Feb. 1909 (draft).

asset' with which the militants had presented them.[103] There was of course a feminist case for militancy. It revealed women's capacity for courage, thus discrediting the anti-suffragists' 'physical force argument'; it also revealed the harm that can be done amid the complexities of modern society when a group withdraws its consent from government. But if its aim was votes for women, the WSPU's strategy was long-term indeed.

The suffragette view therefore exaggerates the militant achievement; and, as has been argued elsewhere, it pays insufficient attention to the undemocratic long-term consequences of the authoritarian structure militancy entailed.[104] It focuses unduly on events between 1906 and 1914, and neglects the crucially important years before and the illuminating period after. It also lends an undue prominence to the campaign for the vote, whose chronology does not necessarily run parallel with that of feminism as a whole; indeed, as has also been argued elsewhere, the suffrage movement was tangential to some other important dimensions of women's emancipation, notably improved health and access to birth control.[105] A longer-term analysis highlights the tactical mistake made by both militants and non-militants when they failed to pursue a strategy that could attract progressive Liberals, and so weakens the feminist dimension (for which detailed evidence and argument are never presented) of the claim that the Liberal party was inevitably doomed. There was a strong liberal, democratic, and even feminist case for resisting any equal franchise strategy in the Edwardian period, especially when advocates of the equal franchise adopted tactical violence. Furthermore, the suffragettes would have attacked any government in power, Liberal or Conservative, and their militancy had begun well before the Liberal government was formed in 1905.[106]

---

[103] J. L. Garvin, *Observer*, 23 Feb. 1913, p. 8; cf. my *Separate Spheres*, ch. 9 for a fuller discussion of militancy's impact on public opinion.

[104] See 'The Act of Militancy: Violence and the Suffragettes, 1904-14', in my *Peaceable Kingdom. Stability and Change in Modern Britain*, Oxford, 1982.

[105] See my 'Women's Health and the Women's Movement in Britain: 1840-1940', in C. Webster (ed.), *Biology, Medicine and Society 1840-1940*, Cambridge, 1981, pp. 15-71.

[106] As emphasized in Manchester City Library, M50/2/1/242: J. A. Spender to Mrs Fawcett, 30 Oct. 1906; and Lloyd George, in *Oxford Chronicle*, 29 Nov. 1913.

V

There is one final modification to the suffragette view: a recognition that the relationship between extra-parliamentary movement and legislative change is complex, and that reforming leaders must therefore do more than merely mobilize and deploy opinion skilfully; their actions must rest on a practicable strategy, and must be directed with shrewd political judgement and tactical sense. Clumsiness, insensitivity, and even coarseness can be found in politicians' handling of women's suffrage as a political issue before 1914, but there were also serious suffragist mistakes, and these were not confined to the militants. Yet the last phase of the suffragist campaign shows that the movement's militant phase had not entirely overlaid the skill at manipulating the political system which had enabled non-militants to produce such rich feminist dividends before 1906.

For the first two years of the war, suffragism as a mass movement virtually disappeared, as the wartime decline in suffragist funds (unlike the funds of non-feminist women's organizations) eloquently displays (graphs 1 and 2); Mrs Pankhurst's organization disbanded, the non-militants diverted their energies elsewhere, and the anti-suffragists went into virtual suspension. The politicians were freed by this and by coalition government to exercise their own judgement in settling the question by methods nowhere envisaged by extra-parliamentary activists before 1914: through an age-restricted female franchise accompanied by further franchise extension to men. Nor was it suffragist pressure that revived the issue in 1916: the patriotic pressure to enfranchise the fighting forces was responsible. 'We did nothing whatever to raise the question of Women's Suffrage . . .', Mrs Fawcett declared in April 1917: 'it was forced upon the consideration of Parliament by the essential facts of the political situation.'[107] Supposing in December 1916 that extra-parliamentary suffragist pressure would help, Northcliffe warned Lady Betty Balfour that 'there is absolutely no movement for Women's Suffrage anywhere'.[108]

[107] *Common Cause*, 27 Apr. 1917, p. 25.
[108] City of London Polytechnic, Fawcett Library Autograph Collection, 7113: Northcliffe to Lady Betty Balfour, 22 Dec. 1916.

Although some effort was made to mobilize suffragist opinion early in 1917, its scale did not compare with what had been organized between 1906 and 1914. On this occasion, the non-militant suffragist leaders were sensitive to the politicians' difficulties. The solution of 1918 was of course illogical and temporary, but it was important to get the women's suffrage principle accepted.

Not only were the Pankhursts inactive as suffragists at this crucial point; all three were at times positively unhelpful.[109] But popular movements can be influential even after they have been disbanded. What of Christabel Pankhurst's view that it was politicians' fear of resumed militancy that really won women the vote in 1916-18? As might be expected, militancy was little discussed in the parliamentary debates. It is Lord Crewe's speech of January 1918 that furnishes Christabel with her sole piece of evidence when attacking Roger Fulford's analysis of 1957. She offers no evidence that this speech influenced a single vote in the House of Lords, by which time the Bill had anyway passed through the assembly which mattered most, the House of Commons. The speeches which do mention militancy—Crewe's, Law's, and Cochrane's —all discuss it in the context of welcoming its absence.[110] Such statements are of course compatible with fear of its revival, but even Crewe's justifications for women's suffrage include women's wartime patriotism and war work as well as the danger of a revived militancy.

In reality there were many reasons for enfranchising women in 1918 besides the fear of resumed militancy, even assuming that such resumption would have been feasible and effective. If fear of militancy influenced politicians at all at this time, it was the fear that Britain would witness post-war militancy on the grander scale experienced by Russia during 1917: a mass violence for which franchise extension in 1918 was (as on earlier occasions) seen as the cure, to which politicians must always in some way defer, and which the WSPU's

[109] A. Rosen, op. cit., p. 260; *H.C. Deb.* 16 Aug. 1916, c. 1960; and see Sylvia Pankhurst's doctrinaire insistence on adult suffrage throughout the delicate negotiations of 1917.

[110] Law, *H.C. Deb.* 28 Mar. 1917, c. 561; Cochrane, *H.C. Deb.* 22 May 1917, c. 2207.

militancy before 1914 had been able occasionally to simulate but never genuinely to evoke.

Though the non-militant achievement at the climacteric of 1916–18 was substantial, the role of the reformer's reason, even when the distractions of militancy had been removed, should not be exaggerated. In many countries at this time, women gained the vote without any preparatory feminist agitation at all. 'Don't you think the whole history is an extraordinary instance of the superior power of sentiment and emotion over reason?' Lady Strachey reflected in April 1917: 'reason drudging away since the days of the French Revolution, hammering against an impregnable wall of senti-ment and prejudice—then the turn of the tide and over we go!'[111] If the half-revolution introduced in 1918 was to gain its completion, there was much subsequent need for the non-militants' political judgement and discretion. That story has yet to be told, but popular demonstrations play only a small part in it, and militancy no overt role at all.

Mrs Pankhurst had long given up political violence, and in the mid-1920s even doubted the wisdom of campaigning for the equal franchise.[112] Suffragists wanted her to be more active in the campaign for equalizing the franchise, but Lady Astor privately discouraged financing her for this purpose, in the belief that (as she told Lady Rhondda in November 1925) 'the Government are certain to give equal suffrage without this'. In November 1927 she feared that demonstra-tions would do harm by implying that Baldwin did not intend to keep his word: 'I am sure that is the wrong line to take, and it is for that reason that I am myself keeping very quiet on this question.'[113] None the less, public demonstra-tions were organized, substantially smaller (as even sympa-thetic observers noted)[114] than pre-war suffrage occasions, and small enough to justify several speakers during debates

[111] Fawcett Library Autograph Collection, 7128: Lady Strachey to 'my dear Mary', 2 Apr. 1917.
[112] D. Mitchell, *The Fighting Pankhursts. A Study in Tenacity*, London, 1967, p. 156.
[113] University of Reading, Nancy Astor Papers, MS 1416/1/1/261: pencilled note by Lady Astor on letter from Lady Rhondda to Lady Astor, 5 Nov. 1925; MS 1416/1/1/263: Lady Astor to Eleanor Rathbone, 24 Nov. 1927 (copy); cf. MS 1416/1/1/634: Lady Astor's secretary to Mrs Wintringham, 14 June 1926.
[114] *Woman's Leader*, 9 July 1926, p. 213.

on the equal franchise Bill of 1928 in emphasizing (as in 1917-18) public apathy on the matter.

Yet beneath the external calm there was a busy susurration of telephoning, leafleting, interviewing, and massaging of opinion by the National Union of Societies for Equal Citizenship (successor-organization to the NUWSS), shrewdly run by Eva Hubback and Eleanor Rathbone, and buttressed by an influential Strachey connection through the London Society for Women's Service. Now that the franchise attached to persons rather than to property, equalizing it presented fewer tactical and strategic difficulties, and prudent suffragist leadership ensured that between 1916 and 1928, feminist self-sabotage no longer materialized. 'Of course the result of getting all these things done in other peoples [*sic*] names is that we shall get no credit for it,' Eleanor told Eva, 'but it seemed the surest way of getting them done.'[115] Their behind-the-scenes pressure on Baldwin to implement his pledge of 1924 on equal franchise ultimately prevailed over Conservative back-bench hostility: 'foregone conclusions do not make for distinguished debates', Baldwin told the King, when reporting on the equal franchise debate in March 1928.[116] By this time both Christabel and Sylvia Pankhurst had long removed themselves, in their different ways, from practical politics. Christabel found in theocracy 'the remedy for the failure of human rule of every form and in every age',[117] while Sylvia's typewriter rattled off dozens of books and press articles embodying her vision of a feminist and socialist utopia.

Joynson Hicks described the equal franchise Bill of 1928 somewhat misleadingly as 'the logical conclusion of a series of Reform Bills, beginning with that of 1832'.[118] In its removal of the sex discrimination, the Bill's pedigree really runs from Mill's unsuccessful equal franchise clause of 1867 through the various unsuccessful equal franchise Bills introduced by suffragists into parliament from 1870, through

[115] Eva Hubback MSS: Eleanor Rathbone to Eva Hubback, 28 Apr. [1927]; I am most grateful to Mrs Diana Hopkinson for allowing me to consult her mother's papers.
[116] Cambridge University Library, Stanley Baldwin MSS, vol. 63: Baldwin to the King, 30 Mar. 1928 (carbon copy), fo. 190.
[117] Quoted A. Rosen, op. cit., p. 270.
[118] *H.C. Deb.* 29 Mar. 1928, c. 1359.

Woodall's unsuccessful amendment of 1884 and even through the Conciliation Bills of 1910–12. But in enfranchising more men and in attaching the vote primarily to persons rather than to property, its pedigree originates with the adult suffrage Bills of Sir Charles Dilke and Geoffrey Howard, and on through the Liberal government's abortive Franchise Bill of 1912 (amendable to include women's suffrage). Its principle of age-restriction was anticipated in W. H. Dickinson's Bill of 1913. The Bill of 1928 finds its immediate ancestor, however, in the franchise measure that was crucial to women, the Reform Act of 1918, whose extension of the male franchise and discrimination against women through an age-restriction would have shocked pre-war feminists.

So muted a role for the extra-parliamentary reformer in the story of women's suffrage lacks inspirational value and has therefore gained little currency. It cannot satisfy the layman who, if he is to go about his daily business undistracted, must normally choose between a shorthand and misleading history or no history at all. Nor does the real sequence of events allow for the attractions of that unadulterated triumph of the oppressed, that rewarding of the brave, which paradoxically has the effect only of depreciating reformers by distracting attention from half the difficulties they face. It is ironic that Michael Foot, a convinced parliamentarian, should recently condone suffragette extra-parliamentary militancy on the ground that 'they . . . were denied the right to speak and act inside Parliament'; so simplistic an analysis ignores the complexity of the motives for suffragette militancy, its ineffectiveness in advancing this particular cause, and the fact that such errors were made by only a minority among Edwardian feminists—not to mention the objective morality of such conduct. Not only is history thereby distorted: a small contribution is thereby made towards weakening parliamentary government for the future.[119]

The suffragette movement, which inspired many romantic or sensational novels in the early twentieth century, made its most lasting impact by creating a romance out of its own history; it thereby neglected to warn later generations against the dangers of the historical parallel, and encouraged them to

[119] *Observer*, 10 Jan. 1982, p. 13.

misunderstand the workings of representative government. This romance entered the mainstream of historical writing through suffragette autobiographical and historical writings, and shimmered in the seductive prose of George Dangerfield; for him, social history should seek 'the reality of fiction, which is the highest reality of all'.[120] His analysis gives insufficient attention to those powerful cohesive influences in any society which are neglected in the written record, and his sources consist entirely of printed material; on women's suffrage this is confined to A. E. Metcalfe's *Woman's Effort*, Sylvia Pankhurst's *Suffragette Movement* and the memoirs of Lady Constance Lytton, Annie Kenney, and Mrs Pankhurst. Such sources will scarcely do justice to the non-militants, let alone adequately comprehend the Westminster view or the situation of the Liberal party.

Fitzjames Stephen once regretted the failure of H. T. Buckle, a progressive historian in his day, to emphasize that 'the existing state of society is the result of each set of efforts, not of either set by itself, and certainly not the result of the forward effort by itself'.[121] For Butterfield, the passion of the Whig historian brings energy and insight, but it also causes him to 'withdraw the effort in the case of the men who are most in need of it'—from the conservatives and the reactionaries, the Cavaliers and the Tories—thereby sacrificing something of history's distinctive contribution to human understanding. In the case of women's suffrage, the opposition to the extraparliamentary crusader included not only conservatives and anti-suffragists but humane and democratic politicians anxiously seeking the truly progressive course, sensitive to the delicate state of public opinion, and alert to the complexities inevitably involved in the political process. Nor were the crusaders' strategy and tactics always above reproach. Still, as Butterfield again rightly points out, 'for the compilation of trenchant history there is nothing like being content with half the truth'.[122]

---

[120] G. Dangerfield, *The Strange Death of Liberal England* (Capricorn edn.), New York, 1961, p. 393.

[121] J. F. Stephen, *Liberty, Equality, Fraternity* (ed. R. J. White), Cambridge, 1967, p. 173; cf. H. Butterfield, op. cit., pp. 35, 39.

[122] H. Butterfield, op. cit., pp. 95, 52.

5

Party, Doctrine, and Thought

Michael Bentley

The trouble is that people who do not accept unilateral approaches too often have no approach at all.

Arnaldo Momigliano, *Studies in Historiography*, 1966, p. 69.

I

We lack a theory of party in its relation to thought for any sub-period of British political history since 1832.[1] Studies abound of parliamentary government, while monographs dealing with the place of 'ideas' in the germination of specific policies are, of course, legion. Indeed it would be strange for a generation conscious of a revival of interest in political thought to remain inert before the challenge of identifying ideology as a motor-force within political action. The focus, however, has been as random as it has been close; and no prospectus has emerged of the period as a whole. By contrast, scholars working in late seventeenth-century and eighteenth-century history have become accustomed to an intellectual framework providing accommodation for the problem of party as a concept. It is possible for students of these periods readily to take on board judgements about this framework because it is built into their apparatus criticus: the relation-ship between ideas and politics presents itself as a pre-condition of understanding rather than as a dark corner to be probed. Yet historians of the very period which witnesses the trans-mutation of political parties in the post-reform environment seem to enter some trauma not unlike that of their subject. Hamlet exits right in a mood of uncertainty and leaves the

[1] The author extends his thanks to graduate seminars at All Souls College, Oxford; Sidney Sussex College, Cambridge; and the London School of Economics and Political Science for their criticism and encouragement in the production of this paper.

stage to Marxists and Whigs. The response to this difficulty need not take the form of labelling types of political inter-action as though they comprised botanical genera susceptible to some Linnaean classification;[2] it might be nothing more pretentious than a traversing of common ground. To deny a foundation to any overarching view of party and its determi-nants, on the other hand, can only foster the degeneration of discussion into the presenting of formularies—a book of common prayer or a cynic's kama sutra.

The problem is a new one to the extent that thought's interrelation with action has recently come to be viewed as problematic in senses different from those stressed by some previous modes of comment. Burke's celebrated definition of party left little room for perplexity about doctrine or 'prin-ciple'; parties were taken to be united by the very promotion of a principle in which their members concurred. The theory enjoyed an afterlife long beyond the passing of parties known to Burke. Anxieties over an encroaching democracy and, later, the Americanization of British party politics found a voice, but the sense of party as an instrument for a constellation of ideas held firm. Realizing thought remained the *raison d'être* of political organizations. Monckton Milnes saw this far through his cognac while staying with Tocqueville in the 1840s. 'Might it not be', he wondered in his notebook, 'the necessary function of men like Peel and Guizot to dissemi-nate, as it were, into the practical life of passing moments the great integral thought of better men like Tocqueville and my-self.'[3] Far from doubts developing about the status of parties as petrified doctrine, indeed, the ascription strengthened in the later decades of the nineteenth century when writers such as Bryce, Dicey, and Ernest Barker provided further buttresses. The legalists who dominated much political speculation in the half-century before the First World War not unnaturally took Law to offer a signpost to Thought. Only examine the patent collectivist tendency of modern legislation and one could not fail to recognize parliament as a means by which thought and doctrine crystallized into enactment.

[2] J. C. D. Clark, 'A General Theory of Party, Opposition and Government, 1689–1832', *Historical Journal*, 23 (1980), 295–325.
[3] J. Pope Hennessy, *Monckton Milnes*, London, 2 vols., 1949–51, i. 241.

Two documents from this period seem in retrospect especially relevant: Dicey's *Lectures on the Relationship between
Law and Public Opinion during the Nineteenth Century*
(1905) and Barker's *Political Thought in England from Herbert Spencer to the Present Day* (1915). 'Politics are not the
same thing as law,' the first conceded, 'but in modern England any revolution in political ideas is certain to correspond
with attitudes in legislative opinion.'[4] The only hint of difficulty comes in 'confound[ing] the accidental division of
parties with central differences of political faith'. And, once
discerned, those faiths can be sought between the lines of the
statute book.[5] Barker approached the subject more directly
but only after prior acquaintance with Aristotle, post-Idealist
Oxford, and Maitland. He looked mostly beyond parliament
for his evidence and dwelt on the impact of Bergson, Sorel,
and the syndicalists in working out a pluralist theory of
sovereignty; and his conclusion was avowedly Burkean. For
Barker, political parties amounted to a form of 'embodied
theory',[6] a view he altered only marginally in later years. As
the Nazis menaced Europe he looked still to party to act as
'a mediator between social thought and political action'; and
if it failed in this function he worried about possible embodiments of new ideas as they 'grip[ped] the mind and dr[ank]
the blood of conviction'.[7]

This strand of thinking suggests the presence of one style
of bridge-building. There were, of course, others. Political
sociology provided a location for much penetrating observation of the nature of the British party system by foreign
commentators of the calibre of Ostrogorski, Lowell, and
Michels. Yet, seen as a whole, these analyses did not lead to
a confrontation with the problem of doctrine. Sovereignty
and party-as-machine dominate the discussion: there is a series

[4] A. V. Dicey, *Lectures on the Relation between Law and Public Opinion in
England during the nineteenth century*, London, 1905, 1914 edn., p. 409.

[5] Ibid. Cf. A. L. Lowell on the evolution of paternalism: 'Without going into
the matter deeply anyone can see this is true by running through the statute
book.' *The Government of England*, London, 2 vols., 1908, ii. 527.

[6] E. Barker, *Political Thought in England*, London, 1915, 13. For Barker's
intellectual background see the autobiography, *Age and Youth*, London, 1953,
and his Cambridge inaugural lecture, *The study of political science and its relation
to cognate studies*, Cambridge, 1928, esp. pp. 8-9.

[7] Ernest Barker, *Reflections on Government*, Oxford, 1942, pp. 89, 120.

of astringencies about the implications of caucus and oli-
garchy for intra-party democracy and Rousseauesque images
of popular authority. About the relationship between politics
and thought little emerges. Ostrogorski invents an intriguing
inverse law (thought becomes greater when politics becomes
less) and isolates periods when 'apathy and indifference'
create a vacuum for theorists to fill. 'The élite of the community, relieved so to speak of their function, ha[ve] recourse
to thought.'[8] Lowell, for his part, recognized that high politics had become a distinctive activity with a tendency to
foster 'short views' rather than long-term strategies.[9] And
Michels dispensed with doctrine altogether in his explanation
of the behaviour of political leaders under the yoke of his
iron law:

> They are enchained by their own past. They have a family, and this
> family must be fed. Moreover, regard for their political good name
> makes them feel it essential to persevere in the old round. They thus
> remain outwardly faithful to the cause to which they have sacrificed
> the best years of their life. But, renouncing idealism, they have become
> opportunists. These former believers, these sometime altruists, whose
> fervent hearts aspired only to give themselves freely, have been trans-
> formed into sceptics and egoists whose actions are guided solely by cold
> calculation.[10]

Closer to home, native John Bullishness needed small encouragement to destroy the bridges built between politics
and any kind of thought. Sir John Macdonnell's definition of
practical politicians as 'those who have agreed to stop thinking'[11] was only half intended as malice: it pointed towards
the difficulties faced by cabinet ministers denied a life-style
congruent with reading and reflection. For some, the dys-
lexia seemed an appropriate accompaniment to democracy's
intrinsic nastiness and another reason for its overthrow.

> Fester and rot, fester and rot
> And angle and tergiversate

[8] M. Ostrogorski, *Democracy and the Organization of Political Parties*, 2 vols.,
1902; Anchor edn., New York, 1964, i. 49–50.
[9] Lowell, ii. 529–30.
[10] R. Michels, *Political Parties*, 1915, Free Press edn., New York and London,
1962, 1968, p. 208.
[11] 'The Referendum *versus* Representative Government', *Contemporary Review* (Mar. 1911), cxix. 303.

> One thing among all things you will not
> Do, that is: *think*, before it's too late.[12]

But defences could be found, then and since. Politicians' insensitivity to doctrine lent itself to ritualization as a facet of national character—a freedom from continental excitability and nostrums too clever by half; 'the fact is that Englishmen, in their public as in their private life, have no great regard for abstract generalizations. They are careless about measures and much more particular about men. Fidelity to persons, rather than to principles, is the spirit of our party life.'[13] Or the assumption could be denied altogether by stressing the intellectual pre-eminence of individual politicians. Gladstone's stature as a thinker left little room for quibble. Morley's as editor and writer seemed no less obvious. More than the *Defence of Philosophic Doubt* gave Arthur James Balfour some claim to an intellectual function. At the very time, again, when R. B. Haldane participated in a high-political conspiracy before 1905 he was immersed also in a *tour de force* of Hegelian ontology in his Gifford lectures.[14] Sir Harold Wilson, in a different generation, brought into high politics his training in economic doctrine. Lord John Russell and Sir Keith Joseph picked up some of it in the evenings. Ramsay MacDonald, rarely identified by his ideological rigidity, has struck his biographer by his doctrinal angularity, just as another writer reminds us of Peel's.[15] Even Lloyd George claimed once to have sat up a tree reading Euclid.

Optimistic, or pessimistic, assessments made before about 1960 of the interaction between political thought and practice converged in their mood of impatience. One is impressed by a breezy confidence about the potential of democracy to maximize reflective governance or an equally uncomplicated alarm over the political structure's impermeability to ideas. Mallock believed he saw conceptions 'borrowed from

---

[12] 'Alf's Tenth Bit' in Ezra Pound, *Collected Shorter Poems*, London, 1952, 1968, p. 283.

[13] Sidney Low, *The Governance of England*, London, 1904, p. 125.

[14] R. B. Haldane, *The Pathway to Reality*, 2 vols., 1903-4.

[15] David Marquand, *Ramsay MacDonald*, London, 1977, p. 454. Cf. Boyd Hilton's remark that '*doctrinally* Peel was anything but "low and dry" '. 'Peel: a reappraisal', *Historical Journal*, 22 (1979), 609.

philosophers by politicians and social reformers'; these were then somehow 'transmitted. . . to thought and opinion generally'.[16] A less celebrated writer paints ideas in the sky as a 'subjective atmosphere . . . a sort of subjective envelop [*sic*] evolved by the units of the Social Organism themselves'.[17] No wonder the intellectual view of politics received short shrift from those whose image of politicians resembled that of Carlyle ('Donothingism in Practice and Saynothingism in Speech'), or Leslie Stephen ('the puniest breed we have had since the days of Pitt'), or Dean Inge ('bottomless insincerity').[18] But again a side-swipe was held to be sufficient reply and a view of human nature thought explanation enough. One buys from Froude a pre-packaged notion of 'mere intellectual culture'[19] and thereby puts the intelligentsia in its place. One buys from Belloc a suspicion of 'mere party men'[20] and goes on to seek the life of the mind.

II

Assumptions on which much of this discussion rested no longer hold sway. A prospectus of likely developments in political history in the 1980s has drawn attention, indeed, to the problem of 'ideology' and its place in the vortex of conviction, tactical calculation, and material interest that plainly informs the behaviour of governing groups.[21] Not all the elements in this new climate have grown out of the historical discipline itself: the burgeoning of sociology and anthropology in the universities since the Second World War has doubtless coloured thinking in some degree. Criticism directed at the possibility and limits of the history of ideas left its mark also.

[16] W. H. Mallock, 'The Unrecognized Essence of Democracy', *Fortnightly Review* (Sept. 1897), 68/62, p. 324.

[17] H. S. Seal, *On the Nature of State Interference*, London, 1893, pp. 78-9.

[18] Thomas Carlyle, *Past and Present*, London, 1843, p. 150; Stephen to Lowell, 30 Apr. 1876 in F. W. Maitland, *The Life and Letters of Leslie Stephen*, 1906, London, p. 289; W. R. Inge, *England*, London, 1926, p. 275.

[19] J. A. Froude, 'A Lesson on Democracy', *Fortnightly Review* (Dec. 1882), 18/32, p. 747.

[20] Hilaire Belloc, 'The Change in Politics', *Fortnightly Review* (Jan. 1911), 95/89, p. 45. For a modern critique of 'merely *party* opinion', cf. Vernon Bogdanor, *The People and the Party System*, Cambridge, 1981, p. 82 and *passim*.

[21] See Peter Clarke's helpful note on a methodology for studying 'Ideas and Interests', in the *Journal of Interdisciplinary History*, 12 (1981), 45-7.

Yet it is noteworthy how much of this reappraisal has aimed neither at the period under consideration here nor at our chosen target. Only one monograph has self-consciously approached the period after 1850 in the light of the critique presented in material dealing with the seventeenth and eighteenth centuries.[22] Nevertheless, the reawakening of Collingwood and Wittgenstein has given rise to numerous implications for those who pay no heed to the intentions of their dramatis personae and regard the language of dead generations as transparent. By representing speech acts as suspensions of sediment historians have underlined the uniqueness of political utterance and the complication of its ingredients. By depicting the practitioners of party politics as victims of a need for self-legitimacy, they have reasserted the role of a 'canon' or 'tradition' in political explanation.[23]

A complementary channel of opinion can be seen irrigating different but adjacent ground. The emphasis of a number of recent monographs in their analysis of 'the structure of political action'[24] recalls categories familiar to Michels or Pareto; the stress falls on a sensitivity to intrigue and conspiracy within a 'sociology of power'.[25] But because this variant of the argument encompasses and even depends on the reconstruction of politicians' intentions—'manipulat[ing] their words to portray their purposes'[26]—a stronger after-taste remains of an evolving view of politics and thought. Concentrating on the primacy of politicians' position within party hierarchies inevitably breeds a historical doctrine in which ultramontane cardinals consume their own church and exchange jokes behind the altar. At this height ideas, principles, and doctrines remain only as a form of self-realization (every

[22] I have in mind Dr Collini's suggestive account of Hobhouse's thought: Stephan Collini, *Liberalism and Sociology: L. T. Hobhouse and political argument in England 1880–1914*, Cambridge, 1979.

[23] Quentin Skinner, 'The Principles and Practice of Opposition: the case of Bolingbroke versus Walpole', in Neil McKendrick (ed.), *Historical Perspectives: studies in English thought and society in honour of J. H. Plumb*, London, 1974, pp. 93–128.

[24] A. B. Cooke and John Vincent, *The Governing Passion: cabinet government and party politics in Britain 1885–6*, Brighton, 1974, pp. 3–23.

[25] Maurice Cowling, *1867: Disraeli, Gladstone and Revolution*, Cambridge, 1967, p. 3.

[26] Andrew Jones, *The Politics of Reform 1884*, Cambridge, 1972, p. 237.

man should have a hobby) at the end of a hard day's work. Conservatism in the great houses shrinks into 'pockets of upper-class antinomianism'; Liberalism on the back benches attenuates into 'little more than a common good nature'.[27] Source criticism leaves behind a detritus of broken reputations among the governing classes: greatness remains only in clear-headedness over the need for complicity. The individual is unable to 'commit' politics. Puncture him and the needle runs on without hindrance through an inner vacuum, a nihilism trained to absorb what is situationally necessary. Point to Gladstone's diary by way of complaint and the quietus comes from the epigraph to volume XXVI

> Where I may think the remnant of my thoughts
> In peace: and part this body and my soul
> In contemplation and devout desires.[28]

How far an entry into high politics requires some such dissociation presents a problem to which no uniform response has been forthcoming from its students. Maurice Cowling's starting-point seems, for example, markedly different from that of John Vincent. Politicians rarely betray at Cowling's hands an obtrusive 'ideological' complexion: they decide what they think as they go along. But the framework in which discussion is set hints repeatedly at an intellectual ambience which implies a readiness to grant significance to doctrinal or religious motivation or constraint.[29] A sense pervades the three volumes concerned with the history of British parliamentary politics since 1867 that lineaments exist between the overt story of this environment and the cosmologies of its actors.[30] The focus, on the other hand, plainly seeks to

---

[27] Cooke and Vincent, p. 65; John Vincent, *The Formation of the Liberal Party 1857-68*, London, 1966, p. 258.

[28] Colin Matthew (ed.), *The Gladstone Diaries*, Oxford, 1968-, vi. 519.

[29] Cf. Maurice Cowling, *The Nature and Limits of Political Science*, Cambridge, 1963; *Mill and Liberalism*, Cambridge, 1963; *Religion and Public Doctrine*, Cambridge, 1980. The distinction made here between Cowling's work and that of the 'high-political school' generally has also been noted in J. P. Parry, 'Religion and the Collapse of Gladstone's First Government, 1870-74', *Historical Journal*, 25 (1981), 72 n. 7.

[30] M. Cowling, *1867*; see also *The Impact of Labour 1920-24*, Cambridge, 1971 and *The Impact of Hitler*, Cambridge, 1975. Especially relevant are *1867*, pp. 1-7 and 311-40; and *Labour*, pp. 1-12.

resolve another relationship, one between the ground rules of cabinet-level politics and the voicing of a 'message' which will promote cohesion and perpetuate authority. Beliefs, doctrines, and ideas seldom escape the quarantine of inverted commas as though refractions have left them with deformed identities.

Despite the obliqueness of some of these currents, many observers felt by the end of the 1970s that something challenging had been said. The response to it proved sporadic and not always helpful; instead an atmosphere of confused recrimination often surrounded the discussion.[31] By historians who had learned to bridge politics and thought in direct ways the problem was left to go away. Pathologies of individual 'ideas' about 'national efficiency' or 'coalition' could still be counted.[32] Biographical material often showed itself susceptible to short-cuts, especially in the bastardized form of the 'political life'; indeed the disease became for a time chronic among the rash of papers and books that focused on Lloyd George. Discussions of policy formation—over Home Rule, for example, or Salisbury's domestic policy, or Liberal social policy—took place in an atmosphere that suggested little permeation of fresh methodologies.[33] Greater sophistication attended work which by its very nature thrust questions about this bridge-building to the centre of the stage. Imperialism and the party system presented one case-study, as did the relationship between 'progressivism' and the Liberal party or socialist theory and the new Labour party.[34] What distanced many of these studies from the adoption of a 'high politics' approach *tout court* amounted to a group of reservations about style, narrative, evidence, morality, and simple verisimilitude. It frequently represented itself, however, as undifferentiated rearguard action in retreat towards a received version of historical truth. Behind the remarks to be made

[31] Cf. Michael Bentley, 'What is Political History?', *Durham University Journal*, 70 (1978), 133-9.

[32] e.g. G. R. Searle, *The Quest for National Efficiency*, Oxford, 1971; R. J. Scally, *The Origins of the Lloyd George Coalition*, Princeton, 1975.

[33] M. Barker, *Gladstone and Radicalism*, Brighton, 1975; Peter Marsh, *The Discipline of Popular Government*, Hassocks, 1978. See also H. V. Emy, *Liberals, Radicals and Social Politics 1892-1914*, Cambridge, 1973.

[34] The historiography of these problems is too extensive to detail here. Some of the contributions to these debates will be discussed below.

here lies an instinct that it ought to prove possible to do better than this even if a preliminary clearing of the battle-ground remains the sole feasible objective.

III

Parties are structures. They do not generally behave as mono-liths but rather display complicated patterns of communication between their various strata—a platitude which several generations of academic analysis and common observation can underpin. They engage in a dynamic, often reciprocal, relationship with other parties and organizations in the system. It follows that a structured view of political activity inside the British parties will establish a closer congruence with observed reality than a view which neglects or overrides these characteristics. Contention enters the discussion at a point at which historians and political scientists take decisions concerning the flow of intra-party influence and *dirigisme* and the relationship subsisting between the structure's components and various forms of pressure and conditioning which originate outside the system. So far as ideas, doctrines, beliefs, and intentions are concerned, however, what seems remarkable is the degree to which bland reflections from first principles eat away at the plausibility of volumes of writing.

Any view of the impact of thought on British politics appears doomed to disappear in self-deception, for example, if it rests on the assumption that senior politicians encounter the same social contacts, party constraints, and rhetorical temptations as those experienced by back-bench stalwarts or constituency activists. Politicians who have lived through periods of office or high-level party responsibility report with great consistency on the singularity of the world they entered. Few cabinet ministers, perhaps none, retained a grip comparable to Gladstone's on the intellectual output of their day; yet even he remarked on the way in which his horizons had become foreshortened by the experience of the premiership.[35] Those horizons, never very long, have closed in noticeably

[35] 'Swimming for his life, a man does not see much of the country through which the river winds . . .', Diary, 31 Dec. 1868, vi. 655. For a different perspective on the same quotation, cf. Boyd Hilton, above, p. 29.

since the middle of last century under pressure of increasing business and instant communication. In the year of Gladstone's accession to the leadership of the Liberal party, 1868, Disraeli defined a long time in politics as three months; Randolph Churchill had reduced it to a fortnight by 1886; Harold Wilson got it down, notoriously, to a week; a Conservative shadow-minister offered twenty-four hours in 1978.[36] Richard Crossman had reminisced ten years before on Winston Churchill's early years. '[T]he marvellous thing then', he wrote in his diary, 'was how much Ministers normally thought out their own policy, talked things out among themselves and wrote their own papers. Now we just haven't the time. . . . [O]ur policy-making functions are virtually eliminated.'[37]

This says more about Crossman's world than Churchill's. Little evidence exists to suggest that thought (understood as the reported deliverances of the intelligentsia) readily informed high-political discussion after the middle of the nineteenth century. Luminous exceptions can soon be identified, of course—a Cornewall Lewis or a Haldane with their philosophical proclivities, a Butler or a Jenkins in more recent years. One recalls the Earl of Malmesbury's bizarre request to Stanley for guided reading on political economy; or Lowe's putative buttonholing by Jevons over the disastrous match tax; or Ramsay MacDonald's reading of serious books in the 1920s; or the currency, in a different climate, of Liddell Hart's theories in Chamberlain's cabinet.[38] But the very paucity of such instances hinders generalization. It is overwhelmingly apparent from the rich material available to historians of this period that a mood of riding or dodging a fast-moving vehicle dominates the sensibilities of politicians

---

[36] Disraeli to Stanley, 16 Aug. 1868, in W. F. Monypenny and G. E. Buckle, *The Life of Benjamin Disraeli, Earl of Beaconsfield*, 6 vols., 1910–20 (2 vol. edn., 1929), ii. 400; R. F. Foster, *Lord Randolph Churchill: a political life*, Oxford, 1981, p. 251; R. Behrens, *The Conservative Party from Heath to Thatcher: politics and policies, 1974–9*, Farnborough, 1980, p. 49.

[37] R. H. S. Crossman, *The Diaries of a Cabinet Minister*, 3 vols., London, 1975–8, ii. 668 (7 Feb. 1968).

[38] Stanley's diary, 15 Mar. 1851, in J. R. Vincent (ed.), *Disraeli, Derby and the Conservative Party: the political journals of Lord Stanley 1849–69*, Hassocks, 1978, p. 56; James Winter, *Robert Lowe*, Toronto and Buffalo, 1976, p. 272; David Marquand, *Ramsay MacDonald*, p. 270; Brian Bond, *British Military Policy between the Two World Wars*, Oxford, 1980, p. 252.

at a high-political level. Among the latter a frequent refrain is contempt of or amusement at those whom Thiers called 'messieurs les istes'. Disjunction imposes itself as the only glaring theme in the careers of such men. Isolation and overwork remain their constant complaint.

Observations of this kind hardly comprise a reliable basis from which to announce a theory of intellectual desiccation within high politics; but perhaps they help suggest that correspondences between 'great men' and their *idées fixes* may have been drawn too confidently. A remnant of Whig typography, after all, appears commonly in the attempt to reveal a continuum of 'character' by hacking away at a mature statesman in order to discover some quintessential acorn that once contained his future.

> Oh gather the thoughts of your early years
> Gather them as they flow,
> For all unmarked in those thoughts appears
> The path where you soon must go.
> .   .   .   .
> The husbandman knows not the worth of his seed
> Until the flower be sprung,
> And only in age can he rightly read
> The thoughts that are thought when young.[39]

From this direction comes a catalogue of examples of lessons learned in youth triggering the behaviour of cabinet ministers like eruptions of a dormant disease. When we must 'always' recognize that the 'mainspring' of Lloyd George's actions lay in 'the principle of moral philosophy which he had read at the impressionable age of sixteen in his deceased father's notebook',[40] a doctrine of explanation has been produced with a self-sufficient apparatus of legitimacy. From that point on it will do to describe an action as 'out of character' to weaken its validity. 'Influence' (a category as full of emptiness as 'tradition') carries one the same way. Derive Joseph Chamberlain's actions from Seeley's thought and Lloyd George's behaviour from Chamberlain's and it becomes possible to

[39] W. E. H. Lecky, 'Early Thoughts', in *Poems*, London, 1891, p. 12.
[40] W. R. P. George, *The Making of Lloyd George*, London, 1976, p. 87.

draw a picture of intellectual influence in politics.[41] Not all individuals, however, appear equally susceptible to biography in this sense of a retrospective skewering of continuities. Is it whiggish to see progress in Chamberlain's biographer recognizing problems in this area or Randolph Churchill's frankly acknowledging complication in the episodic structure of his biography?[42]

Early thoughts and episodes cannot be wished away. By definition, senior politicians cannot be born: they have to be made. The making of a minister will include a steeping in a number of ideological environments—family dining-room, seat beneath the pulpit of a Sunday, marquee society with its vol-au-vents and imperial savagery; hard-nosed selection committees, the search for an identity on the back benches and the smoking room. Here the custodians of the party phylacteries enjoy their salad days and the freedom of that 'heedless rhetoric' taken by Disraeli (a man who knew about these things) to be 'the appanage of all who sit below the gangway'.[43] Gladstone either forgot this difference or never knew about it. At any rate it took Sidney Herbert to remind him that there did exist differences between the parties: 'the differences [were] on the back benches'.[44] For both Gladstone and Disraeli, however, ideas and principles bit into their sense of practice only in so far as they forced an entry into a world preoccupied by the problems of executive government. Neither Gladstone nor his colleagues showed much interest in 'party Liberalism' with its slogans and demagoguery.[45] Joseph Chamberlain demonstrates a sensitivity to both perspectives

[41] R. T. Shannon, 'John Robert Seeley and the Idea of a National Church', in R. Robson (ed.), *Ideas and Institutions of Victorian Britain: essays in honour of George Kitson Clark*, London, 1967, pp. 266–7; George, p. 128. Cf. Mallock's selection of a different discipleship for Chamberlain: 'Mr. Hyndman follows Marx; Mr. Chamberlain emulates Mr. Hyndman' (*Property and Progress*, 1884, p. 190).

[42] Richard Jay, *Joseph Chamberlain*, Oxford, 1981; R. F. Foster, *Lord Randolph Churchill.*

[43] In the House of Commons, March 1868, Monypenny and Buckle, op. cit. (2 vol. edn.), ii. 357. The phrase seems to have caught Harcourt's eye in the parliamentary reports: 'I should not regret having a little heedless rhetoric below the gangway before I go into the dull harness of office'. A. G. Gardiner, *The Life of Sir William Harcourt*, London, 2 vols., 1923, i. 189.

[44] Gladstone's diary, 4 Feb. 1855, *Diaries*, v. 15.

[45] The distinction is amplified in Vincent, *The Formation of the Liberal Party*, pp. 11–14.

over a long career. In an early letter, written before he entered
parliament, he identifies the salient characteristics of Alfred
Illingworth, a back-bencher whom he admired. 'His principles
are matters of belief & conviction & not the result of pressure.'[46] He might have said the same words ten years later as
a junior minister in Gladstone's second government. Ten
years beyond that, would there not have been just the trace
of a smile? Lloyd George's relationship with conviction similarly seems to have been more straightforward in 1890 than
it was to become after 1908. The implication of bundling
together a few such illustrations argues against treating a
'party' as though it carried within its strata a consistent weight
of intellectual or ideological commitment. It argues against
accepting without persuasive evidence that Edwardian Liberals
'were on the whole keenly aware of the principles involved in
their activities' or that their legislation concealed ideological
complexities 'not always voiced but omnipresent in every
move of the policy planners and executors'.[47]

Within party hierarchies an intellectual disposition has
little value as a promotion mechanism and may seriously in-
hibit success. Crossman presents a modern cameo of the
difficulty. As an intellectual who 'made it' he confutes any
iron law that academics cannot become effective politicians.
But his admiration during the heady days of the first Wilson
government was won most consistently by the 'intensively
unreflective' George Brown, 'a pure man of action . . . who
bashes around. He is doing a wonderful job.' And as optimism
turned to sourness he blamed the government's lack of ideas
and controlling strategy on the men who ran the party at the
top and who had reached the top precisely because they were
trimmers; 'and we wouldn't have been elected if they hadn't'.[48]
Many of the private archives of leading politicians carry a
similar, if less pungent, patina. Intellectuals committed to the
propagation of ideas rarely impose their image of political
purpose on colleagues, at least for any length of time. On the

[46] Quoted in D. W. Bebbington, *The Nonconformist Conscience: chapel and politics 1870-1914*, London, 1982, p. 20.
[47] Michael Freeden, *The New Liberalism: an ideology of social reform*, Oxford, 1978, pp. 249, 195.
[48] *Diaries*, i. 100; ii. 627.

other hand, the public evidence reads far more ambivalently and demands consideration.

Rhetoric is an intellectual art-form—the manifesto, the public letter, the leading article, the radio broadcast, the television interview, above all the formal set speech—which has provided the political structure with a central promotive criterion since the eighteenth century. The content of rhetorical statements from modern politicians bears little relation to that pressed into the elegant periods of Burke or Sheridan. But the function of such statements continues to be that described exquisitely by Croker in 1822, to provide 'that *flow* of ideas and language which can run on for a couple of hours without, on the one hand, committing the government or, on the other, lowering by commonplaces or inanities the status of a Cabinet Minister'.[49] Because rhetoric is creative, its content sometimes runs beyond truth. It was Robert Lowe's failure to understand this that led to his censure by a more experienced colleague, Sir Charles Wood, following one of Lowe's less discreet performances. 'Charles says that any blockhead can speak the truth, but that nobody wanted it and Lowe will never be forgiven by the party.'[50] Lies, on the other hand, must be avoided also when they generate false expectation and limit options. Consequently rhetoric offers an important subject for scholarship. It will provide few *aperçus* into intention and strategy: it seems unlikely that Lloyd George 'discussed the thinking' behind one of his appointments in a public speech.[51] But neither will it support a role of subservience to tactical considerations and merit unthinking dismissal. What a politician can legitimately or realistically include in his communication with his public interacts with what can be done privately or in cabinet. If thought leaves its mark somewhere in British politics this is the place to seek the traces.

[49] Louis J. Jennings (ed.), *The Croker Papers*, 3 vols., London, 1884, i. 231.

[50] Clarendon to Lewis, 14 Dec. 1858, in Sir Herbert Maxwell (ed.), *The Life and Letters of George William Frederick, Fourth Earl of Clarendon*, London, 2 vols., 1913, ii. 172.

[51] John Campbell, *The Goat in the Wilderness*, London, 1978, p. 185. For an analysis of complexity in rhetoric, see the interpretation of Salisbury's 'Hottentot' speech of 15 May 1886 in Cooke and Vincent, *The Governing Passion*, pp. 79-82.

IV

Political ideas do not in themselves comprise an apparatus: the ghosts cannot become a machine. But in the British historical experience they have tended, in their potential to affect political practice, to manifest a distinct sociology— one that has proved capable of curtailing or enhancing their potency among politicians. Thought does not, that is to say, necessarily exercise sway in this area in proportion to its intelligence, originality, or appropriateness. Its *source* often predetermines its power. Instances occur, needless to say, when individual ideas or thinkers transcend this difficulty and penetrate the political structure in an obvious and significant way. Perhaps an article in a weekly review is picked up by a minister at a moment when he feels receptive. Perhaps sheer serendipity throws an individual into conversation with a politician in a train.[52] For the most part, however, the British class environment (and the part played by educational provision in deepening it) creates an atmosphere in which such randomness rarely matters. Quite as markedly as any political élite, the intelligentsia possessed, during the period we are considering, a house style of background, vocabulary, and timbre. Because it reinforced its separateness from that élite as successfully as it maintained its differentials from other social sectors, moreover, its relationship with high politics reflected little mutual understanding. Disraeli's excitement at coming across intellectuals during a visit to Oxford —'I saw in the flesh Jowett, Max Müller and Ruskin!'— would say more for congruence if he could have stifled the feeling that he had been watching ornamental carp in a tank.[53]

[52] Witness the remarkable (but consciously sought) conversations recorded in the diaries of the Conservative back-bencher Sir Arnold Wilson during the 1930s. See his *Walks and Talks*, London, 1934; *Thoughts and Talks*, London, 1938; *More Thoughts and Talks*, London, 1939.
[53] Disraeli to Gathorne Hardy, 12 Dec. 1873, in A. E. Gathorne Hardy (ed.), *Gathorne Hardy, First Earl of Cranbrook: a memoir*, London, 2 vols., 1910, i. 332. It is true that Gladstone's Home Secretary, H. A. Bruce, reports 'some good talks with Mat. Arnold' and recommends the reading of Mill (*Letters of the Rt. Hon. Henry Austin Bruce, G.C.B., Lord Aberdare of Duffryn*, 2 vols., priv. circ., 1902, i. 248, 252); but then Bruce was a ministerial oddity whose passion for education, like A. H. D. Acland's and H. A. L. Fisher's in later generations, overtook his political ability.

Crossman's depiction of a quondam academic among his colleagues, a man 'who kn[ew] his way about the academic
world and the U[niversity] G[rants] C[ommittee]', flounder-
ing like 'a fish out of water' following his translation to high
politics,[54] suggests that Mind in the 1960s could be deemed
no less wet.

Certainly the party and intellectual structures offer many
points of personal contact; indeed Oxford itself provides an
example of how this could occur during the years when Christ
Church acted as a nursery for statesmen, or when Balliol
stocked the higher civil service, or when All Souls failed to
divest itself of embarrassing alumni in Neville Chamberlain's
cabinet. Elections there could also catch the national eye on
occasion—Peel's withdrawal in 1829, Gladstone's defeat in
1865, the 1938 by-election when the Master of Balliol squared
up to a Fellow of All Souls—and recall the frictions generated between the clerisy and party exigencies. Yet distance
has been more noticeable than friction in the relations between these two sectors. It has been bridged mostly by the
written word and especially in the high journalism which
established itself in London after the Crimean war and reached
a high point of influence in the second half of the nineteenth
century. The presence of an intellectual component in this
writing became so apparent that it earned remark at the time:
the Warden of Merton pointed out with some satisfaction
that about a quarter of the articles written for periodicals
such as the *Contemporary Review* and the *Fortnightly Review*
emanated from the common-rooms of Oxford and Cambridge.[55] Closer to Westminster, however, in the clubs and
eating-houses where one could not order dinner without implying a party plot, this presence thinned out. Earl Spencer
reminded his son of the dangers these places posed for his
education. 'Pray remember', he told him in 1879, 'that in
what is called Society, and at Clubs such as the Marlborough
and Whites or even Brooks, you may find excellent Liberals;
but not the thinkers of the party.'[56]

[54] See Crossman's reflections on the problems of Vivien Bowden: *Diaries*,
i. 42 (2 Nov. 1964).
[55] Christopher Kent, 'Higher Journalism and the mid-Victorian Clerisy', *Victorian Studies*, 13 (1969/70), p. 189.
[56] Spencer to C. R. Spencer, 21 Dec. 1879, in Peter Gordon (ed.), *The Red*

Granted that thinkers tend to broadcast their message from afar, questions arise about the function of what they have to say within party politics. The modern history of the British political intelligentsia does not, for example, suggest the operation of a cohesive pressure group. On the two occasions when the intelligentsia spoke with some kind of unity in the later part of the nineteenth century (in favour of Gladstone's moralizing in 1876 and against it in 1886) neither its support nor its opposition activated Liberal strategy.[57] 'Educating the party' sounds a plausible role for the intelligentsia until the idea comes under scrutiny; possibly enough has been said to cast doubt on the likelihood of an external agency achieving so grand an object within organizations like those presented in political parties. Obviously some significance remains unless one adopt an image of politics as some kind of collective solipsism which denies anyone's world access to anyone else's. And if, as has been contended here, political rhetoric offers the best evidence of such contact, then we have to decide which interpretative framework seems most appropriate in which to consider it. Some would say that Lord John Russell's midnight oil shows through in his speeches and requires no further elaboration; or that Lloyd George's quotations from Rowntree or Alfred Marshall on the platform provide evidence enough for his 'doing some homework in the social sciences'.[58] Yet more than mere quibbling may leave one restive over these direct correlations and wondering about ways of refining them.

Part of the problem stems from confusing the function of thought as a decoration prepared by politicians (or bought from their researchers) in a couple of hours in the House of Commons library with a more fundamental role in guiding their behaviour and conditioning their thinking. 'We want

Earl: the papers of the fifth earl Spencer 1835–1910 (Northants Record Soc., xxxi), Northampton, 1981, i. 139. Cf. W. F. Lord, 'The Creed of Imperialism', *Nineteenth Century and After*, 66 (July 1909), 30.

[57] For analyses of the problems raised by the Bulgarian atrocities and the Home Rule issues see R. T. Shannon, *Gladstone and the Bulgarian Agitation*, Edinburgh, 1963, and Christopher Harvie, *The Lights of Liberalism: university liberals and the challenge of democracy*, London, 1976, pp. 218–42.

[58] John Prest, *Lord John Russell*, London, 1972, p. 191; Don M. Cregier, *Bounder from Wales*, Colombia and London, 1976, p. 132.

to know', as Ramsay MacDonald once said with a nod towards Liberal party headquarters, 'what the Liberal intelligence is thinking, not what 42 Parliament Street is compiling.'[59] Private correspondence, memoranda, and diaries serve as the best available control over the possibility of deception; but they do not survive evenly and may themselves encourage forms of deception when they leave large holes for speculation. This is ambiguity enough. But when historians raise questions about the gestation of policy within governing groups whose activities are surrounded by variables and/or about the working of a congested parliamentary milieu, those ambiguities expand alarmingly. The point has some urgency when it is recalled that these areas form the mainstream of recent enquiry about political thought in its relations with action. Rhetoric frequently appears in such enquiries as a means of locating 'ideas' defined in some closely confined sense as issues in party life: disestablishment, home rule, national efficiency, manhood suffrage, tariff reform, direct action, anti-waste, 'arms and the covenant'. But these issues take their existence and character from that part of the political environment in whose deposited evidence tactical considerations appear at their most thickly textured. The danger thus appears of asking questions which rhetorical evidence cannot resolve and ignoring questions about which rhetoric might prove suggestive.

Nineteenth-century politicians employed between themselves a revealing terminology about their views of ideas and beliefs. They often spoke less of a man's having an idea or maintaining a belief than of his *holding a language*. Archaic though the phrase seems, it allows the modern eye a fuller vision of the interrelated assumptions on the basis of which political problems were approached than atomic analyses sometimes imply; and it may be that a more 'molecular' understanding of political ideas—one that stands back from party slogan and catch-cry and examines networks of assumption and symbiosis within the public statements of politicians —would release this form of political study from some of its difficulties. An enquiry along these lines would seek evidence for correspondence and dissonance between the public language of politicians and the private; and it would place the

[59] Quoted in Emy, *Liberals, Radicals and Social Politics*, p. 128.

language of the platform and the parliamentary report side by side with the message of intellectuals, churchmen, journalists. The criterion on which a political 'idea' might then be recognized would lie not in its capacity to translate into a jingle short enough to fit a banner but rather its potential for sustaining a distinct and definable political language.

Attention has recently focused on the degree to which an 'organic' conception of society, popularized by Darwinist writers and taken up more generally in the last quarter of the nineteenth century, explains a number of political ideas pressed with some enthusiasm by both individualists and Liberals.[60] The argument offers a case in point. By refusing to force the history of this idea into a 'Liberal versus Conservative' framework and by concentrating instead on the uses made by politicians of all party ascriptions of what they picked up from an array of writing recommending the regarding of modern society as a living organism comprising interdependent cells, historians have successfully demonstrated how contradictory positions in party politics might be built from varying emphases detectable in biological theorists and their imitators. An 'embodiment' view of party would have provided no reason for such deep-digging. Nor could it have stimulated scholars to wonder whether Spencerean individualism and many versions of imperialist or socialist speculation could be explored in the same way as idea-systems capable of giving rise to a diversity of political languages which might be assimilated, even if in a rudimentary or foreshortened form, by politicians seeking to justify policy decisions and validate their behaviour. In explicating the material in this fashion, further, one moves towards a mode of criticism. If, for example, the influence of idealist thought on political practice has been called into question in recent years, its significance may gain ground again if it can be demonstrated that the vocabulary of organic sovereignty and self-realization appears as a notable component of Liberal rhetoric after 1890.

---

[60] Among recent studies see especially Stephan Collini, *Liberalism and Sociology*, pp. 13-50 and 147-208; Collini, 'Hobhouse, Bosanquet and the State', *Past and Present*, 72 (1976), 86-111; Michael Freeden, *The New Liberalism*, esp. pp. 25-70; Peter Clarke, *Liberals and Social Democrats*, Cambridge, 1978, *passim*.

This approach invites internal complexities of its own which must be left to a separate occasion. Under scrutiny here is the relationship between this view of the evidence and what political historians do when they write histories of party practice. It seems that the place of thought in the record rarely amounts to that of an engine driving politicians forward towards the achievement of conceived policy objectives: on both a priori and evidential grounds this role seems hard to cast. More convincing is a conception of thought as a reservoir of political possibility. Politicians do not know what the intellectuals know; but perhaps their version of what is *knowable* (and thus available) takes much of its character from the mild atmospherics created by the intelligentsia. More pressing stimuli and constraints undoubtedly exist, however. Some of them originate, as we have seen, in the structural nature of party itself. Some derive rather from prescriptions built into parties which help determine how their members will respond to certain types of idea. If 'thought' comes to politicians as a range of working models of practice and legitimacy from which to choose, speculation of this kind cannot of itself predict which model will obtain the best fit with a party man's sense of the realistic and rational. Equally important as explaining the significance of what is available must therefore be the exercise of working out why so little is chosen.

V

Doctrine can be understood both as an intellectual domain and as a mechanism whose function consists less in complementing thought than in obviating it. The ambivalence confuses discussion when these two senses elide from one to the other. Witness Leslie Stephen in 1902: 'We are sometimes invited to regret the insensibility of Englishmen to "ideas". The regret may be softened by the reflection that in politics an idea means a device for saving thought. It enables you to act upon a little formula without taking the trouble to ask whether it be or be not relevant to the particular case.'[61] No great weight can be supported by so tongue-in-cheek a remark;

[61] Leslie Stephen, 'The Good Old Cause', *Nineteenth Century and After*, 51 (Jan. 1902), 23.

but it does typify a conflation of ideas-in-general with a supposed special sub-category of ideas-in-politics. Clarity demands that these senses be separated and we shall be speaking here of 'doctrine' as an embodiment of the formulaic, non-reflective aspect of political thinking to which Stephen pointed. The two senses plainly involve one another to some degree: thought, in the sense considered so far, will include examples of doctrine defined as prescriptive statements of personal belief. But where doctrine suggests an explanatory problem is rather in its role as a nexus of assumptions and recommendations historically evolved within organized political groups and making itself felt as an appurtenance of party.

Inside the party system doctrine often assumes the form of personal luggage carried by an individual—a type of sentiment of which religious conviction perhaps presents a paradigm. Since, moreover, religion has entered into the central regions of policy discussion at a number of points since the 1830s, individual perspectives about it have merged into those of party élites over issues such as disestablishment in 1868-9 and 1910-20, ritualism in the 1870s and 1890s, prayer book revision in the 1920s, and pacifism in the 1930s and 1960s. They provide vital components in compiling an understanding of leading politicians ranging from Peel, Gladstone, and Salisbury to Baldwin, Lansbury, and Cripps. Out of the prosopography, however, no generalized photo-fit emerges of doctrine's place in politics. In their usual location —biography—these individual perspectives need not bear the burden that a theory would impose. Think of the creaking planks in Trotsky's blaming God for the policies of the first Labour government:

MacDonald's ministers reek of piety and make a show of it in every possible way. MacDonald himself is a Puritan: he looks at political questions, if you can call it looking, through the glass of the religion that inspired the revolutionary petty-bourgeoisie of the seventeenth-century. His colleague, Henderson, the Home Secretary, is the president or vice-president, or something of the sort, of the Christian evangelical societies. Every Sunday the Home Secretary in the Labour government pronounces a devout sermon.[62]

[62] Speech to the Tbilisi soviet, 11 Apr. 1924, in R. Chappell and A. Clinton (eds.), *Trotsky's Writings on Britain*, London, 3 vols., 1974, i. 195; cf. his attack on Lansbury's Christian pacifism, ibid., ii. 59-64. It should be observed that

Expanding personal cosmologies into an explanation for the behaviour of groups gives rise to difficulties that go beyond the question of representativeness; for in rooting political action in a network of private belief it neglects the complications inherent in high politics and foists on doctrine a role which the archival evidence suggests it to have been rarely capable of playing.

Casting doctrine in this way followed from an acceptance of the 'embodiment' view of party's relation with ideas: once concede that ideas comprise the *fons et origo* of political activity (and that doctrine amounts to a specialized segment of those ideas) and the conclusion becomes unavoidable. If Disraeli taught the Conservative party its doctrines after 1846, then the legislation of his 1874 government becomes the embodiment of that teaching. 'The aspirations of *Sybil* and "Young England", the doctrines in which Disraeli had "educated" the party for thirty years, the principles laid down in the great speeches of 1872, were translated into legislative form; it was Tory Democracy in action.'[63] Correlations of this kind typically take their evidence from the years when parties feel young—exciting points of origin as in the Labour party's experience after 1906 and the Social Democratic Party's more recently; or moments of doctrinal renewal, as in the Tory party following its shedding of Peel in 1846 or the Thatcherite retuning which led a Conservative back-bencher to denounce 'doctrinal purity' as 'a strange posture for a Tory'.[64] But old parties do not often feel young and young ones soon age. Seen as a whole, the history of doctrine in British politics since the mid-nineteenth century leaves an impression of mature institutions overmastering threats from theorists by the use of doctrine rather than by the defeat of it.

Whether an aspiring politician travels light or carries the world on his shoulders, after all, he tends to come to his party as a novice seeking acceptance. His party existed (normally)

Maurice Cowling's monumental study of 'public doctrine' and religious disposition does not seek to explain the operation of the political structure; see his *Religion and Public Doctrine in Modern Britain*, Cambridge, 1980.

[63] Monypenny and Buckle, ii. 709. Cf. Paul Smith's revision of their position in his *Disraelian Conservatism and Social Reform*, London, 1967.
[64] Patrick Cormack MP, reported in *The Times*, 20 Oct. 1981.

and possessed doctrines and ambiences and unspoken identities long before he entered the novitiate; it will perpetuate them when he is gone. Sometimes, to be sure, the story has proved otherwise: in 1681 a man had more to say about the matter, as he did in 1906 or 1980. But for most of the period we are considering, politicians came to their parties as apprentices to an existing mode of practice and heirs to a history. Of the doctrines with which they felt familiar and comfortable their parties had long since learned to be authors more than creatures. The parliamentary reformer Thomas Hare included this thought in his list of reservations about the parliamentary system in 1859. 'It is not usually the political tenet which has caused the party,' he wrote, 'but the party which has created the tenet.'[65] Behind this need to create tenets lies an imperative about identity rather than a wish to educate. Doctrine defies the erosion that simple passage of time inflicts on a party's image of itself and its purpose; by placing beyond question or argument certain facets of party outlook it provides a core of continuity. To this extent Disraeli looked as much backwards as forwards after 1846. He began with a view of tory identity and a sense that 'things must be done by parties, not by persons using parties as tools'. He proceeded, in speeches 'about the "hierarchy of classes" . . . incomprehensible to the country gentlemen and indeed not easily comprehended by anyone', rhetorically to reclaim identities which Peel no less deliberately had lost.[66] His 'education' contained no lessons beyond a reminder of what right-thinking tories had known intestinally since the days of Liverpool and Wellington.

From time to time doctrine appears easily recognizable in the residue of shared instincts discernible beneath the ephemera of party dialogue. Three economic doctrines—free trade, tariff reform, and 'monetarism'—have enjoyed periods of prominence in this way and exemplified the power of a doctrine in jelling party sentiment. All of them have provoked intellectual statement and theorizing: economic analyses and

[65] Quoted in Vernon Bogdanor, *The People and the Party System*, p. 107.
[66] Disraeli to Manners, 17 Dec. 1845, quoted in R. Stewart, *The Politics of Protection: Lord Derby and the Protectionist party 1841–52*, Cambridge, 1971, p. 76; Stanley's diary, 30 June 1849 in Vincent (ed.), *Diaries*, p. 11.

prognostications, histories, even ethical philosophies. Yet among politicians from John Russell to John Biffen their function has been to deepen a consciousness of party lineage and close down the possibility of admitting counter-theses dangerous for stability. Among Liberals at all levels of the party structure, for example, the importance of free trade in performing this service during the later years of 'historic' Liberalism seems striking in both public and private evidence.[67] More often, however, doctrine makes less overt impact; it lurks within views of how a party should operate and what elements should make up its collective persona. Edward Stanley's reflection in the wake of 1846 that Conservative leaders seemed 'out of place' leading an agitation implies an important Conservative doctrine about the place of open argument and discussion in a party that instinctively rates privacy above policy.[68] Doctrines of this kind come no closer to finding expression in rule-books than does clubhouse etiquette in a golf manual; and for much the same reasons. But the existence of a corpus of *savoir-faire* inside party organizations imposes constraints on how its supporters behave and enters into their understanding of loyalty to the group.[69]

---

[67] See Michael Bentley, *The Liberal Mind 1914–29*, Cambridge, 1977, pp. 152–4.

[68] Stanley's diary, 26 June 1849, Vincent (ed.), *Diaries*, p. 11; cf. the brilliant evocation of Conservative doctrine in the 1880s in Cooke and Vincent, *The Governing Passion*, pp. 61–83.

[69] The distinction drawn here between 'thought' and 'doctrine' to some extent runs parallel with one drawn in Dr H. M. Drucker's *Doctrine and Ethos in the Labour Party*, London, 1979, though it was formulated independently of that highly stimulating study. My understanding of thought's distance from doctrine echoes that observed by Dr Drucker between 'doctrines' ('ideas which have been argued about and agreed by a group of people') and a collection of dispositions (tenderness towards leaders; attitudes to party funds; the need for formality in party practice; demands for sacrifice) which make up an 'ethos', though I confuse matters by using 'doctrine' to mean something close to Dr Drucker's 'ethos' and 'thought' to mean, in its party connotations, something akin to his 'doctrine'. But Dr Drucker identifies doctrine by its flexibility or openness and ethos by its sociological anchorage. I am more struck by the *closed* character of doctrine (in my sense) and the role of party practice (as opposed to its class background or cultural experience) as a generator of identity. I also see difficulties in the way of expanding Drucker's model into a form which would fit the doctrinal history of the Conservative and Liberal parties, just as it seems to me no accident that Cooke and Vincent are at their most illuminating in their chapter on the Conservative party.

Blurredness over the meaning of doctrine calls into question the crisp distinction often made in rhetoric and correspondence between 'men' and 'ideas'. The logical demarcation hardly presents a problem; nor does the certainty of ungrooved politicians like Lord Randolph Churchill ('persons more than principles determine political events')[70] or academic commentators who despair in the search for ideology. 'Nothing, indeed, [was] more curious', to Sidney Low in 1904, 'than to observe the unimportance of formal statements of doctrine, compared with the significance attributed to the utterances and assertions of influential men.'[71] One can miss, however, the extent to which a man's utterance and assertion over a period of years turn him into a doctrinal symbol—an animated bundle of ideas implied by association. Such men have a power, as part of their charisma, to tie sympathy to a particular party with which they are associated; and they do so by appearing to stand (or indeed standing) for a collection of dispositions with which party colleagues and the electorate find it possible to identify. Contemporaries knew what it meant to be a Peelite, a Gladstonian, an Asquithian, even if they would have shown themselves unable to list the recommendations or detect all the nuances enclosed in the name. Grey, Baldwin, and Macmillan might have had adjectives created around them if events had worked out more propitiously. Did Joe Chamberlain 'stand for' anything? Ostrogorski asked a supporter of Chamberlain which party he followed and received the reply 'I follow Mr. Chamberlain.' He then asked if this meant that his interviewee supported the Liberal Unionists; but he 'merely repeated with an air of calm resolution, "I follow Mr. Chamberlain".'[72] It seems no more likely that reductionism of this kind involved nothing but blood and bone than that the evidence of Asquith's remarkable personal support during his declining years can be explained by reference to a compelling personality. If doctrine reaches its audience through means other than 'formal statements', so do individuals act as emblems for its message.

---

[70] Quoted in Foster, *Lord Randolph Churchill*, p. 220.
[71] Sidney Low, *The Governance of England*, pp. 127–8.
[72] Ostrogorski, *Democracy and the Organization of Political Parties*, i. 323 n.

The message, when it is written, is written positively: it announces a central role for itself in the formulation of party policy. The Liberal party claimed to be charged with innovatory doctrines when it challenged Balfour's government with 'ideas' which, as Haldane rightly judged, turned out to be no ideas in fact, 'merely objections to other people's ideas'.[73] Conservative doctrines about nationalization, similarly, receive a face-lift in their public promulgation. Even when the content of party doctrines appears evangelical, however, its function for the party which seeks to evangelize will tend to be negative. Doctrine constrains behaviour among those who subscribe to it and places barriers against the absorption of inappropriate ideas; it comprises the filter through which 'thought' must pass before its adaptation to a party purpose. It follows that explanations of party practice which take no account of this element in the complex exclude material arguably crucial to any conception of deep structure. It follows, on the other hand, that treatment of doctrine as a category co-extensive with either political thought generally conceived or with party calculation will force the evidence available into too small a space.

VI

A brief review of three elements in the modern history of party in Britain provides an insecure platform from which to attempt a detailed analysis of the historiography. But perhaps enough has been said to awaken unease over certain forms of cheerfulness about party ('Party government is responsive to all forms of pressure'[74]) and about policy ('Policy is of course based on theory'[75]). The raising even of simple questions such as those suggested here implies a rudimentary style of criticism on which others may wish to dilate in their own areas of interest: to go beyond that point will take one into a degree of detail inappropriate to general comment. Yet it seems

[73] Quoted in D. A. Hamer, *Liberal Politics in the Age of Gladstone and Rosebery*, Oxford, 1972, p. 323.
[74] James Jupp, *Political Parties* (1968), p. 107.
[75] E. J. Hobsbawm, *Industry and Empire*, 1968 (Pelican edn., 1969), p. 225.

natural to wonder which parts of the political story covered here might be brought under close scrutiny.

Judged from the standpoint of a historian interested in the interaction between party history and the history of thought, the period after 1850 presents numerous challenges. The reformulation of Liberal policy during the 1860s, the doctrinal content of Disraelian Conservatism before 1874, the place of imperialist ideology in high politics after 1885, the character of social-democratic politics after 1906, the value-structure of inter-war Conservatism, the relationship between various socialist theories and the Labour party between 1931 and 1951, the network of assumptions that held together consensualist politics after the Second World War and the doctrinal aspects of their suppression at the end of the 1970s— all these problems present case-studies of manifest richness. More books and theses directed at them—many good ones already exist—will not necessarily fill the gap: the need is not for more of the same. The seriousness and sensitivity of studies in these areas will become validated, as it seems to me, by the depth and integrity of their source-criticism. It goes without saying that highly trained historians already demonstrate their scrupulousness and thoroughness in their use of material; but the historiography, taken as a whole, has spent less time than it might in relating the internal logic of projects to the most plausible means of achieving their objectives. Harmless incompetence plays a part—that familiar absence of acumen sorrowfully noted in penultimate paragraphs of reviews in the learned journals. But among first-class scholars a resistance remains that consorts oddly with their acuity elsewhere.

Possibly the tendency comes out of a post-*annaliste* catholicity which prescribes the piling up of layers of context and a variety of sources, each of which is regarded as capable of throwing light on the object in question. The experience of the 'revolution in government' debate in the 1950s and 1960s and the direction taken by some historians of Edwardian Liberalism more recently show the difficulties in which historians can find themselves as they try to make 'thought' and 'practice' run together in some convincing way. The last chapters of such books can be painful: a slow slog 'towards a conclusion' through types of evidence glaringly inapposite to the purpose.[76] Much might be gained by beginning with a view of evidential possibility; at any rate, it is hard to see what could be contentious in a methodological sense about doing so. In the case of 'progressivism', for example, it seems plain that the diaries and letters of politicians will not provide the best place to look for analyses of social theory. They will, however, provide the best (and conceivably the only) chance of finding out whether politicians knew very much about a world in which they can too easily be assumed to have membership. What this latter procedure suggests about progressive politicians presents few gifts to theory. On the contrary, one is left with the stark conclusion that evidence of this kind simply does not exist in sufficient weight to support the contention that the 'new Liberalism' successfully injected its politicians with an ideology of which they were conscious.[77]

The argument cannot end there. But it could have *begun* there and thus liberated historians for the next phase of the discussion which becomes not so much historical as epistemological. For the question now arises: must explanations of interaction between politics and thought subject themselves to the operation of a verification principle drawn from the survival of such evidence? An affirmative answer seems tenable: the historian can study only that which has survived; to suggest that sources *ought* to exist cannot come within his brief. Yet the harshness feels uncomfortable. Those scholars who work on 'high-political' sources are as keenly aware as are their critics that the evidence survives non-randomly, that it emphasizes near-sight in its creators, that an 'executive' tone can be predicted from its *raison d'être*. Then there are anxieties about the interpretative framework which high politics encourages in its students. It hardly suffices to have grounds for adopting positions about the evidence; one must also have grounds for changing those positions. But the

[76] Emy, *Liberals, Radicals*, pp. 281–98. Dr Freeden likewise loses some of his force in the last chapter of *The New Liberalism*.

[77] See an important unpublished Ph.D. thesis, R. E. Ellins, 'Aspects of the New Liberalism 1895–1914' (University of Sheffield, 1980). For a counter-example showing rejection of this position about evidence, cf. T. J. Dunne, 'Ireland, England and the Empire 1868–86: the ideologies of British political leadership' (unpublished Ph.D. dissertation, Cambridge, 1976).

attitudes of high-political writers readily become self-sealing and suggest no compelling reason for subjecting the overall strategy to review. Many writers interested in the problem of authenticity in political evidence have proved quicker to adduce reasons for deciding what is unacceptable in historical commentary than to provide accounts of what evidence would need to be presented in order to reverse their decisions. If it should turn out, in the house-clearance of some Liberal dowager, that Asquith, Crewe, and Grey each wrote a couple of impeccably private letters endorsing the urgency of social reform in terms more naturally associated with Lloyd George and Winston Churchill, would the resistance of high-political writers to the 'progressivist' case change colour? If three cabinet ministers seem insufficient, how many does one need? If two letters seem too few, how many will suffice?

Converting the raw stuff of political history into a museum catalogue of extant relics brings dangers of its own. It has been the theme of this essay none the less that worse dangers accrue when relics are ignored or deemed unworthy of archaeology. The way forward appears to lie in determining which frames of reference are relevant for the discussion of thought and politics. Party doctrines, in the sense we have been considering them, have so far received very little attention from historians for all their critical function on the boundary of party. This is not the place to dilate on the importance of an idea which has in any case been considered elsewhere in a study of the impact of the First World War on Liberal doctrine and party identity.[78] What requires reporting is simply that high-political evidence can yield conclusions by no means antagonistic to the thesis that doctrine constitutes a significant component of political explanation. Ideology need not be permitted its indiscriminate character as a bundle of ideas loosely assumed to trigger behaviour. Not that the presence of an intellectual climate—the contiguity of an intelligentsia whose pronouncements do not amount to party statements—can be excluded from the reckoning. We have seen that thought's history no more reflects party's than

[78] Bentley, *The Liberal Mind, passim.* For a contrasting study representing ideology as a linear tradition, see A. Bullock and M. Shock, *The Liberal Tradition from Fox to Keynes*, London, 1956.

does the history of intellectual preoccupations find a fit with that of politicians'; but in establishing what was available for politicians to select as justificatory theory, the intelligentsia has at once conditioned practice and provided the raw material for an academic subject of enquiry. Exploiting this and most other aspects of the relationship between politics and thought will demand only the abandonment of the ' "intellectualist" fallacy' that depicts action as the hand-maiden of rationality.[79] For in this unexplored hinterland, that fallacy, last seen nesting elsewhere in 1908, sits undisturbed in its roost.

[79] Graham Wallas, *Human Nature in Politics*, London, 1908, pp. 1-166.

6

The Politics of Keynesian Economics, 1924–1931

Peter Clarke

I

In speaking of the politics of Keynesian economics, one might legitimately have in mind a topic to which considerable attention has been paid over the years. There is a fecund literature about how, and why, and when, and to what extent, and from whom, the Keynesian revolution in economics encountered political resistance or acceptance.[1] The present essay does not purport to contribute to that literature. Thus it is not concerned with the impact of Keynes but with a prior question about the political considerations which may have influenced Keynes during a crucial stage in his economic thinking. It is implicitly directed against two reductionist approaches, each with its own temptations. Although the two are methodologically distinct, they are able to enjoy a sort of peaceful coexistence which it is one object of this essay to provoke and disturb.

The first approach has its stronghold in the technical history of economic theory, whereby Keynes can be placed within a self-contained tradition of economic thought and his

---

[1] See especially Donald Winch, *Economics and Policy*, London, 1969; Robert Skidelsky, *Politicians and the Slump*, London, 1967; 'The reception of the Keynesian revolution', in Milo Keynes (ed.), *Essays on John Maynard Keynes*, Cambridge, 1975, pp. 89–107; Susan Howson and Donald Winch, *The Economic Advisory Council, 1930–1939*, Cambridge, 1977; and Roger Middleton, 'The Treasury in the 1930s: political and administrative constraints to acceptance of the "new" economics', *Oxford Economic Papers*, 34 (1982), 48–77. For its sources, this essay is manifestly under a considerable debt to Donald Moggridge's exemplary edition of recent volumes in *The Collected Writings of John Maynard Keynes*. I have cited this edition wherever possible, abbreviated as follows: *JMK*, v and vi: *A Treatise on Money* (2 vols., 1930); *JMK*, ix: *Essays in Persuasion*; *JMK*, xiii and xiv: *The General Theory and After*; *JMK*, xix: *Activities, 1922–1929*, Parts 1 and 2; *JMK*, xx: *Activities, 1929–1931*. I am grateful to Michael Bentley, Stefan Collini, Michael Hart, Murray Milgate, Mary Short, John Thompson, and Donald Winch for their helpful comments on an earlier draft.

conceptual contribution to it appraised accordingly. It is the internal logic of the development of a discipline which is to the fore here, and the frame of reference is fundamentally teleological. The aim is to identify the Keynes patent on certain functional parts of the working model which economists have assembled and tested in use. Keynes's thought can thus be reduced to his apprehension of a number of original propositions, the essence of which can be captured in their fully-developed exposition. This essay, however, is less concerned with Keynes's thought than with his thinking. Why and how did he arrive at certain conclusions? Was he led to them or driven to them? The path of reasoning by which he got there should certainly be examined, but so should his reasons for choosing it.

But if economics is not a walled garden, it follows that one does not jump over the wall into a peculiar territory, called politics, where the rules are different. It is surely no less reductionist to suppose that the significance of Keynesian policies can be comprehended simply by putting the sharp enquiry, *cui bono*? The methodology of high politics has taught historians to identify some of the tactical functions which issues can serve, but this does not exhaust the question of their substantive content. How is it that self-serving ideas become current in one form rather than another? Accepting, for the sake of argument, the high-political dictum that politicians' interest in ideas is governed by solipsism, one might suppose that there would be nothing like a slump for fostering economic panaceas. It would follow that Keynes was saying what politicians wanted to hear. But why Keynes rather than Hobson or Major Douglas? And why the striking vicissitudes over time in the reception accorded to Keynesian ideas? Adapting a famous metaphor, one might say that a concentration on the imperatives of high politics neglects supply in favour of demand—an explanation relying on one blade of a pair of scissors to cut through the problem. This essay cannot provide a methodological paradigm to banish such difficulties. It can try to illuminate a necessarily complex dialectical relationship between the formulation of sophisticated ideas, with their own rules of congruence and logic, and the political predispositions helping to determine their thrust.

II

On 14 September 1930 John Maynard Keynes finished writing the *Treatise on Money*, which had occupied him for much of the previous seven years. He told his mother: 'Artistically it is a failure—I have changed my mind too much during the course of it for it to be a proper unity.'[2] In the preface, written the same day, he said virtually the same, that 'there is a good deal in this book which represents the process of getting rid of the ideas which I used to have and of finding my way to those which I now have. There are many skins which I have sloughed still littering these pages.'[3] It was, however, a work to which he attached considerable importance—the 'strict logical treatment of the theory' which he had promised his fellow members of the Macmillan Committee on Finance and Industry the previous March.[4] The theoretical nature of the *Treatise* did not, therefore, divorce it from the practical policy questions which the Macmillan Committee was considering in 1929-31. The rather technical brief of the committee was likewise related to broader issues of economic policy, on which Keynes was giving advice to the authorities at this time, chiefly under the auspices of the Economic Advisory Council. This advice in turn had direct political bearings, especially in so far as it touched on proposals which were matters of party controversy.

Now Keynes was no political innocent. His authorship of the pamphlet *Can Lloyd George Do It?* during the 1929 election campaign had given him a prominent polemical role as an advocate of public works. The *Treatise*, however, suggested the primacy of cheap money in promoting recovery. Nor was this the only source of bewilderment about Keynes's views at this time. A notorious opponent of Britain's return to the Gold Standard, he spoke up against devaluation. An advocate of a national treaty to reduce all incomes, he poured scorn on wage cuts. A free trader all his life, he began arguing for tariffs. The relationship between these matters is what first needs to be established.

When the *Treatise* was published, it was generally agreed

[2] *JMK*, xiii. 176.   [3] *JMK*, v. xvii.
[4] *JMK*, xx. 136 (evidence of 6 Mar. 1930).

that its most original contribution to economic analysis was the emphasis laid upon the distinction between saving and investment.[5] This was enhanced in late revisions of the book in 1929–30. The notion itself had been 'gradually creeping into economic literature in quite recent years', and Keynes paid tribute to the work of his Cambridge colleague, D. H. Robertson, here.[6] None the less, the way Keynes put the concept to work opened up a whole new field. In a homely exposition, added at a late stage to Volume Two, he pointed out that it was usual to think of the world's wealth as having been accumulated by thrift, whereas the truth was that another economic factor—enterprise—was really respons-ible. 'If enterprise is afoot, wealth accumulates whatever may be happening to thrift; and if enterprise is asleep, wealth de-cays whatever thrift may be doing.'[7] Saving in itself achieved nothing until investment employed the resources thus made available. Investment depended on entrepreneurs, and their confidence was best generated by cheap credit and infla-tionary expectations. Keynes's chapter, 'Historical Illustra-tions', is virtually a hymn to inflation. What use could be made of monetary policy to encourage enterprise by facilitat-ing investment? This was the practical question to which Keynes's theory gave rise.

In the *Treatise* Keynes declared that 'the real task' of monetary theory was 'to treat the problem dynamically' in order 'to exhibit the causal process by which the price level is determined, and the method of transition from one posi-tion of equilibrium to another'.[8] He considered that this was the chief failure of the quantity theory (the contention that a rise in the price level was the result of an increase in the money supply). Keynes held that equilibrium supplied the unique condition under which it was true. He stated his argu-ment initially for a closed system, where the problem was to balance saving and investment. Since they responded inversely

---

[5] See reviews by Norman Angell, *Time and Tide*, 8 Nov. 1930; A. C. Pigou, *Nation*, 24 Jan. 1931; Barbara Wootton, *The Listener*, 26 Feb. 1931; anon., *New Statesman*, 31 Jan. 1931.

[6] *JMK*, v. 154 n.

[7] *JMK*, vi. 132. The stages in the composition of the *Treatise* can be followed from material in *JMK*, xii, ch. 2.

[8] *JMK*, v. 120.

to changes in interest rates, the way was open for the banking system, as 'a free agent acting with design', to control the final outcome. It could *achieve* a balance by throwing the weight of official interest rates to one side or the other. 'Booms and slumps', Keynes maintained, 'are simply the expression of the results of an oscillation of the terms of credit about their equilibrium position.'[9] If this was a relatively simple task inside a closed system, it became appallingly difficult when considered within the real world of the international economy. For not only had saving and investment to be kept in equilibrium, so also had the country's international earnings and its foreign lending. Since the banking system had to work with the same instrument on these two different problems, it followed that 'the conditions of international equilibrium may be incompatible for a time with the conditions of internal equilibrium.'[10] How, then, could it be supposed that a balancing act of such complexity could ever be brought off?

Keynes worked out his answer in chapter 13 of the *Treatise*, 'The *modus operandi* of Bank Rate'. This was a rigorous theoretical account, designed to cover all possibilities. In order to assess where the weight of analysis fell, however, it is necessary to bear in mind the special conditions which were at the forefront of Keynes's own mind. Britain's return to the Gold Standard at an overvalued parity in 1925 set the conditions of the problem. The existing monetary mechanism coped best when it followed the market, up or down, not when it tried to fight the market: in particular, it was 'singularly ill adapted' to impose lower real earnings via high interest rates.[11] Yet the 1925 measures had required credit restriction, 'with the object of producing out of the blue a cold-blooded income deflation'.[12] Bank Rate had been given the job of reducing British costs to a level which would restore international competitiveness. Keynes claimed that neither economists nor bankers had been clear enough about the causal process involved, and hence 'apt to contemplate a deflation too light-heartedly'.[13] For the chain of causation here was: first, the deliberate choking of investment by high interest rates; second, its effect in inflicting abnormal losses

[9] *JMK*, v. 164–5.   [10] *JMK*, v. 165.   [11] *JMK*, v. 245.
[12] *JMK*, vi. 163.   [13] *JMK*, v. 244.

upon entrepreneurs; third, the consequent withdrawal of offers of work; fourth, the reduction of money earnings as a result of unemployment.

Backed by this analysis, in February and March 1930, Keynes conducted his evidence to the Macmillan Committee like a seminar. He expounded the *modus operandi* to the committee, inviting admiration for its jewelled mechanism. It was, he stressed, 'not a doctrine peculiar to myself', but the classical theory underpinning all notions of 'traditional sound finance in this country'.[14] His orthodox exposition prepared the ground for the more disturbing contention that the return to Gold, requiring wage reductions of 10 per cent, had the effect of 'setting Bank rate policy a task it had never been asked to do before in the economic history of this country'.[15] The external constraints had to be met, and could be met; but the price was an interest rate structure inappropriate for the achievement of an internal equilibrium. When Keynes thereupon broached his own distinction between saving and investment, he was able to produce Bank Rate as the key to the position. But it was a key which would not turn in the lock. As Keynes acknowledged, 'if we did not belong to an international system I should have said there was no difficulty whatever; one could simply reduce the Bank rate to that level where savings and investments were equal'.[16] Under those conditions, 'the rate of interest would always tend to fall to the yield of the next thing which was worth doing'.[17] When international conditions dictated higher rates, the mechanics of the system should in theory have produced lower costs and lower prices. 'But if you jam the machine halfway through so that you have a chronic condition in which business men make losses, you also have a chronic condition of unemployment, a chronic condition of waste; and the excess savings are spilled on the ground.'[18] It was when Bank Rate was used to regulate income downward that this 'jam' or 'hitch' occurred, preventing the process from working through to its final conclusion, and creating 'the worst possible condition, to be left in this jammed state'.[19]

---

[14] *JMK*, xx. 53 (evidence of 20 Feb. 1930).   [15] *JMK*, xx. 56 (ibid.).
[16] *JMK*, xx. 84 (evidence of 21 Feb. 1930).   [17] *JMK*, xx. 79 (ibid.).
[18] *JMK*, xx. 75 (ibid.).   [19] *JMK*, xx. 82 (ibid.).

Keynes had thus begun by investing some of the classical propositions with his own lucidity. Pigou acknowledged that the *Treatise* gave 'an account of the *modus operandi* of bank rate much superior, as it seems to me, to previous discussions'.[20] It was when Keynes used this as a basis on which to build his own distinctive analysis that his efforts found less ready acceptance. As long as saving and investment remained undifferentiated, increased saving seemed a plausible solution to the problem of under-investment; likewise, investors would presumably be attracted once wage costs were cut back to realistic levels. But at this stage in the argument Keynes pointed to the mental leap he required from his hearers, claiming that 'it makes a revolution in the mind when you think clearly of the distinction between saving and investment'.[21] In practice, wage cuts had never been an easy way out, but in theory they had constituted a simple answer. Keynes now challenged this. He had constructed his own squirrel cage, and he was to spend most of 1930 and 1931 darting around inside it, exploring possible exits.

III

What were the main features of this cage? The fundamental constraint on Britain's international position was inadequate foreign earnings. They were insufficient to finance British investments abroad. The Bank of England therefore stepped in to safeguard the gold reserves, which backed the exchange rate of sterling. Its sole weapon was a high interest rate, which indeed discouraged foreign lending but only at the cost of domestic enterprise. With home investment held back, and foreign lending blocked off, the result was that 'a certain amount of our savings is spilled on the ground' in a wasteful dissipation of potentially useful resources. Savings were eaten up in financing business losses rather than profitable investment. 'Our investment abroad is fixed by the cost of production, our investment at home is fixed by rate of interest, and the two together fall short of our savings, and the difference

---

[20] Review of the *Treatise* by Pigou, *Nation*, 24 Jan. 1931.
[21] *JMK*, xx. 87 (evidence of 21 Feb. 1930).

is accounted for by the loss to the business world.'[22] To what solution did this way of posing the problem point? The logic of the analysis was such that in itself it did not imperatively demand any single remedy, but rather established criteria by which a range of remedies might be judged. This was the technical virtue of formal economic analysis, but it did not foreclose the political choices that then arose.

Before the Macmillan Committee, Keynes spoke blandly of 'classifying the suggested remedies in such a manner as to fit in neatly with this general analysis and diagnosis'. This served to declare his professional credentials, which were accepted by his colleagues with little demur. The chairman, indeed, cut in to supply the right word when Keynes was, for once, momentarily at a loss.[23]

'I propose, as a scientist to be—'
'Remorseless.'

The remorseless method involved a systematic appraisal of the relevance of a variety of proposals. At this stage Keynes identified seven classes of remedy, as follows.

1. *Devaluation.* Revaluation of gold (the usual way of putting it) was an obvious possibility in view of Keynes's contention that the return to Gold in 1925 lay at the root of Britain's immediate problems. But an opportunity missed was an opportunity lost, so far as Keynes was concerned, and he did not see devaluation as desirable in 1930, because of the consequences for credit and confidence. It was a last resort, if all else failed.

2. *A national treaty.* This would provide for an agreed reduction of all domestic money incomes. It was really a way of living with the Gold Standard by short-circuiting deflation as the path to a lower level of domestic costs. Keynes had advocated it on these grounds in 1925, but by 1930 he pretty clearly recognized that it was not practicable. 'Its feasibility is almost entirely a matter of psychological and political, and not economic factors', he commented.[24]

---

[22] *JMK*, xx. 95 (evidence of 28 Feb. 1930).
[23] *JMK*, xx. 99 (ibid.).
[24] *JMK*, xx. 102 (ibid.).

3. *Bounties to industry.* These, too, constituted a theoretically attractive possibility in that they would use taxation to place the burden of maintaining competitive prices upon the whole community rather than upon certain sections of industry. 'It may be', Keynes argued, 'that our social feelings have caused us to fix wages at a higher level than the economic machine grinds out. If we were to balance that by a bounty that would be the public subscribing to meet the difference out of the common purse.'[25] This was a variant on a plea he had made earlier in the year for seeing the social wage rather than high earnings as the economically viable road to social amelioration.[26]

4. *Rationalization.* This was the vogue word in 1930 for schemes to cut unit costs, especially through economies of scale. Clearly any improvement in efficiency was desirable; the real question was whether this alone could be relied upon to turn the situation round.

5. *Tariffs.* Protection was an old political battle-axe with a new economic cutting edge. New because several of the traditional free-trade arguments now struck Keynes as inverted arguments for tariffs. Would tariffs not increase the profits of entrepreneurs at the expense of the rest of the community? 'That is precisely what we want. . . .' Would they not act as 'a surreptitious way of decreasing real wages'? Or induce a rise in prices? Indeed, 'also something we want', said Keynes.[27] Moreover, the classical theory of free trade bore a striking likeness to the *modus operandi* of Bank Rate—in fact, it was mere prolegomenon in so far as trade transactions worked through international gold movements to *activate* changes in Bank Rate. Thereafter, the precision of the compensating effects depended likewise upon the fluidity of wages and the flexibility of employment. But again, the immediate problem was what to do 'supposing we get jammed at the point of unemployment'? The choice was not between making more or less suitable articles according to a perfect international

[25] *JMK*, xx. 108 (ibid.).
[26] 'The question of high wages', *Political Quarterly*, Jan.–Mar. 1930, in *JMK*, xx. 3 ff.
[27] *JMK*, xx. 113 (evidence of 28 Feb. 1930).

division of labour, but between making something (albeit un-suitable ideally) and making nothing. Keynes's conclusion was therefore that 'the virtue of protection is that it does the trick, whereas in present conditions free trade does not'.[28] Protection was thus helpful even if it was 'not anything like adequate to the situation'.[29]

6. *Home investment.* Keynes called this 'my favourite remedy' without further ado.[30] He proceeded to justify it by a process of elimination. New employment, he reasoned, might arise from exports (though the snag there was high wages); or from import substitution (the protectionist solu-tion). Alternatively, consumption might rise at home. Al-though the spending power of the newly employed would create a favourable repercussion, 'you cannot start the ball rolling in this way'.[31] Less saving would also be of some advantage, though it was 'very low in my category of reme-dies . . .'.[32] There remained a fourth possibility: that of creating new capital assets. 'It is the only remedy left, if one holds that the other three remedies are either impracticable in the position today or are inadequate, or are in themselves undesirable.'[33] There were various devices by which private enterprise might be encouraged to invest more at home, but the crux of the case was 'that it must be Government invest-ment which will break the vicious circle'.[34]

7. *International measures.* High interest rates were choking investment, so reducing them would pave the path to recovery. Cheap money in one country, however, was not much of a slogan. Concerted action by the central banks was, therefore, in the long term, the most important thing of all.

Keynes endorsed all these proposals as having some point. 'While I have my preferences, practically all the remedies seem to have something in them', he claimed.[35] Rather than argue for one panacea, in season and out, therefore, he sug-gested that almost any of them might be worth a trial, given

[28] *JMK*, xx. 114–15 (evidence of 28 Feb. 1930).
[29] *JMK*, xx. 125 (evidence of 6 Mar. 1930).
[30] Ibid.
[31] *JMK*, xx. 126 (ibid.).
[32] *JMK*, xx. 127 (ibid.).
[33] *JMK*, xx. 128 (ibid.).
[34] *JMK*, xx. 146–7 (ibid.).
[35] *JMK*, xx. 99 (evidence of 28 Feb. 1930); cf. 125 (evidence of 6 Mar. 1930).

particular circumstances. Thus, as far as his Macmillan Committee evidence goes, devaluation was a last resort; a national
treaty was a spent hope; bounties were probably impracticable; rationalization was insufficient in itself; tariffs were
helpful at the margin; public works remained the favourite
emergency measure; and in the long term the international
economy needed cheap money. In the *Treatise*, Keynes commended four solutions: rationalization, tariffs, public works,
and cheap money. But this was *given* that the Gold Standard
obtained (no devaluation), and *given* also that wage reductions were ruled out; so only bounties failed to make both
lists.

The close correspondence here is hardly surprising, since
Keynes was putting the finishing touches to the *Treatise*
while giving his evidence to the Macmillan Committee. But it
serves to show that there is little reason to charge Keynes
with inconsistency on the ground that his polemical advocacy
of public works in 1929-30 did not match up with his
theoretical prescription of cheap money in the *Treatise*. The
economic reasoning was the same in both cases, in that both
met his criteria for stimulating investment. Thus the *Treatise*
insisted that 'the great evil of the moment' lay in 'the unwillingness of the central banks of the world to allow the market
rate of interest to fall fast enough', and asserted that 'we cannot hope for a complete or lasting recovery' until such a fall
had taken place.[36] But whether to leave a long-term solution
in the hands of central bankers—hands tied by national constraints and paralysed by mutual suspicions—was a question
of practical judgement. Even in the *Treatise*, therefore, Keynes
added that 'there remains in reserve a weapon by which a
country can partially rescue itself when its international dis-
equilibrium is involving it in severe unemployment,[37] and
this was, of course, domestic investment promoted by the
Government.

IV

Keynes can be called inconsistent, therefore, only in the sense
that he was led to investigate various methods of escaping

[36] *JMK*, vi. 185, 344.   [37] *JMK*, vi. 337.

from the squirrel cage; but it formed a structure within which all his moves were circumscribed; and his set aim was to get out. This consistency of approach, if not of methods, can be seen in four further attempts at analysis of the problem which he made, in slightly differing contexts, six months either side of the *Treatise*'s publication in October 1930. Indeed, the main difference between them is one of emphasis, depending largely on the starting-point in each case. How the remedies presented in his evidence to the Macmillan Committee (numbered as Evidence 1 to 7 above) fared under those conditions can be followed in remorseless detail.

The first of these statements was his letter to the Governor of the Bank of England, Montagu Norman, of 22 May 1930.[38] This started, naturally enough, with the international difficulties on account of which the Bank felt inhibited from taking further action. 'But that is why I twist and turn about trying to find some aid to the situation', Keynes countered. Again his analysis turned on the *Treatise* proposition that unemployment *must* stem from an excess of savings over investment. In which case, only an increase of investment, at home or abroad, was a real solution. Increased foreign investment implied higher exports (which implied lower costs); or lower imports (which implied lower costs or tariffs); or more loans. Any of these were compatible also with increased home investment; but this would not materialize unaided. A further alternative —'a counsel of despair'—was to decrease savings. Thus *given* the Gold Standard, and *given* existing interest rates (which eliminated Evidence 1 and 7), the options were to cut domestic costs (Evidence 2 and 4), to resort to protection (Evidence 5), and to stimulate home investment (Evidence 6).

Two months later Keynes tried again, this time in response to the Prime Minister's questions to the Economic Advisory Council.[39] His scheme remained the same. 'Our dilemma in recent years, as I see it, is that if we raise the rate of interest sufficiently to keep our foreign lending down to the amount of our favourable balance, we raise it too high for domestic

---

[38] *JMK*, xx. 350–6. Since section (iv) does not advance the argument, but merely substantiates it in detail, readers who find this rebarbative are advised to take it on trust and move on to section (v).

[39] *JMK*, xx. 370–84 (Keynes's answers, 21 July 1930).

enterprise.' The touchstone in appraising remedies was therefore whether they increased either the foreign balance or the
outlet for savings at home. The former could be accomplished
in five ways. First, by decreasing the costs of production
(rationalization, tax deductions, or wage cuts—really reiter-
ating Evidence 2 and 4). Second, by protection (Evidence 5),
which was the quickest, easiest method. Third, by import
boards (a new idea). Fourth, by arrangements with the Domi-
nions, of which Keynes was sceptical. Fifth, by increasing
world trade, which was primarily an international rather than
a local matter (Evidence 7). This cluster of measures would
work on the foreign balance; the alternative was to concentrate on the problem of home savings, for which four proposals were enumerated as appropriate (all of them varieties of
Evidence 6). A home development programme, to which 'the
greatest possible importance' was attached, came first. Next,
subsidies to private enterprise. Thirdly, there were ways of
helping domestic enterprise to afford high interest rates. On
inspection, two of these merely restated options already considered—a decrease in costs (Evidence 2 and 4) and protection (Evidence 5)—so the only new consideration was the
desirability of promoting confidence. Keynes's fourth proposal on home investment was to make lenders accept less.
How? A tax on foreign loans was one possibility; so was an
outright embargo upon them; and lower world interest rates
would clearly help, though to say this only reiterated the
desirability of international measures (Evidence 7). The residual means of influencing lenders turned on confidence,
already adumbrated as a factor influencing borrowers; and by
this route Keynes came to a specific Budget proposal. Confidence, he told MacDonald, should be sought by postponing
improvements in the social services, by looking for economies
in 'abuses of the dole', and finally—the square at the bottom
of every snake and the top of every ladder of Keynes's board
—tariffs (Evidence 5).

His third survey of the problem took shape in the Report
of the Committee of Economists for the Economic Advisory
Council in October 1930.[40] Keynes's influence upon the

[40] See Keynes's memorandum for the committee, dated 21 Sept. 1930, in
JMK, xiii. 178–200; his 'Proposal for tariffs plus bounties', 25 Sept. 1930, *JMK*,

report was considerable, but in its drafting he was in the hands of formidable professional colleagues, only one of whom (Stamp) was in full accord with him. That he managed to carry Pigou and Henderson with him in the final report, and Robbins for a good part of the way, is evidence of Keynes's adroitness in committee work rather than of like-minded unanimity between the experts. The marks show. Keynes seems to have bought assent for his proposals by accepting his colleagues' way of specifying the problem. Thus Keynes's draft of the report defined the remedies at the outset as confronting the problem of a disparity between wages and prices.[41] Forced to start from here, Keynes proceeded to classify the options in terms of their relevance to this relationship.

The initial class of remedies were those which permitted present wages to be paid: by tackling restrictive practices, conditions for the dole, and productivity (Evidence 4). Next came those which involved raising prices. This might be achieved through a rise in world gold prices or by a sterling devaluation (Evidence 1). An intermediate category followed, which gave Keynes plenty of elbow-room. It became, in the first place, a means of justifying measures to promote home investment—the 'confidence' package for the Budget, including tariffs (Evidence 5), fiscal incentives to favour domestic projects, and, of course, public works (Evidence 6). It also turned into an advocacy of ways of increasing investment abroad, one method again comprising tariffs (Evidence 5). Finally, it ushered in, naked and explicit, the tariff-bounty proposal (Evidence 3 and 5) which Keynes had been working out.[42] The final group of remedies were for wage cuts (Evidence 2 and 4). In Keynes's original scheme, the classes covering Evidence 3, 5, and 6 were preferred, with 1 better than those parts of 2 and 4 which implied wage

xx. 416-19; and the 'Draft Report', 4 and 6 Oct. 1930, *JMK*, xx. 423-50. The final report, 24 Oct. 1930, is printed in Howson and Winch, *The Economic Advisory Council*, pp. 180-227, which gives (pp. 71-2) an authoritative account of its composition.

[41] *JMK*, xx. 429 (draft report).
[42] 'Proposal for tariffs plus bounties', 25 Sept. 1930, *JMK*, xx. 416-19, introduced into section XII (b) of the Report, Howson and Winch, pp. 212-13.

cuts.[43] In the agreed Report, after concessions to Henderson and Pigou, the emphasis on wage cuts received fuller endorsement in Section VII, but Sections IX, X, and XI elaborated the variants under Keynes's umbrella category covering Evidence 3, 5, and 6.[44]

The fourth document stating Keynes's overall view on economic policy in this period is the Macmillan Report, published in June 1931, especially Addendum I as signed by Keynes and five other members. The Report accepts Keynes's account of the *modus operandi* of Bank Rate.[45] In other sections drafted by him, it rejects devaluation as inexpedient, and indicates the opening for government enterprise in breaking the vicious circle.[46] In the Addendum, Keynes was able to impose his own logic more cogently. He stated the alternatives as being: more exports, import substitution, or further home investment. The practical courses open to achieve this were three. First, real wages might be reduced. The available means were: devaluation, which was theoretically best fitted for this task (Evidence 1); tariffs and bounties (Evidence 3 and 5), which produced the same effects while not disturbing confidence; and a national treaty (Evidence 2), despite its practical difficulties. Second, there might be some control on imports or aid to exports—tariffs again (Evidence 5). Third, there might be an encouragement of home investment, requiring government initiative in such fields as housing, the re-equipment of staple industries, and railway electrification (Evidence 6). In the year or so since Keynes had outlined his seven options in evidence before the committee, therefore, the proposal for tariffs (Evidence 5) had been combined with bounties (Evidence 3) as a functional alternative both to devaluation (Evidence 1) and to a national treaty (Evidence 2); and was also advocated as a support for a public works programme (Evidence 6). Rationalization (Evidence 4) had

[43] *JMK*, xx. 429 (draft report).

[44] Moreover, even in section VII, Keynes largely succeeded in drawing the teeth of the wage-cut recommendation by adding his own summary (par. 51), in which clause (v) stated that 'every other remedy with any serious balance of argument in its favour should be tried first'. (Howson and Winch, p. 195.) This paragraph alone was put in the summary of conclusions (p. 219).

[45] Report of the Committee on Finance and Industry, Cmd. 3897 (1931), pars. 215 ff.

[46] Ibid., pars. 256, 316 (authorship from *JMK*, xx. 309).

faded considerably, meanwhile, and international measures (Evidence 7) looked even less promising as a short-term answer.

V

It can be seen, therefore, that, wherever Keynes began in analysing the problem, he always ended up with the same handful of remedies. He was constrained within these options by his commitment to the theoretical proposition of the *Treatise*, that '*if* our total investment (home *plus* foreign) is less than the amount of our current savings (i.e. that part of their incomes which individuals do not spend on consumption), then —in my opinion—it is absolutely certain that business losses and unemployment *must* ensue'.[47] True or false? 'I can only say', Keynes told Norman, 'that I am ready to have my head chopped off if it is false!'[48]

Which course Keynes advocated at any one time depended partly on what was taken as given. Saving exceeded investment because Bank Rate was too high. The only way to reduce it was by international action, which in this sense was at the top of the list as a theoretically sound long-term solution. But from a local point of view, it was at the bottom of the list as a likely source of relief. Devaluation was admitted to be the most direct means of escape from the shackles imposed by international commitments; but until the summer of 1931 Keynes accepted the existing exchange rate as given. This left four real options: rationalization, tariffs (and bounties), wage cuts, and public investment. *Something* had to be done. It was Keynes's opinion that 'we should probably abolish our existing economic system if present conditions looked like lasting indefinitely'.[49] As to which of the relevant policies should be tried, Keynes told MacDonald that 'the peculiarity of my position lies, perhaps, in the fact that I am in favour of practically all the remedies which have been suggested in any quarter'. It was the negative attitude that was unforgivable— 'the repelling of each of these remedies in turn'.[50]

[47] *JMK*, xx. 350 (Keynes to Norman, 22 May 1930); cf. *JMK*, v. 161–2.
[48] *JMK*, xx. 351 (Keynes to Norman, 22 May 1930).
[49] *JMK*, xx. 273–4 (comments on Brand's memorandum, 7 Apr. 1931).
[50] *JMK*, xx. 375 (answers to the Prime Minister's questions, 21 July 1930).

How far could economics be expected to provide the correct answers? Keynes held a generally high opinion of his calling and expressly urged that the Government should take professional advice. He encouraged the Prime Minister to appoint a committee consisting solely of professional economists, who had 'a language and a method of their own', so that issues could be properly isolated. 'There is no reason', he added, 'why the results should not be expressed in a manner intelligible to everyone.'[51] He stated more than once that economics was at an awkward transitional stage, making it difficult to expound to laymen.[52] Technical questions had to be settled among economists—not least whether the theoretical framework of the *Treatise* was generally acceptable.

Meanwhile, however, it was no good leaving everything to the experts. 'In a sense there are no experts', he told a radio audience in 1931.[53] So the fact that public works were 'agreeable to common sense' was a strong recommendation, although there were also some cases 'where uninstructed common sense tends to believe exactly the opposite of the truth'.[54] The worst combination was the sort of bastard economic reasoning he detected behind the Treasury View, 'half-way between common sense and sound theory; it is the result of having abandoned the one without having reached the other'.[55] Expert appraisal might properly be conceived as a filter, separating cogent propositions from plausible fallacies. The real choices could thus be made apparent through professional skill. But, as the Report of Economists put it, at this point 'wider considerations of policy must necessarily come in than those merely of economic cause and effect'; and on these, 'economists, like other people, differ among themselves'.[56] Likewise the Addendum to the Macmillan Report concluded that the ultimate differences were 'not so

[51] *JMK*, xx. 368 (Keynes to MacDonald, 10 July 1930).
[52] *JMK*, xx. 269 (Macmillan evidence, 5 Dec. 1930); 477 (lecture on 'The internal mechanics of the trade slump', 6 Feb. 1931).
[53] *JMK*, xx. 515 (CBS broadcast, 12 Apr. 1931).
[54] *JMK*, xx. 129 (Macmillan evidence, 6 Mar. 1930); 305 (Macmillan Report, Addendum I).
[55] *JMK*, xx. 130 (Macmillan evidence, 6 Mar. 1930).
[56] *JMK*, xx. 449–50 (draft report of committee of economists, Oct. 1930).

much matters of theory as of the practical judgement of probabilities and of what is most prudent'.[57]

Whereas Keynes's economic analysis endorsed a range of proposals as relevant to Britain's current predicament, his own political predispositions naturally affected the relative priorities which he assigned to them. Some remedies were innocuously uncontentious. Nearly everyone nodded approvingly when the desirability of rationalization or of international measures to promote recovery was preached. Conversely, nearly everyone shook their heads sagely when devaluation was mentioned. The other remedies, however, were more highly charged politically.

This was most obvious in the case of protection. For a quarter of a century the Conservatives had been identified with tariffs, while the Liberals were immemorially free traders. Hence the unmistakable *frisson* in the Macmillan Committee when Keynes revealed his sympathy for tariffs in his evidence of 28 February 1930.[58] He argued that protection was 'radically unsound, if you take a long enough view, but we cannot afford always to take long views . . .'. In treating protection as a technical question of this kind, rather than as a moral absolute, he immediately sensed himself to be on dangerous ground, confessing that it was 'extremely difficult for anyone of free trade origin, so to speak, at this juncture to speak in a way that he himself believes to be quite truthful and candid without laying himself open to misrepresentation and to being supposed to advocate very much more than he really does'.[59] The chairman delicately drew attention to the 'political considerations' and 'gibes about inconsistency' which this new topic was bound to arouse.[60] He was 'frankly rather concerned' about whether it fell within his committee's terms of reference, since 'a report dealing with tariff reform' would be 'an unexpected result of our appointment'.[61] Worthy recommendations about credit, banking, and finance were no doubt what Macmillan had envisaged, but it suddenly

---

[57] Cmd. 3897, Addendum I, par. 53; printed in *JMK*, xx. 307.
[58] *JMK*, xx. 113 ff.
[59] *JMK*, xx. 120 (evidence of 6 Mar. 1930).
[60] *JMK*, xx. 121 (ibid.).
[61] *JMK*, xx. 123 (ibid.).

came home to him that 'our Report might become a document of first-rate political importance'.[62]

A large part of Keynes's advocacy of tariffs was an attempt to dissipate the conventional political connotations of the issue. When he made a public declaration of his position in March 1931, he suggested that 'Free traders may, consistently with their faith, regard a revenue tariff as our iron ration, which can be used once only in emergency.'[63] The question then was whether the emergency had arrived, not whether the traditional free trade case had been misconceived. But the controversy he provoked was not, of course, conducted by such a reappraisal but by wheeling out the time-honoured maxims which had seen service against Joseph Chamberlain, not to mention Lord George Bentinck.[64]

Keynes concluded that 'new paths of thought have no appeal to the fundamentalists of free trade', who had forced him 'to chew over again a lot of stale mutton, dragging me along a route I have known all about as long as I have known anything', and which was nothing but 'a peregrination of the catacombs with a guttering candle'.[65] He was, however, fully ready to exploit the ideological purchase of the protectionist cry. Indeed he laid increasing emphasis upon it as a means of promoting confidence among business men because it matched their general prejudices. Keynes was hoping, moreover, to achieve a more ambitious finesse, by marrying his own proposals for public works with those for import duties. 'For the bad effect of the former on business confidence and on the foreign exchanges would be offset by the good effects of the latter; whilst both would increase employment.' In his own mind, this combination made good economic sense, with the principle being the same on both counts.[66]

---

[62] *JMK*, xx. 125 (ibid.).

[63] *JMK*, ix. 238 ('Proposals for a revenue tariff', *New Statesman and Nation*, 7 Mar. 1931).

[64] Cf. A. J. Balfour's complaint a generation earlier: 'Those who are protectionists are assumed to be protectionists after the manner of Lord George Bentinck. Those who are free traders are assumed to be free traders after the manner of Mr Cobden.' (*Economic Notes on Insular Free Trade*, London, 1903, p. 3.)

[65] *JMK*, xx. 505 (*New Statesman and Nation*, 11 Apr. 1931).

[66] *JMK*, xx. 488 (foreword to Rupert Trouton, *Unemployment: its causes and their remedies*, London, 1931); cf. 300–1 (Addendum to the Macmillan Report);

In the case of protection, Keynes was seeking to discuss it as a technical economic device, by ignoring its emotive political and social overtones. When it came to wage cuts, however, he acted in a contrary fashion. In the *Treatise* his analysis showed that an equilibrium rate of interest, appropriate to the needs of home investment and the foreign balance, was only feasible if 'the money rate of efficiency earnings of the factors of production' were flexible.[67] Since every other means of achieving this mobility had been covered under other heads, the remedy of income reduction stood as one prominent option every time Keynes had to produce an exhaustive list. He did not deny that the economic position would be improved by wage cutting: indeed the fact that 'the resistance to it has been tenacious and on the whole successful' was cited to explain 'why the phase of unemployment had been so exceedingly prolonged'.[68]

Keynes, however, never showed much stomach for breaking down this resistance. After the General Strike, when such a policy might have been feasible, 'Mr Baldwin decided—quite rightly—that it would be socially and politically inexpedient to take advantage of the situation in this way.'[69] Keynes repeated in 1930 that it was 'impracticable and undesirable to seek the remedy of reducing wages'.[70] In the *Treatise* he described an attempt to cut wages as 'a dangerous enterprise in a society which is both capitalist and democratic'.[71] He gave the Macmillan Committee his opinion 'that for centuries there has existed an intense social resistance to any matters of reduction in the level of money incomes'.[72] Listening to the employers' evidence, he found their unwillingness to recommend this solution 'truly remarkable', even when they had been pressed to fall back upon it.[73] The Addendum

386 (*Manchester Guardian*, 14 Aug. 1930); 416 (proposal for tariffs plus bounties, 25 Sept. 1930).

[67] *JMK*, v. 165.
[68] *JMK*, xix. 772 (book review in *Britannia*, 2 Nov. 1928).
[69] *JMK*, xix. 763 ('How to organise a wave of prosperity', *Evening Standard*, 31 July 1928).
[70] *JMK*, xx. 11 ('The question of high wages', *Political Quarterly*, Jan.–Mar. 1930).
[71] *JMK*, vi. 346.   [72] *JMK*, xx. 64 (evidence, 20 Feb. 1930).
[73] *JMK*, xx. 377 (answers to the Prime Minister's questions, 21 July 1930).

to the Report foresaw 'immense practical difficulties, perhaps insuperable difficulties', in the way of such cuts, and warned that 'the social costs of an attempt which failed would be incalculable'.[74] Keynes had, at the drafting stage, categorized such an endeavour as requiring 'the utmost determination and ruthlessness, an iron will, and a readiness to face, almost for certain, a violent social struggle'.[75] When he prepared a memorandum for the committee of economists, advocating the tariff-bounty proposal, he contrasted it with a direct attempt to reduce money wages, which could only be enforced 'as a result of a sort of civil war or guerilla warfare carried on, industry by industry, all over the country, which would be a hideous and disastrous prospect'.[76] In response to Hubert Henderson's charge that this was to run away from the problem, these references were cut out of the agreed report.[77] But in saying, during his exchanges with Henderson, that 'an assault on wages' represented a 'view which I have hitherto been rejecting and still on the whole, I think, reject',[78] Keynes had conveyed a disingenuous impression of the strength of his opposition. Did he merely think—'on the whole'—that 'a hideous and disastrous prospect' should be rejected?

Keynes's persistent approach was thus to admit the theoretical possibility of the wage-cut remedy but to discount it as impracticable. The requisite mobility of wage rates was simply 'not one of the alternatives between which we are in a position to choose. We are not offered it. It does not exist outside the field of pure hypothesis.'[79] Having closed this avenue, Keynes could blandly suggest that 'if we are to avoid putting wages lower we must look around for some other method'.[80] Thus, despite his readiness to admit that there was something in 'practically all the remedies that have been suggested in any quarter', he managed to 'twist and turn about' in a way that always led him away from the most widely canvassed

[74] *JMK*, xx. 308 (par. 53, iv).

[75] *JMK*, xx. 280 (notes on the majority draft, 20 May 1931).

[76] *JMK*, xx. 419 (25 Sept. 1930).

[77] Compare *JMK*, xx. 416-19, with Howson and Winch, pp. 212-15; Henderson's memorandum is in *JMK*, xx. 452-6.

[78] *JMK*, xx. 365 (Keynes to Henderson, 6 June 1930).

[79] *JMK*, xx. 497 (letter to the *New Statesman and Nation*, 16 Mar. 1931).

[80] *JMK*, xx. 322 (radio talk, *The Listener*, 26 Feb. 1930); he had argued in the same steps in a letter to *The Times*, 15 Aug. 1929, *JMK*, xix. 833.

common-sense remedy of all. As Henderson trenchantly noted on Keynes's draft for the economists' report, after half-recognizing the case for cuts, it 'runs right away from it, and proceeds to twist and wriggle and turn in a desperate attempt to evade the logic of the situation'.[81] Henderson, moreover, was surely right in identifying Keynes's politics as the fundamental explanation of the course taken in his economic reasoning.

VI

No one was better placed to acquire an insight into Keynes's political values than Hubert Henderson. He had been appointed editor of the *Nation* by Keynes in 1923, after the paper had been taken over as an organ of the sort of Liberalism with which the Summer Schools were associated. As editor and chairman of the board, the two men worked closely together. Keynes wrote for the *Nation* himself, and used it to launch his most telling public initiatives—especially, it may be noted, in bringing the issue of unemployment to the fore. In his economics Keynes was finding that the tradition in which he had been brought up was no longer relevant to the new problems of the 1920s. But the same was not really true in his politics. Despite the vicissitudes of the Liberal party in recent years, and despite the novelty of Labour's rise to office, Keynes's political outlook in the mid-1920s remained in essentials that of the new Liberalism which had flourished in the Edwardian period when he was a young man.

There are four salient respects in which Keynes can be identified with the new Liberalism. In the first place, he proclaimed the end of *laissez-faire*—'not enthusiastically, not from contempt of that good old doctrine', he claimed in 1924, 'but because, whether we like it or not, the conditions for its success have disappeared'.[82] Two years later he was pointing to the Conservative party as the place 'for those whose hearts are set on old-fashioned individualism and laissez faire in all their rigour'.[83] This decisive rejection of the

[81] *JMK*, xx. 453 (Henderson's memorandum, 13 Oct. 1930).
[82] *JMK*, xix. 228 ('A drastic remedy; reply to critics', *Nation*, 7 June 1924).
[83] *JMK*, ix. 300 ('Am I a Liberal?', *Nation*, 8 Aug. 1925).

economic navigation of the older Liberal tradition cleared the decks for a new agenda in politics.

Secondly, salvation could not be looked for in socialism and class warfare. Keynes therefore rejected, on the one hand, the theoretical prescription of doctrinaire state socialism, 'because it misses the significance of what is actually happening'. For example, he insisted that there was 'no so-called important political question so really unimportant, so irrelevant to the reorganisation of the economic life of Great Britain, as the nationalisation of the railways'.[84] On the other hand, he also rejected the class war as the appointed means of achieving socialism. He could 'conceive nothing worse for us all than a see-saw struggle on class lines between the Haves and the Have-Nots'.[85] Moreover, the appearance in the latter guise of trade-unionists—'once the oppressed, now the tyrants'— merely masked their 'selfish and sectional pretensions'.[86] Hence the fundamental inadequacy of this whole approach. 'I do not believe', he wrote in 1927, 'that class war or nationalisation is attractive or stimulating in the least degree to modern minds.'[87]

Thirdly, therefore, Keynes envisaged 'a reformed and remodelled Liberalism, which above all, shall *not*, if my ideal is realised be a *class* party'.[88] The experimental use of the state to achieve the ends of social justice did not imply a strategy of catastrophe but rather the application of hard thinking to see how the system could be made to work more acceptably. Keynes concluded 'that capitalism, wisely managed, can probably be made more efficient for attaining economic ends than any alternative system yet in sight, but that in itself it is in many ways extremely objectionable'.[89] Even when it functioned well, it was unfair; when it functioned badly, it became intolerable. Keynes was seeking 'the development of new methods and new ideas for effecting the transition from the

---

[84] *JMK*, ix. 290 ('The End of Laissez-Faire', 1926).

[85] *JMK*, xix. 324 (letter of support to the Liberal candidate in Cambridge, 18 Oct. 1924).

[86] *JMK*, ix. 309 ('Liberalism and Labour', *Nation*, 20 Feb. 1926).

[87] *JMK*, xix. 640 (speech on 'Liberalism and Industry', 5 Jan. 1927).

[88] *JMK*, xix. 441 (lecture on 'The economic transition in England', 15 Sept. 1925).

[89] *JMK*, ix. 294 ('The End of Laissez-Faire').

economic anarchy of the individualistic capitalism which
rules in Western Europe towards a regime which will deliberately aim at controlling and directing economic forces in the
interests of social justice and social stability'.[90]

Finally, this meant in practice that there was a large
amount of common ground between Liberalism and ordinary
or moderate Labour. If Liberals were 'inclined to sympathise
with Labour about what is just', then their task was 'to guide
the aspirations of the masses for social justice along channels
which will not be inconsistent with social efficiency'.[91] As
things stood in the mid-1920s, there was little immediate
likelihood of 'a progressive Government of the Left capable
of efficient legislation' unless co-operation with Labour was
established,[92] and Lloyd George's efforts in this direction
were a major reason why Keynes swung into his orbit, despite
the strong pull of old Asquithian loyalties.

These four corner-stones of the new Liberalism were built
into the foundations of Keynes's political thinking. He specifically described his aspirations as 'the true destiny of a New
Liberalism'[93]—an odd turn of phrase if it was merely a random choice of words. This outlook not only made him a
committed Liberal in party terms but also placed him self-
consciously on the left of the British political spectrum—'I
am sure that I am less conservative in my inclinations than
the average Labour voter', he reflected.[94] It meant, moreover, that Keynes looked on the Liberal party not as a route
to power (in which case 'I agree that one is probably wasting
one's time')[95] but rather as a means of putting policies on to
the political agenda. There was some consolation in 'supply-
ing . . . Labour governments with ideas'.[96] Keynes's stance,

[90] *JMK*, xix. 439 ('The economic transition in England', 15 Sept. 1925).

[91] *JMK*, xix. 639–40 ('Liberalism and Industry', 5 Jan. 1927).

[92] *JMK*, xix. 327 ('The balance of political power at the elections', *Nation*, 8 Nov. 1924).

[93] *JMK*, xix. 439 ('The economic transition in England'); cf. 647 ('Liberalism and Industry') and *JMK*, ix. 305 ('Am I a Liberal?'). The balance of historical evidence thus seems to me to invalidate the philosophically plausible view stated by Maurice Cranston, 'Keynes: his political ideas and their influence', in A. P. Thirlwall (ed.), *Keynes and Laissez-Faire*, London, 1978, pp. 111–14.

[94] *JMK*, ix. 308–9 ('Liberalism and Labour').

[95] *JMK*, xix. 733 (Keynes to J. L. Garvin, 9 Feb. 1928).

[96] *JMK*, ix. 310 ('Liberalism and Labour').

furthermore, gave a specific direction to his proposals on tackling unemployment. It is not just that these were first published in a Liberal journal, subsequently discussed under Liberal auspices, and increasingly identified as the policy of the Liberal party in the late 1920s: there are also indications that their origin was more political than economic.

Now it would be foolish to deny the centrality of the Gold Standard in conditioning Keynes's thinking on economic policy in these years; but all is not as it seems. When, in his advice on different occasions up to the summer of 1931, Keynes ruled out devaluation as a remedy, he was accepting Churchill's decision to return to Gold as a *fait accompli*. His advocacy of other courses, as has been seen, ran logically from this premiss. It is accordingly no surprise to find Keynes, in April 1929, defending his consistency by claiming 'that I began advocating schemes of National Development as a cure for unemployment four years or more ago—indeed, as soon as I realised that, the effect of the return to Gold having been to put our money rates of wages too high relatively to our foreign competitors we could not, for a considerable time, hope to employ as much labour as formerly in the export industries'.[97] He wrote in the same vein in May 1929 that, since the return to Gold, he had 'spent the four years trying to find the remedy for the transitional period and to persuade the country of its efficacy'.[98] His unemployment proposals could thus be viewed as an economic response to the imposition of the Gold Standard. There is only one snag in this account. Churchill announced the return to Gold in April 1925; Keynes's article, 'Does unemployment need a drastic remedy?', had been published in the *Nation* nearly a year previously, in May 1924.

Taking his cue from Lloyd George, Keynes in this article for the first time outlined proposals for national development as a cure for unemployment. The seeds of some of his most fruitful notions were planted here. He was already claiming that 'we must look for succour to the principle that *prosperity is cumulative*'. He contended that 'the mind must be averted' from wage cuts, in favour of seeking 'to submerge

[97] *JMK*, xix. 812–13 (letter to the *Evening Standard*, 30 Apr. 1929).
[98] *JMK*, xix. 824 (review of the Treasury White Paper, *Nation*, 18 May 1929).

the rocks in a rising sea'.[99] In response to his critics, he defied them to 'maintain that England is a finished job, and that there is nothing in it worth doing on a 5 per cent basis'.[100] Such notions were developed in a series of statements over the next five years or so, bringing Keynes into close co-operation with Lloyd George's efforts to revitalize Liberalism. Whatever Keynes's motives for becoming involved in a crusade against unemployment, mere chronology suggests that they cannot simply be ascribed to the economic consequences of Mr Churchill.

The Liberal proposals to cure unemployment, authoritatively outlined in the 'Yellow Book' of 1928, were peculiarly Keynes's responsibility.[101] He obviously intended that they should help the party electorally. The pamphlet he wrote with Henderson during the 1929 election campaign, *Can Lloyd George Do It?*, took a robustly partisan line and drew him directly into party political controversy. But the results of the 1929 election dealt a mortal blow to the Liberals' chance of power, and they were condemned to a peripheral role once MacDonald's Labour government took office. Keynes remained an advocate of the 1929 programme through thick and thin. 'I am keener than ever on schemes of home development', he wrote in May 1931, 'and indeed on much of the Yellow Book.'[102] For his collaborator, Henderson, however, the intervening period had been one of disillusionment and reappraisal, confronted with the responsibilities of his new post as secretary to the Economic Advisory Council.

Henderson's doubts surfaced by May 1930, when he told Keynes of his 'shifting of opinion from my position a year or so ago', i.e. the publication of *Can Lloyd George Do It?*. No longer believing a public works programme would be merely transitional, he denounced any impression that its cost would be trifling as 'a sheer fake and fraud'.[103] By October 1930

---

[99] *JMK*, xix. 221 ('Does unemployment need a drastic remedy?', *Nation*, 24 May 1924).

[100] *JMK*, xix. 228 (reply to critics, *Nation*, 7 June 1924).

[101] *Britain's Industrial Future*, London, 1928; for Keynes's contributions see *JMK*, xix. 731. There is a good account of this episode in John Campbell, *Lloyd George: the Goat in the Wilderness*, London, 1977, ch. 7.

[102] *JMK*, xx. 527–8 (Keynes to Aubrey Herbert, 29 May 1931).

[103] *JMK*, xx. 358 (Henderson to Keynes, 30 May 1930).

the world slump had convinced him that it was no use bilking 'the disagreeable reactionary necessity of cutting costs (including wages)'. Rather than face up to it earlier, he acknowledged that he had 'in recent years supported recourse to temporary expedients and makeshifts'; but he now found it 'impossible to maintain such an attitude any longer'.[104] He could not accept that public works were in any real sense an alternative. Keynes seemed to him in danger of 'going down to history as the man who persuaded the British people to ruin themselves by gambling on a greater illusion than any of those which he had shattered'.[105] Henderson, moreover, had no doubt about the explanation of this extraordinary perversity. It seemed to him that 'the really important issues' which had arisen to divide them were 'of a broad and almost temperamental nature'.[106] He told Keynes of his feeling that 'you're over-moved by a sense that it's inconsistent with your self-respect to accept anything savouring of a conservative conclusion'.[107] The plain moral of economizing was that 'drawn by the ordinary, conservative, unintellectual businessman', and it was no doubt 'disagreeable to admit that the ordinary businessman can possibly be right'.[108] If only Keynes had 'considered the question really objectively and without regard to Left prepossessions'![109]

VII

As Henderson must well have realized, a Keynes lacking 'prepossessions' would have trodden a different path from 1924 onward. By 1931, however, the claims of 'objectivity' were hardly likely to deflect him: rather the reverse. After the return to Gold, Keynes had once written 'I am trying with all my wits, now in this direction and now in that, to face up to the new problems, theoretically and practically, too'.[110] Theoretically, he had not at this juncture succeeded in estab-

---

[104] *JMK*, xx. 452-3 (Henderson memorandum, 13 Oct. 1930).
[105] *JMK*, xx. 364 (Henderson to Keynes, 5 June 1930).
[106] *JMK*, xx. 454 (Henderson memorandum).
[107] *JMK*, xx. 360 (Henderson to Keynes, 30 May 1930).
[108] *JMK*, xx. 452 (Henderson memorandum).
[109] *JMK*, xx. 363 (Henderson to Keynes, 5 June 1930).
[110] *JMK*, xix. 450 (*Manchester Guardian Commercial*, 2 Nov. 1925).

lishing much of a hold, at least as far as any justification for public works was concerned. In his early drafts of the *Treatise* he maintained that capital expenditure financed by public borrowing could 'do nothing in itself to improve matters' and might 'do actual harm'.[111] No hint here of a gap between savings and investment which state action could be summoned to close. As late as the summer of 1927 Keynes was commending the use of tax revenue so long as the Government 'itself *saves* it in some shape by diverting it into productive channels',[112] when the option of *investing* it in this way was how the *Treatise* would have made the point. It was at this stage that Keynes's activities as a publicist threatened to outrun even his formidable technical capacities as an economist. Although the author of *Can Lloyd George Do It?*, brimming with common sense and self-confidence, had been well into his stride by 1924, the author of the *Treatise* was still groping for the right words several years later. It was only when they were both summoned to appear before the Macmillan Committee that they turned out to be the same person.

---

[111] *JMK*, xiii. 23 (draft from 1924–5).
[112] Italics supplied. *JMK*, xix. 676 ('The Colwyn Report', *Economic Journal*, June 1927).

7

The Making of Unemployment Policy, 1931–1935

John Stevenson

I

'The word today written on the hearts of the British people and graven on their minds'—unemployment. So wrote Lloyd George in the Liberal 'Orange Book' of 1929, *We Can Conquer Unemployment.*[1] Few aspects of British policy between the wars have attracted more attention than the policies pursued by governments towards the issue of unemployment and the consequences of these policies for the standing army of never less than a million unemployed whose plight, with the conduct of foreign policy, was to provide by the eve of the Second World War one of the major indictments of the performance of British politicians in the 1930s. Certainly, the experience of the 'forced Keynesianism' of the war years and the high levels of employment enjoyed for thirty years after 1945 were to reinforce an interpretation of the nature and context of economic policy which had a relatively simple plot and uncomplicated characters. As in the debate over appeasement, the pursuit of the 'guilty men' of domestic policy in the 1930s drew heavily not only upon a genuine and often deeply felt concern for the consequences of the policies pursued by governments, but also upon the comforting reassurance of hindsight. Subsequent economic history seemed only to confirm what had been obvious to a progressive minority all along: that governments of blinkered and reactionary old men had conducted the wrong economic strategy in the face of the slump, had shown themselves unthinkingly harsh in their treatment of the unemployed,

---

[1] *We Can Conquer Unemployment: Mr. Lloyd George's Pledge*, London, 1929, p. 5.

and had sacrificed the unemployed and the depressed areas on the altar of financial and economic orthodoxy.[2]

This judgement and the record upon which it was based have come under closer scrutiny in recent years.[3] As so often with the development of historical research, fresh enquiry has proceeded in parallel with the growing volume of source materials. In one direction, the opening of the state papers for the inter-war years held at the Public Record Office, following the Public Records Act of 1967, provided the material for a much more detailed discussion of the evolution of policy in a wide range of fields, including economic and social affairs.[4] Further, the opening of the administrative record was matched by the availability of the cabinet papers and the systematic cataloguing of the papers of cabinet ministers, MPs, and officials.[5] A still unbroken wave of memoirs, diaries, and letters has also added considerably to the volume of material relating to the domestic politics and political processes in the 1930s.[6] At another level of political activity, the publications and behaviour of significant pressure groups, such as Political and Economic Planning, have now been more thoroughly explored, while the burgeoning of interest in 'Labour History', trade-unionism, and popular or would-be popular movements has provided a growing body of material relating to their impact upon policy-making.[7]

[2] For a typical statement of this view see, for example, N. Branson and M. Heinemann, *Britain in the Nineteen Thirties*, London, 1971, pp. 6–7: 'The Tory leadership of the period, indeed, was notably aged, backward-looking and inert.'

[3] See especially, D. Winch, *Economics and Policy: a historical survey*, London, 1969; J. Stevenson and C. Cook, *The Slump: society and politics during the Depression*, London, 1979.

[4] The Act introduced the so-called 'thirty-year rule', covering most classes of records for the inter-war years, though excluding certain categories of material. For a guide to the type of administrative material made available see B. Swann and M. Turnbull, *Records of Interest to Social Scientists, 1919 to 1939: Introduction*, Public Record Office Handbooks, No. 14, London, 1971.

[5] See C. Hazlehurst and C. Woodland, *A Guide to the Papers of British Cabinet Ministers, 1900–1951*, London, 1974, and C. Cook, with P. Jones, J. Sinclair, and J. Weeks, *Sources in British Political History*, 5 vols., London, 1974–.

[6] For a useful guide, see C. L. Mowat, *Great Britain Since 1914*, London, 1971, especially ch. 4.

[7] J. Pinder (ed.), *Fifty Years of Political and Economic Planning: looking forward, 1931–1981*, London, 1981; see also the annual bibliographies of material relating to the Labour movement in *The Bulletin of the Society for the Study of Labour History*.

Amidst this plethora of source materials, it might be supposed that historians have been in a superior position to
account for the actions of governments and the positions
taken up by individuals, particularly in relation to key areas
such as unemployment policy. The argument of this essay is
that this is not so, that the availability of a wider range of
source materials has, if anything, fragmented our understanding of the political processes at work in domestic policy after
1931 and that, rather than resolving controversy, the greater
availability of sources, allied to fresh angles of approach and
perspective, has served to expose important questions about
the way in which decisions were taken and policy formulated
in Britain during the 1930s. The purpose here is to examine
one main strand of policy between 1931 and 1935, that relating to unemployment, primarily with a view to assessing the
relevance of the systems of interpretations which have been
applied to politics in general.

II

The rationale and record of governments on unemployment
from 1931 has to be considered on more than one level. First,
there was the overall economic strategy, translated through
budgetary and fiscal policy; second, there were the ameliora-
tive measures specifically employed to deal with unemployment; third, there was the question of unemployment relief.
But although such a division makes for neat analytical categories, it has to be remembered that these layers of policy
were interdependent. The broad thrust of government
thinking about the economy, and concern for the exchange
rate and the trade and credit balances, had profound implications for the scale and nature of the assistance given to the
depressed areas, as well as for the level of unemployment
relief. Conversely, the sheer scale of the problem of unemployment by the early 1930s and the commitment of governments
of whatever persuasion to paying some form of unemployment relief, however exiguous, had important repercussions
for budgetary and fiscal strategy, and ultimately the government's credibility in managing the economy with confidence
and security. On occasion the tail could indeed wag the dog.

For example, it has not always been fully reflected in the literature that the summer crisis of 1931 which led to the dis-integration of the Labour cabinet and the formation of the National Government was not directly one of unemployment or industrial depression, but one mediated through the ques-tion of a deficit in the Unemployment Insurance Fund. As Sidney Pollard has written:

The Bankers and the Governments concerned were not trying to increase employment or salvage industry, but merely to right the unbalances of the budget, trade and credit. . . . The fault, if any, lay with the still general belief that the limits of Government economic action lay in pro-viding financial stability on the one hand and assisting those who fell into pauperism because of the failure of the economy to employ them on the other.[8]

The broad attitudes of governments of both parties were dominated from the late 1920s, if not earlier, by the belief that the problems facing the British economy and the un-employed were a result of the temporary dislocation of the world economic system caused by the First World War. During the 1920s a return to 'normalcy' in the form of a revival of the German economy, the creation of a sound basis for inter-national trade, including a restoration of the Gold Standard, and the fostering of business confidence were seen as the keys to economic recovery. According to prevailing econo-mic theory, long-term economic depression was impossible, because supply and demand would always tend to balance out within a market framework. As labour became available through unemployment, wages would fall, allowing more labour to be employed until an equilibrium was reached. Something approaching full employment was expected to be normal, providing the market mechanism was allowed to work properly. Although there were always likely to be groups marginal to the labour market who were employed in booms rather than slumps because of physical, mental, or moral weaknesses, problem groups of seasonal or casual wor-kers, or those thrown out of work because of some techno-logical change or the trade cycle, orthodox economic theory did not admit to large-scale, long-unemployment unless it

[8] S. Pollard, *The Development of the British Economy, 1914–1950*, London, 1962, p. 227.

was the product of exceptional circumstances. This view dominated thinking in both academic and governmental circles not only in the 1920s but for most of the inter-war years. The proper business of government was therefore seen to lie in reviving the market mechanism and restoring the financial stability and confidence of the years before 1914. While it was accepted that government could facilitate the labour market through labour exchanges and mitigate the worst effects of unemployment through unemployment insurance, the prevailing view was that the role of government lay primarily in providing the right conditions for the return to 'normalcy' rather than large-scale intervention in the economy.

Current economic opinion also stressed the need for a balanced budget, preferably one in which the government attempted to minimize its activities, covering the basic costs of defence, administration, and social services, but otherwise interfering as little as possible in the general running of the economy. Shortfalls in government revenue in relation to expenditure would have to be matched by increases in taxation. This desire to restrict government influence over the economy led time and time again to the pursuit of 'economy' in order to balance the books. Within this context, as well as the repercussions of 'economy' on such areas as defence, education, and the social services, there was constant pressure upon the level and terms of unemployment benefit, particularly as it came to play an important role in the total government budget. Moreover, budgetary orthodoxy also conditioned attitudes towards such solutions as public works or a massive injection of government funds to boost the economy. An Unemployment Grants Committee was set up as early as 1921, but the funds allocated to it were small and by 1928 provided work for only a tiny fraction of the unemployed. According to an official statement of policy in this area by the Treasury in 1929, reductions in unemployment were to be looked for in greater flexibility over wages, efficiency, and industrial change. Public works schemes diverted investment from its 'normal' channels into what were seen as inevitably less productive and efficient ones. As elsewhere in economic activity, 'normalcy' meant allowing the investment market to operate with the minimum of intereference from the state.[9]

In theory, at least, the Labour party might have been expected to pursue less orthodox policies. Its constitution of 1918 committed it to a socialist programme, and the provision of 'work or full maintenance' had been one of the earliest objectives of the Labour movement. At local level, in places such as Poplar, Labour leaders such as George Lansbury, in their role as local politicians, had backed this up in the early 1920s by championing the cause of the unemployed and offering the highest possible level of relief, which led, inevitably, to clashes with a central government bent on economy. But there were fundamental difficulties for the Labour governments of 1924 and 1929–31, in that, while committed to socialism, they were in fact operating within a capitalist system and accepted the orthodox economic and fiscal constraints which affected other inter-war governments.[10] As a result, the Labour party did little that was novel during its brief period of office in 1924 and, when it came to power in 1929, accepted the current orthodoxy that a balanced budget, a sound currency, and the restoration of business confidence were the priorities. Philip Snowden, the Labour Chancellor, was fully committed to the Treasury line and prepared to defend it with sincere conviction as the proper policy for any responsible government to pursue. Labour's policies were therefore confined to providing a rather more generous level of unemployment relief on less restrictive terms and a modest boost to public works. Through the Unemployment Grants Committee, Labour spent £77 million on public works, employing, with local authority schemes assisted by central government, no more than 200,000 people at their peak, less than a tenth of the unemployed. The limited scope of these schemes was, however, recognized by Snowden when in 1930 he told the House of Commons: 'You are never going to settle the unemployed problem, you are never going to mitigate it to any extent, by making work.'[11]

[9] Pollard, *Development of the British Economy*, p. 209.
[10] Skidelsky, *Politicians and the Slump*, London, 1967, pp. 422–34.
[11] Figures for the sums expended on public works and the numbers employed vary from one authority to another. These figures can, however, be regarded as at

In spite of the opposition of lesser Labour ministers such
as Oswald Mosley, the trade union leader Ernest Bevin, and
the economist J. M. Keynes, the Labour government steered
an orthodox economic course. Its break-up in 1931 was primarily the result of the clash between its commitments to
maintain a generous level of unemployment relief and the
pursuit by its leaders, MacDonald and Snowden, of an orthodox national economic policy. As the slump worsened, the
cost of unemployment benefit to the Government had risen
from £51 million in 1929 to £125 million in 1931 and was
causing serious disquiet in financial circles. If anything, the
Labour government had loosened the purse-strings further by
the Unemployment Act of 1930, which allowed people with
a minimum of contributions to claim benefit and abolished
the clause demanding that benefit be paid only to those
'genuinely seeking work'. Even so, half a million people were
receiving the 'transitional benefits' paid for by the Treasury,
having exhausted their entitlement to benefits under the
Insurance Scheme. The government's expenditure on unemployment benefit became the centre of the battle to restore
confidence in the economy. The May Committee Report,
published on 1 August 1931, recommended drastic economies to reduce the budget deficit. Cuts in government expenditure totalling £96 million were suggested, of which £66
million would be saved on unemployment relief. Faced with
a foreign exchange crisis which, it appeared, could only be
met by cuts unacceptable to the majority of the Cabinet, the
Labour government resigned in August 1931. While the
debate on MacDonald's so-called 'treachery' does not concern us here, it reflected none the less the general economic
orthodoxy of the leading Labour politicians between the
wars. MacDonald and Snowden were persuaded, in the
former's case by the King, that in a national crisis they had
a duty to remain in a new administration. MacDonald, himself, as his biographer David Marquand has made clear, was
convinced that only the orthodox line of 'economy' could

the higher level of estimates: see Pollard, *Development of the British Economy*,
p. 254; D. H. Aldcroft, *The Inter-War Economy: Britain, 1919–1939*, London,
1970, pp. 312–14.

save the country from a disastrous foreign exchange crisis and the threat of runaway inflation.[12]

The National Government formed on 24 August 1931 was to remain in power for the rest of the 1930s. Confirmed in office by a landslide victory in the general election of autumn 1931 and by a large majority again in 1935, it pursued the economic policies advocated by the Treasury, the great majority of academic economists, and the leaders of industry. Until Keynes's *General Theory* appeared in 1936 there was no obvious alternative strategy available, while the lessons offered by foreign countries were by no means clear. The examples of Fascist Italy, the USSR, and Nazi Germany represented totalitarian solutions to unemployment, often admired for their achievements, but politically unacceptable in Britain, while, in America, Roosevelt's 'New Deal' had yet to prove itself. Hence the main objectives the National Government set itself were governed by orthodox principles: to balance the budget, economize on government spending, and restore business confidence.[13] In response to the crisis of 1931 emergency measures were taken to raise extra taxation and to make economies; unemployment relief was cut and the means test introduced. Strict control was applied to such measures as public works, so that the limited schemes undertaken by the Labour government were effectively wound up in 1931–2 and most local authorities were forced to economize on relief expenditure during the worst years of the slump. The reasoning behind the government's policy of curtailing public works at the trough of the depression was revealed in cabinet discussions in 1932. A memorandum on unemployment submitted to the Cabinet emphasized the 'grave danger to the stability and prosperity of the country', but committed itself only to pursuing voluntary schemes which involved 'little capital cost to the nation'. The cabinet proceedings recorded the opinion that:

most of those who had been in office during the last five years were agreed that, whatever the past attractions of a public works policy, its application had been in many cases ill considered and its disadvantages now far outweighed such advantages as it might once have possessed.

[12] D. Marquand, *Ramsay MacDonald*, London, 1977, pp. 621–37.
[13] Pollard, *Development of the British Economy*, p. 209.

They continued:

Experience has taught us that they [relief works] do less good in the direct provision of work than harm in the indirect increase of unemployment by depleting the resources of the country which are needed for industrial restoration.

An allotment scheme undertaken with the help of the Society of Friends, physical education for men, and training in domestic service for women were seen as the only positive measures that could be taken. They suggested that voluntary agencies should concentrate upon teaching the unemployed clothing repairs, handicrafts, gardening, and other 'useful' occupations.[14]

The one initiative of the National Government concerning the unemployed was the Special Areas (Development and Improvement) Act, 1934. It was increasingly apparent that the problem of the older industrial areas would not be solved by a mere upturn in world trade. In 1932 industrial surveys of some of the most depressed areas were carried out by a number of universities and published by the Board of Trade. They concluded that the collapse of export markets and the exhaustion of local resources was such that there was little hope of revival in the staple industries on a sufficient scale to employ the resident work-force. As a result the Government appointed four special investigators to examine conditions in Scotland, west Cumberland, Durham and Tyneside, and South Wales. Their reports confirmed the picture shown by the Board of Trade studies. In spite of the revival which was beginning to be felt in the south-east and the midlands, these areas were still suffering from massive unemployment. Some areas of South Wales were described by Sir Wyndham Portal as 'derelict'; while Sir Arthur Rose calculated that the depressed areas of Scotland had a permanent 'surplus' of 64,000 men.[15]

Under the Act as it was implemented from 1934, two unpaid commissioners were appointed to co-ordinate 'the economic development and social improvement of the

[14] Public Record Office, CAB 27/490: Report of Unemployment Committee, 30 Sept. 1932 and Cabinet Minutes, pp. 1–12.
[15] Cmd. 4728, Ministry of Labour, Reports of Investigations into the Industrial Conditions in Certain Depressed Areas, 1934.

depressed areas' with the aid of a £2 million grant. Grants were also given to local authorities and to voluntary agencies, such as the National Council of Social Service, to initiate improvement schemes for water supply and sanitation, hospital building, and other amenities. Assistance and encouragement, too, was to be given to land resettlement schemes. Though help was given to some larger projects, such as the location of a new steel works in Ebbw Vale, there remained a widespread feeling that the funds and powers of the commissioners were inadequate for the purpose. By 1938, the commissioners had actually spent about £8.5 million, but only 121 new firms had been set up, creating 14,900 jobs. When he resigned as commissioner in November 1936, Sir Malcolm Stewart admitted that 'no appreciable reduction of the number of unemployed has been effected'. Eventually the Government did extend the powers of the commissioners by the Special Areas (Amendment) Act, 1937, to allow them to remit rates, rent, and taxes for firms settling in the Special Areas. Trading estates were set up with all facilities laid on, in which firms could lease premises. Those at Treforest in South Wales, Team Valley, near Gateshead, and North Hillington, near Glasgow, provided work for over 5,000 people by the outbreak of the war. None the less, fewer than 50,000 new jobs were created under the Special Areas legislation. Many areas, such as Lancashire, for example, were left outside the scope of the legislation, and the policy had an air of expediency rather than that of a well-considered and whole-hearted attempt to solve the problems of the depressed areas.[16]

In order to relieve something of the labour surplus in older industrial areas an industrial transfer programme had been inaugurated by the Ministry of Labour in 1928. The scheme aimed to give financial assistance for the transfer of people from the depressed areas to more prosperous regions. Training centres to teach the adult unemployed new skills were established, and there were also separate Juvenile Instruction Centres. Between 1929 and 1938 the centres handled over 70,000 men, of whom 63,000 found work. Another 100,000 were covered by centres in the depressed areas which were

[16] Pollard, *Development of the British Economy*, pp. 132–3; Aldcroft, *Inter-War Economy*, p. 103.

intended to restore the morale and fitness of the long-unemployed. It has been calculated that a third of the latter received employment up to 1938. Between 1928 and 1937, 190,000 people were assisted to transfer to other areas, of whom over a quarter eventually returned to their home area. Transference was a natural corollary of the National Government's policy, easing the flow of labour from areas where it was not required to the regions in which industry was more buoyant. The policy was adopted by the Commissioners for the Special Areas. Sir Malcolm Stewart wrote:

> Transference of individuals and families out of the Special Areas must in my view be regarded as one of the essential measures of relief. My policy is, therefore, aimed at making clear the desirability of encouraging the younger persons to take every opportunity of obtaining employment outside the areas.[17]

In the six years 1927-33 almost 20,000 juveniles under the age of 18 were transferred from the depressed areas. Almost the same number were transferred in the three years 1934-6, reaching a peak in 1936 when 16,000 juveniles were involved. The effects of transference, however, can be exaggerated. Even at its peak it was overtaken by the much larger volume of voluntary migration. Moreover, it was most difficult to operate when it was most needed, in the early thirties; the Cabinet recorded in 1932 that owing to the difficulty in obtaining jobs even in prosperous areas it was being forced to consider closing all Transfer Instruction Centres. The areas from which the transfers were drawn also felt that they were being drained of their youngest and most active workers by the scheme.[18]

The National Government regarded most of these schemes as temporary expedients to meet an exceptional emergency. Its policies came to be regarded as mistaken, in that in pursuing deflation in the face of depression, it worsened rather than alleviated the problem of unemployment. Hindsight was to suggest that the Keynesian solution of government-led expansion, or that practised *ad hoc* by countries such as

---

[17] Quoted in W. Hannington, *The Problem of the Distressed Areas*, London, 1937, pp. 116-17.

[18] See, for example, the comments in J. Gollan, *Youth in British Industry*, London, 1937, pp. 170-2.

Sweden, offered a better approach, but it is also the case that, up to the 1940s, from the standpoint of a majority of economic experts, the National Government ploughed its economic furrow with a dull obstinacy which, while it infuriated opponents, nevertheless retained a logic and coherence. Even some of the sternest critics of British society in the 1930s were prepared to admit by the late 1930s that the National Government had, on its own terms, seen Britain through the worst effects of the slump.[19]

III

At this level, Donald Winch has argued that the dominant feature of British economic policy-making in the 1930s was its fragmentation: recovery was sought piecemeal. Capital expenditure solutions for unemployment were repeatedly rejected or so curtailed as to demonstrate government's unwillingness to consider them as the appropriate means for coping with the problem of unemployment. Winch cites Runciman, President of the Board of Trade, at the World Economic Conference in July 1933, restating the Treasury view on a scheme for a co-ordinated expansion of demand: 'We have terminated our schemes for dealing with unemployment by way of capital expenditure works, and we shall not reopen these schemes, no matter what may be done elsewhere.' Nor had attitudes changed significantly by January 1935 when Lloyd George sought to place himself at the head of a progressive movement closely modelled on Roosevelt's New Deal policies. In stating the Government's position, Chamberlain reasserted the orthodox view on increased expenditure on a public works programme:

There may be circumstances when it is right and sound to follow a policy of that kind, but not for the purpose of providing employment, because the whole experience of the past shows that, for the purpose of providing employment, this policy of public works is always disappointing. In that respect the experience of this country is no different from that of other countries which have tried the same thing. . . . The quickest and most effective contribution which any Government can

[19] Stevenson and Cook, *The Slump*, pp. 280–1.

make towards an increase of employment is to create conditions which will encourage and facilitate improvements in ordinary trade.[20]

Again, towards the end of 1937, fears that a renewed downturn in the economic cycle was imminent led to a campaign mounted in the Economic Advisory Council by Keynes and other prominent individuals such as Sir Arthur Salter, H. D. Henderson, and Sir Josiah Stamp, supported by *The Times*, and by a letter signed by a number of Oxford economists, for the Government to undertake a public works policy, received scant attention from Ministers.[21]

Such persistent resistance to any departure from orthodoxy has led Frederic M. Miller, in an important article, to argue that the National Government did, in fact, have an unemployment policy, but one which was regarded as so totally wrongheaded in progressive circles by the late 1930s and so completely eclipsed by the pro-Keynesian consensus following the war years, that it has been obscured. This policy, according to Miller, was the 'free enterprise' approach, which had two principal characteristics:

First, the government's policy of minimal direct intervention to relieve unemployment was directed towards achieving its central objective of ensuring that the depression would cause no fundamental changes in existing economic and social relationships. Immediate political considerations were subordinated to this overriding goal. Secondly, the government's approach, though not all of its particular actions, was based on a rational, comprehensive and widely accepted theoretical framework.[22]

Working primarily from the cabinet papers, Miller has described the National Government's approach to the unemployment problem as 'based on a fatalistic view of the economy combining short term optimism and longer term pessimism' in which the Conservative ministers who dominated domestic policy after the victory of the National Government in 1931 accepted the premiss that the 'Great Crash' of 1929–30 was a cyclical phenomenon which would reverse itself, while unemployment would still remain high because of the structural

[20] Winch, *Economics and Policy*, pp. 220–2.
[21] Ibid., pp. 222–3.
[22] F. M. Miller, 'The Unemployment Policy of the National Government, 1931–1936', *Historical Journal*, 19. 2 (1976), 453.

basis of unemployment: 'Ever since the 1928 report of the Industrial Transference Board, it had been recognised by senior civil servants and leading Conservatives and Liberals that the collapse of the old export staples would leave about 300,000–500,000 unemployed for many years.' This was the basis for Chamberlain's estimate in 1932 that irreducible medium-term unemployment, including normal 'frictional' unemployment, might be as high as one million.[23]

Although the National Government repeatedly sought the awaited 'turning-point' in the trade cycle, a search which obtained some degree of encouragement from the revival of world trade from 1933 and, by the mid-1930s, a spurt into a level of domestic economic growth which has been described as 'the largest and most sustained period of growth in the whole of the inter-war period',[24] an underlying 'pessimism' ran through the whole period, founded essentially on fears about the implications of demographic trends and the inevitable return of a downswing in the economic cycle.[25] The Government's own predictions in 1934 were that unemployment would average almost as much in 1940 as it had in 1932: approximately a fifth of the employed working population. Hence Miller concludes:

The obvious implication was that, despite disclaimers, the cabinet would never be able to turn with a clear mind to the problem of structural unemployment (the depressed areas) let alone deal with the 'normal' 3 per cent frictional unemployment, for another general crisis was inevitable, and excessive government spending could set it off prematurely.[26]

Assisted by a policy of protection, the reduction of interest rates, and the abandonment of the gold standard, the National Government was able to claim, without obvious hypocrisy, that it was doing the best it could to steer the economy through deep, perilous seas. The emphasis, however, was less upon the 'management' of the economy in the sense in which Keynesians understood it, than it was upon a responsible attitude on the part of the Government towards

---

[23] Miller, 'Unemployment Policy of the National Government', p. 455.
[24] Aldcroft, *Inter-War Economy*, p. 44.
[25] Miller, 'Unemployment Policy of the National Government', pp. 456–7.
[26] Ibid., p. 456.

budgetary and fiscal policy. Two of the most important sources
of recovery in the mid-1930s, the housing boom and falling
commodity prices, owed little to the actions of government.
Nor did the committees appointed to deal with improving
employment prospects devote much attention to foreign
trade, cheap money, or the development of industrial car-
tels.[27] Primarily, the sphere of government activity was seen
as maintaining a policy of minimum intervention in line with
the majority of economic advice.

IV

In this context, the system of unemployment relief provided
a crucial element in respect both of the effects of the depression and of the politics of the unemployment question. As
early as 1921 a majority of industrial workers were covered
by the National Insurance scheme introduced in 1911 and
greatly extended as a consequence of the First World War.
The terms under which unemployment benefit was given
when Britain first began to experience mass unemployment
in the early 1920s offered a sum of money equal to about a
third of the average wage, with six weeks of contributions
required for each week of benefit, up to a maximum of fifteen weeks. Workers had to prove themselves available for
work by 'signing on' every day at the labour exchange during
working hours. Several large groups of workers lay outside
the provisions of National Insurance, notably agricultural
workers, domestic servants, and the self-employed. Up to
1929, if unemployed and without other means of support,
these groups had to rely upon the Poor Law and, thereafter,
on the Public Assistance Committees of the local authorities.
This system of unemployment relief, however, soon ran into
serious difficulties. As unemployment rose to unexpectedly
high and persistent levels during the 1920s, a series of acts
were passed to provide levels of benefit outside those originally provided under the insurance scheme. Workers who had
not paid enough contributions to qualify for 'standard benefit', or had exhausted their benefit allowance of 15 weeks
(extended to 26 in 1921), qualified for special payments,

[27] Miller, 'Unemployment Policy of the National Government', p. 459.

variously termed uncovenanted benefit (1921), extended benefits (1924), transitional benefits (1927), and transitional payments (1931), paid in anticipation of future contributions. These *ad hoc* solutions destroyed the actuarial basis of the unemployment insurance fund and demonstrated the failure of the original schemes of 1911 and 1921 to cope with the extent of unemployment between the wars.[28]

By 1931 the burden of financing unemployment benefit was costing the Government £125 million per year, only £44 million of which was being met by contributions. Recognition that the exceptional nature of unemployment had outstripped the original insurance scheme was contained in the next phase of legislation, the Unemployment Assistance Board Acts of 1934-5. Under these measures, the locally paid transitional payments were to be funded by the Treasury out of general taxation, and responsibility for the payments was to be taken over by a new body, the Unemployment Assistance Board. The Board applied uniform rates and a standardized means test, both to those who had exhausted 'standard benefit' and to those who fell outside other provisions. The Unemployment Assistance Board represented an important attempt to rationalize provision for the unemployed. The introduction of the new regulations, however, provoked an outcry when it was found that the rates to be paid were sometimes lower than the locally administered transitional payments. A Standstill Act had to be introduced in February 1935, modifying the operation of the scheme so that the old rates were kept wherever they were more favourable and delaying the absorption of people relieved under the Public Assistance Committees into the UAB scheme. Not until 1937 were the majority of the unemployed relieved under the PACs transferred to the UAB.

The existence of a system of unemployment benefits played a crucial part in the politics of unemployment policy. The provision of some kind of unemployment pay provided an important pre-condition for the pursuance of a non-interventionist strategy towards the economy by maintaining the majority of the unemployed at a subsistence or near-subsistence level.

[28] B. B. Gilbert, *British Social Policy 1914-1939*, London, 1970, especially chs. 2 and 4.

During the 1920s nice observance of insurance principles was virtually cast aside and benefit rights extended to all the insured class on practically the same terms as to those who conformed to the original insurance contract. The addition of dependants' benefit from 1921 also indicated a wider application of insurance to provide something approaching a full maintenance payment. Faced with the alternative of turning anything up to half a million under-insured unemployed on to the Poor Law, benefit as a right, without enquiry into means, had been extended to practically anyone who could prove that he had worked in an insured trade at some time. In the words of one contemporary expert on unemployment insurance this was the crucial period when unemployment benefit became part of the 'moral economy' of sections of the working classes:

> The rates of benefit were raised, lowered and raised again. . . . It was not their sumptuousness that made benefits attractive; it was the fact that they could be drawn as a legal right without inquiry into personal circumstances. These were the years when British workers acquired the habit of possessing this legal right to a fixed sum during unemployment. They came to regard the local employment exchange as a bank where, subject to the rules, they always had a balance, and this sense of rights entered into the very grain of British social life. The money they could draw might be far less than their needs, or they might not need it at all. In the former case only the very exceptional family applied to the poor law for a supplementary aid. The majority carried on somehow.[29]

Thus, in contrast to most other countries, Britain had already established by 1931 a system of unemployment benefit in large part independent of a means test. Indeed, according to R. C. Davison, the idea of such a test came to be viewed with 'a fierce repugnance':

> To the typical independent British worker, insurance benefit was welcome, but after the experience of those early post-war years, allowances which depended upon the result of a home visitation and the assessment of house-hold income were psychologically and ethically distasteful.[30]

Under these circumstances it was almost inevitable that one area in which political disturbance would occur was over the issue of entitlement to benefit as in the application of the

[29] R. C. Davison, *British Unemployment Policy: the modern phase since 1930*, London, 1938, pp. 5–6.

[30] Ibid., p. 6.

means test in 1931-2 and over the level of scales in the UAB crisis of 1934-5.

But while sensitivity to the nature and level of unemployment relief was something which forced itself into all political and economic calculations, the provision of unemployment relief acted not only to retain a degree of moral legitimacy for a policy of 'natural recovery' but also a critical outwork of government policy over which the major political battles could often be fought without seriously affecting the main thrust of policy. Miller has put the point succinctly: 'When sorely pressed or in the streets, the government made marginal improvements in the relief system and preserved its limitation on public capital expenditure.'[31] This had a bearing upon the whole conduct of policy towards the unemployed and helps to account for what must be regarded as one of the most significant features of the whole unemployment question between the wars, namely its relatively small and episodic impact upon both the political process and the conduct of day-to-day politics. The issue raised by this statement is a fundamental one, going to the heart of perceptions of the political process as a whole. Historians have inevitably interpreted the role of unemployment policy within the context of their own framework of belief as to how decisions are taken and what they perceive as the decisive arena of political action: be it the streets, the House of Commons, the Civil Service, the Cabinet, or even a smaller group of 'top' politicians.

It was perhaps hardly surprising that contemporary activists in unemployed movements should credit themselves with a decisive influence upon the behaviour of the Government. There does, however, appear to be rather more evidence of this on some occasions than others. For example, the first major wave of protest over unemployment came with the application of the National Economy Orders of 1931. Under two Orders in Council the new National Government took up the economy campaign on unemployment relief which had destroyed the Labour Cabinet: namely a 10 per cent cut in benefit scales and the introduction of a means test on the non-contributory or transitional benefit section, applying to those who had exhausted their statutory entitlement or

[31] Miller, 'Unemployment Policy of the National Government', p. 454.

failed to qualify for it—precisely the category to whom benefits had been so generously extended in the 1920s. The National Economy Orders effectively put unemployment insurance benefits on a two-tier basis, differentiating between insurance benefit drawn as of right, and the supplementary transitional scheme operating on the basis of need. As well as the reduction in rates and in duration for the statutory unemployment benefit, claimants had to prove thirty contributions in the two years preceding the claim, that is that they had worked thirty weeks in the available time. These restrictions excluded over half the registered unemployed, so that over a million claimants were transferred to a system of means-tested relief. No one in this group was entitled to draw more than his benefit rate, including the fixed dependants' allowances, but could draw less or nothing at all, according to the amount of personal or household resources. The 'means test' was to attract a notoriety and bitterness which has barely abated fifty years later. While it undoubtedly took on a symbolic significance for those campaigning on behalf of the unemployed, and was to be translated into the mythology of the Labour movement, there is ample evidence that the means test aroused deep hostility amongst a large section of the unemployed. In part, this was because many of the people subjected to the 'test' were coming under scrutiny for the first time. Skilled workers and sections of the 'respectable' working class now found themselves undergoing a household investigation by the local Public Assistance Committee, the successors to the Poor Law Guardians. Clearly, for many, the transfer to a body tainted with the relief of 'pauperism' and the household investigation provided a genuinely bitter experience. Complaints of people being disallowed benefit or having it reduced to very low levels were legion.[32] Moreover there was something of a revolt amongst those charged with administering the system, the local Public Assistance Committees. Several Labour-controlled authorities refused to operate the new regulations at all, but were also joined in opposition by a number of independent or Conservative-controlled PACs.[33] Hence, by the winter of

---

[32] Stevenson and Cook, *The Slump*, pp. 68–70.

[33] Ibid., pp. 69–70; Branson and Heinemann, *Britain in the Nineteenth Thirties*, pp. 27–8.

1931–2 it was clear that there was considerable discontent among some sections of the unemployed, not only because they were out of work but also because of the rates and operation of unemployment relief. There was manifest dissatisfaction from sections of local government, from the Labour party and the TUC, and from sympathetically inclined Conservative MPs.[34] Extra-parliamentary protest was mobilized by the communist-led National Unemployed Workers' Movement. Agitation on the issue of relief rates and their administration provided the background to a series of demonstrations during 1931 and 1932, including a national hunger march to London. The autumn and winter of 1931 witnessed a number of clashes between police and unemployed demonstrators, reaching a climax in the autumn of 1932 when there was serious rioting in Belfast and Birkenhead, and in London, upon the arrival of the NUWM's National Hunger March to present a million-signature petition calling for the abolition of the Means Test and the restoration of the 10 per cent cut in unemployment relief. In some respects this was an impressive campaign by the NUWM which by 1932 was claiming up to 100,000 members. The organization and mobilization of people concerned about unemployment was effective in reaching public opinion as well as impinging itself upon the police, whose concern for public order led them not only into conventional policing operations but also into infiltration of the movement.[35]

The impact of this activity in 1931–2 upon policy-making and the actions of government, however, was strictly limited. In many respects, the NUWM campaign fell a prey to a problem familiar to extra-parliamentary movements before and since. The difficulties involved in employing the 'moral force' of a mass petition to parliament backed up by large-scale demonstrations were as ruthlessly exposed for the NUWM in 1932 as they had been for the Chartists at Kennington Common, eighty-four years earlier. In fact, pursuing what was, in effect, a militant, but cautiously conceived policy of mass

[34] Miller, 'Unemployment Policy of the National Government', pp. 460–1.

[35] See R. Hayburn, 'The Police and the Hunger Marchers', *International Review of Social History*, 17 (1972), and J. Stevenson, 'The Politics of Violence' in G. Peele and C. Cook (eds.), *The Politics of Reappraisal, 1918–1939*, London, 1975.

demonstrations, the NUWM risked falling between two stools, courting sufficient disapprobation to lose it 'respectable' support, principally from the official TUC and Labour party leadership, and the serious disruption of police surveillance, arrest, and obstruction, while failing to make any decisive impact upon the government.[36]

This is confirmed by the political response of the National Government in 1932 to the call of the NUWM and other groups for some decisive action. The extra-parliamentary agitation was easily isolated as a public order question, in which the NUWM was publicly charged with mischievous and subversive intent and treated accordingly. Attempts by the NUWM to press its campaign seemed only to end in bans, baton charges, or arrests. During 1932 no less than 400 of the movement's activitists had been arrested, including the major part of its executive committee. Elsewhere, criticism within parliament was met by the formation of a new cabinet committee on unemployment in September 1932. It was, on the whole, a low-key affair, chaired by a Parliamentary Secretary, Lord De La Warr, but excluding the Chancellor of the Exchequer, Neville Chamberlain. Firmly rejecting the call for a capital expenditure programme, the committee's main response lay in a grant of £10,000 towards the expenses of the National Council of Social Service in providing occupational centres for the unemployed. It was quite deliberately conceived as doing in one step something to prevent the physical deterioration of the unemployed and as a means of forestalling demands for heavier expenditure of other kinds.[37] Combined with minor adjustments to the rules for granting unemployment relief, highlighted in some of the protests from PACs, there was little else that the committee felt able to do within the confines of its broad economic strategy.[38] Similarly, projects put before a new and more important cabinet committee on trade and employment by an advisory panel of industrialists and business men foundered on the

[36] J. Stevenson, 'The Politics of Violence', pp. 161–4.

[37] CAB 27/490: Report of Unemployment Committee, September and October 1932.

[38] The Transitional Payments (Determination of Need) Act of 1932 instructed local authorities to disregard 50 per cent of any disability pension or workmen's compensation while savings of up to £25 were not to be counted against benefit.

arguments of Chamberlain and Horace Wilson that government spending had to be kept to an absolute minimum. It
would not be a difficult argument to sustain that the extra-
parliamentary agitation of 1931-2 had a minimal impact
upon the decisions taken by government. If we have any definite evidence about effective pressures leading to concession
or movement, they appear to lie in the reactions of the
government's supporters rather than its critics.

V

Once unemployment began to decline from the spring of
1933 something of the pressure to act was taken off the
government. For almost a year there was no major debate
on unemployment in the House of Commons. The year
1934-5, however, was to witness one of the most interesting
and suggestive episodes arising out of unemployment in the
period, the crisis surrounding the Unemployment Assistance
Board Act. The attempt to set up a centralized system for
the payment of unemployment benefits had its origins in a
desire both to rationalize the confusing patchwork of unemployment benefits and to defuse the political complications arising from the unwillingness of some local authorities
to implement the means test regulations. Bentley B. Gilbert
has noted that as early as 15 October 1932 Neville Chamberlain indicated in his private correspondence that he and the
Minister of Labour were at work on a scheme to remove the
relief of the able-bodied unemployed from the local authorities and to put it 'outside of party politics'.[39] By the end of
1932 the civil servants in the Treasury and in the Ministry of
Labour were at work on the new machinery to administer
unemployment benefit. Part I of the Unemployment Act,
setting up an Unemployment Insurance Statutory Committee, independent of the Treasury, to supervise the unemployment insurance fund and putting the financial basis for the
new unemployment benefits on a fresh footing, proved
straightforward enough. Part II of the act establishing a
national Unemployment Assistance Board to administer
benefits proved more contentious. It is a significant indication

[39] Gilbert, *British Social Policy*, pp. 177-9.

of the role of unemployment benefit as the main area for
conflict over unemployment that the debate on Part II of
the Unemployment Act occupied twenty-seven days of discussion, the longest period spent on any single piece of legislation before the House since the First World War. Once it
was passed, one of the most difficult problems lay in devising
new, universal scales of benefit. Chamberlain presided over
the committee drawing up the new scales, making adjustments for rent and special circumstances and ending a mass
of local anomalies. Debates on the new scales were held in
December 1934, and while there was some concern from
Labour members that the scale for transitional benefits was
below that being currently paid by some Public Assistance
authorities, the issue attracted relatively little attention, and
the Government's declaration that the unemployed would be
better off as a result of the new scheme was widely accepted.
The UAB was to assume responsibility for two main groups
of unemployed on specific 'appointed days'. On 7 January
1935 the UAB was to take over the 800,000 unemployed
receiving transitional payments and on 1 March another
200,000 relieved by the Public Assistance Committees.[40]
Protest began in the second week of January, especially in
Wales and the North. The new scales in these areas were
quickly found to fall below those already being received. By
the last days of January a large-scale wave of protest was
taking place in South Wales. A demonstration of 50,000 in
the Rhondda on 20 January was followed on the 27th by
demonstrations by an estimated 100,000 people. During the
following week the volume of protest increased. On 3 February an estimated 300,000 people were marching and demonstrating in South Wales. Complaints also flowed in from other
areas of high unemployment, especially Scotland, Cumberland, Lancashire, and Durham. The protests were also becoming more widely based as trade unions, local authorities, local
Labour party branches, and groups sympathetic to the unemployed joined in the clamour.[41]

When Parliament reassembled on 28 January 1935 it was

[40] Gilbert, *British Social Policy*, pp. 178–84.
[41] F. M. Miller, 'The British Unemployment Assistance Crisis of 1935', *Journal of Contemporary History*, 14 (1979), 335–8.

against a background of widespread complaint and indignation. The Minister of Labour, Oliver Stanley, found himself
attacked on all sides over the operation of the new scheme.
Many government supporters joined in the criticism of the
act, forcing Stanley into hasty negotiations with the Board
as to how to revise the scales and avert the crisis. Faced with
a major political crisis in parliament and a growing volume of
protest outside, Stanley was forced on 5 February to announce
a legal standstill authorizing relieving officers to apply whichever scales were most favourable to the applicant. Within
eight days a Standstill Act was rushed through the House of
Commons regularizing the position. The attempt to take the
unemployment issue 'out of politics' had ended in dismal
failure, indeed it had produced one of the most severe defeats
of any government in the inter-war years.

The interpretation of these events and their significance
has followed closely the spectrum of analyses offered by historians as to how the political process operated. Some have
stressed the role of the street demonstrations in effecting a
reversal of policy. This has been emphasized by the historians
of the South Wales Miners' Federation, who have noted that
Stanley's decision followed the day after the first major
violence of the campaign in South Wales when, during a
women's march on the UAB offices in Merthyr Tydfil, the
building was ransacked and its windows broken. Clearly
implying the direct effect of the popular movement in South
Wales upon the decision, they conclude: 'It [the standstill
order] was a great victory, the only time in the 1930s when
direct action caused a government to change its course and
capitulate to demands from outside Parliament.'[42] F. Miller
in his case-study of the UAB crisis has also emphasized this
point, arguing that although Parliament was the 'means by
which the force of the protest was conveyed to the Government it reacted only after massive demonstrations took place
in South Wales and Scotland and began to spread elsewhere'.[43]
Miller's account of the crisis, however, is capable of bearing
a different interpretation, especially his stress upon the

---

[42] H. Francis and D. Smith, *The Fed: A History of the South Wales Miners in
the Twentieth Century*, London, 1980, p. 261.
[43] F. M. Miller, 'The British Unemployment Assistance Crisis of 1935', p. 331.

importance of the Northern Tory Group and the negotiations between ministers and the UAB in the days up to the
standstill order. Within the context of a more wide-ranging
analysis of the significance of the UAB crisis, Middlemas has
also given credence to the direct impact of popular disorder
upon the decision of the Government to concede, writing:

> Uproar in the House of Commons may have had some impact, but on
> the evidence available, including the post-mortem after Stanley's inevit-
> able resignation, the two main reasons were discovery that the actuarial
> basis of the scales had been wildly wrong and the fear of very wide-
> spread popular unrest involving over one million of the unemployed.
> The decisive factor may have been the events of 5 February in Sheffield,
> when 10,000 demonstrators crowded into the main shopping streets
> outside the City Hall; the Riot Act was read, troops were assembled,
> and the revolutionary spectre of 1919 briefly reappeared. Until then,
> Stanley and Chamberlain were inclined to fight; after, they accepted
> responsibility for the débâcle.[44]

The plausibility of this explanation, however, is somewhat
diminished because the so-called 'decisive factor', the disturbances in Sheffield, did not in fact take place on the day
Middlemas states, the 5th, the day of the standstill, but on
the 6th, the day *after*.

More generally, the difficulty with analyses which place
so much emphasis upon the threat of disorder as the principal
factor in the Government's decision on the issue beg the
question of why the Government gave way on this occasion
but not on others, for example in the agitation over the
means test in 1931–2. Historians who wish to emphasize the
role of popular agitation in forcing the hand of the Government in 1935 must inevitably stress the scale of the protest
movement in that year compared with earlier years. This is
not entirely convincing. There was, for instance, no violence
in 1935 to compare with the riots which took place in, for
example, Belfast and Birkenhead, in 1932. If there was a difference, it was that the protest was more broadly based,
drawing increasingly, in the days leading up to the standstill
order, upon the Labour party, the TUC, local authorities,
and sections of 'middle opinion' including the churches,
chambers of trade, and ex-servicement's organizations. This

---

[44] K. Middlemas, *Politics in Industrial Society: The experience of the British
system since 1911*, London, 1979, p. 233.

also manifested itself in the all-party criticism of the Government, something which had been far less prominent in 1931–2.

But 'respectability' and a broad basis of support were not in themselves guarantees of influencing governments. The experience of the Jarrow Crusade of 1936, perhaps the most 'respectable' of all unemployed protests, certainly one enjoying widespread sympathy and support, suggests that something more was required in order to sway government decisions. Indeed, comparison of the impact of protests over the administration of unemployment relief with the operation of other pressure groups in the 1930s, such as the child-poverty lobby in its campaign for family allowances, only serves to emphasize the difficulties encountered by even the most articulate and well-supported campaigns in obtaining their ends until the right circumstances presented themselves, crucially, within the corridors of power.[45]

If the 'populist' explanation of the introduction of the standstill leaves something to be desired, it is clear that the attempts to place it within other 'models' is no easier. Middlemas, for example, attempts to integrate the 1935 crisis into his thesis of the development of the tendency or bias towards a 'corporate triangle between government, employers and unions' in which a form of equilibrium was so valued by the partners that compromise by governments was an accepted part of the inter-war political scene. The UAB crisis of 1935 was an example of miscalculation, in which 'the government wisely gave way'. Even so, Middlemas admits that 'It is not easy to answer the question of why they gave way on a measure of such importance, so long prepared, and so closely associated with Chamberlain, the Chancellor.'[46] Indeed, although the UAB scheme was intended to set up an independent non-political body to deal with unemployment benefit, there is little doubt that the deciding influences in the crisis were those of the politicians. In spite of the awkwardness of the relationship of Chamberlain and Stanley to the semi-autonomous UAB, it was the Cabinet's victory in the struggle with the UAB in the days up to 5 February which determined

---

[45] See J. Macnicol, *The Movement for Family Allowances, 1918–45*, London, 1980, especially pp. 169–76.

[46] Middlemas, *Politics in Industrial Society*, p. 232.

first the standstill order and then the modification of the whole process of administrative rationalization. When the Board refused to go beyond permissive revisions to defuse the outcry over the new scales, Stanley and Chamberlain abandoned any pretext of the Board's non-political status and brought pressure to bear on it in order to obtain an end to the crisis.[47]

But an explanation of these events which depends upon the motivation of politicians raises its own difficulties. Some members of the Board expressed the issue in narrow, electoral terms. Violet Markham wrote to Davison that:

At the first sign of trouble [the government] made no effort to stand firm. They flung in the towel and ran like hares—ran from the very principles they had set up the Board to implement. They did this, of course, because a General Election is on the horizon, and they were concerned not with principles, but with votes.[48]

Certainly electoral considerations must have had an impact. By-election and municipal election results were running against the Government during the autumn and winter of 1934-5. In the Putney by-election on 28 November 1934 an extremely safe Conservative seat registered a swing of 26.9 per cent and was almost captured by Labour after the Conservatives had taken 81 per cent of the votes in 1931. Although the result of the Liverpool Wavertree by-election was not to come until the day after the standstill order, 6 February, showing a large reversal of the Conservative position (owing partly at least to the candidature of Randolph Churchill as an Independent Tory taking 23.9 per cent of the vote), party organizers were already becoming concerned about the impact of the unemployment question upon election results.[49]

Characteristically, however, a much more detailed investigation of relationships within the higher echelons of the Government has suggested to Maurice Cowling that the significance of the crisis lies in a more complex evaluation of the political process. Cowling has emphasized the fears of

[47] F. M. Miller, 'The British Unemployment Assistance Crisis of 1935', pp. 340-4.
[48] Ibid., p. 342.
[49] J. Stevenson and C. Cook, *The Slump*, pp. 119, 246.

a Labour recovery and electoral success from 1933, especially should the National Government lose the support of the Liberal component of the domestic electorate:

For the government the danger was that an election might produce a Labour majority in the House of Commons (without any vast increase in the Labour vote) if Cecil, Samuel and Lloyd George between them stuck Liberal pins in the broad-based balloon which had taken off in 1931.[50]

In a government run by the 'Big Six', Baldwin, Chamberlain, MacDonald, Thomas, Simon, and Runciman, in which the major domestic decisions were made by Chamberlain and Baldwin, Cowling argues that whatever other issues impinged on politics between 1933 and 1935 only the UAB crisis and the India Bill presented any serious threat to the Government. Acknowledging the sensitivity of the unemployment question, particularly as mediated by the issue of unemployment assistance, he has put forward the view that the issue 'cut no ice with serious politicians' until the UAB reorganization was implemented in 1934–5.[51] The administrative blunder about the new relief scales has been described by Cowling as 'inflicting the deepest damage to the morale of the Conservative Party' and precipitating a conflict between Chamberlain and important sections of Liberal opinion at a time when their continued support was seen as essential. Its role within the rivalries of the 'Big Six' was to strengthen Baldwin's position at the expense of Chamberlain. Its importance has therefore to be seen primarily in the context of the manœuvres and thought-processes of a relatively small group of people, rather than in terms of wider political structures determining events and policies. But while the significance of the UAB crisis can be interpreted in these terms, the way in which decisions were taken still leaves room for the role of wider processes, such as electoral fears and back-bench revolt. What it has done is to shift the emphasis of political history towards the contingent adjustments and personal relationships of politicians at the highest level of politics.

---

[50] M. Cowling, *The Impact of Hitler: British politics and British policy, 1933–1940*, Cambridge, 1975, p. 41.
[51] Ibid., pp. 42–3.

VI

A consideration of unemployment policy in these years suggests a number of problems and potential confusions for political historians. Those who have analysed earlier political
crises and confrontations have become familiar with a series
of debates about the relative weight to be attached to different elements in the decision-making process and the sources
of political action. As we have seen, historians of different
persuasion have chosen to interpret events in their own way.
To an extent, some confusion exists about what exactly is
being explained and the level of causality at which their analysis attempts to intervene. Clearly, historians can have quite
different views of the political process, ranging from the completely deterministic to the entirely contingent, views which
usually influence the level of politics on which they concentrate their expertise. Hence debates on particular events are
informed by quite distinct assumptions as to how the political process works and the nature of political consciousness.
These assumptions are not always adequately stated, perhaps
because of the reluctance of historians to be seen to be constructing 'models'. While a beginner's textbook on British
government or politics will provide any number of such
models of the decision-making process or of policy-formation,
these remain a virtual dead-letter amongst historians seeking
their distinctive interpretation of particular events.[52]

If anything, the development of historical research and the
greater availability of source materials have served to emphasize rather than reconcile differences in interpretation. Historians have usually chosen to research more deeply into the
sources that have most bearing upon what they consider to
be the critical levels of political activity. Frequently, what
some historians come to regard as the highest-grade ore of
historical research is regarded by others as nothing but fools'
gold. For example, in the case of the present study—unemployment policy—considerable doubt has been cast upon

[52] See, for example, R. Rose, *Politics in England: An Interpretation*, London,
2nd edn., 1974, and B. Jones and D. Kavanagh (eds.), *British Politics Today*, Manchester, 1979, especially M. Burch's essay, 'Policy-making in central government',
pp. 108–18, and B. Jones, 'Pressure Groups', pp. 119–30.

the relevance of the public records to an elucidation of the means by which decisions were made. C. L. Mowat, for example, in his review of the cabinet papers released by the Public Records Act noted:

What difference will this new source of information, the Cabinet papers, make to the hitherto accepted narrative of events or ascription of causes? . . . That it will deepen our knowledge of what happened, of the information on which ministers or Cabinet decided to act, is clear enough; but what the papers do not say about motives or passions, the information they failed to supply to the government, will remain important, and light on these things will still have to be sought elsewhere.[53]

Similarly, the Crossman diaries have cast doubt on the cabinet minutes as historical evidence. More generally, the documentary record from the Public Record Office has been questioned by two economic historians who are concerned whether it reflects very accurately upon the most important processes in decision-making.[54] Hugh Heclo and Aaron Wildavsky in their study of the Treasury, moreover, have laid stress upon the 'chat in the corridor' in the taking of decisions, formation of opinion, and channelling of information. Historians of Britain's war economy have also suggested that the paper record is an often misleading approach to the question of decision-making in the war period.[55] On the other hand, there is the question of the relevance of private papers as the effective source of historical truth. Not the least of the contributions of the so-called 'high politics' approach has been

[53] Mowat, *Great Britain Since 1914*, p. 68, cited in A. Booth and S. Glynn, 'The Public Records and Recent British Historiography', *Economic History Review*, 2nd ser. 32. 3 (1979), 304.

[54] Booth and Glynn, 'The Public Records', pp. 303–15, noting: 'The enormous volume of research undertaken in the field of political science directed towards an answer to the question "Where does power lie in Britain?" makes it exceedingly naive for economic and social historians to accept, without question, that the crucial centres of power are to be found within the Cabinet and departments.' (p. 314.)

[55] H. Heclo and A. Wildavsky, *The Private Government of Public Money*, London, 1974, pp. 68–75; W. K. Hancock and M. M. Gowing, *British War Economy*, London, 1949, both cited in Booth and Glynn, 'The Public Records', p. 306. Booth's own work on Special Areas legislation has also cast doubt on the relevance of the public record as an explanatory tool for the political processes involved, see A. Booth, 'The Timing and Content of Government Politics to Assist the Depressed Areas' (unpublished Ph.D. thesis, University of Kent, 1975).

its emphasis on the importance of the higher echelons of politics. Writing of an earlier period, the 1880s, Alastair Cooke and John Vincent have stressed the importance of seeing Westminster as a relatively closed world, so that:

Explanations of Westminster should centre not on its being at the top of a coherently organised pyramid of power whose bottom layer was the people, but on its character as a highly specialised community, like the City of Westminster or Whitehall, whose primary interest was inevitably its own very private institutional life.[56]

This argument is carried forward by the authors in their discussion of the archival base upon which historians rely, notably the 'single crucial distinction between politicians who just did their particular jobs, and politicians who took it upon themselves to create the general situation'. Unimportant men leave unimportant archives is the message of this analysis: 'There are no interesting papers, except at the top, because there was nothing of much interest, except at the top, to put on paper', or more fully:

historical investigation of the structure of politics suggests that, at least in a parliamentary system where high politics is an arcane and esoteric craft whose meaning is not even intelligible to many members of the cabinet, the idea of a 'structure' is an unhelpful metaphor drawn from Meccano and fluid dynamics. It is also untrue, in that it implies that different areas of political activity are united by sharing in a common system of information and mutual response, rather than separated by concealment, dissimulation, and mutual inattention. . . . True, party leaders had their own abstract views of what society was like and what people wanted, but these conceptions were formed, on a very small factual basis, by interpreting what they read in the newspapers in the light of the opportunities they saw in high politics.[57]

This radical detachment of the very highest echelons of politics from the 'pyramid of power'—even from the influence of many members of the Cabinet—offers an important argument which can be applied as well to the unemployment policies of the National Government as to the issues of the 1880s. Cowling, while far from exactly replicating them and applying his own distinctive view of the 'political consciousness' of the principal actors in politics, offers a similar

---

[56] A. B. Cooke and J. Vincent, *The Governing Passion: Cabinet Government and Party Politics in Britain, 1885–86*, Brighton, 1974, p. 22.

[57] Ibid., p. 57.

detachment of the main elements in decision making. Here again, the emphasis is upon sources in the highest levels of politics—an approach which is dismissed by others as far too narrow an appreciation of the political process.

To an agnostic in these matters, it appears that there remain many difficulties in assessing the development of and the crucial levels of influence in the making of unemployment policy in these years. No 'model' fits very neatly into the differing circumstances and decisions considered here and a greater wealth of sources has served less to conclude debate about how the political process worked than to stimulate it. Whatever else, the sentiments expressed in the first sentence of this essay serve as something of an ironic commentary upon an issue which affected hundreds of thousands of people deeply. There is no overwhelming evidence that a prior concern of the public, even a substantial and deserving minority of them, would be arbitrated directly or proportionately into decision-making or policy formulation at the higher levels of politics. Where power lay in inter-war British politics and how it could be mobilized remains, on the evidence of unemployment policy, still very much an open question.

8

Misinformation, Misconception, Mistrust:
Episodes in British Policy and the Approach of War, 1938–1939

D. Cameron Watt

I

British historians have devoted as much, if not more, effort and time to the question of the origins of the war of 1939 and to the issue of appeasement than those in any other country, with the possible exception of Germany. Since 1945 the emphasis has shifted entirely from the search for, and identification of, those who could be held responsible for the collapse of the inter-war security system, to the discussion of the policies of the 1930s in the light of the dilemmas faced in the 1950s by a Britain declining in power while overcommitted in strategic and economic terms. The post-war historians of the Churchillian right, Sir Lewis Namier, Sir John Wheeler-Bennett, Sir Charles Webster, and others, have given way to two main groups: neo-conservatives concerned to rehabilitate the conservative leaders of the inter-war years (of whom Professor W. N. Medlicott and the late Professor Bassett were the forerunners), and neo-populists concerned to rehabilitate the pacifist anti-war liberal traditions in terms of which the policies of Chamberlain and Halifax were defended.[1] Characteristic of this latter group is Mr Taylor's remark that the spirit of Munich represented all that was best in Britain. A great deal of careful work, much of it as yet still in the form of Ph.D. theses, has gone into the examination of the role of extra-European anxieties in the Far East and the Mediterranean in influencing British policy towards Germany. There has been some interesting and useful work on the

[1] For a comment on these developments see D. C. Watt, 'Appeasement. The Rise of a Revisionist School?', *Political Quarterly* (1965).

strategic factor, work headed by Professor Norman Gibbs's monumental official history of *Grand Strategy* between the wars.[2] And a good deal of attention is now being paid to the development of the British rearmament programme,[3] to the influence of the Treasury,[4] to the whole question of Britain's external balance of payments and trade. The emphasis has switched dramatically from the search for 'guilty men' to the detailed study of all aspects of British policy-making.

Central to this interest has been the assumption that official policy was basically determined by official anxieties over the decline of British power and the rise of numerous different threats to that power from both traditional and newly-emerged adversaries. This assumption of the *Primat der Aussenpolitik* has been challenged only once, by the Cambridge historian, Maurice Cowling, in his *Impact of Hitler*.[5] His argument that British policy after Munich represented an attempt to set the stage for a forthcoming General Election has as yet found few followers. There have, however, been a number of interesting studies of the development of political attitudes and of public opinion towards the perils of an approaching war in Europe, though they have not so much been concerned to argue the *Primat der Innenpolitik* as to show that these were much less of a restraint on government action than its defenders have alleged, or to call attention to the difference between the actual realities of these factors and government perceptions of them.[6]

The measure of agreement in method among British historians is such that the main historical controversy generated

---

[2] Norman Gibbs, *Grand Strategy*, vol. I, *Rearmament Policy*, London, 1974.

[3] Notably by R. A. C. Parker: 'British Rearmament, 1936-1939: the Treasury, Trade Unions and Skilled Labour', *English Historical Review*, 96 (1981). See also J. P. D. Dunbabin, 'British Rearmament in the 1930s: a Chronology and a Review', *Historical Journal*, 18 (1975).

[4] See, for example, Robert Paul Shay Jr., *British Rearmament in the Thirties. Politics and Profits*, Princeton, N.J., 1977; George C. Peden, *British Rearmament and the Treasury, 1932-1939*, Edinburgh, 1979.

[5] Maurice Cowling, *The Impact of Hitler. British Politics and British Policy, 1933-1940*, Cambridge, 1975.

[6] See, for example, Roger Eatwell, 'Munich, Public Opinion and Popular Front', *Journal of Contemporary History*, 6 (1971); D. C. Watt, 'British domestic politics and the onset of war. Notes for a discussion', in Centre Nationale de la Recherche Scientifique, *Les Relations Franco-Britanniques de 1935 à 1939*, Paris, 1975.

by the concentration on the origins of the war of 1939–45 has been that provoked by A. J. P. Taylor's *The Origins of the Second World War*, an attempt to argue that the war of 1939 was no more and no less planned, and no more and no less 'accidental', than the war of 1914, both stemming, in Mr Taylor's view, from the inherently expansionist ideology of German nationalism. Indeed Mr Taylor has tended to argue both that the war of 1914 was intended and that the war of 1939 was unplanned, an 'accident' rather than a design. He has attracted a great deal of denunciation, specifically because the indictment at Nuremberg of the survivors of Hitler's regime, at American instigation, and over French and Soviet objection, included the charge of 'conspiracy to commit aggression' and to launch aggressive war. Mr Taylor himself has come to believe more and more in the role of accident in history; and his professional admiration is reserved for those who, like Bismarck, he believes were most successful in turning accident to their advantage.[7] But the issue of design or accident is still a very real one, and it is to this that the remainder of this paper is devoted.

II

An essential element in the design or accident controversy in the past has been a once widely-accepted version of events,[8] which represented Hitler as following a preconceived programme which had as its first aim the absorption of Czechoslovakia and as its second the conquest of Poland, both being conceived as preliminary stages to a drive into western Russia. British policy, in this version, is represented as being bound up with the continuation of the appeasement of Germany right up to the German entry into Prague. Even thereafter, although British opinion was outraged by this unmistakeable proof that Hitler's aims reached beyond the mere recovery of the German frontiers of 1914 and the ingathering

[7] An attempt to assess Mr Taylor's work in the field of diplomatic history may be found in D. C. Watt, 'Some Aspects of A. J. P. Taylor's Work as Diplomatic Historian', *Journal of Modern History*, 49 (1977).

[8] Now only encountered among Soviet historians, and, as the recent TV series, 'Churchill, the Wilderness Years' (ITV, 1981) was to show, among British mediamen.

of those German minorities who were being oppressed by the dominant racial groups in the artificial multinational states set up by Versailles, the British government still hankered after appeasement. It dragged its heels when confronted with the offer, by the Soviet foreign minister, Maxim Litvinov, of a Russian alliance.[9] And it jumped at the prospect of a new appeasement deal offered by its contacts with Helmut Wohltat, the State Secretary to Goering's Four Year Plan Organization:[10] it was even prepared to entertain the last-minute hopes offered on the one hand by the missions undertaken by M. Dahlerus, the self-appointed and unofficial Swedish mediator between Marshal Goering and the British government[11] and on the other, even after the German attack on Poland had begun, by the Italian offer of mediation. Outraged public opinion dragged the Chamberlain government into war as it had thwarted the negotiations with Wohltat and driven Chamberlain into taking up Litvinov's offer, but too late and too unenthusiastically to convince Litvinov's successor of the seriousness of British intentions.

There is something to be said for this version; but not much.

III

This is not the point to go into detail about Hitler's intentions, since this is not the theme of my paper. But since an important factor in British policy was the picture of those intentions presented to politicians by their sources of information, both overt and clandestine, it is worth devoting a little space to them. The first point to make is that if Hitler took seriously the programme outlined to his immediate entourage

[9] For the Russian offer of a Treaty of Mutual Assistance against Aggression of 18 Apr. 1939, see *Documents on British Foreign Policy, 1919–1939 (DBFP)*, 3rd ser., London, 1949–55, vol. V, No. 201.

[10] On which see below, pp. 250–3.

[11] On which see *DBFP*, 3rd ser., vol. VI, No. 192 and Appendix IV, *passim*; vol. VII, Nos. 67, 209, 236, 237, 299, 349, 402, 406, 418, 458, 470, 477, 478, 509, 529, 587, 592, 613, 762, and Appendix (i), Nos. (ii)–(vii); *Documents on German Foreign Policy, 1918–1945 (DGFP)*, Series D, Washington, 1949–60, vol. VI, Editors' Note, pp. 10, 1088–1093; vol. VII, No. 312; Birger Dahlerus, *The Last Attempt*, London, 1947.

on 5 November 1937,[12] the course of the Czech crisis had rendered it largely academic. It would seem from the anger and irritation vented by him on Britain's leadership in the immediate aftermath both of the May weekend crisis[13] and of the Munich conference,[14] that he regarded the outcome of the latter as at least a major personal setback, and as evidence of Britain's unremitting hostility. The inception of the Z-Plan for the rapid expansion of the German Navy, the *Reichsmarine*,[15] the award on 6 January 1939 of priority in the allocation of armour plate to the *Reichsmarine* over the *Luftwaffe* and the army,[16] confirms the picture set out in the military orders of 26 November 1938.[17] Hitler's priority was now to drive Britain off the European continent by smashing France. It is to be noticed, however, that there is no time scale mentioned. The first stage of the Z-Plan was not to be ready until 1942 at the earliest.

While Hitler appears to have been determined in his aims, there appears to have been a good deal of uncertainty in his mind as to how to achieve them. As a result one can definitely distinguish two alternative lines of policy being urged on him and followed up by their advocates, while a third group may be fairly seen at work in the background. The main rivalry lay between Goering and von Ribbentrop, a rivalry in which the two protagonists were at times to swap policies. In the

[12] For the text of this much discussed document, see *DGFP*, Series D, vol. I, No. 19.

[13] On the May Week-End Crisis see D. C. Watt, 'Hitler's visit to Rome and the May Crisis of 1938: a Study in Hitler's Reponse to External Stimuli', *J. Cont. Hist.*, 9 (1974) and 'The May Week-End Crisis of 1938: a Rejoinder to Mr. Wallace', *Slavonic and East European Review*, 44 (1966); W. V. Wallace, 'The May Week-End Crisis of 1938', *Sl. and E. European Review*, 41 (1963); G. L. Weinberg, 'The May Crisis, 1938', *J. Modern History*, 29 (1957).

[14] On Hitler's anti-British statements after Munich, see D. Dilks (ed.), *The Diaries of Sir Alexander Cadogan, O.M., 1938–1945*, London, 1971, p. 116; ibid., entry of 14 Nov. 1938; Cabinet papers, F.P. (38), 127/627. See also David Irving (ed.), *Breach of Security: the German Secret Intelligence file on Events leading to the Second World War*, London, 1968, pp. 48–51, and footnotes thereto. For a British protest see *DBFP*, 3rd ser., vol. III, No. 302, Halifax to Berlin, 11 Nov. 1938.

[15] On the Z-Plan see Jost Dülffer, *Weimar, Hitler und die Marine*, Düsseldorf, 1973, pp. 429 ff.; Michael Salewski, *Die deutsche Seekriegsleitung, 1935–1945* 3 vols., Frankfurt, 1970–3, vol. I, pp. 53 ff.

[16] See *DGFP*, Series D, vol. VII, Appendix III K No. (iv).

[17] *DGFP*, Series D, vol. IV, No. 411.

background at least, for the period up to February 1939, one can discern a third policy pursued by the SS, in much the same way as they had run Karl Wolff and the extremists among the Sudetendeutsche Partei against Henlein in 1937-8.[18]

Ribbentrop's policy, to which he remained firmly wedded until the events of March and April 1939 forced him to abandon it and take over Goering's line, called for a negotiated settlement with Poland designed to protect Germany's eastern frontier in the event of a conflict in the west;[19] for a tripartite alliance with Italy and Japan designed to distract the United States and divide Britain's forces;[20] and for a courtship of all those elements in France which were less than wholehearted about their *entente* with Britain so as to divide France and Britain from one another.[21] Goering's policy, in which he would appear to have been backed by, among others, Erich Koch, the Gauleiter of East Prussia,[22] called for a bilateral alliance with Italy, conflict with Poland, and, from at least mid-March 1939, a *rapprochement* with the Soviet Union. The SS line involved the encouragement of separatist nationalism among the inhabitants of Carpatho-Ukraine, the search for a Slovakian Henlein to spearhead the break-up of the Czecho-Slovak state, and was uniformly hostile to Italy.[23]

[18] On the SS and Czechoslovakia see Ronald Smelser, *The Sudeten Problem 1933-1938: Volkstumspolitik and the Formulation of Nazi Foreign Policy*, London, 1975.

[19] On Ribbentrop's negotiations with the Poles, see *DGFP*, Series D, vol. V, ch. I *passim*; vol. VI, Nos. 4, 12, 18, 61, 64, 73, 74, 79, 85, 88, 90, 101, 108, 115, and 118. See also Marian Wojciechowski, *Die Polnisch-Deutschen Beziehungen 1933-1938*, Leyden, 1971.

[20] See Mario Toscano, *Le Origini diplomatichi dell Patto d'Acciaio*, Florence, 1956; see also the essay by Ohata Tokushiro, 'The Anti-Comintern Pact 1935-1939', in James William Morley (ed.), *Deterrent Diplomacy. Japan, Germany and the USSR, 1935-1940; Selected Translations from Taikeiyo senso̅ no michi: Kaiser gaikoshi*, New York, 1976.

[21] On German–French relations see Eberhard Jaeckel, *Frankreich in Hitlers Europa: die deutsche Frankreichpolitik im Zweiten Weltkreig*, Stuttgart, 1966.

[22] See the Italian records cited in Mario Toscano, 'L'Italia e gli Accordi Tedesco-Sovietici dell' Agosto 1939', *Revista di Studi Internazionali*, 18 (1951), esp. 577-9, 34 bis. For an English translation of this article see M. Toscano, *Designs in Diplomacy. Pages from European Diplomatic History in the 20th Century* (trans. and ed. G. Carbone), Baltimore and London, 1970, pp. 51-6.

[23] The picture of SS activities is much more difficult to put together. See, however, Henry Delfiner, *Vienna broadcasts to Slovakia, 1938-1939: a case study in subversion*, New York, 1974. On German support for the Carpatho-Ukraine

Behind this struggle for the second place in Hitler's state lay the comparative failure of the Four Year Plan to achieve its aims. The synthetic oil programme was way behind schedule.[24] Access to Romanian oil became of extreme importance. Germany's foreign exchange reserves were almost exhausted. German heavy industry was becoming increasingly unwilling to follow the orders of the Four Year Plan. Schacht was staging his final stand for sound finance at the portals of the Reichsbank. State Secretary Brinkman, Goering's deputy in the Four Year Plan, suffered an open breakdown early in March, which only the most strenuous efforts succeeded in keeping from the world press.[25] And on top of this Ribbentrop's own grand design ran into serious trouble. The Japanese Cabinet could not agree on an alliance which would operate against Britain and America. Mussolini provoked a conflict with France he was unable to follow through. And, despite six months of negotiations with Poland, the Polish government would not take Ribbentrop's bait. Relations with Russia broke down entirely not only because of Ribbentrop's cancellation of the January 1939 mission to Moscow, but because Germany could not meet Russia's financial requirements.[26] And, finally, even after the SS had been slapped down over the Carpatho-Ukraine, the wooing of the Slovaks failed entirely.[27] No Slovak Henlein was forthcoming. Instead, the Czechs precipitated the crisis by their ill-judged and ill-informed attempt to use force against the Slovaks.[28] The diplomatic preparations for the absorption of rump-Czechia were unusually badly bungled even by Ribbentrop's standards of mismanagement.

and its withdrawal see *DGFP*, Series D, vol. IV, Nos. 112, 119, 140, 141, 146, 165, 210, 215, 230, 235, 236, and 237; vol. VI, No. 77, and Editor's Note on p. 90.

[24] See Philippe Marguerat, *Le IIIe Reich et le pétrol roumain, 1939–1940*, Geneva, 1977.

[25] For the version of this speech which reached London see Foreign Secretary's memorandum, 25 Jan. 1939, CAB 23/97.

[26] See *DGFP*, series D, vol. IV, document Nos. 486, 495; ibid., vol. V, document Nos. 125. 126; ibid., vol. VI, No. 332.

[27] For an account of this from the Slovak side see Milan Stanislav Durica, *La Slovacchia e le sue relazioni politiche con la Germania, 1938/1945*, vol. I. *Dagli Accordi di Monaco all'inizio della seconda guerra mondiale*, Padua, 1964.

[28] See the accounts of this in J. Hoensch, *Die Slowakei in Hitlers Ostpolitik*, Cologne, 1965; Gerhard L. Weinberg, *The Foreign Policy of Hitler's Germany: starting World War II, 1937–1939*, Chicago, 1980.

In the three weeks following the march into Prague and the Memel, Hitler found himself confronted with a British guarantee for Poland,[29] a projected Anglo-Polish alliance, the clear failure of Ribbentrop's Polish and Japanese policies, a British and French offer to Romania,[30] and what would seem to be evidence of Soviet interest in renewed talks with Germany.[31] By the end of May he had made the destruction of Poland his first priority,[32] concluded the Pact of Steel with Italy[33] alone, had frustrated the British blockbuilding exercise in south-east Europe by pressure on Romania,[34] and had decided to take up the Russian alternative very seriously.[35] He had also set a timetable for war against Poland and activated the Danzig issue.[36] From that point on, although there may have been some discussion of provoking a coup in Danzig itself, and at one point he may have had hopes of an Anglo-Japanese war over Tientsin which would have made his other measures designed to distract Britain unnecessary,[37] he seems simply to have played a waiting game until the end of July, at which point it was time to set off the fuse marked 'Danzig customs officers' and provoke the conflict. His belief in the reluctance of Britain to come to Poland's aid apparently

[29] Announced to Parliament on 31 Mar. 1939; see *Parliamentary Debates (Parl. Deb.)*, 5th ser., House of Commons, vol. 345, col. 2415; *DBFP*, 3rd ser., vol. IV, No. 582.

[30] On the British and French guarantee for Romania see *DBFP*, 3rd ser., vols. IV and V *passim*: for the text see *Parl. Deb.*, 5th ser., H. of C., vol. 346, col. 13.

[31] See D. C. Watt, 'The Initiation of the Negotiations leading to the Nazi–Soviet Pact: a Historical Problem', in C. Abramsky and Beryl Williams (eds.), *Essays in Honour of E. H. Carr*, London, 1974.

[32] The revised orders for 'Operation White' were issued on 10 May 1939, see *Trial of the Major War Criminals*, Nuremberg, 1948, vol. XXXIV, Document 126-C.

[33] The pact was signed on 22 May 1939. *DGFP*, Series D, vol. VI, No. 426.

[34] See *DGFP*, Series D, vol. VI, Nos. 195, 227, 234, 337, 354, 376, 428, 488, 504, 561, 567.

[35] For Hitler's decision to explore the possibility of an agreement with the Soviet Union see *DGFP*, Series D, vol. VI, document Nos. 424, 441, 446, 450, 451, 452, 453, 465, 478, 490, 514. See also Watt, 'Initiation' (n. 31 above).

[36] Ludwig Denne, *Das Danzig-problem in der deutschen Aussenpolitik 1934–1939*, Bonn, 1959.

[37] For German monitoring of the Tientsin Crisis see *DGFP*, Series D, vol. VI, Nos. 526, 548, 719, 735, and 762. See also Bradford A. Lee, *Britain and the Sino-Japanese War, 1937–1939. A Study in the Dilemmas of British Decline*, Stanford, 1973, ch. 7 *passim*; Peter Lowe, *Great Britain and the Origins of the Pacific War. A Study in British Policy in East Asia, 1937–1941*, Oxford, 1977, ch. III *passim*.

remained unshaken until the afternoon of 25 August when his troops actually had to be recalled from their assault positions.[38]

IV

British reactions to the experience of the Czech crisis and Munich have to be divided quite clearly into those connected with domestic politics and those connected with the formulation of British foreign policy. The first were overt. Euphoria at the avoidance of war had trapped Chamberlain on his return from Munich into public statements he was to beg parliament not to take too seriously only a few days later.[39] But the resignation of Duff Cooper, the vigour and vehemence of the attack launched by Churchill, Eden, their respective group of supporters, as well as by the official Liberal and Labour opposition parties in the parliamentary debate on the Munich agreement, forced Chamberlain and the Cabinet to defend the agreement in absolute terms as a positive gain for peace, and a basis for the attainment of a new understanding with Germany.[40] The private conversations of Chamberlain and other members of the Cabinet, now available to us in private papers[41] and in the Public Record Office, suggest that if there were any serious hopes of such an advance they were seriously weakened by the reports of German behaviour on the international committee administering the transfer of the Sudeten territories, and by the accurate and detailed reports of Hitler's virulently hostile remarks at Chamberlain's expense which reached the Cabinet from their clandestine sources of information in Germany.[42] The Foreign Office and the Department of Overseas Trade did persist, it is true,

[38] On the course of events on 25 August 1939 see *DGFP*, Series D, vol. VII, Appendix I, Halder Diary, entries of 25 and 26 Aug. 1939.

[39] In the debate of 5 Oct. 1938.   [40] Ibid.

[41] See especially Birmingham University Library, Neville Chamberlain Papers; Cambridge University Library, Hoare Papers; Churchill College, Cambridge Library, Inskip Diaries; entries of Cadogan diaries, notes cited n. 14 above; Cowling, *The Impact of Hitler*, pp. 279–83. See also David Dilks (ed.), *Retreat from Power. Studies in British Foreign Policy of the Twentieth Century*, London, 1981, vol. I, p. 150.

[42] Hoare Papers, xxi, i (13)5: notes of a conversation between Lord Templewood and Lord Halifax, 5 Dec. 1951.

in the effort to open economic talks with Germany,[43] and hopes were also pinned to the industrial contacts in progress between the Federation of British Industry and the Reichsgruppe Industrie.[44] A deal of theoretical work was also put into the composition of a new approach to air disarmament, involving a redrafting of the rules of air warfare, but the status of the documents concerned never advanced beyond the planning stage.[45]

Much more significant are the exacerbation of Anglo-German relations consequent upon Hitler's and Goebbels's resentment of British public reaction to the Kristallennacht;[46] Chamberlain's repeated rejection of the idea of according Germany a free hand in economic expansion into south-east Europe[47] and the steady advance of the Foreign Office's efforts to convince a reluctant Treasury and Board of Trade to shore up the economies of Turkey, Greece, and Romania against German pressure;[48] the Cabinet's somewhat confused

[43] On which see *DGFP*, Series D, vol. IV, ch. II *passim*.

[44] For the British records of the meeting between a delegation from the Federation of British Industry and representatives of the *Reichsgruppe Industrie* on 15–16 Mar. 1939, see FO 371/229251, C 2991, C 3008, 8/18. See also *Foreign Relations of the United States, 1939 (FRUS, 1939)*, Washington, 1939, vol. I, pp. 77–8, Kennedy to Hull, 20 Mar. 1939; pp. 110–12, British Board of Trade to US Embassy, London, 4 Apr. 1939. For a general discussion of the issues of 'economic appeasement' see Berndt Jürgen Wendt, *Economic Appeasement. Handel und Finanz in der britischen Deutschland-Politik, 1933–1939*, Düsseldorf, 1971; C. A. Macdonald, 'Economic Appeasement and the German "moderates", 1937–1939. An Introductory Essay', *Past and Present*, 56 (1972).

[45] On which see Uri Bialer, *The Shadow of the Bomb. The Fear of Air Attack and British Politics, 1932–1939*, London, 1980, pp. 119–26.

[46] On Hitler's remarks about no longer setting any value on friendship with Britain see *DBFP*, 3rd ser., vol. III, No. 315. On Hitler's speech to the German press on 10 Nov. 1938, see Wilhelm Treue, 'Hitlers Geheimrede vor der deutschen Presse', *Vierteljahresheft für Zeitgeschichte*, 6 (1958).

[47] The Prime Minister was confronted at Munich with a draft statement prepared by Sir Horace Wilson, offering Germany a free hand in south east Europe, which he rejected. See G. J. van Kessel, 'The British Reaction to German Economic Expansion in South-Eastern Europe, 1936–1939' (unpublished Ph.D. thesis, London University, 1972), pp. 155–7. For Chamberlain's rejection of a similar proposal by Mr Pirow, the South African Defence Minister, who was about to visit both Berlin and Rome, see D. C. Watt, 'South African Efforts to mediate between Britain and Germany, 1936–1938', in K. Bourne and D. C. Watt (eds.), *Studies in International History: essays in honour of W. M. Medlicott*, London, 1967. On 14 Oct. 1938 Chamberlain approved a new Anglo-Romanian wheat agreement, even though, as he said, 'the Germans will probably be annoyed at it'. Chamberlain to Halifax, 14 Oct. 1935, Halifax Papers, FO 800/Hal (38)92, cited in van Kessel, p. 158.   [48] van Kessel, *passim*.

appreciation of the collapse of the German economy and its rather less justified belief in the conflict for Hitler's ear between 'moderates' and 'extremists', a complex of views which encouraged once again the idea that a loan or some financial aid to solve Germany's desperate weakness in foreign exchange might possibly defuse the extremists' arguments;[49] and finally the continuing speculation that Hitler's next move would involve a drive for the Ukraine.[50] This speculation fed apparently on the reports of SS work and propaganda in eastern Czechoslovakia on the one hand and the fairly accurate picture built up in part from informants in Tokyo, in part from other less historically accurate sources of information, of the course of German–Japanese negotiations. The Cabinet appears to have had no picture whatever of Ribbentrop's negotiations with Beck until quite late in the day,[51] and, unlike the Russians, they appear to have missed the significance of the German insistence on widening the terms of the pact with Japan to make it operate against the Anglo-Saxon naval powers. In November 1938 Chamberlain became so convinced by the reports that Hitler was envisaging a new *Drang nach Osten*, that he made this one of the major points to be raised with Mussolini on his forthcoming visit to Rome in January 1939,[52] the main preparations for which were already being discussed in the middle of that month.[53]

The most important point about these rumours, and Chamberlain's willingness to entertain them, is that they make nonsense of the idea that it was only when Hitler marched into Prague that the Cabinet and Chamberlain saw him in his true colours. There was no way a German attack into the Ukraine could be represented as a mere revision of the terms of Versailles. It is equally clear that, far from wishing to divert Hitler eastwards, Chamberlain hoped to use his new-found link with Mussolini, the link which had after all brought Hitler back from the brink of war to Munich, to urge

---

[49] Macdonald, 'Economic Appeasement', op. cit.

[50] See *DBFP*, 3rd ser., vol. III, Nos. 298, 505, 516, 536: the question was raised by Chamberlain in his meeting with Mussolini on 12 Jan. 1939; see ibid., No. 500(3).

[51] *DBFP*, 3rd ser., vol. III, Nos. 526, 531, 561; ibid., vol. IV, Nos. 546, 598, 600.

[52] Ibid., vol. III, ch. VIII, *passim*.   [53] Ibid.

the Italian dictator to restrain Hitler once again. Perhaps the biggest error in the British approach to Italy after the initial misconstruction of Hitler's current thinking was Chamberlain's belief that Mussolini either could or would play brakeman to Hitler's war-chariot.

V

From this fantasy world the Cabinet were to be very quickly recalled to a totally different nightmare. In the third week of January the Cabinet found itself confronted with a Foreign Office dossier built up from a variety of intelligence sources seeming to show that a German attack in the west was imminent.[54] This attack would *either* open with a major air attack on London *or* with the occupation of Belgium and the Netherlands with the aim of acquiring bases from which such attacks could be launched. One could accept that these reports might have been based on a misapprehension of Keitel's orders of 26 November 1938, but for three things. The Keitel orders specifically excluded Belgium from the operation of the attack envisaged on France—'*nicht wie im 1914*'. The intelligence reports specifically mentioned a date—mid-February. And their emphasis on alleged German plans for a full-scale air attack on London ran largely contrary to existing Luftwaffe doctrine and capabilities. It did, however, fit so exactly with the worst anxieties of those responsible for British defence planning as to give rise to the strong suspicion that this was more than a mere coincidence.

This impression is heightened when one attempts to identify the German sources of these reports. They are referred to in one place as 'Vansittart's Germanophiles',[55] in another as the sources whose information had proved accurate in the

---

[54] There is a considerable literature on this 'war-scare': see Sidney Aster, *1939: the making of the Second World War*, London, 1973, pp. 43–9; Bialer, pp. 159–60; Gibbs, *Grand Strategy*, pp. 498–500.

[55] Inskip diaries, entry of 28 Jan. 1939; see also J. Harvey (ed.), *The Diplomatic Diaries of Sir Oliver Harvey 1937–1940*, London, 1970, entries of 27–8 Jan. 1939; Brian Bond (ed.), *Chief of Staff: the diaries of Lieutenant-General Sir Henry Pownall*, vol. I, London, 1972, entry of 23 Jan. 1939; Dilks, *Cadogan Diaries*, entries of 17, 19, 23 Jan. 1939.

Czech crisis the previous year.[56] They seem to have included Karl Goerdeler, Herman Rauschning, and the Sudeten German Socialist, Dr Ernst Jäckh. Behind these men lay the anti-Hitler opposition in the General Staff and the Abwehr. It seems a reasonable supposition that having failed to turn Britain against Hitler in 1938 by telling the truth about Hitler's plans, someone (and the action matches Oster's exaggeration of British offers made in November 1939 in the desperate effort to persuade the Reichswehr leadership to overthrow Hitler) decided to doctor the reports so as to trick the British at their most sensitive spot, the fear of a 'bolt from the blue' which would devastate London in the first forty-eight hours of war.

The anonymous originators of these reports scored even better than they knew. Although Chamberlain remained sceptical, the Cabinet authorized approaches to the Netherlands, France, Belgium, and to President Roosevelt.[57] Even more to the point, they authorized staff talks with the French on the assumption of a joint engagement in a continental war.[58] This step led inevitably to the doubling of the Territorial Army[59] and the introduction of conscription.[60] At the same time every hope the Treasury might have entertained of restraining the rate of rearmament in the light of the steady deterioration of Britain's financial and overseas trade position was swept away. Morally, if that be the right word, the Cabinet were already braced for war with Germany at the end of January 1939.

The change in mood can be seen in two other spheres, the diplomatic and the military. In the diplomatic sphere much

[56] See FO 371/22061, C864/15/18. See also Halifax's remarks in the Foreign Policy Committee of the Cabinet on 23 Jan. 1939, CAB 27/624, FP (36) 35th meeting, pp. 117–18.

[57] See *DBFP*, 3rd ser., vol. III, Nos. 5, 8, 18, 20, 26, 27, 28, 29, 39, 40, 41, 42, 45, 48, 49, 50, 54, 55, 57, 58, 64, 70, 72, 75, 78, 80, 81, 86, 94; *FRUS, 1939*, vol. I, pp. 2–6, 9; *Documents Diplomatiques Français, 1932–1939*, 2e Série (1936–1939), Tome XIII, Nos. 445, 454; *Documents Diplomatiques Belges, 1920–1940, La Politique de Sécuritée Extérieure*, vol. V, Nos. 50, 51, 52, 53, 54, 55, 56.

[58] On the issue of authorization for Anglo-French staff talks, see Gibbs, *Grand Strategy*, pp. 654–7.

[59] Peter Dennis, *Decision by Default; peace-time conscription and British defence, 1919–1939*, London, 1972, pp. 197–9.

[60] Dennis, pp. 206–21.

quiet and patient work was put into encouraging the Balkan states to settle their differences and combine to withstand German economic pressure. At the same time Lord Halifax persuaded Chamberlain of the necessity of improving Anglo-Soviet relations lest Soviet isolation give way to German blandishments. A new Russian-speaking ambassador, Sir William Seeds, was sent to Moscow.[61] And the Prime Minister, with other senior members of his cabinet, turned up at a reception at the Soviet Embassy in London, arousing surprise and not a little suspicion in the breasts of their hosts. Stalin's reference to the vain expectations entertained by the capitalist powers that the Soviet Union would pull their chestnuts out of the fire, made in his speech of 11 March 1939, could well have been provoked by that incident.[62]

In the military strategic sphere the other major development was the initiation of a major debate on the issue of Italy. Italy, it was felt, in part on the basis of Italian behaviour in August and September 1938, could not be relied on to stay neutral in the event of war with Germany.[63] Perhaps it would be best to abandon the attempt to keep the Mediterranean neutral, downgrade the priority given to reinforcing the Far East, and plan for a pre-emptive strike against Italy to knock her out of the war in its opening stages. These discussions are less significant for their outcome, which was negative, than for the evidence they present, again well before 15 March, of a change in the mood of the policy-making élite against Germany and Italy.

VI

How then did it happen that, in the first ten days of March, not only did Chamberlain indulge in a highly euphoric interview with the lobby correspondents[64] but also put the

[61] Aster, pp. 152–5: for Sir William Seeds's report on his first conversation with Litvinov, see *DBFP*, 3rd ser., vol. IV, No. 24.

[62] For relevant extracts from this speech see Jane Degras (ed.), *Documents on Soviet Foreign Policy*, Oxford, 1953, vol. III, pp. 315–22.

[63] For the debate on a pre-emptive strike against Italy, see Lawrence W. Pratt, *East of Malta, West of Suez; Britain's Mediterranean Crisis, 1936–1939*, Cambridge, 1975, pp. 167–75. See also D. C. Watt, 'Britain, France and the Italian Problem, 1937–1939', in *Les Relations Franco-Britannique* (see n. 6 above).

[64] D. C. Watt, *Personalities and Policies: studies in the formulation of British foreign policy in the 20th century*, London, 1965, p. 179, n. 2.

unfortunate Sir Samuel Hoare up to his 'Golden Age' speech only the day before Hitler suppressed the Czech state?[65] The answer is a complicated one. But it must begin with the failure of the reported German assault on the Low Countries to manifest itself. This could have been because, as I argued above, there was no truth in the reports. It could also have been because something had changed Hitler's mind. Chamberlain may well have believed this. His letters to his sisters certainly suggest so.[66] What then had changed Hitler's mind? The evidence suggests that five factors combined to induce in Chamberlain that singularly ill-timed moment of euphoria. The first was his conviction that the British rearmament effort was beginning to impress Hitler.[67] Certainly in the air British aircraft production was beginning to overhaul that of Germany, and the air defence of Great Britain, having profited immensely from the chaos which had overtaken its hasty mobilization in September 1938, was beginning to take what, to the Prime Minister, was an impressive shape.[68] The worst area of British armaments was at sea, where refits and modernization had reduced Britain's battle fleet from fifteen to eleven capital ships.[69] But that was less alarming *vis-à-vis* Germany than it was against Japan.

The second factor was a spurious one. It had to do with the attitude of the United States; and it is worth a little digression on the subject on which research is only now concentrating: British perceptions of that country.[70] It is not too much to say that the British regarded the United States at this period as a kind of *dea ex machina*, to be called upon in Britain's hour of need, but a goddess, it was devoutly hoped, whom they would never need so to evoke. Chamberlain did not see the United States as a European power; nor did he see

[65] Sir Samuel Hoare, Viscount Templewood, *Nine Troubled Years*, London, 1954, pp. 328-9.
[66] See, for example, his letters to Hilda Chamberlain, of 5 Feb. and 19 Feb. 1939: Neville Chamberlain Papers, University of Birmingham.
[67] *FRUS, 1939*, vol. I, pp. 14-17, Kennedy to Hull, 17 Feb. 1939, reporting on a conversation with Chamberlain.
[68] Ibid.   [69] Pratt, *East of Malta*, pp. 170-1.
[70] See the excellent studies by Callum A. Macdonald, *The United States, Britain and Appeasement, 1935-1939*, London, 1981, and David Reynolds, *The Creation of the Anglo-American Alliance, 1937-1961; a study in competitive cooperation*, London, 1981.

the Soviet Union in that light either. In his view, the price of calling either or both of these powers in to the support of the European balance would be much too high. Throughout the 1930s indeed there was very little evidence to suggest that either would come if they were called upon. But in the months before Christmas 1938 Chamberlain had received clandestine assurances from the President that, in the event of Britain finding herself at war with Germany, American neutrality legislation would be circumvented.[71] Such assurances at least partially allayed the fear that America would not answer a call; they did nothing, of course, to allay Chamberlain's fears that the price of American aid would be more than Britain and the Commonwealth could pay without permanently conceding American hegemony in the economic field. And what Chamberlain really needed was not clandestine assurances of action in the event of war, but open assurances that could work to prevent it.

Chamberlain thought he could discern such assurances in Roosevelt's New Year message to Congress,[72] and still more in the remarks he made to members of the Senate Foreign Relations Committee at the end of January 1939, a version of which was immediately leaked to the press, to the effect that America's frontier now lay on the Rhine.[73] These remarks were not without impact in Berlin, even on Hitler. Unfortunately, Roosevelt immediately denied them, fearing that they might hamper the repeal of the 1937 neutrality legislation which was to form the major legislative task he was to set before Congress in the spring and summer of 1939. America was further of use in restraining Japan and (the third factor), Chamberlain was naturally aware of the impasse into which the German-Japanese negotiations had stumbled.

The fourth factor contributing to Chamberlain's outburst

[71] These assurances were given via Lord Murray of Elibank. For his visit to Hyde Park in Oct. 1938 and his subsequent communications with Chamberlain, see D. C. Watt, 'Roosevelt and Chamberlain: the Appeasers', *International Journal*, 78 (1973); Reynolds, *Creation*, pp. 47-8; Elibank papers, National Library of Scotland, vol. 8809.

[72] For the text see Donald B. Schewe (ed.), *Franklin D. Roosevelt and Foreign Affairs, 1937-1939*, New York, 1979, vol. 8, No. 1503.

[73] For the circumstances of this meeting and Roosevelt's subsequent denial of the remarks attributed to him by senators present at this meeting, see Schewe, *Roosevelt*, vol. 8, Nos. 1565, 1574.

of euphoria was the conviction that German inactivity could be ascribed to the influence of the moderates around Hitler.[74] Everything, in the words of the song, seemed to be going his way. British intelligence reports pointing to a German attack on Czechoslovakia in March were simply ignored.[75] Chamberlain had been less than wholly convinced by the evidence cited in January on the imminence of a German attack on the Low Countries. These reports had not been substantiated. In the case of Czechoslovakia, however, they were to be substantiated immediately and humiliatingly, and Chamberlain's misconceptions revealed for what they were. He was not inclined to put much faith thereafter in the moderates around Hitler, or in Hitler himself. He did not, on the other hand, abandon the idea of deterrence.

The final element in giving rise to Chamberlain's euphoria was a consequence of the return to Berlin of Sir Nevile Henderson.[76] From mid-November until mid-February he had been in England, seriously ill with a cancerous growth behind his tongue. During his absence the British Embassy, under Sir George Ogilvie-Forbes (who had succeeded Sir Ivone Kirkpatrick as Counsellor in early December), was able to report their suspicions of Germany and the state of Nazi Anglophobia without ambassadorial censorship. On his return to Berlin Henderson took rigorous control of all reporting, rebuking those responsible for the part they had played in exacerbating relations between Germany and Britain.[77] Reporting from Berlin resumed its Pollyannaish optimism right up to the moment of Hitler's entry into Prague.[78] This would have added to Chamberlain's relief by supporting the hypothesis that the 'moderates' around Hitler were winning the battle against his more extreme advisers.

---

[74] Macdonald, 'Economic Appeasement', op. cit.

[75] On which see David Dilks, 'Appeasement and Intelligence', in Dilks, *Retreat from Power*, vol. I, pp. 158–60.

[76] On Henderson's embassy see Vaughan B. Baker, 'Nevile Henderson in Berlin; a re-evaluation', *Red River Valley Historical Journal*, 2 (1977).

[77] I was given a first-hand description of this rebuke by one of the junior embassy staff present.

[78] See, for example, Henderson's reports of 3 and 9 Mar. 1939; *DBFP*, 3rd ser., vol. IV, Nos. 172, 195.

VII

It will be seen from much of the foregoing that the real significance of the crisis which followed the march into Prague corresponds very little with that accorded to it in the conventionally accepted model of the development of British policy. Its main significance lies not in that it confronted the Cabinet for the first time with a Hitler intent on territorial expansion rather than treaty revision—for they had already largely accepted that; nor that it confronted them with a cynical and hardly concealed exercise of the use of force to compel the weak to observe the outward appearance of legality in inviting the dismantling of their political existence— for they had already seen this in the annexation of Austria. It is true that the open presence of these elements in Hitler's acts made it much easier to win public support for action that had hitherto been merely discussed behind locked doors. It enabled the Cabinet also to abandon the parliamentary defence of the Munich agreement, and to end the increasingly unreal, yet still acrid, contention within the Conservative parliamentary party. But all of this was inevitable sooner or later. The 'march into Prague' simply provided the occasion for it.

   The main significance of the crisis of 15–19 March is that it created the occasion for a major British diplomatic offensive in eastern Europe, what the German Foreign Ministry, in providing a title for the new series of files which recorded the British moves, called the *Einkreisungspolitik*, the policy of encirclement. And the occasion for this was not the 'march into Prague', which the Cabinet were inclined to accept, though with a mental note that Hitler's basic untrustworthiness was now proven beyond a peradventure, but the story of the alleged German ultimatum to Romania which the Romanian Minister to the Court of St. James, M. Tilea—and his colleague in Paris—unloaded on the Foreign Office, the War Office, and the press on 16 March.[79] This story was untrue, a fact which it took less than twenty-four hours to discover. What Tilea's motives were for his action have never been

[79] On the Tilea 'ultimatum' see Aster, *1939*, ch. 3, *passim*; Martha Bibescu, *Journal Politic, 1939–1941*, Bucharest, 1980, entries of 16–19 Mar. 1939; V. Moisuc, 'Tratatul economic Romano-German dur 23 Marte 1939', *Analele*, 12 (1967).

properly determined. His verbal testimony, given on two
occasions to different doctoral candidates at LSE,[80] was to
the effect that he was acting on instructions telephoned to
him from the Romanian court. He was, in fact, going well
beyond them, possibly in conjunction with Max Ausnit, the
Romanian Jewish millionaire, who shared with Tilea a desire
for closer trade relations with Britain.[81] In the time it took
to discover his falsity, however, the attempt to create a European front in protection of Romania was initiatied.

It is worth pausing a moment at this point to consider the
central role played by Romania in British thinking at this
time. Subsequent events were to distort matters, leaving the
impression that the central role in British policy between
March and August 1939 was played by the protection of
Poland, the first country to be guaranteed by Britain. This
impression is erroneous. In the scheme to create a diplomatic
grouping that would deter Hitler from further movement
along the road he had apparently chosen, a 'dam' as Sir
Alexander Cadogan called it,[82] the key position was always
played by Romania. Romania was Poland's ally. Romania
was also linked to Turkey, Greece, and Jugoslavia by the
Balkan pact. British influence over Greece was considerable,
and greatly feared by the Greek dictator, General Metaxas.[83]
British relations with Turkey had been growing closer throughout the 1930s, something incidentally the Soviet authorities
appear to have disliked and resented.[84] In Prince Paul of
Jugoslavia Britain had an old friend and the Foreign Office

[80] To the late Dr Frank Marzari, then a student at LSE: 'The Balkans, the
Great Powers and the European War, 1939–1940' (unpublished Ph.D. thesis, London University, 1966); and to Dr Sidney Aster, 'British Policy towards the
U.S.S.R. and the onset of the Second World War', (Ph.D. thesis, London University, 1969).

[81] These and various later paragraphs on Romanian policy are based on the
hitherto unpublished work of Dr Dov Lungu, sometime research fellow at LSE,
who was allowed access to the Romanian archives. See also the German intelligence reconstruction based on intercepted Jugoslav and other Balkan diplomatic
cipher traffic, in David Irving (ed.), *Breach of Security*, p. 28, n. 23.

[82] Dilks, *Cadogan Diaries*, entry of 26 Mar. 1939.

[83] See John Koliopoulos, *Greece and the British Connection, 1935–1941*,
Oxford, 1977.

[84] D. C. Watt, 'The Sa'dabad Pact of July 8, 1937', paper presented to the
Conference on the Great Powers and the Middle East, 1919–1939, University of
Tel Aviv Centre for Middle Eastern Studies, May 1982.

a very valuable informant.[85] Romania's treaty link with Poland, it was true, was limited to action against the Soviet Union, but it was hoped that that treaty could be made more general in its scope.

British concern over Romania had begun at least a year earlier, with the Foreign Office's urging that steps be taken —in Romania—to resist German economic imperialism in the Balkans. That a clearer policy had not emerged was the fault of the Treasury and the Board of Trade, where consciousness of Britain's own economic and financial weakness made officials reluctant to consider any economic proposals that could not be justified on purely commercial grounds. British gestures towards the support of Romania's economy were therefore grudging and only partially adequate.[86] There are, however, gaps in our knowledge of the significance of Anglo-Romanian relations in this period. We have very little documentation on the King's visit to London in November 1938. We have very little evidence on the role of Lord Lloyd as an intermediary, a distinguished visitor to Romania and of known importance in the development of British clandestine activities.[87] We do not know what the Economic Intelligence Centre was reporting on the Romanian and German economies. And we know very little of the role of the British oil interests and the advice they proffered, if any.

What is clear is that the discovery that the information on which the British action was initiated was false did nothing to cause the British to abandon it. It depended on, and developed from, the concern to withstand German economic expansion in the Balkans that had been generated the previous summer. The reports from M. Tilea were effective precisely because they hit the central point of British anxieties about and concerns to resist that expansion. And in the block-building policy on which Britain now embarked in the Balkans Romania

[85] See J. B. Hoptner, *Jugoslavia in crisis, 1934–1981*, New York, 1982. See also Neil Balfour, *Paul of Yugoslavia*, London, 1980; Dilks, *Cadogan Diaries*, entry of 6 Oct. 1938.
[86] van Kessel, pp. 198–201; see also FO 371/22460, R 9438/223/77, Halifax to parliament, 17 Nov. 1935; FO 371/22466, R 9213/223/77, R 968/223/77, Chamberlain minute, 17 Nov. 1938. For the Romanian view, see N. Petrescu Comnène, *I Responsabile*, Milan, 1949, pp. 378–96; Lungu, op. cit.
[87] Lord Lloyd's papers in the Library of Churchill College, Cambridge, are at present closed to research.

not Poland, was the essential element. The guarantee to Poland, and the other guarantees which were to follow, including that given to Romania itself, were decided on in an emergency and superimposed on the block-building policy, rendering it largely impossible.

VIII

The guarantee to Poland has recently been the subject of an important study by Simon Newman, whose thesis I do not altogether support.[88] His thesis is essentially that by the time the guarantee to Poland was made, the British, or perhaps better said the driving force in the Foreign Office behind the guarantee, were aware that the reports of imminent German action against Poland were false. The idea that the guarantee was intended as a deterrent to German action is therefore, in his view, one which they urged on the Cabinet knowing it to be unnecessary and provocative, as a means of forcing the Cabinet's hand, committing it to a policy of resisting Germany, and outwitting the continuing influence of those who wanted to do nothing to exacerbate Anglo-German relations.

Dr Newman's thesis, in my view, outruns the available evidence. He has, however, put his finger on the driving role played by Lord Halifax, egged on thereto by Sir Alexander Cadogan,[89] to whom the expelled *News Chronicle* correspondent, Mr Ian Colvin, poured out the misinformation tending to point to the immediacy of the German threat to Poland, which had been planted on him by his contacts in the German bureaucratic and military opposition to Hitler.[90] Somewhat the same perception, allied to his conviction in

[88] Simon Newman, *March 1939: the British guarantee to Poland*, Oxford, 1976.

[89] Dilks, *Cadogan Diaries*, entry of 29 Mar. 1939.

[90] The late Ian Colvin's version of his experience may be found in Ian Colvin, *Vansittart in Office*, London, 1945, pp. 304–10. See also Dilks, *Cadogan Diaries*, entry of 29 Mar. 1939. Dr Newman attached little importance to the impact of Mr Colvin's views on Lord Halifax and the Foreign Office, save as a welcome means of stampeding the Prime Minister and the more cautious members of the Cabinet in the desired direction. See Newman, pp. 82–7, who implies that Noel Mason-Macfarlane, the somewhat unconventional British military attaché in Berlin, was behind Colvin. Aster tends to agree with Newman while calling attention to the singularly fortunate, not to say fortuitous, timing of War Office reports of the imminence of a German coup against Danzig: Aster, pp. 99–110.

the primacy of domestic politics, seems to have led Mr Cowling to his conclusion that the motive force behind British
policy at this time was Lord Halifax's drive to reunite the
Conservative party for the forthcoming general election.[91]
The Foreign Office, and Lord Halifax, were opposed by elements determined not to be lured into a policy of withstand-
ing Germany, as is shown by the efforts they made to water
down the effect of the guarantee in the British press on the
day it was announced, efforts which the Foreign Office were
at some pains to counter.[92] But to move from this opposition
to Mr Newman's thesis is, I think, unwarranted.

The factors underlying the making of the guarantee were,
I would suggest, these. In the first place there was no love for,
and precious little trust in, Colonel Beck to be found in London. His gratuitous and belated participation in the dismem-
berment of Czechoslovakia had been neither forgotten nor
forgiven.[93] The regime of the Colonels enjoyed a reputation
for deviousness, megalomania, total national self-centredness,
and greed. The German–Polish Non-Aggression Pact, the
Polish role in frustrating not only French plans for an Eastern
Locarno in 1934-5 but all British plans to find an alternative,
Colonel Beck's grandiose traipsings around central and
northern Europe in 1937-8, all had combined in British eyes
to enhance this picture. British policy-makers knew that
German–Polish negotiations had been in train, but they knew
virtually nothing about their content; nor were they informed of their final breakdown. Indeed Dr Newman makes
clear that they profoundly distrusted Colonel Beck and
thought it quite possible that he was in the process of reaching an accommodation with Hitler.

The reports which Mr Colvin brought with him, and which
were supported by the British military attaché in Berlin,
General Mason-Macfarlane,[94] and by the American ambassador

[91] Cowling, pp. 27-83, 88-91.

[92] See Franklin Reid Gannon, *The British Press and Nazi Germany, 1936–
1939*, Oxford, 1971, p. 265; Newman, 208-9.

[93] For British suspicions of Colonel Beck see the sources cited in Newman,
pp. 171-3.

[94] On Mason-Macfarlane's report, see, in addition to the sources cited in n. 90
above, Mason-Macfarlane's own papers. See also Ewen Butler, *Mason-Mac: the
Life of Lieutenant-General Sir Noel Mason-Macfarlane*, London, 1972.

in Poland, Anthony J. Drexel Biddle IV (which were passed on to the British),[95] caught the Cabinet, as they caught the senior policy advisers in the Foreign Office, at a moment when they were in a state of alarm, apprehension, and frustration, as much over the effects of events abroad on British opinion at home as over the course of those events themselves. The political effect of Mr Chamberlain's speech of 19 March to his Birmingham constituents, and of the immediate British initiative had been lost in frustration and mistrust. M. Litvinov's counter-proposals had been embarrassing, to say the least,[96] and the idea of a close Anglo-Soviet association in a kind of Popular Front style block against Hitler threatened to alienate more states than it would win over. Poland and Romania, the states immediately threatened, would have nothing to do with the Soviets;[97] a vital chance of securing Italian neutrality appeared to have been lost; hopes of attracting Franco's Spain (whose Atlantic islands threatened Britain's vital trade routes) away from his Axis supporters had dwindled;[98] and opinion among the Boers and French Canadians, momentarily aroused against Germany by the German march into Prague, was ebbing back into isolationism.[99] In the meantime Hitler had followed up the destruction of Czechoslovakia with the annexation of the Memelland.[100] Under the circumstances it is hardly surprising that Foreign Office advisers started writing soothing reports of the kind Dr Newman quotes. They were arguing with their own more agitated nerves. For if Hitler did plan a coup against Danzig or the Corridor and nothing were done to forestall him, no one abroad would ever take any British government seriously again.

[95] Sergent minute, 29 Mar. 1939, FO 371/23015, C 4505/54/18.
[96] For Litvinov's proposal of 19 Mar. 1939 and for British comments see *DBFP*, 3rd ser., vol. IV, pp. 421, 433, 446, 461, 538; *FRUS, 1939*, vol. I, pp. 98-9.
[97] See *DBFP*, 3rd ser., vol. IV, pp. 450, 464, 471, 479, 518.
[98] See *DBFP*, 3rd ser., vol. IV, pp. 507, 509; Aster, *1939*, p. 175; CAB 83/49, COS 902(39); CAB 23/99, CAB 27(39) 10 May 1939; CAB 24/286, CAB 108(30) 10 May 1939; Hugh Dalton, *The Fateful Years*, London, 1957, p. 238.
[99] On reactions among the Boers and the French Canadians see R. Ovendale, *Appeasement and the English-Speaking World*, Cardiff, 1975, pp. 220-1, 223-6, 227-31. See also Hugh Dalton Diaries, entries of 20 Mar. and 13 Apr. 1939.
[100] On 22 Mar. 1939.

The effect in domestic politics could be worse. For while the Foreign Office, backed by the Chiefs of Staff, might seek to dismiss the reports of an imminent attack on Poland as part of a war of nerves rather than genuine, and win the agreement of Chamberlain and the Cabinet, parliamentary opinion was far less accessible to them. The professionals of the British Foreign Office have always been well aware of the effect on a government's standing abroad created by lack of majority support for its policies in parliament, or from public opinion. Indeed, one often finds them warning their political masters, demonstrating a degree of sensitivity sometimes more acute than that displayed by their political overlords. Harold Nicolson's diaries bear witness to the agitated state of opinion in parliament.[101]

Added to this was the general conviction, very largely shared by Foreign Office advisers, that Hitler was not only capable of improvising major actions at very short notice (as against Austria in March 1938, for example) but that this was his normal manner of operating. It was thus not all that easy to exclude the possibility that he would move from the absorption of Czechia to a new adventure against Poland, in three weeks.

Dr Newman's deduction that Halifax and Chamberlain used the reports of an imminent German attack on Poland to push the idea of a guarantee of Poland through the Cabinet, in order to embroil Hitler with Poland and secure war in the east rather than the west, goes too far. It makes no sense save as an immediate response to what was perceived as an emergency, and as a deterrent. Dr Newman argues rather speciously that he who wills an event also wills its consequences. But human motives do not easily conform to such *obiter dicta* conceived *a priori* by someone who has only the written evidence to guide him. It is true, and ironic, that here, as in the summer of 1938, the British were anticipating rather than precipitating Hitler's actions. Hitler's remarks to von Brauchitsch on 25 March make it clear that he was losing patience with Poland.[102] The OKW planning staff began

[101] Nigel Nicolson (ed.), *Harold Nicolson; Diaries and Letters, 1933-1939*, London, 1966, entries of 29 Mar.–3 Apr. 1939.
[102] *DGFP*, Series D, Vol. VI, No. 99.

drafting *Fall Weiss* around 27–8 March.[103] The Polish rejection of Hitler's 'offer'[104] led logically to his signature of the
initial orders for *Fall Weiss* on 3 April. Even then the political
preamble to the draft he signed put preparations for a conflict
with Poland firmly within the context of a war with France
and Britain on the western front.[105] It was not until 23 May
that he was to begin talking of war against Poland alone, a war
in which France and Britain were expected to stand aside.[106]
The British guarantee to Poland was misconceived—possibly;
that it was based on a combination of mistrust of Poland and
misinformation as to the imminence of an attack on Poland
seems clear; that it was intended to precipitate a war between
Germany and Poland so as to win more time for Britain seems
to me an unproven hypothesis.

IX

The establishment of the British guarantee for Poland made
the problem of Anglo-Soviet relations acute. British perceptions of Soviet policy were coloured by a variety of considerations of which distaste for the Soviet system and Soviet
efforts to implant it in India and east of Suez were only
important in the case of a few individuals.[107] One of the difficulties the historian faces in attempting to assess British
attitudes to the Soviet Union at this point is the absence of
access to the data provided by Britain's intelligence services.
It would appear that the military purges and the chaos which
was reported to have overtaken the Red Army manœuvres
in 1937 had left British military observers with little confi-

[103] See the account by Walter Warlimont, then in charge of the planning section of the OKW, *Im Hauptquartier der Wehrmacht, 1939–1945*, Bonn, 1966.

[104] *DGFP*, Series D, vol. VI, No. 149.

[105] See *DGFP*, Series D, vol. VI, No. 185, enclosure II, part 2, 'Military Conclusions'. 'The great objectives in the reconstruction of the Wehrmacht will
continue to be determined by the antagonism of the Western Democracies.
"Operation White" constitutes only a precautionary complement . . . not . . .
the necessary prerequisites for a military conflict with the Western opponents.'

[106] *DGFP*, Series D, vol. VI, No. 433.

[107] The only substantial work at present on British attitudes to the Soviet
Union is G. Niedhart, *Grossbritannien und die Sowjet-Union, 1934–1939. Studien
zur britischen Politik der Friedensicherung zwischen den beiden Weltkriegen*,
Munich, 1972.

dence in the Red Army's effectiveness as an attacking force,[108] though it was expected to function effectively in the defence of Soviet territory. Lack of confidence was particularly apparent in the capacity of the Russian General Staff, damaged as it was rightly assumed to have been by the effects of the purges, to cope with the problems of movements and supply for any sizeable body of forces.

In its diplomacy the Soviet Union was seen to be retreating into isolationism. Its commitment to Republican Spain was being liquidated.[109] Foreign consulates were being closed down. No Soviet initiatives were being taken. There were persistent reports that Litvinov was due to be dismissed.[110] Munich had destroyed the Soviet Union's one point of involvement in central Europe. At the same time the Cabinet were confronted with the persistent rumours of a German attack on the Ukraine.

Under these circumstances Lord Halifax and his advisers had begun to worry whether a sense of its isolation and of anxiety over German plans might not drive the Soviet leadership towards an accommodation with Hitler. At the end of January 1939 Lord Halifax had initiated an attempt at improving Anglo-Soviet relations. He had also put paid to a rather stupid agitation against the Anglo-Soviet trade treaty. Sir William Seeds, a Russophile, educated in Russia before the revolution, had replaced Sir Esmond Ovey as ambassador, and had used his first audience with Litvinov[111] to urge British friendship on his surprised and suspicious host. At the same time a number of ostentatiously friendly gestures towards the Soviet Embassy in Britain culminated, as mentioned above, in the appearance of Neville Chamberlain and Lord

[108] For British military views on the effects of the purges on the Red Army as a military force see G. Niedhart, 'der Bündniswert der Sowjetunion im Urteil Gross-Britanniens, 1936–1939', *Militärgeschichtliche Mitteilungen*, 10 (Feb. 1971).

[109] There has been no real study of the Soviet liquidation of their commitment to Spain, in the winter of 1938-9; but see David T. Cattell, *Soviet Diplomacy and the Spanish Civil War*, Berkeley, 1957, pp. 124-5.

[110] See *DBFP*, 3rd ser., vol. III, No. 217, Chilston to Halifax, 18 Oct. 1938; *DGFP*, Series D, vol. IV, Nos. 476, 477, Tippelskirch to Berlin, 3 and 10 Oct. 1938; *Foreign Relations of the United States, the Soviet Union, 1933–1939*, pp. 591-2, Kirk to Hull, 31 Oct. 1938; ibid., p. 737, Kirk to Hull, 22 Feb. 1939.

[111] For Seeds's report of 26 Jan. 1939 of his first meeting with Litvinov, see *DBFP*, 3rd ser., vol. IV, No. 24.

Halifax at a Soviet Embassy reception, the first visit by a British prime minister to the Embassy since 1917.

This was followed by the unhappy episode of the Anglo-Soviet trade talks[112]—a product of the vaulting ambition of Robert Hudson, MP, the parliamentary under-secretary of the Department of Overseas Trade. Hudson's ambitions would normally never have seen the light of day, a parliamentary under-secretary being so very junior a minister that any step out of line brings immediate rebuke from both his minister and the permanent officials of the department. But the Department of Overseas Trade was unique, a hybrid sub-department stranded between, nominally dependent on, yet actually independent of, the Board of Trade and the Foreign Office. In practice this meant that Hudson was his own master, having no senior cabinet minister above him. Hudson's feelings lay towards the right of the Conservative party. He disliked and resented the disproportionate number of senior cabinet posts lavished on the Conservative's partners in the National Government, the National Liberals and the National Labour. Nor was he, with his landed gentry background, particularly drawn to the lawyers and provincial business men of Chamberlainite conservatism. Over the turn of the year he had led an unsuccessful conspiracy against Sir Thomas Inskip and Leslie Hore-Belisha, respectively the Minister for the Co-ordination of Defence and the (Jewish) Minister of War.[113] For this he had been severely rebuked by Chamberlain. Nothing abashed, he now looked to the trade negotiations in Moscow for a political coup which would reinforce what he took to be the new line in British foreign policy, taking care that the British press were fed with reports about the importance of his mission. His attempt to issue a final communique celebrating the trade treaty as a

---

[112] On the Anglo-Soviet trade-talks and the role of Robert Hudson see Aster, 'British Policy', pp. 287–90. For Hudson's personal ambitions see his remarks to the *Daily Express* correspondent, Sefton Delmer, who accompanied him to Moscow: Sefton Delmer, *Trail Sinister*, London, 1961. For personal testimony in confirmation of these reports see the letters of Seeds, Delmer, and Ashton-Gwatkin of the Foreign Office Economic Section to Aster, therein cited; see also Aster, *1939*, pp. 154, 156; *DBFP*, 3rd ser., vol. IV, Nos. 505, 519, 528, 531, 533, 545, 593, 608.

[113] Cowling, p. 331, n. 180; Aster, *1939*, pp. 243–5, citing PREM 1/244 of 9 Dec. 1938; Inskip diary, entry of 17 Jan. 1939.

manifestation of the new spirit in Anglo-Soviet relations was, however, too much for the Foreign Office, who called him to heel and attempted to censor the communique as drafted[114] in order to remove the passages referring to Anglo-Soviet political co-operation. The effect was only to increase the suspicions which Seeds's and Chamberlain's unwonted friendliness had aroused.

British perceptions of the Soviet Union's position at this stage suffered from three areas of misunderstanding. The British did not appreciate that the main weight of Hitler's resentment had turned against *them* and that his anti-Soviet line was in abeyance. They did not appreciate that, from their knowledge of the course of the German–Japanese negotiations, Litvinov and the Soviet leadership were quite certain that Britain rather than the Soviet Union was the country most under threat of German attack.[115] The British assumed that Soviet fears of German attack would make a *rapprochement* with Britain welcome. Such was to prove far from the case. In point of fact the Soviet leadership, possibly as a result of garbled reports of the content of the Chamberlain-Mussolini talks,[116] had come to believe that Britain was aiming to precipitate a German–Soviet conflict. (The reverse would appear to have been the case. Expecting a German victory, the British disliked the prospect of a German–Soviet war for the accession of strength victory over the Soviets would bring to Germany.) The result was that neither the degree nor the basis of Soviet suspicions of British motives was ever clearly appreciated in London.

This difficulty was made greater by the personality of I. M. Maisky, the Soviet ambassador.[117] It is one of the

[114] *DBFP*, 3rd ser., vol. IV, Nos. 505, 593; ibid., vol. VI, No. 13; Aster, *1939*, p. 264.

[115] The Soviet ambassador to Rome remarked as much to his American colleague on more than one occasion: see *FRUS, 1939*, vol. IV, pp. 4, 9-10, 16. See also Litvinov's remarks, made in early Jan. 1939 to Grzbowski, the Polish ambassador in Moscow, and related by him to A. Rosso, his Italian colleague, who reported them to Rome on 13 Jan. 1939, cited in Mario Toscano, 'L'Italia e gli Accordi Tedesco-Sovietici'. See above, p. 219 n. 22.

[116] See the remarks of V. Potemkin, Soviet deputy Foreign Minister to Grzybowski, as reported by Rosso to Rome, 12 Mar., 13 Mar., and 5 Apr. 1939 in Toscano, 'L'Italia e gli Accordi Tedesco-Sovietici'.

[117] On Maisky, see Sidney Aster, 'Ivan Maisky and Parliamentary Antiappeasement', in A. J. P. Taylor (ed.), *Lloyd George: Twelve Essays*, London,

tragedies of this period that Maisky, who was a convinced Anglophile and would have seen an Anglo-Soviet alliance as the triumphal crown of his career, was one of the major obstacles to its achievement. The trouble was that the Britain Maisky admired was the Britain of the Webbs, Bernard Shaw, the *New Statesman*, the Union of Democratic Control, the Hampstead and Highgate educated *rentiers*. His contacts in British politics were with dissident Conservative reformers and with Labour intellectuals. And instead of wooing the makers of policy to persuade them of the need for Soviet friendship, he tried to organize parliamentary and public pressure against them to constrain them into a Popular Front-style alignment. To do this he regularly broke the convention by which diplomatists do not reveal to outsiders the content of their conversations with representatives of the government to which they are credited; still worse, on occasion he actually misrepresented what was said to him and was forced to apologize. He was allowed a latitude in what was essentially intervention in British domestic politics which would have earned an American, a German, or a French ambassador a severe rebuke on the first occasion and a demand for his recall on its repetition. As a result British ministers and diplomatists distrusted him, resented his behaviour, and were loath to confide in him. This was bad enough; what was worse was his regular acceptance of the interpretations put on official British policy by its political opponents. The recently published volumes of Soviet documents on the Soviet efforts for peace before the outbreak of the Second World War[118] contain a number of examples of his reporting, for instance, Lloyd George's interpretation of Chamberlain's motives as if they were indeed valid evidence for something more than the degree to which seventeen years of frustrated ambition had soured Lloyd George's never enormous capacity for understanding the motives of his enemies.

This was particularly unfortunate in a number of cases. What one must assume to have been the real Soviet objections

1971. For Maisky's own memoirs, see I. M. Maisky, *Who helped Hitler?*, London, 1964.

[118] See V. M. Falin *et al.* (eds.), *Soviet Peace Efforts on the Eve of World War II*, 2 vols., Moscow, 1973, *passim.*

to the British policy of guarantees were never clearly put by
Maisky or any other Soviet representative to their British
counterparts. Maisky indeed gave Halifax to understand that
the guarantee for Poland would not be unwelcome to his
government, and seemed as bewildered by Litvinov's hostile
reaction as was Halifax himself.[119] Yet the British scheme,
to achieve a block yet avoid an alliance, to deter Hitler without confronting his potential victims with the choice between Nazism or the Soviets, besides carrying a certain element the Soviets were unlikely to find as convincing as Lord
Halifax did, placed the larger risk in case of failure on the
Soviet Union, while conferring the larger advantage in the
event of success on its British originators. Stalin and Molotov, it can hardly be doubted, saw this very clearly. Indeed,
if one strips away the Stalinist rhetoric from Molotov's
speech of 31 May,[120] or from Zhdanov's article in *Pravda*
of 29 June,[121] this is the main burden of their complaint. But
the rhetoric of anti-Fascism, and the accusations of insincerity which accompanied it, prevented the British from ever
appreciating this simple point, just as they never appreciated
the Soviet conviction that, far from their needing British aid
against Germany, it was for the British, being most in danger,
to court them.

This was perhaps the most unfortunate of the many British
misunderstandings, since it prevented their accepting the
various warnings that reached them as to the progress of the
German–Soviet negotiations. It is a curious comment on
American morals that they would pass on to the British
Biddle's warnings in March, which were unconfirmed, and
refuse to pass on the accurate information on German–Soviet
talks given by Hans von Herwath of the German Embassy in
Moscow, to Charles Bohlen.[122] The Foreign Office apparently

[119] *DBFP*, 3rd ser., vol. IV, Nos. 565, 589, 597; vol. V, Nos. 3, 4, 13.
[120] Jan Degras (ed.), *Documents on Soviet Foreign Policy*, Oxford, 1953, vol.
III, pp. 332-40.
[121] *Soviet Peace Efforts on the Eve of World War II*, vol. II, pp. 116-18.
[122] On which see Charles Bohlen, *Witness to History, 1929-1969*, New York,
1973, pp. 69-84; for Hans von Herwath's own account of his actions and the reasons
why he did not himself contact the British Embassy in Moscow, see Johnnie von
Herwath, *Against Two Evils*, London, 1981, pp. 141-67. For the American Embassy reports see *FRUS, 1939*, vol. I, pp. 318, 319, 321-30, 332-3, reports of 17,
20, 22, and 25 May, 6, 9, 13, 19, and 29 Jun., 1, 2, 10, 11 Jul., and 6 Aug. 1939.

believed all such reports to be just another underhand Soviet
form of pressure on them to accommodate themselves to
Soviet demands.[123] Nor did they appreciate the degree to
which Soviet suspicions that some new piece of appeasement
was in preparation fed upon Britain's reluctance to play the
role in which the Soviets had cast them.

We do not, of course, know all the information that was
reaching the Cabinet. We do know that the leader of the
British delegation to the Moscow talks, Admiral Drax, was
warned before his departure of the suspicions of the Soviets
entertained by the head of the Secret Intelligence Service,
whose past experience in India had predisposed him, as it had
a number of his deputies, to suspicions of the Soviet Union.[124]
But the real motive for British reluctance to adopt Litvinov's
proffered alliance was fear that a Soviet alliance would press
the card of an anti-Bolshevik crusade into Hitler's hands. The
prospect of Franco's Spain, with its Atlantic islands, let alone
Japan and Italy, being aligned against Britain implied a
worsening of Britain's strategic position at its most vulnerable
spots.[125] Balanced against a strengthening of the diplomatic
front in eastern Europe, the bargain could still have been
regarded as a bad one. But if the diplomatic front would dis-
integrate with Poland and Romania refusing to have anything
to do with Soviet support, the point of the manœuvre disappeared entirely. The aim of British policy after all was still
to contain and deter Hitler rather than to defeat him.

In retrospect the negotiations between Britain, France, and
the Soviet Union were doomed to failure. The rock on which
they broke was the Soviet conviction that Britain and France
needed Soviet aid, whereas the Soviet Union had no need of
Britain and France. It was therefore up to Britain and France,
as suitors for Soviet support, to pay whatever price the Soviet
Union felt was adequate recompense for the position it was
being asked to occupy. Once it occurred to someone in

[123] See for example, *DBFP*, 3rd ser., vol. V, No. 413, n. 2.

[124] For Drax's record of their encounter see Churchill College, Cambridge,
Drax Papers.

[125] COS 902, 10 May 1939. The Chiefs of Staff later changed their minds
about the relative advantages of an alliance with Russia as against alienating Spain.
French anxieties about Spain were expressed at the Anglo-French staff talks in
Apr. 1939, Gibbs, *Grand Strategy*, pp. 672-3.

Moscow to see what price Hitler would pay for Soviet neutrality the negotiations assumed the classic model of all such negotiations between potential belligerents and a potential neutral, where the belligerent who can bargain with the territory of his enemies can always outbid those who can only offer the territory of their allies. The Nazi–Soviet pact is merely a historical repetition of the Treaty of London of 1915.

What is surprising, in view of the desperate need of a western front the Soviet Union was to experience after June 1941, is that current Soviet historiography still largely accepts the Soviet estimation of Russia's situation in the summer of 1939. Thus one still hears references from Soviet or pro-Soviet historians to the decision to send Sir William Strang rather than Lord Halifax himself to Moscow, or to the slow means of transport chosen to get the Anglo-French military missions to Moscow in July (a sea voyage)——matters of supreme unimportance once the basic premiss that it was for London and Paris to make the running is questioned, as it clearly must be in the light of the subsequent course of German–Soviet relations.[126] The subject of Soviet misconceptions, misinformation, and mistrust in 1939 is clearly worth a major investigation in itself.

X

The guarantee to Poland was intended to be merely a device of a transitional nature to cover the period until a more stable block could be built up, bringing together all the powers of central and south-eastern Europe threatened by Hitler. In recommending the guarantee for Poland to the Cabinet on 30 March 1939, Halifax had noted that it might upset the Franco-British approaches to the Polish and Romanian governments, initiated the previous day, to persuade them to make their alliance against the Soviet Union also operative against an enemy on their western frontiers.[127] His views were to be only too thoroughly borne out by subsequent experience.

The essence of the British reaction to the occupation of

[126] Aster, *1939*, pp. 264–6.
[127] Public Record Office, Cabinet Office Papers CAB 23/98, minutes of 30 Mar. 1939.

Prague and M. Tilea's report of the alleged German ultimatum was, as noted above, to find means of containing Hitler
by constructing a dam against further German expansion.
This dam was to consist basically of the Balkan *Entente*
Powers (with due allowance made for Jugoslav vulnerability
to Italian pressures) plus Bulgaria (it was hoped to settle Bulgaria's frontier problems with her neighbours), and Poland.
Romania occupied the key position, not only by virtue of the
link provided by her membership of both the Balkan *Entente*
and Romano-Polish alliance, but also because German control
of her oil and wheat could create a major breach in the
economic blockade of Germany should war break out.

The fundamental weakness in the British policy of dam
building was that it conflicted with the basic instincts of the
states which were envisaged as comprising its component
parts. The Little *Entente* had begun as an alliance against
Hungary, and the Balkan *Entente* was intended as a constraint
on Bulgaria. But, despite the existence in each case of military institutions within the *Ententes*, neither organization
had ever been envisaged by its members as anything more
than a political grouping, especially as a pressure group within
the League. The idea that it might have to function as a much
tighter political organization, possibly even as an alliance,
against a power of Germany's size and coherence, was not
one any of the states cast by the British as members of the
block found attractive, even the Turks who were much
tougher in outlook than any of their would-be partners. For
Beck, as for Gafencu, all hopes of avoiding conflict were
pinned on guarantees or alliances, not on blocks. A war
would mean an end to the policy of independence; it would
mean having to choose between the Soviet Union or Germany, neither of them powers likely to encourage the Polish
or Romanian governments in the pursuit of freedom between
the blocks.

The Balkan block conceived by the British was to be
guaranteed by the major powers, by Britain and France herself, by the Soviet Union, and, it was hoped, by Italy. The
block was envisaged essentially as a device for stabilizing
what was otherwise a dangerously loose state of affairs likely
to tempt, if not to challenge, Hitler to fresh intervention. As

such it was attractive neither to the Soviet Union nor to Italy; the Soviet leadership said very little at the time, or later, directly relevant to the British proposals. But their insistence on an Anglo-French–Soviet alliance shows their basic mistrust of the device of guarantees. The Italian leadership, as Mussolini was soon to demonstrate, was more interested in what it could pick up on the cheap than in stabilizing the situation. Mussolini's fury at Hitler's annexation of Czechia was focused on the lack of warning given to him and his consequent loss of face,[128] not on the annexation *per se*, which he regarded since Munich as inevitable. His fury expressed itself therefore not in a switching of allegiance away from Hitler and an abandonment of his conflict with France, but in the decision to annexe Albania. This in turn led the British briefly to the assumption that German and Italian action had been concerted, and to alarm about stability in the Mediterranean.[129] The decision to offer guarantees to Greece and Turkey followed automatically, though the reports of an imminent Italian attack on Corfu which sparked off that decision were as false as Tilea's 'ultimatum'. More than that, as John Koliopoulos has shown, the British were careful to extract assurances from Mussolini that no action against Greece was planned before going ahead with the guarantee.[130]

The British decision to press for a guarantee of Greece thus involved two serious miscalculations, that the Italian action against Albania was concerted with Germany (whereas the opposite was the case) and, secondly, that the giving of a guarantee to Greece and Turkey would stabilize the eastern Mediterranean and ease progress towards the desired Balkan block. It involved, however, a further miscalculation—that France would share Britain's views. France did not. The principal point of French concern was still Romania.[131] The price of a French guarantee for Greece was a British guarantee

---

[128] Count G. Ciano, *Ciano's Diary, 1939-1943*, London, 1947, entries of 16–23 Mar. 1939.

[129] *DBFP*, 3rd ser., vol. VI, No. 138.

[130] See Koliopoulis, *Greece and the British Connection*, pp. 110-13.

[131] On French uneasiness at this time, and on M. Daladier's panicked reactions to the Italian attack on Albania and to M. Cretzianu's appeal in Paris, see *DBFP*, 3rd ser., vol. V, Nos. 20, 21, 22, 23, 31, 34, 48, 49, 51, 53, 65, 96, 115, 144; Alexander Cretzianu, *The Last Opportunity*, London, 1962, p. 22; Georges Gamelin, *Servire*, Paris, 1947, pp. 403-7.

for Romania, which had now officially revived the story of a German ultimatum originally given circulation by Tilea. And where Tilea was clearly acting outside the limits of his government's instructions, this new alarm was voiced by the State Secretary of the Romanian Foreign Minister, M. Cretzianu himself.[132] The British paid this price with the utmost reluctance in the face of a flat French refusal to settle for less. (As it was, it must be doubted whether the French realized that the price they in turn would have to pay for agreeing to the British proposal to guarantee Turkey was the final cession to Turkey of their Syrian province of Alexandretta.[133]) This reluctance was to be fully justified.

With the guarantees to Romania and Poland all hope of, indeed the only leverage available for, forcing the Balkan states into a common grouping disappeared. The Romanians had no real life-or-death conflict with Germany, to compare with the issue of Danzig and the Corridor. Their fears focused on Hungary as Germany's stalking-horse. Once the Anglo-French guarantee was given, the principal aim of Romanian policy came to be the giving of assurances of friendship and neutrality to the Axis powers. Gafencu's behaviour in his visits to Berlin and Rome is more than a little nauseating, though not directly in conflict with Britain's aims.[134] But his decision to press the Turks not to conclude the alliance, which was an essential part of the guarantee they had accepted from Britain and France, a decision implemented on his visit to Ankara in June 1939, spells the defeat of British policy. Instead of a dam, a structure each component of which is linked to its neighbour, they were left with a series of bilateral or unilateral guarantees, the states of eastern Europe linked not to one another but to Britain and France as if by some kind of dental bridge-work. If the guarantees were intended to embody what modern deterrence theory would

[132] *DBFP*, 3rd ser., vol. V, No. 37. Lungu maintains, convincingly, that had Poland been willing to accept the transformation of the Polano-Romanian alliance against Russia into one against Germany, Romania would have supported British plans.

[133] On which see the memoirs of the French ambassador in Ankara, 1938–40, René Massigli, *La Turquie devant la Guerre*, Paris, 1964, *passim*.

[134] On Gafencu's visits to Rome and Berlin see *DBFP*, 3rd ser., vol. V, Nos. 278, 279, 287; *DGFP*, Series D, vol. VI, Nos. 227, 234, 303, 342; GFM, 169/82587; *Ciano's Diary, 1939–1943*, entries of 1-3 May 1939; Lungu, op. cit.

call a system of 'trip-wires', then their very number proved destructive of their 'credibility'.

More than that: there is evidence to suggest that it was either the issue of the guarantee to Romania or the complexity of the arrangements into which Britain and France had stumbled which played an important role in the Soviet decision to explore the question of an agreement with Germany. In mid-April, after Litvinov's offer of an alliance to Britain and France, an offer which was followed by a lengthy conference in Moscow to which both Maisky and Merekalov, the Soviet ambassador in Germany, were summoned,[135] M. Potemkin, Litvinov's deputy, was despatched on a round tour of the Balkan capitals. He visited Bucharest, Sofia, Warsaw, and Ankara.[136] But on arriving in Istanbul he broke his tour for three days before travelling on to Ankara. In that break the news came of Litvinov's dismissal. From what records we have of his conversations in the Balkans it would appear that his enquiries were devoted to establishing how far the British exercise in block-building had progressed, and what were its prospects.[137] It would seem from the fact that he escaped Litvinov's fate that his report met with Stalin's approval, though whether it was the extent of the British effort or its apparent failure which made up the core of his report the Soviets have not yet revealed.

The story of the failure of British policy in relation to Romania is essentially one of misjudgement and misinformation, the latter being supplied by the Romanians with some help from the Greeks. So far as the latter are concerned the principal fault was the misjudgement of the Italian action against Albania, which was taken much too seriously. The insistence on a French guarantee for Greece laid Britain open to unanswerable pressure to guarantee Romania. And once the Romanian authorities had received a guarantee from

[135] On this conference see I. M. Maisky, *Who Helped Hitler?*, pp. 119–23; see also George Bilainkin, *Maisky, Ten Years Ambassador*, London, 1942, p. 246.

[136] On the Potemkin 'Rundreise' see Frank Marzari, 'Western-Soviet Rivalry in Turkey', pt. I & II, *Middle Eastern Studies*, 7 (1971); see also *DBFP*, 3rd ser., vol. V, Nos. 292, 322, 343; Massigli, *La Turquie*, pp. 191-3.

[137] The most detailed reports on Potemkin are of German provenance: see *DGFP*, Series D, vol. VI, Nos. 320 n. 4, 324, 336, 337, 342, 346, 349, and 355; see also German Foreign Ministry Photostats, 7798/E566124; *DBFP*, 3rd ser., vol. V, Nos. 378, 427, and 457.

Britain (which they took without themselves offering any reciprocal arrangement), there was no way Britain and France could control the Romanian government save by threatening to withdraw it, something which their own view of Romania's strategic importance made impossible.

XI

By June 1939 the only factor delaying the outbreak of the Second World War was Hitler's time-table: this may itself be the explanation of the otherwise mysterious June 'week-end crisis'.[138] Since we still lack any detailed study of the processes of German military planning against Poland, it remains unclear whether the 'week-end crisis' of 30 June–1 July was simply a *crise de nerfs* or an attempt by Goebbels and the SS to trigger off the alternative policy, which formed part of the military planning, of a *coup de main* limited in its operation to Danzig alone. The delay between mid-May 1939, when the Kalthof incident first provided Hitler with the excuse for awakening the Danzig–Polish conflict,[139] and the last weeks in July, when he actually invoked it, is difficult to understand. It could be he was waiting to see whether the Anglo-Soviet negotiations would, after all, prove successful; it could also be that he delayed to see whether Britain might not stumble into a Far Eastern conflict over Tientsin which would, after all, give him the Japanese alliance and the British distraction which had inspired him to keep the negotiations with Tokyo alive for so long. These are still areas where we are remarkably ignorant.

On the Hudson–Wohltat talks on the other hand, it is now clear that we are confronted not with a historical but with a historiographical problem. Since the publication of Dr Metzmacher's article in the *Vierteljahresheft für Zeitgeschichte* in

---

[138] On the 'week-end' crisis of 30 Jun.–1 Jul. 1939 see *DBFP*, 3rd ser., vol. VI, documents Nos. 155, 170, 174, 176, 180, 183, 184, 186, 197, 198, 201, 211, 212, 219, 223, 231, 236, 241, 249, 262, 263, 264, 275, 289, and 293 n. 1; *FRUS, 1939*, vol. I, pp. 195–7.

[139] On the Kalthof 'incident' of 20 May 1939 see *DBFP*, 3rd ser., vol. V, Nos. 575, 577, 579, 585; *DGFP*, Series D, vol. VI, Nos. 417, 418; *I Documenti Diplomatici Italiani, Ottavo Serie*, vol. XII, No. 37; *French Yellow Book*, No. 129.

1966,[140] the enormous discrepancies between the British and German records of these conversations can at last be understood. There are two separate stories how the conversations happened and how they became known to history; and of these understanding the second is the essential preliminary to unravelling the first.

The facts of the Wohltat-Hudson conversations became known at the end of July 1939 through an indiscretion to the British press.[141] The effect on the Soviets was to confirm the expectations of those Soviet observers who believed the Chamberlain government to be preparing for a new round of appeasement of Hitler at Poland's expense.[142] So far as British public opinion was concerned, the episode was a nine days' wonder, swiftly overtaken by the outbreak of war.

The historiography of the episode began with the publication in 1948 by the Soviet Union, in retaliation to the State Department's publication of *Nazi-Soviet Relations, 1939-1941*,[143] of two volumes of *Documents and Materials Relating to the Eve of the Second World War*.[144] The first volume of these was a mixed bag of Polish and German documents of only limited interest. The second consisted of selections from the papers of Herbert von Dirksen, the last German ambassador to Britain.[145] Among these were reports by both von Dirksen and Wohltat on the conversations held in July 1939 with Halifax, Sir Horace Wilson, and Robert Hudson. They revealed what seemed to be a far-reaching British attempt to buy Germany off, with a very large loan, joint access to colonial raw materials, an Anglo-German condominium in Central Africa, and so on. The publication of the British records of

[140] Helmut Metzmacher, 'Deutsch-Englische Ausgleichsbemühungen im Sommer 1939', *Vierteljahresheft für Zeitgeschichte*, XIV (1966).

[141] First publication came in a report in the *News Chronicle* on 22 Jul. 1939; Aster, pp. 248-9.

[142] For Soviet reactions see *Soviet Peace Efforts*, vol. II, p. 159. The Soviet Editors of this volume chose to reprint Wohltat's reports on these meetings. For a recent Soviet view see Vilnis Sipols, *Diplomatic Battles before World War II*, Moscow, 1982, pp. 232-5. Dr Sipols is one of the editors of *Soviet Peace Efforts*; see also P. Fedoseyev *et al.* (eds.), *The Origins of the Second World War*, Moscow, 1982; Aster, 'British Policy towards the USSR', p. 371, n. 2.

[143] *Nazi-Soviet Relations, 1939-1941*, Washington DC, 1949.

[144] 2 vols., Moscow, 1949.

[145] They fell into Soviet hands with the Soviet occupation of Dirksen's family estates in East Prussia in 1945.

these conversations in 1953, in volume VI of the third series of *Documents on British Foreign Policy 1919-1939*[146] by Sir Llewellyn Woodward, largely failed to make any real historiographical impact, despite the wide differences between the British and German records.

There the matter largely rested until the work of the German historian, Helmut Metzmacher, was published in 1966. This work, based on interviews with and memoranda by Wohltat, made it clear that the initiative in opening the conversations had lain with Wohltat himself, acting with the tacit understanding of Goering, his aim being to try to obtain from the British an alternative to the conflict he felt to be inevitable and of which Ribbentrop was denying the possibility to Hitler. He felt that something was being achieved when the indiscretion mentioned above alerted Ribbentrop to the facts of the talks and the participation in arranging these talks of the ambassador. But faced with the threat of severe disciplinary proceedings, both Wohltat and von Dirksen felt obliged both to exaggerate the nature and scope of the conversations, and to represent the initiative as having come from the British side. In making up the picture of the negotiations and of the alleged British offer they drew most heavily on Wohltat's interview with Robert Hudson. For, while Halifax and Sir Horace Wilson had conducted themselves with care and caution, Hudson had gone very much further, taking it upon himself to revive proposals put to Germany in March 1938, as revised in internal discussions in the aftermath of Munich.

The British cabinet records now available, when taken with the Neville Chamberlain and other papers, make it clear that Hudson was acting entirely on his own responsibility. He seems to have seen the nature of the prizes he dangled before Wohltat as very much conditional on the abandonment by Hitler of his existing line of conduct, even of withdrawal from Czechia. This part Wohltat, desperate to ward off Ribbentrop's threats, omitted entirely from his report. The incident left Chamberlain convinced that the original indiscretion had

[146] See *DBFP*, 3rd ser., vol. VI, document No. 370 for the record of Mr Hudson's conversation with Wohltat of 20 Jul. 1939; for Sir Horace Wilson's records of his conversation of 18 Jul., ibid., No. 354; see also ibid., Nos. 423, 424, 425, 439, 440, 442, 458, 509, 533, 557, 509; *Parliamentary Debates*, 5th ser., *House of Commons*, vol. 350, cols. 1025-28.

been engineered by the Soviets,[147] and inclined to exonerate Hudson. The professionals of the Foreign Office were privately furious;[148] but with the August crisis already breaking they had their hands too full to do anything except write an occasional acid minute.

The episode was important for its defeat of the motives inspiring its originator, Wohltat. It convinced Hitler that the will to appeasement still flourished in the Chamberlain cabinet. It awoke new suspicions of Britain in France, Poland, and the United States. It must have confirmed those of the Soviet leadership. Historiographically it distorted understanding of British policy in the summer of 1939 for nearly twenty years. It is only now, in the work of Aster and others, that it is being seen in its proper perspective in the West; Soviet historians remain unshaken in their original views.

XII

The three qualities this paper has examined stem from three different, though allied, sources. Much of the misinformation was spread deliberately by elements seeking to manipulate the British government. Among outstanding examples of this are those who provided the reports which gave rise to the war-scare of January 1939, and M. Tilea and those who in the last week of March 1939 reported the imminence of a German attack on Poland. In each case they nudged the British government one step closer to war.

The principal areas of misconception lie in the British image of Germany's moderates; British hopes of a Balkan–Polish block; British misunderstanding of Roosevelt's position in February 1939; and most serious of all, British misconceptions of Soviet policy. The misconceptions originated mainly in the British inability to postulate the realities of a totalitarian society on the one hand, or a genuinely divided one such as the United States on the other. The Chamberlain cabinet were far from ill-informed about German and European

[147] Chamberlain Papers, Chamberlain to Ida Chamberlain, 23 Jul. 1939.
[148] See Vansittart Minute, PRO Foreign Office Records FO 371/22990, C 10521/16/18; see also letters and minutes in C 10698/16/18; see also *Harvey Diaries*, p. 303. Sir Alexander Cadogan was on holiday. His comments are not recorded.

politics, the Foreign Office still less so. But it was not until 25 March 1939 that Sir Alexander Cadogan could confide to his diary his amazement that events were conforming so closely to the prognostications of his predecessor, Sir Robert Vansittart.[149] British élite opinion lacked either the education or the experience properly to assess the realities of the policy-making processes in the two future super-powers. The concept of a dam and the naïve deterrence theory that underlaid it has been commented on elsewhere.

As for mistrust, it underlay three of the most vital areas, relations with the Soviet Union, relations with Colonel Beck, and relations with the sources of so much of the information which was obtained from Germany. Of these the first was the most tragic, though the suspicion was clearly mutual and rooted in the experience of the 1920s.

It is equally easy to point to the areas of misinformation and mistrust on the German side, the misjudgement of British reactions to the occupation of Czechia, and Hitler's acceptance of Ribbentrop's assurances that British resistance to him would collapse in the moment of crisis. In view of the controversy aroused by Taylor, still more of the appearance of a right-wing school of revisionism which seeks to exonerate Hitler, it is essential to abandon the position taken by many historians of a refusal to speculate. On the German side it is very difficult to argue that Hitler did not want war in 1939, and scheme and plan for it. He did not want the war he got; it was from his point of view four years or so too early before the Z plan had come to fruition. As a manipulator and stage manager Hitler was a comparative failure, and he was served by dolts.

On the British side a vital part in triggering British responses was played by misinformation. But the steps actually taken were taken on a rational calculation of the pros and cons of each step, taken in the laboured and measured machinery of consultation, recommendation, and decision which is the British system of government. It did end with Britain at war with Germany; and this can only be regarded as a mistake by those who deny Hitler's unique embodiment of the European tradition of state authoritarianism and who seriously believe that the world is not a better place for his defeat.

[149] Dilks, *Cadogan Diaries*, entry of 25 Mar. 1939.

9

The Labour Government of 1945–1951:
The Determinants of Policy

Henry Pelling

I

The general election of 1945 was not decided by party mani-
festos. Doubts about the qualities of Winston Churchill as a
peacetime leader, residual criticism of the National Government's policy of 'appeasement' and dissatisfaction with pre-
war rearmament, a sympathy for the type of 'planning'
apparently evident in the conduct of military operations both
by the Western Allies and by the Russians—all these were
factors in the outcome of the election.[1] But of course the
Labour party did have a manifesto, *Let Us Face the Future*,
drafted in the main by Herbert Morrison, who was chairman
of the National Executive's Policy Committee; it had been
approved by the 1945 Party Conference; and, in accordance
with the doctrine of 'the mandate' which was especially
prevalent on the left (although originally promulgated on the
right),[2] its elected members determined to suit the action to
the word. Clement Attlee, the new Prime Minister, had written less than ten years earlier: 'I am convinced that whenever
this mandate has been given, the Labour programme must be
carried out with the utmost vigour and resolution.'[3] He and
his colleagues were especially fortunate, in that they came to
power at the end of a long war, during which they had experienced office as members of a coalition government, and
with many controls of the type that they might have wished
to impose already in force as a result of wartime conditions.

---

[1] See my 'The 1945 General Election Reconsidered', *Historical Journal*, 23
(1980), 399–414.

[2] On the history of the doctrine, see C. S. Emden, 'The Mandate in the Nineteenth Century', *Parliamentary Affairs*, 11 (1958), 260 ff. I owe this reference to
Mr Floyd Parsons.

[3] C. R. Attlee, *The Labour Party in Perspective*, London, 1937, p. 286.

II

The power structure of the Labour party had not by 1945 been subjected to any substantial academic analysis, for the publication of Professor R. T. McKenzie's *British Political Parties* still lay ten years in the future. McKenzie was to argue that, rather than the Labour party being more 'democratic' than the Conservative party, it was more authoritarian in that its leader was more rarely changed than the leader of the Conservative party; and that the apparent domination by the party conference and the National Executive elected at the conference was little more than a myth. So far from Ramsay MacDonald having been forced out of the leadership in 1931 by a party revolt, Professor McKenzie argued, he had decided to leave of his own accord: 'whether in fact MacDonald parted company with the Labour Party with regret or relief, he did so, in effect, of his own volition'.[4] But this is not really what happened. Although the National Executive showed some weakness in the financial crisis, agreeing to 'leave matters in the hands of their Ministerial colleagues',[5] the leaders of the TUC asserted their complete opposition to MacDonald's policy, and in effect executed a *coup d'état* within the party, which led to the break-up of the Government and—when MacDonald formed a new 'National' Government—to his expulsion from the party.

Professor McKenzie has been criticized by other students of the history of the period for ignoring the role of the trade-union leadership within the Labour party. From 1931 onwards, the secretary of the General Council of the TUC, Walter Citrine, and the secretary of the largest of the unions, Ernest Bevin, resolved to play a leading role in politics as well as in industry. The National Joint Council, which was used for liaison between the General Council and the party, was reorganized to provide the General Council with a majority of seats; and it was decided that it should henceforth meet monthly so as to determine and make pronouncements about major questions affecting the movement as a whole.[6] In 1934

[4] R. T. McKenzie, *British Political Parties*, 2nd edn., London, 1963, p. 387.
[5] *Labour Party Conference Report* [*LPCR*], 1931, p. 4.
[6] *LPCR*, 1932, p. 67.

the National Joint Council was renamed the 'National Council of Labour'.[7]

The NCL's importance *vis-à-vis* the parliamentary party was very evident in the years between 1931 and 1935, when initially the party had only forty-six MPs and the veteran left-winger George Lansbury—at first the only Cabinet Minister to survive the 1931 débâcle—was the parliamentary leader. Lansbury, himself a pacifist, could not adequately express the rather more robust standpoint of the movement as a whole in the face of the growth of fascism on the continent: he retired shortly after receiving a harsh rebuff from Ernest Bevin at the 1935 party conference,[8] and was succeeded on a temporary basis by Clement Attlee, a mild-mannered lecturer and social worker who had also survived the 1931 election by holding a very strongly working class constituency in East London. Partly because of the party's wish to avoid an imposing leader like MacDonald, partly because the rival candidates tended to cancel each other out, Attlee survived as leader for altogether twenty years.

During the war, Winston Churchill had good reason to appreciate the extent to which his Labour colleagues were dependent upon the extra-parliamentary elements of their party. In the crisis of May 1940, which brought Churchill to power, Attlee would not accept office until he had received the support of the National Executive, which was in session at Bournemouth during an annual conference;[9] and just five years later, when the conference was meeting at Blackpool after the 'German War' had ended, Attlee's advice to continue the coalition was rejected by the Executive and by the conference and he and his colleagues resigned in order to fight an immediate general election.[10] It was no wonder, therefore, that when Professor Harold Laski, the Chairman of the National Executive, challenged Attlee's right to accompany Churchill to Potsdam as more than an 'observer', Churchill at once jumped to the conclusion that the National Executive was to take control if Attlee and his colleagues won the election.

This, however, was not to be the case. The very fact that

[7] *LPCR*, 1934, p. 14.
[8] *LPCR*, 1935, p. 178.
[9] *LPCR*, 1940, pp. 123–34.
[10] Pelling, '1945', pp. 402–3.

258   *Henry Pelling*

the issue had been raised by Churchill was enough to enable Attlee to assert his authority within the movement to an un-precedented degree. Moreover, the conflict with Churchill during the election did much to build up Attlee's personality with the electorate. After his broadcast reply to Churchill's initial attack, Attlee replied by letter to a series of messages, of course intended for publication, which Churchill showered upon him. Attlee wrote in his autobiography: 'All the corre-spondence was published. Sometimes his letter reached me at a very late hour at night, but I always contrived to get my replies into the Press the same day as his letters.'[11] Another reason for the strength of the Labour government *vis-à-vis* both National Executive and TUC was the fact that Ernest Bevin, having entered parliament to serve as Churchill's Mini-ster of Labour, loyally supported Attlee, 'the little man' as he called him, from inside the Labour cabinet.[12]

It is true that Attlee's personal position came under threat at times. Laski, the new chairman of the National Executive, thought that he should have given way on the eve of the elec-tion, but the proposal, which he made in a personal letter to Attlee himself, was ignored by the leader after consultation with the Chief Whip.[13] Morrison also thought that the new parliamentary party should be given a chance to select a fresh leader on assembling after the election: but by that time Attlee had already been invited by the King to form a govern-ment and had undertaken to do so. When the parliamentary party met, Attlee's reputation was at its height: full confi-dence in him as leader was expressed on the motion of Arthur Greenwood, with Ernest Bevin seconding, and he received a 'three-minute ovation'.[14] Later on, in 1947, when there was an economic crisis, there was criticism of Attlee, and indeed, as I shall relate in due course, a further attempt to replace him, this time by Bevin; but Bevin himself gave no support to the project and Morrison was disappointed not to have been regarded as the natural successor.[15] Although there were to

[11] C. R. Attlee, *As It Happened*, London, 1954, p. 145.
[12] F. Williams, *Nothing So Strange*, London, 1970, p. 222.
[13] Chuter Ede, diary, 28 May 1945, BL Add. MS 59701.
[14] *Town-Crier* (Birmingham), 4 Aug. 1945.
[15] Hugh Dalton, *High Tide and After*, London, 1962, pp. 240–5.

be two resignations from the Cabinet in 1951—Aneurin Bevan and Harold Wilson—there were no more challenges to Attlee as leader.

III

Let Us Face the Future was the product of many years in opposition before the war as well as of some reconsideration while the war was taking place. It contained a programme of reforms which a Socialist government could be expected to accomplish within the period of one parliament, that is, five years. It involved a number of measures of nationalization—of the Bank of England, of the coal and power industries, of transport, and of the iron and steel industry. All of these proposals, except for that for iron and steel, had appeared in the 'Immediate Programme' adopted at the 1937 party conference. Iron and steel was added as the result of an amendment from the floor of the 1944 conference, put forward by a young left-wing delegate, Ian Mikardo, and carried against the advice of the Executive.[16] Actually, Mikardo's resolution was more all-embracing: it demanded 'the transfer to public ownership of the land, large-scale building, heavy industry, and all forms of banking, transport and fuel and power'—but the addition of this one major industry to the list of what could be done within one parliament was thought to be an adequate concession to the view that the conference had expressed.

In addition, *Let Us Face the Future* contained pledges accepting and going somewhat beyond the Coalition Government's commitments which had followed the Beveridge Report of 1942—notably the acknowledgement of full employment as an object of national financial policy, the payment of family allowances, and the creation of a national health service. Planning for these objects within Whitehall had been going on for the two years preceding the election, and Labour ministers, who played an especially important part on the domestic side of government during the war, had a major role in the determination of coalition policy. In the case of education, the Labour manifesto was largely content

[16] *LPCR*, 1944, pp. 163, 167, 168.

to accept the proposals of the Coalition Education Act, passed in 1944 on the initiative of the Conservative Minister, R. A. Butler.

In the latter part of the war Labour's National Executive had also thrashed out a statement of the principles that should animate foreign policy. The major responsibility for the statement, which was called 'The International Post-War Settlement', lay with Hugh Dalton, who was serving as President of the Board of Trade in the Coalition, but who was regarded as the party's most likely candidate for the post of Foreign Secretary.[17] The statement called for 'the closest possible Anglo-American–Russian cooperation', for support for the world organization of the United Nations—not then in existence—for the preparation of colonial territories for self-government, and for the control of Palestine by a Jewish 'majority'. There was no reference to Palestine in *Let Us Face the Future*, but at the 1945 conference, just before the election, Labour's policy as declared in the longer statement of 1944 was re-affirmed by Dalton.[18]

IV

It was therefore the Party Conference, and the National Executive annually elected by Conference, which took the responsibility for Labour's programme. The National Council of Labour had ceased to operate as an effective guiding force, partly because in 1940 Ernest Bevin, its most powerful personality, had entered Government and Parliament; partly because in 1941 representatives of the Co-operative Union had been admitted to membership on an equal basis with those of the TUC, and this made it unduly cumbersome.[19] But trade-union votes still counted for the great majority of those exercised at the conference, and in choosing the National Executive. The principal new factors affecting policy after the 1945 election were, on the one hand, the legacy of commitments made by the Coalition Government and the economic

[17] For an account of the drafting of the statement, see J. T. Grantham, 'Hugh Dalton and the International Post-War Settlement', *Journal of Contemporary History*, 14 (1979), 713–29.

[18] *LPCR*, 1945, p. 103.   [19] *LPCR*, 1942, p. 3.

weakness of the country; and, on the other hand, the views of the enormous Parliamentary Labour party, much of it consisting of youngish men from middle-class occupations who had won marginal constituencies and who were determined to ensure that the party programme was put fully into effect. Herbert Morrison, as Leader of the House, secured good relations between the government and the parliamentary party by establishing a Liaison Committee, by encouraging the development of back-bench policy groups, and by suspending the disciplinary standing orders.[20]

On the whole, the parliamentary policy groups had little influence in shaping the decisions of the Government. It is true that as early as October 1945 Lord Winster's proposals for civil aviation, submitted to the Cabinet at that time, incorporated 'very substantial modifications' urged upon him by the PLP Civil Aviation Group.[21] Throughout 1945-6 the Defence and Services Group, under the chairmanship of James Callaghan, was active in the cause of more rapid demobilization, and not without effect.[22] But Ernest Bevin, although he took care to bring major foreign policy issues before the Cabinet, regarded the parliamentary party's External Affairs Group with hostility. Hugh Dalton later wrote that Bevin had made the mistake of allowing the Group to choose itself, with the result that it included 'all the pacifists, and fellow-travellers, pro-Russians and anti-Americans, and every sort of freak harboured in our majority'.[23] Dalton, of course, had taken care to ensure that the Finance Group mostly consisted of his friends. Even so, the Foreign Secretary had little difficulty in appealing beyond the External Affairs Group to the parliamentary party as a whole, and indeed to the party conference.

The first serious clash of the External Affairs Group with Bevin occurred in March 1946. Bevin was pressing for an early

[20] B. Donoughue and G. W. Jones, *Herbert Morrison*, London, 1973, pp. 367-71.

[21] Minutes, Liaison Committee, PLP, 29 Oct. 1945: microfilm in British Library of Political and Economic Science (BLPES).

[22] Callaghan to M. Webb, 4 Dec. 1946, Attlee Papers, Box 9, University College Library, Oxford. (These papers have lately been transferred to the Bodleian Library, Oxford.)

[23] Dalton, *High Tide and After*, p. 23.

general election in Greece so as to be able to establish a stable government and then withdraw British troops. But the back-benchers thought that haste would result in a government not fully representative of the Left, and so 'by a large majority' they urged the postponement of elections.[24] The issue was taken to a full meeting of the parliamentary party, with about 300 MPs present. Bevin attended and asked for loyalty: he wanted to know if he was supported by '50 per cent of the party, or 60 or 70 or 80 per cent'. His aim, he pointed out, was to encourage a mutual withdrawal of troops by Britain in Greece and by Russia in the Balkans. His policy was endorsed 'overwhelmingly, there being only six dissentients'.[25]

Foreign affairs, in any case, were not easily susceptible to manifesto declarations. Labour foreign policy still had to take account of the permanent interests of the powers. Denis Healey, at that time the International Secretary at the party's headquarters at Transport House, quoted Vyshinsky, the Deputy Foreign Secretary of the Soviet Union, to this effect in a pamphlet in which he argued the case against the left-wing advocates of a distinctive 'Socialist' foreign policy: 'The class struggle does not alter geography. It is still the case that a ship travelling from the Aegean to the Black Sea must pass through the Dardanelles.'[26]

Attlee had replied in the same vein to an amendment to the Address in November 1946, when Richard Crossman and other back-bench Labour MPs, to the number of 57, had called on the Government to 'recast its conduct of international affairs' so as to secure the collaboration of 'Nations striving to secure full Socialist planning and control of the world's resources'.[27] Although the Labour MPs did not wish to divide the House on the amendment, the issue was forced by two ILPers and it was apparent that about a third of the parliamentary party chose to abstain. According to his Private Secretary, Pierson Dixon, Bevin, who was attending a meeting of the Council of Foreign Ministers in New York, found

[24] Minutes, Liaison Committee, 19 Mar. 1946.
[25] Press Statement, Minutes, Liaison Committee, 27 Mar. 1946; 'Criticism of the Foreign Policy of the Secretary of State', Circular to Heads of Mission, PRO FO 371/54801.
[26] Labour Party, *Approach to Foreign Policy*, London, 1947, p. 14.
[27] *H.C. Deb.*, vol. 430, 526 (18 Nov. 1946).

the result 'upsetting'.[28] He made his riposte at the party conference at Bournemouth the following June, when he referred
to the Crossman amendment as a 'stab in the back'. He strongly
implied that this was what could be expected of middle-class
members of the party: 'I grew up in the trade union, you see,
and I have never been used to this kind of thing.' With union
support, his policy was endorsed so overwhelmingly that
there was no need for a card vote.[29]

Bevin would have liked to preserve more of Britain's world
power than he was able to. Early in 1947 he complained to
Attlee about the constant retreats and withdrawals that were
being insisted upon at the time.[30] But they were really being
imposed upon the Government, not by ideology, but by the
Treasury's urgent need for the retrenchment of overseas expenditure. Thus, the partition of Germany and its occupation,
and the Soviet Union's refusal to allow grain shipments from
its zone for the benefit of the Western zones, involved for
both Britain and the United States a heavy financial burden.
As Keynes wrote in February 1946: 'Our present policy, by
which we have become involved in paying her [i.e. Germany]
large reparations, might rank as the craziest ever if we did not
remember last time.'[31] This situation led the American State
Department to propose to Britain a merger of the British and
American zones, in the hope that they would soon become
by joint efforts economically viable. After some hesitation,
Bevin urged the Cabinet to accept this offer, and it did so in
July 1946.[32] This was an important turning-point in international relations, for it meant a renewed association between
Britain and the United States, in the occupation of the heart
of Europe. The merger took formal effect on 1 January 1947.
The Russians continued to press for the payment of reparations from current production in Germany; but Bevin replied,
as he later told the British Cabinet, that 'he could not accept
any change in reparations policy which would impose a further

[28] P. Dixon, *Double Diploma*, London, 1968, p. 241.
[29] *LPCR*, 1947, p. 179.
[30] Bevin to Attlee, 1 Jan. 1947, in N. Mansergh (ed.), *The Transfer of Power,
1942–7*, vol. ix, London, 1980, pp. 431 f.
[31] 'The Overseas Deficit', CP (46) 58, 8 Feb. 1946, PRO CAB 129/7/43.
[32] Cabinet Meeting, 25 July 1946, CAB 128/6/46.

burden on the British taxpayer'.[33] At this time the British Ambassador in Moscow, Sir Maurice Peterson, noticed a 'growth of tension between the Soviet Union and the Anglo-Saxon *bloc*, as Britain and the United States are consistently called here'.[34]

It was the same desire for economy which led the Cabinet to authorize the announcement to the United States early in 1947 that Britain could no longer supply financial assistance to Greece and Turkey, which had hitherto been in the British area of influence. No prior notice was given to the United Nations, but President Truman accepted the commitment with remarkable alacrity, declaring, in what became known as the 'Truman doctrine', that 'it must be the policy of the United States to support free peoples who are resisting attempted subjugation by armed minorities or by outside pressures'.[35] Dalton, Chancellor of the Exchequer at the time, later took credit for forcing this decision upon the Foreign Secretary and through him upon the American President.[36]

In the case of India, Labour policy and the Government's need for economy were in unison. It was while MacDonald was Prime Minister at the time of the second Labour government that dominion status had first been formally recognized as the object of British policy. The Government of India Act, 1935, passed by the National Government after a struggle with its own right wing, provided for the establishment of, first, elected provincial governments, and then a federal government at the centre; but the Congress party in 1939 refused to operate the Act during the war, and full powers were returned to the Provincial Governors. In 1942 an attempt was made, by the Cripps mission, to secure the support of the Indian parties for the war in return for a promise of independence as soon as victory was achieved. The mission, which was not favoured by the Prime Minister, Winston Churchill, was the result of a combination of factors: the Japanese advance into Burma, the pressure from the United States, and the conviction of Labour ministers that action was essential.

[33] Cabinet Meeting, 2 May 1947, CAB 128/9/194.

[34] Sir M. Peterson to Bevin, 22 Oct. 1946, FO 371/56883.

[35] F. O. Wilcox and T. V. Kalijarvi, *Recent American Foreign Policy: Basic Documents, 1941–1951*, Westport, Conn., 1972, p. 817.

[36] Dalton, *High Tide and After*, pp. 206–9.

Attlee wrote a paper in which he argued that 'we need to do in India what Durham did in Canada'.[37] But the mission proved a failure, Gandhi being reported as describing the offer as 'a post-dated cheque on a crashing bank'.[38] For the remaining war years, constitutional advance was abandoned.

When the war ended, it was accepted in Whitehall that Indian independence would be achieved as soon as appropriate arrangements could be made. In 1946 a three-man mission of Cabinet Ministers was sent to India in order to seek a constitutional settlement; but the Indian parties were bitterly divided, and the mission returned without success. Meanwhile there was a gradual collapse of law and order in the subcontinent, and the then Viceroy, Lord Wavell, asked the Cabinet for the declaration of a date of British withdrawal: in his opinion, British rule could not be enforced beyond March 1948.[39] This was the moment of Bevin's truculence about withdrawals already referred to;[40] Attlee, however, realizing that there was no alternative, decided to accept Wavell's recommendation but to send out Mountbatten, the King's first cousin, to succeed him and to conduct the procedure of withdrawal with appropriate dignity. Mountbatten did so, and actually brought forward the date for the transfer of power to August 1947. The reality of the situation was well brought out by Hugh Dalton, who wrote in his diary: 'If you are in a place where you are not wanted, and where you have not got the force, or perhaps the will, to squash those who don't want you, the only thing to do is to come out. . . . I don't believe one person in a hundred thousand in this country cares tuppence about it, so long as British people are not being mauled about out there.'[41]

The independence of India did not take place as happily as had been hoped, for instead of the handover being made to one newly independent state, there were two mutually hostile successor states in the subcontinent. And the communal rioting of 1946 was succeeded by an even more bitter conflict

---

[37] WP (42) 59, 2 Feb. 1942, in Mansergh, *Transfer of Power*, vol. i, 1970, p. 110.

[38] I. Stephens, *Monsoon Morning*, London, 1966, p. 31.

[39] P. Moon (ed.), *Wavell: The Viceroy's Journal*, London, 1973, p. 399.

[40] See above, n. 30.

[41] Dalton, *High Tide and After*, p. 211.

amounting to virtual warfare. Something of the Anglo-Indian connection was maintained, however, by the willingness of both successor states to join the Commonwealth, which ceased to be simply a white man's club and became multi-racial in character. All this was in line with Labour party policy; but it also owed not a little to the special knowledge of the Indian problem which had been acquired by Attlee, dating from his work on the Simon Commission in the later 1920s.[42] He had himself taken charge of the India Committee of the Cabinet until the summer of 1947.

The Government's policy in Palestine formed an unhappy contrast to its performance in India. Once in office, Attlee and Bevin took little notice of the commitment to a 'Jewish majority' which had been accepted by the Labour Party Conference in 1944; they were prepared to sacrifice the cause of Zionism for British *realpolitik*. When President Truman, under the influence of the large Jewish minority in the United States, demanded the immediate admission to Palestine of 100,000 Jewish immigrants, Bevin retorted at the 1946 Party Conference, 'They do not want too many Jews in New York.'[43] It was true that the Foreign Office was seriously concerned about Arab reactions to any large Jewish immigration. The Arabs, after all, controlled the oil supplies of the Middle East, which were already vitally important for the British economy; and the Chiefs of Staff wished to be able to use Palestine as a military base for the Middle East.[44] In addition, as Attlee had reminded Truman as early as September 1945, the British Government had to take account of reactions among the 'ninety million Moslems' of India.[45] The Zionist lobby discovered that, whatever its success at party conferences, it was a different matter to get pledges translated into policy. But here again the desire for economy proved the determining factor: in September 1947 the Cabinet decided to relinquish the Mandate and make an early withdrawal of British forces

[42] For Attlee's own account, see F. Williams, *A Prime Minister Remembers*, London, 1961, ch. 13.

[43] *LPCR*, 1946, p. 165.

[44] Sir Norman Brook to PM, 14 Jan. 1947, Prime Minister's Briefs, CAB 21/2243.

[45] Attlee to Truman, 16 Sept. 1945, quoted Williams, *A Prime Minister Remembers*, p. 190.

from Palestine because, as Dalton said, 'the maintenance of British forces in it merely led to a heavy drain on our financial resources and to the creation of a dangerous spirit of anti-semitism'.[46]

V

In the domestic sphere the Government had a far better chance of fulfilling its election pledges, for it was not there quite so much at the mercy of external pressures. Both the parliamentary party and the membership in the constituencies were keen to see the enactment of the full programme of nationalization, as the first steps to the creation of a Socialist state. The first nationalization bill was that for the Bank of England, and even Churchill, remembering his difficulties with Montagu Norman in the 1920s, was sympathetic to this. In the case of coal and the railways, reorganization was essential whatever the complexion of the government, and the trade unions had long favoured nationalization. But some disagreement arose over the extent of the nationalization of road haulage, which the railway MPs regarded as necessary in order to preserve railway freight traffic.

Herbert Morrison's account of the progress of the Transport Bill is instructive. He says that both he and the Minister of Transport, Alfred Barnes, wished to eliminate the 'cut-throat competition' of road and rail services, and were therefore keen on taking into public ownership, not the small local hauliers but 'the big firms, including those with their own fleets for carrying their own goods (the holders of 'C' licences)'. But partly owing to his own illness in 1947, and partly as a result of opposition from the Co-operative Societies who in many cases had large transport fleets, 'the C-Licence firms were cut out of the Bill'.[47] Certainly this resulted in a considerable reduction of the Transport Commission's effective power to co-ordinate all forms of transport across the country.

On the nationalization of iron and steel, however, Morrison was himself inclined to caution. This was the one item of

[46] Cabinet Meeting 20 Sept. 1947, CAB 128/10/149.
[47] H. Morrison, *Autobiography*, London, 1960, p. 259; D. N. Chester, *Nationalisation of British Industry, 1945–51*, London, 1975, p. 136.

public ownership which had been introduced into the programme against the wishes of the party leadership. As it happened, 1947 was a year of acute economic crisis, and it was
easy for opponents of the measure to argue that this was not
the time to risk the disruption of output owing to a change
of ownership, which in any case was bound to be strongly
resisted by the owners because of the profitability of the industry. It was also true that the leader of the principal trade
union concerned—Lincoln Evans, General Secretary of the
British Iron and Steel Trades Association—was lukewarm
about nationalization.[48] Under these circumstances Attlee
encouraged Morrison to explore the possibility of a compromise scheme with Sir Andrew Duncan, the most prominent
of the steel magnates. Together they produced a scheme
whereby there was to be an Iron and Steel Board to control
the industry but not to own it: the industry was to remain in
private hands unless it or parts of it became inefficient.[49]

The issue was repeatedly debated in the Cabinet in the
course of 1947, for the last opportunity of nationalizing the
industry before the end of the Parliament, assuming that
the Lords exercised their delaying power of two years, was in
the 1947–8 session. Morrison's proposed compromise was
supported by several members of the Cabinet, including
Lords Addison and Jowitt; but the Prime Minister, to Morrison's indignation, played only a chairman's role, and there
was strong opposition: both Dalton and Cripps were in favour
of early nationalization, and Aneurin Bevan felt so strongly
that he threatened to resign.[50] Early in August the compromise was definitely abandoned in favour of nationalization,
but the question of date was for the time left open.[51] The
matter was discussed at a special meeting of the parliamentary
party, when a motion to insist on nationalization in the
1947–8 session was hotly debated but, in the end, by a small
majority, not put.[52]

Within the Cabinet the actual difficulty of shaping the bill

[48] G. W. Ross, *The Nationalisation of Steel*, London, 1965, p. 129.
[49] Morrison, *Autobiography*; Dalton, *High Tide and After*, pp. 252-3.
[50] 'Reorganisation of the Iron and Steel Industry', CP (47) 185, CAB 129/19/
210; Morrison, *Autobiography*, p. 296.
[51] Cabinet Meeting 7 Aug. 1947, CAB 128/10/118 f.
[52] PLP Minutes 11 Aug. 1947: microfilm in BLPES.

was present in the minds of Ministers, who had had plenty of problems already with earlier nationalization bills. In the case of iron and steel, the firms often had interests in engineering and in shipbuilding as well as in the basic work of manufacture. It was argued that to delay until 1948–9 was quite feasible if the nationalization bill was preceded by a measure to reduce the Lords' delaying power from two years to one. The final decision, which was in favour of this course, was only made in mid-October.[53] The Parliament Act (Amendment) Bill took precedence over it in November 1947.

There was renewed debate as the details of the Iron and Steel Bill were thrashed out in the spring of 1948. Attlee had resigned himself to its enactment, although, as he told Dalton, he 'did not think it was a good choice as it had too ragged an edge'.[54] The members of the existing Iron and Steel Board —a board of control left over from wartime, and all employers in the industry—were hotly against it. Sir Archibald Forbes, the chairman, wrote to the Minister of Supply to say 'In my view the introduction of a dislocating factor in the form of proposals for public ownership would inevitably lead to a loss of production and slowing down of development projects.'[55] The civil servants took fright at this themselves: Plowden, the chairman of Cripps's Economic Planning Board, sent him a letter in May to say that the bill would threaten short-term output and would also arouse hostility in the United States, at a time when Britain was increasingly dependent upon American aid. His letter ended: 'I respectfully submit that to introduce at the present time a Bill for the nationalisation of the iron and steel industry is an act of economic irresponsibility.'[56] At a Cabinet meeting on 7 June Morrison put up his last fight for the limited bill that he had already proposed; but the decisive argument came from Ernest Bevin, who pointed out that if there was no take-over it would be 'inconsistent

[53] Cabinet Meeting 14 Oct. 1947, CAB 128/10/170; telegram, PM to Addison, 15 Oct. 1947, PREM 8/1059.

[54] Dalton, unpublished diary, 26 May 1947, BLPES. This and later quotations from the unpublished papers of Hugh Dalton appear by permission of the Librarian, BLPES.

[55] Forbes to Minister of Supply, 28 Apr. 1948, Appx. to CP (48) 123, CAB 129/27/21.

[56] Plowden to Chancellor of Exchequer, 24 May 1948, copy with Norman Brook to PM 27 May 1948, Prime Minister's Briefs, CAB 21/2244.

with the policy of seeking to promote the socialisation of the Ruhr steel industry'.[57]

The Iron and Steel Bill was introduced in the following November and, having been subjected to much delay owing to the bitterness of the opposition in both Commons and Lords, received the Royal Assent only in November 1949. By then it had long become clear that it would not be fully operative by the time of the next general election. In the end there was no need to use the Parliament Act in its new form because the Government, which had great difficulty anyway in forming a new control board, accepted the compromise of having the bill on the Statute Book before the election rather than insisting on its immediate operation.[58]

VI

More immediately tangible reforms, so far as most people were concerned, were the extension of the national insurance system, the creation of the National Health Service, and the putting into effect of the Butler Education Act. Two Welshmen were in charge of the first two of these tasks. James Griffiths, the Minister for National Insurance, helped to bring into operation the Caretaker Government's Family Allowances Act and extended the range of national insurance and national assistance. Aneurin Bevan, after some tiffs with the doctors, secured the establishment of a National Health Service which, except in respect of the nationalization of the hospitals—an idea which emerged from the minds of his civil servants—was not very different from what had been planned under the Coalition government.[59] All these schemes came into operation in July 1948. Meanwhile Ellen Wilkinson, as Minister of Education, had secured the raising of the school-leaving age to fifteen. Successive Chancellors of the Exchequer had to find the finance for these schemes, but none of them aroused

---

[57] Cabinet Meeting 7 June 1948, CAB 128/12/162.

[58] Cabinet Meeting 10 Nov. 1949, CAB 128/16/98; Ross, *Nationalisation of Steel*, pp. 115 f.

[59] H. Eckstein, 'The Politics of the B.M.A.', *Political Science Quarterly*, 26 (1955), 345–59; H. Eckstein, *The English Health Service*, Cambridge, Mass., 1959; J. E. Porter, *The Making of the National Health Service*, London, 1981, p. 178.

issues of principle between Government and Opposition, or Government and back-benchers.

What had embarrassed the Government, however, was the fact that at the end of the war, as Churchill had foreseen, the country was virtually bankrupt and could not recover without substantial assistance from the United States. The problem was highlighted by the sudden conclusion of the war against Japan, only three months after the end of the European war, instead of—as the planners had been expecting—eighteen months later; and by President Truman's abrupt termination of Lend-Lease one month later. Whitehall had been relying upon the continuation of Lend-Lease for some months at least in order to tide the country over the difficult period of transition back to its pre-war pattern, when exports could once more pay for imports of essential raw materials and foods. The incoming Labour government decided to ask Lord Keynes to negotiate for a dollar grant, or failing this, a loan on easy terms from the United States: after weeks of negotiation, Keynes secured a rather smaller sum than had been requested, in the form of a loan, and with the condition that the British Government would make sterling convertible to dollars one year after enactment. The belief that multilateral trading could be resumed after only twelve months was, as the British negotiators well knew, a highly optimistic expectation.[60]

Under the circumstances it was fortunate that the Labour government inherited from the Coalition an elaborate system of import controls and rationing. But the machinery for economic recovery was, to begin with, distinctly defective. During the war the Treasury and the Board of Trade had been downgraded in importance, and the Lord President's Committee fulfilled the task of allocating manpower, which was the most important function at a time when the United States was willing to sustain the country with Lend-Lease supplies. In Attlee's Cabinet, of course, Dalton as Chancellor of the Exchequer and Cripps as President of the Board of Trade at once recovered much of the old authority for their

[60] R. N. Gardner, *Sterling–Dollar Diplomacy*, new edn., New York, 1969, p. 230; Dalton, unpublished diary, 14 Dec. 1945: 'The terms of the loan will not stand long unaltered.'

departments, but Morrison as Lord President was senior to them in the cabinet hierarchy and claimed to control the domestic economy. Cripps made a bid in August 1945 to win control of the Economic Section of the Cabinet Office, but Morrison ensured that it remained subordinate to himself.[61] But the Lord President, who knew little about economics, and who spent most of his time leading the House of Commons and controlling the enactment of the nationalization programme, could not formulate a plan for national recovery. The Lord President's Committee served a useful purpose in reconciling differences among ministers on a wide range of relatively unimportant issues on the domestic front.[62] Early in 1947 Morrison suffered a thrombosis, and was out of action for three and a half months.[63]

Meanwhile Dalton was only too well aware of the delicacy of the national finances, and he tried his hardest to persuade his colleagues, especially those who spent money abroad, to cut their budgets. He had relatively little success, for A. V. Alexander, the Minister of Defence—'Albert Victorious', as Dalton derisively called him—did not favour rapid demobilization; and Bevin, for reasons of foreign policy, was inclined to side with Alexander.[64] The American loan, which was originally intended to last until 1949, began to show signs of running out in 1947, and this became very obvious after the disastrous failure of the experiment in convertibility, which had to be terminated after only five weeks. It was in this situation that Cripps, despairing of the existing system of government, conceived the idea of replacing Attlee as Prime Minister with Bevin, who, he assumed, would at once recognize the economic problems to be faced and would provide strong leadership on the domestic front.

This attempted 'palace revolution' had little chance of success. Dalton was willing to go along with it if Morrison could be persuaded to join in; but Morrison thought that he

[61] J. M. Lee, 'Reviewing the Machinery of Government, 1942-1952' (mimeo, 1977), p. 40; Sir James Meade's diary, p. 92 (27 Jan. 1946), BLPES. Sir James was then Head of the Economic Section.

[62] See files of Lord President's Committee, CAB 132/1 ff.

[63] Donoughue and Jones, *Morrison*, pp. 391-7.

[64] Dalton to Attlee, 20 Jan. 1947, Dalton Papers 9/3/2, BLPES; Dalton, *High Tide and After*, pp. 194-8.

himself was entitled to the succession.[65] Furthermore, Bevin could not be tempted by suggestions that he should take the premiership. Nevertheless Cripps visited Attlee and invited him to give way in favour of Bevin. Fortunately for him, Attlee, who had been the intended victim of so many plots already, took no offence; in fact he recognized that there was a serious economic problem which was not being properly dealt with by the Government. Attlee therefore invited Cripps himself to take the new post of Minister for Economic Affairs, which meant that he took over from Morrison the responsibility for planning production. This could be done without too much embarrassment because Greenwood, who as Lord Privy Seal had had general oversight of the social services, had lately retired from the Government and Morrison could take over his committees.[66] There was also to be an Economic Policy Committee to consist of the 'Big Five' leaders of the Government—Attlee, Morrison, Bevin, Dalton, and Cripps —together with (presumably because of his personal loyalty to Attlee) Addison, who was leader of the House of Lords. The Committee's brief was 'to exercise a general oversight over the work of economic planning in relation to both external and internal economic questions'.[67] Cripps was succeeded at the Board of Trade by the young Harold Wilson, previously his Secretary for Overseas Trade. But Cripps had only been in his new office for six weeks when Dalton, before presenting an autumn budget to the Commons, outlined his proposals a few minutes in advance to a journalist who promptly rushed them into print.[68] The indiscretion obliged Dalton to resign his office, and this enabled Cripps to become Chancellor as well, and so the danger of a clash between the Treasury and a new Economic Affairs department was eliminated.

'Economic planning' in practice meant no more than maintaining rationing of food and raw materials, allocating licences, and stimulating production, especially for the dollar markets. Cripps himself set an example of 'austerity' which the country

[65] See above, n. 15.
[66] Morrison to Attlee, 19 Sept. 1947 and Attlee to Morrison, 23 Sept. 1947, Morrison Papers, Nuffield College (by courtesy of Sir Norman Chester).
[67] Economic Policy Committee, 1st meeting, 9 Oct. 1947, CAB 134/215.
[68] Dalton, *High Tide and After*, pp. 276–86.

recognized as highly principled, if severe. The unions were somewhat restive at the reintroduction of the direction of labour and the imposition of a virtual standstill upon wages, and when the Government's White Paper on 'Personal Incomes, Costs and Prices' was published in February 1948, a special Committee of the TUC General Council met Attlee, Cripps, and other ministers to ensure that measures were taken to restrict prices and profits as well as wages.[69] But even so, the TUC accepted the White Paper only on the basis that 'the system of collective bargaining and free negotiation' was retained 'unimpaired' and that existing wage differentials were respected.[70] No wonder, therefore, that Cripps complained a few months later that 'Labour is still moving far too slowly into the under-manned industries. The attractions of the home market are still diminishing the pressure on manufacturers to export.'[71]

The gloom of Crippsian austerity, such as it was, was lightened by the promise of the Marshall Plan. This fresh initiative, tentatively offered in June 1947 by General Marshall, Truman's new Secretary of State, was eagerly grasped by Bevin as a means of putting Europe back on her feet again with the aid of American dollars. Bevin at once proposed an international conference of European Powers, to meet in Paris and to devise a plan for the implementation of the proposal. The Soviet Union decided not to participate, and persuaded the Eastern European countries under its aegis not to do so either. Although this confirmed the division of Europe between West and East, it also made it easier for Congress to be persuaded to vote the necessary funds for the scheme to be implemented in 1948. The West/East conflict was sharpened by the revival of the Communist International in the form of the 'Cominform', by the doctrine of the 'two camps' into which the world was divided (i.e. 'peace-loving' and 'imperialist'), and then early in 1948 by the consolidation of Communist control in the one Eastern European country which had so far partially resisted it, Czechoslovakia. The attempt to squeeze the Western Powers out of Berlin by

[69] *The Times*, 12 and 19 Feb. 1948.
[70] *TUC Report*, 1948, p. 290.
[71] Cripps, press conference, *Daily Telegraph*, 15 July 1948.

a land blockade, which precipitated the Berlin air-lift, was counter-productive for the Soviet Union because it led to a build-up of Western air power and to the return of American bombers to British bases.

All these events weakened the critics of Bevin's policy within the Parliamentary Labour party. In the spring of 1947 Crossman and other colleagues had published a pamphlet called *Keep Left*, arguing the case for rejecting any alignment with the United States against the Soviet Union. In another pamphlet, *Keeping Left*, which came out just at the time of the 1950 general election, they acknowledged that the pamphlet had been 'out-dated' within a few weeks owing to Marshall's Harvard speech and the Soviet refusal to take part in the Marshall Plan. The later pamphlet declared that the government 'was right to resist the Russian efforts, through the Cominform, to sabotage Western recovery; it was right to resist the Berlin blockade; and finally, it was right to accept the division of Germany as a *fait accompli* and take part in setting up the West German Government'.[72]

This reflected the views of the more left-wing members of the Cabinet themselves: it was known that Aneurin Bevan had been an advocate of sending an armoured column through on the autobahn from West Germany to 'relieve' Berlin;[73] but this drastic proposal was more than the Western governments, on the advice of their Chiefs of Staff, were prepared to attempt. Fortunately, the Berlin air-lift proved successful; it led to a Russian climb-down and withdrawal of the blockade in the spring of 1949. But in the meantime the Western nations had been driven together into a new defensive alliance known as the North Atlantic Treaty. Even this was accepted by the authors of *Keeping Left*: 'By committing America to the defence of Europe, the Atlantic Pact diminishes the risk of military aggression.'[74]

It now became possible for the National Executive, loyal as it was to the Government in this period, to isolate the few Labour MPs whose speeches and actions indicated that they remained sympathetic to the Communist party, and to expel

---

[72] R. H. Crossman *et al., Keeping Left*, London, 1950, pp. 18 f.
[73] Cabinet Meeting, 26 July 1948, CAB 128/13/59; M. Foot, *Aneurin Bevan*, vol. ii, London, 1973, p. 230.   [74] Crossman *et al., Keeping Left*, p. 19.

them one by one. In all, four MPs were deprived of party membership for left-wing deviation, and one—an opponent of steel nationalization—for similar offences on the right of the party.[75] It was to be a feature of the 1950 general election that none of them was able to retain sufficient support to alter the result in his constituency, all being successfully opposed by newly adopted loyalists. *Tribune*, which had been the weekly organ of the left in the 1930s, was now so short of money that it sought and obtained a subsidy from the party chest—a factor which could not but effect the vigour of its criticism of government policy.[76]

The weak link in the Labour party's resistance to Communism was in the trade unions. Some unions, such as the Welsh and Scottish Miners and the Electricians, appeared to be irrevocably under Communist control; but in the Engineers —a large union and one with a constitution almost as elaborate as that of the United States of America—the conflict was being constantly waged in ballots for union posts. 'Private and confidential' instructions went out from Morgan Phillips, the Party secretary, to his regional organizers to secure support for the more 'moderate' candidates at such elections.[77] These efforts, combined with the loyalty that Attlee and Bevin could command among the trade-union hierarchy, ensured that the Communist party was held at arm's length at the conferences of both the TUC and the Labour party.

VII

It was the task of the National Executive to prepare a programme for the next election. Morrison was still chairman of its Policy Sub-Committee; for research assistance he had to use, not his own civil servants, but the small research department at Transport House headed by Michael Young, who with precocious ability had headed during the war the independent research body called Political and Economic Planning. But Young's qualities could not make up for the absence of

[75] H. G. Nicholas, *British General Election of 1950*, London, 1951, pp. 251 f.

[76] NEC Minutes 27 Oct. 1948 (s.v. 'Policy and Publicity'); and 25 Jan. 1950 (s.v. 'Finance and General Purposes').

[77] See, e.g. M. Phillips to J. W. Raisin (organizer, London District) 24 May 1948, M. Phillips Papers, Box XIV, Labour Party Library.

coherent thought on the part of the political leaders. The Policy Sub-Committee's draft manifesto, *Labour Believes in Britain*, contained a curious mixture of industries or firms which on one ground or another were proposed for nationalization, for no other real reason than to demonstrate that the party had not lost its faith in public ownership. Industrial assurance, oil refining, Imperial Chemicals Ltd., ship-building, sugar, meat wholesaling, water supply, and cement were all included. This list was submitted to a private conference of ministers and members of the Executive at Shanklin, on the Isle of Wight, in February 1949. Not many trade-union leaders were at the meeting, but those directly concerned were consulted in advance: their views tended to be rather mixed. Co-operative leaders were also asked to comment, and they were distinctly hostile wherever the interests of their own movement came under threat.[78]

To add to the lukewarm character of the occasion, the very pioneer of the public corporation, Herbert Morrison himself, was now in favour of slowing down the process of nationalization and of consolidating existing publicly owned bodies. With his keen political sense, he thought that it was now necessary to appeal to Liberal voters and to those of the middle class who had been alienated by aspects of Labour policy since 1945. 'To scorn this problem, or to adopt a contemptuous attitude to this section of the community and to show lack of sympathy with their real difficulties, is suicidal.'[79] Morrison was hinting at the folly of the comments of his two colleagues, Shinwell and Bevan, the former of whom had said that he did not care 'two hoots' for anyone except 'the workers' and the latter had described 'the Tories' as 'lower than vermin'.[80] Both these comments had probably helped to strengthen Conservative party recruitment.

Although at Shanklin the left, including Bevan and Michael Foot, defended the idea of pressing on with nationalization,

[78] NEC Minutes 23 Feb. 1949. On co-op views, see 'Joint Meeting with Co-operative Representatives, 16 March 1949', NEC Minutes 23 Mar. 1949. On trade-union views, see M. Phillips Papers, Shanklin Box, esp. RD 232 ('Sugar Industry') and RD 270 ('Industrial Assurance').

[79] Morrison, 'Some Considerations as to the next General Election', RD 173, M. Phillips Papers, Shanklin Box.

[80] *The Times*, 26 May 1947 (Shinwell); and 5 July 1948 (Bevan).

and although no decisions were made at the meeting, the effect was to limit still further the list of proposals. In the draft chemicals and ship-building were dropped, and industrial assurance was not to be 'nationalized' but 'mutualized', which meant that the companies were to continue in existence but to be owned by their policy-holders. As the Nuffield General Election survey for 1950 justly commented, nationalization was 'played down' by Labour spokesmen. What Richard Crossman was to call the 'battering-ram of change'—that is to say, the policy of a radical party—was very much weaker than it had been five years earlier.[81]

The results of the election also showed that the electorate had lost much of its enthusiasm for a Labour government: the party stayed in power, but with a majority in the Commons of only five seats. The 'tidal wave' of 1945 (Morgan Phillips's phrase) had passed;[82] and it was to the party's credit that it polled so well when so many influences were against it. One was the redistribution of constituencies, which alone cost the party twenty-five seats, or fifty of its majority.[83] Another disadvantage was the devaluation of sterling as recently as the autumn of 1949: it was this factor that made Morrison think that the dissolution should be delayed, but Cripps was afraid of another sterling crisis in the spring.[84] A further disadvantage was, of course, the continuation of rationing and shortages, albeit eased to some degree by assistance from the United States under the Marshall Plan. On the credit side for Labour, there was the creation of the 'welfare state'—a term only just coming into circulation in the election year—and the maintenance of full employment, a boon particularly appreciated by the manual workers and their families. So although Labour polled numerically as well as in 1945, the Conservatives secured a greater accession of strength, some of it deriving from greatly improved organization. Dalton thought that a small majority was the 'worst possible situation . . . office without authority or power'.[85] A fresh

[81] Nicholas, *1950 Election*, p. 81; R. H. S. Crossman, *Inside View*, London, 1972, p. 89.

[82] NEC Minutes 24 Oct. 1945 (s.v. M. Phillips, 'Report on Party Development'). [83] Nicholas, *1950 Election*, p. 4.

[84] Dalton, unpublished diary, 7 Dec. 1949.

[85] Dalton, unpublished diary, 26 Feb. 1950.

government, such as that of 1964, might have rejoiced in the limited opportunity thus afforded; but many of the Labour leaders of 1950 had been continuously in office since 1940; and even the back-benchers who had survived the election, being mostly the members for the safer seats, were older than the Conservatives and so less able to face the test of prolonged hours of attendance in the Chamber imposed upon them by an Opposition ever on the alert for an opportunity to defeat the Government.[86] It is not surprising that the Cabinet soon abandoned any hope of passing controversial legislation of any kind. By the summer Attlee and his colleagues were waiting for a suitable occasion for a fresh general election.

But in June 1950 there suddenly began the invasion of South Korea by Communist forces from the North. The American reaction was swift, and soon Truman was calling upon all members of the United Nations to assist in the defence of South Korea. Both Government and Opposition, with the lessons of the 1930s in their minds, had no difficulty in agreeing that British troops should be sent to join what was called the 'United Nations command'. The force that was sent was nevertheless a small one, and American stock-piling of raw materials from the sterling area helped to improve the dollar balance, thus enabling Britain to dispense with Marshall Aid in December 1950. But the danger of a European war was considered to be serious; and in consultation with their allies in the North Atlantic Treaty the Government agreed to make a substantial increase in the military budget. Cripps had retired owing to illness in October; and his successor, Hugh Gaitskell, in planning his 1951 budget proposed some economies on the health service, in particular partial payment for false teeth and spectacles. This led to strong objections from Aneurin Bevan, and another threat of resignation. Nevertheless Gaitskell stood firm, and announced the changes. Bevan might have been persuaded to stay if Cripps had not left office owing to illness in the previous October—because he always respected Cripps's judgement— or perhaps even if Attlee had not been ill at the time, leaving Morrison in charge of the Cabinet. The resignation of both Bevan and Harold Wilson took place before the month of

[86] D. E. Butler, *British General Election of 1951*, London, 1952, pp. 13 f., 37.

April 1950 was out. It was a bad month for the Government, for it was also the month of Ernest Bevin's death: he had been succeeded as Foreign Secretary by Herbert Morrison. It was of this period that Dalton later said that the Government was 'suffering from an acute exhaustion of ideas'.[87]

Attlee was convinced that an early general election was desirable in order to escape from the existing political dead-lock. He allowed his concern for the King's health to have an influence here: George VI was to make a trip to Australia in the spring of 1952. 'I do not think it would be fair', Attlee wrote to Morrison, 'to let him go away with the possibility of a political crisis hanging over him. He takes things hard and is apt to worry when he is away.'[88]

Morrison favoured a later date, in the hope that world events would turn in the Government's favour; he was not impressed by Attlee's concern for the King, telling him that 'for the sake of the country and the world, a victory for Labour is of prime importance'.[89] But Dalton, like Attlee, was for an early election, fearing that things might otherwise get worse; and Attlee in fact decided to hold the election in October 1951. In one respect, at least, the Labour programme was an improvement: both wings of the party had been able to agree to drop the old so-called 'shopping list' of industries for nationalization, and to substitute for it a phrase about taking over 'concerns which fail the nation'. But what probably proved decisive in the election was an increase in the cost of living, occasioned by the Korean war. There was a swing to the Conservatives of 1.1 per cent;[90] and with the existing slight bias of the electoral map in the Conservative favour, this gave the Conservatives a majority of twenty-six seats over Labour, although Labour secured the higher total vote—in fact the highest vote that any party had yet received in any British election. Attlee resigned forthwith and Chur-chill took office once more.

[87] Dalton, *High Tide and After*, p. 370.
[88] Attlee to Morrison, 27 May 1951, Morrison Papers.
[89] Morrison to Attlee, 6 July 1951, ibid.
[90] Butler, *1951 Election*, p. 242.

VIII

What, in short, was the achievement of the Attlee Government? The enactment of the 1937 programme would seem to have been the most obvious success from the point of view of the Labour party itself. That meant nationalization of the basic industries, though not of iron and steel, which, although formally under public ownership by the autumn of 1951, remained in limbo, for although the companies had been bought out, they had not been reconstructed in any way.[91] But the public ownership of these industries did not mean the positive planning of the economy, although this had been expected a few years earlier to be one of the concomitants of nationalization. In 1944 Attlee wrote to Laski about the Coalition Government's success in promoting 'the whole concept of State planning and the control of the financial machine by the Government and not by the Bank of England and the City'.[92] And similarly the election programme *Let Us Face the Future* spoke of achieving reconstruction by 'drastic policies of replanning and by keeping a firm constructive hand on the whole productive machinery'.[93] However, in accordance with Morrison's concept of the semi-autonomous public corporation, the industries that were nationalized were left with a substantial degree of independence. They were expected to balance their books, 'taking one year with another';[94] the separate power industries and transport industries were left to compete with each other; and only in 1949, when there was concern about the possible need for positive action from the Government in the event of an economic slump, was it realized that existing legislation provided no powers for Governmental instructions to the supposedly publicly owned corporations. The Attorney-General reported that 'the policy of the nationalisation acts does not seem to have been expressed in such a way as to enable the nationalised industries to be used as instruments for promoting economic

[91] Ross, *Nationalisation of Steel*, pp. 146 f.
[92] Attlee to Laski, 1 May 1944, quoted K. Martin, *Harold Laski*, London, 1953, p. 161.
[93] Labour Party, *Let Us Face the Future*, London, 1945, p. 4.
[94] D. N. Chester, *The Nationalisation of British Industry, 1945–51*, London, 1975, p. 562.

results outside their own immediate field'.[95] Nor did nationalization work as well as its supporters had hoped: by late 1948 Herbert Morrison was advocating the idea of a common efficiency unit; and in 1949 the Prime Minister thought that, unless some such machinery were set up, the demand for closer control by Parliament would be difficult to resist.[96]

For the country as a whole, however, the Government's principal achievement was its success in coping with the economic crisis of 1947, both in boosting production to 50 per cent above the pre-war level and in securing a rapid expansion of exports to 67 per cent above pre-war. This was done without sacrificing the wartime achievements of 'fair shares' and 'full employment'.[97] Indeed the wartime controls and rationing were, in this period of Crippsian 'austerity', to some extent strengthened. By 1949 it was recognized inside the Government that there were dangers in their continued retention, as J. M. Fleming of the Cabinet's Economic Section warned Sir Edwin Plowden: 'Apart from the time taken up by both civil servants and the public, and possible threats to respect for the law, controls on production have tended to freeze the pre-war pattern of industry and to check efficient firms at the expense of the inefficient.'[98] Harold Wilson made rather a show of eliminating various types of restriction in 1948–9—this was his so-called 'bonfire of controls'—but there were many of them that had to remain beyond the period of the Labour Government: it was much to the disappointment of Winston Churchill that food rationing persisted in the early 1950s, even though by that time the country was beginning to obtain the benefit of a favourable shift in the terms of trade.

Full employment was the greatest boon that Government was able to confer upon its working-class supporters—and we have seen that this was probably the main reason for its retention of such widespread popularity in working-class constituencies. The policy of full employment, which had been incorporated in a White Paper of 1944, involved the

[95] Chester, *Nationalisation of British Industry*, p. 984.
[96] Ibid., pp. 962, 965.
[97] See the statistics in D. Jay, *Change and Fortune*, London, 1980, p. 211.
[98] Fleming to Plowden, 19 Jan. 1949, Prime Minister's Briefs, CAB 21/2245.

application if necessary of Keynesian techniques of demand management. No such techniques were in fact required during the period 1945–51, as the economy continued to be under full stretch throughout. But fiscal policy differed sharply from the pattern followed after the First World War, when the object had been to restore the pre-war value of sterling, culminating in the return to the Gold Standard in 1925, with severe side effects upon industry and employment.[99] It was true that Britain's foreign trade was even more seriously out of balance in the 1940s than in the early 1920s: but a solution was found, first of all by the dollar loan, and then by the Marshall Plan. It is no doubt true that without this assistance there would have been widespread unemployment owing to the inability of the country to afford to pay for the raw materials required for industry: Sir Stafford Cripps, as Chancellor, admitted in July 1948 that unemployment might have risen to about 1,500,000 'unless we had accepted a very much lower standard of living, too low to allow us to produce efficiently'.[100] Conservative spokesmen made some play of this admission; they pointed out that Britain's welfare state depended upon the fruits of free enterprise in the United States. From another point of view, though, the problem was that Britain had made a much greater proportionate effort during the war than the United States had done. Furthermore, some European countries which secured Marshall Aid still had relatively heavy unemployment, and this was true of the United States itself. At least Britain was the first of the recipient countries to be able to dispense with the assistance at the end of 1950.[101]

The sphere in which Government attracted most opposition from its own supporters was foreign policy. This was largely a product of the popular illusions about the beneficent character of the Soviet regime, which had always been widespread in the labour movement and which, after a setback in 1939–41 (the period of the Nazi–Soviet Pact), was fostered not only by the military achievements of the Red Army but also by the conscious efforts of the Ministry of

[99] On this, see D. E. Moggridge, *The Return to Gold, 1925*, Cambridge, 1969.
[100] Cripps, press conference, 15 July 1948.
[101] Jay, *Change and Fortune*, p. 201.

Information, even though the Minister himself in this period was a Churchillian Conservative.[102] But in 1948, with the Communist coup in Czechoslovakia, the Berlin Airlift, and the beginning of Marshall Aid, the disillusionment of the great bulk of the Labour party's membership was completed; and in 1949 Bevin was able to commit the country to the provisions of the North Atlantic Pact without serious opposition. For the rest, the retreat from Empire was the most important feature of the period, dictated as much by the needs of economy as by party principle. Britain's withdrawal from India, under Attlee's personal supervision, was conducted with dignity; and if dignity was lacking in the case of the withdrawal from Palestine, it is difficult to see how the internal conflict there could have been prevented from emerging. In retrospect the reputation of Ernest Bevin as Foreign Secretary remains as high as does that of Attlee as the first post-war Prime Minister.

[102] I. McLaine, *Ministry of Morale*, London, 1979, pp. 201 ff.

10

The High and Low Politics of Labour: Keir Hardie to Michael Foot

Kenneth O. Morgan

The 'high politics' interpretation of modern British history has usually applied most naturally to the established Gilbertian world of the Conservative and Liberal parties. Maurice Cowling's analysis of the manœuvres that surrounded the passage of the 1867 Reform Act; John Vincent and A. B. Cooke's discussion of the party conflicts during the Irish home rule crisis of 1885-6; above all, Maurice Cowling's account of the response to the growing threat from organized labour manifested both by the Lloyd George coalition and its various Asquithian and Tory die-hard critics in the 1920-2 period, all relate most easily to the rhetoric and conventions of the older parties.[1] In so far as Labour does fit into this pattern, however, it has usually been seen as rapidly accommodating itself to the traditions, even the charades, of the capitalist enemy, down to Jimmy Thomas's dress shirt. Mr. Cowling has stressed the willingness, even the enthusiasm, of Labour politicians such as MacDonald, Thomas, Snowden, and Clynes in the 1922-4 period—a time of extraordinary flux after the downfall of Lloyd George and resultant divisions within both the two older parties—to view politics in the enclosed, parliamentary terms of their opponents.[2] While using 'sob stuff' in their speeches to placate socialist sentimentalists in the constituencies, in practice they connived at the Tories' parliamentary game. They dismissed external demands from 'direct action' militants, ILP Clydesiders, or 'wild men' in general; they emphasized, instead, their own moderation, decency, and loyalty to Crown and constitution.

[1] Maurice Cowling, *1867: Disraeli, Gladstone and the Revolution*, Cambridge, 1967; A. B. Cooke and John Vincent, *The Governing Passion*, Hassocks, 1974; Maurice Cowling, *The Impact of Labour, 1920–1924*, Cambridge, 1971.
[2] Cowling, *Impact of Labour*, pp. 425-7.

Indeed, a general, non-militant tendency amongst academics, both historians and political scientists, has been to underline the similarities between the Labour party, whether in office or in opposition, and the Tory and Liberal enemy. In the Labour party also, the leadership and the parliamentary party has been firmly in control. Grass-roots activists, whether in the annual conference, on the national executive constituency section, or in local branch or divisional pressure upon MPs, have been kept at arms' length and effectively impotent.[3] The pronouncements of Labour leaders, from Keir Hardie in February 1907 to Michael Foot in September 1981, both men of the Labour left, have confirmed a view that emphasizes the primacy of the parliamentary leadership, responding to national rather than party needs, and stresses the basic similarities of Labour to the older parties in practice and policy-making. Philip Snowden in 1923 proclaimed confidently that a future Labour government would 'err rather on the side of conservatism than of "extremism"'.[4]

Indeed, it has been a traditional source of criticism from constituency parties on the Labour left, ranging from the ILP before 1914 to the Labour Co-ordinating Committee in 1980–1, that the parliamentary leadership, whatever its ritual deference to theories of inner party democracy and its token responsiveness to the socialist demands of the rank and file, has in fact pursued a consensual caution that has instinctively sought the middle ground. Labour's policies, in effect, emerged time and again as little different from those of the defenders of capitalism. Herbert Morrison's view of the need for 'consolidation', with the consequent need not to alienate middle-class or professional sympathizers by too extreme or aggressive a policy—a view elaborated in the later 1940s in opposition to Aneurin Bevan's demand for more nationalization—has been writ large over the entire eighty-year history of the Labour party. Labour's leaders, as Tony Benn insisted in the later 1970s, are believed to have constantly preached social revolution, but to have contemplated and achieved

[3] This is argued most effectively in R. T. McKenzie, *British Political Parties* London, 2nd edn., 1963, a book that has significantly little to say about the role of the trade unions.

[4] Philip Snowden, *If Labour Rules*, London, 1923, p. 18. This booklet is a classic statement of the 'high politics' view of Labour in government.

something much less dynamic. Ralph Miliband's account of the evolution of the party down to 1960 sees the socialist promise of a working-class upsurge constantly frustrated by the dogma of parliamentarism.[5]

And yet it is also a part of Labour's tradition—perhaps of its necessary mythology—that it has always been a different kind of party, a crusade, born anew in the working-class struggles of the late Victorian era. Labour partisans have always claimed that it was a democratic party in a unique sense, that policy within the Labour party (and in marked contrast to the Conservatives) has been the result of pressure from below rather than edict from above. In this respect, party leaders from Hardie to Foot have insisted that the primacy given to the annual party conference in the 1918 constitution and embodied down to the Brighton conference of October 1981, was no mere window-dressing. It is not the case, so Labour's leaders have frequently insisted, that we are all high politicians now. On the contrary, the Labour party still remains a people's movement, where pressures and policies evolve from social and economic forces deep within the mines and mills, slums and terrace houses where the movement was cradled, far removed from the narrow, privileged, class-ridden hot-house world of Westminster and Whitehall.

At first sight, this may seem to be simply a conflict of view between the academics—detached, cloistered, committed by instinct and professional habit to exalting traditions of continuity and consensus—and the Labour politicians, forced to mouth a populist rhetoric for reasons of party morale, even one actually divorced from reality. Yet, a survey of the Labour party from its inception in 1900 down to the troubled 1980s may suggest a less clear-cut view. Neither the scholarly critique of the Labour party as simply cast in the 'high politics' mould, nor the politicians' assertion of the imperatives of inner party democracy can be swallowed whole. The Labour party, throughout its history, has been to some degree a differently structured and motivated party, for all the apparent gradualism, or 'opportunism', of such leaders as MacDonald, Attlee, Gaitskell, Wilson, and Callaghan. There has been, over the eighty-year period, a tension (not always

[5] Ralph Miliband, *Parliamentary Socialism*, London, 1961.

creative) between the parliamentary superstructure and the political and industrial pressures boiling up below. The conflict of principle embodied so dramatically in the struggle between Denis Healey and Tony Benn for the deputy-leadership in 1981 is by no means new or unique. It relates to deep stresses latent in the evolution of the party. There is no simple answer to the 'high and low politics' dualism within the Labour party. As will be seen, a bland, generalized verdict on Labour's constitutional normality is often based on the relatively untypical behaviour of the Labour party during the years of the Attlee government in 1945–51, the only time in its history when Labour has functioned effectively and decisively as a party of power. Merely to pose anew the question of the relationship of the labour movement to 'high politics' may take us a little closer to understanding the ambiguities and complexities of the British variant of modern mass industrial politics.

I

In the earliest years of Labour history, from its foundation at the Memorial Hall, Farringdon Street, in February 1900, down to Ramsay MacDonald's acceptance of office as Labour's prime minister just twenty-four years later, the Labour party seemed to be the very apotheosis of 'low politics'. It was the voice of the workers and the underprivileged, the voiceless and the inarticulate, those on the outside looking in. The highly flexible nature of the Labour Representation Committee in 1900—Keir Hardie's famous 'labour alliance' of affiliated political socialists and trade-unionists—emphasized the centrifugal, haphazard nature of the party. Down to 1918, it had no coherent structure, no local party machinery, no clear framework for the formulation of policy. Head Office strove with some effect to impose central control over the selection of candidates and over party finance and propaganda. But the going was always hard, even for a party secretary as dominant as Arthur Henderson after 1911. Labour in the constituencies was a congeries of local representation committees, Labour unions, trades councils, and the like. The annual party conference was a rare, fleeting opportunity to bring these miscel-

laneous *ad hoc* bodies together. The Independent Labour
Party always retained its own organization and ethos. The
fact that such Labour leaders as Hardie, MacDonald, and
Snowden sprang from the ILP gave it a special relationship to
the Labour party as a whole. In its emphasis on localism and
devolution, in its insistence that it had no formal leader and
that its executive was only an 'Administrative Council' (for
all its obvious controlling influence upon the ILP membership from 1896 onwards),[6] the ILP coloured the outlook of
the early Labour party. In addition, the position of the trade
unions was a recipe for fragmentation, sectional and individualistic as most of them were, devoted to their own social and
economic objectives rather than to the primacy of parliamentary politics.

By 1914, it is true, the party had established a kind of
'high politics' commitment to traditional forms of political
activity. MacDonald, in particular, the party's leader from
1911 to 1914, symbolized the old style of parliamentarism
translated into Labour terms. In March 1914 he even came
fairly close to accepting Lloyd George's proposal of the formal coalition between the Labour and Liberal parties.[7] This
owed much to MacDonald's personal skill as a parliamentary
tactician, compared with the previous chairmen of the PLP
since 1906, Hardie, Henderson, and George Barnes. But it
was a difficult feat of political equilibrism for MacDonald,
committed as he also was to the ILP style of socialist activism,
and devoted to upholding Labour's structural and ideological
independence. The upsurge of the 'new unionism' in 1910–
14, especially the kind of quasi-syndicalist 'direct action'
approach associated with bodies such as the Miners' Unofficial Reform Committee in South Wales and the shop stewards
amongst the Engineers, emphasized the challenge to Labour
viewed simply in traditional high politics terms. More omi-
nously, there was the Triple Alliance of miners, railwaymen,
and transport workers in the spring of 1914, an ambiguous
creation but one which challenged the simple view that the

---

[6] Notably in resisting the fusion of the ILP with the Marxist SDF: see Kenneth O. Morgan, *Keir Hardie: Radical and Socialist*, London, 1975, pp. 87–90.
[7] Memorandum in MacDonald Papers (PRO 30/69; 8/1); ILP National Administrative Council minutes (London School of Economics library), 17 Mar. 1914.

Labour movement could be carried along by its parliamentary spokesmen on the traditional road of high politics pursued by the Asquiths and Balfours.

The outbreak of war in 1914 considerably enhanced the rank-and-file pressure within the Labour movement. Indeed, for a time the parliamentary leadership almost disintegrated, since men like MacDonald, Snowden, and Jowett, who were opposed to the war, were isolated outcasts. Henderson was more significant as the architect of the Unions' 'treasury agreement' with the government in March 1915 than as a parliamentary figure. What the war immediately emphasized was the primacy of the trade unions within the Labour movement. Their membership doubled from 4,145,000 in 1914 to 8,334,000 at the start of 1920. Their role within a quasi-corporate war economy was massively reinforced, notably through their control of the labour market and entry into skilled trades. The unions led working-class protests against unpopular government policies such as the 1915 Munitions of War Act, and military conscription in 1916. They were driven into more radical postures by their radical wing, as the shop stewards transformed the outlook of the Engineers, and rank-and-file militants extinguished what was left of the old Lib-Labism of the miners. The War Emergency Workers Committee, on which the unions were dominant, grew steadily in influence to campaign on behalf of 'socialist unity'.[8] The Bolshevik revolution in Russia added powerfully to the leftwards currents sweeping through the Labour movement. Even Henderson noted how they reinforced the 'democratic consciousness' of the masses, while Lloyd George considered him to be infected with 'the revolutionary malaria'. When the Labour party constitution was drawn up in 1917-18, it was the unions who dominated at all levels, as they had dominated the discussions that preceded the Nottingham conference. They controlled the decision-making process of the annual party conference through the block vote. They had controlling influence on (and largely elected) the National Executive, which interpreted the policy resolutions passed by the

[8] Royden Harrison, 'The War Emergency Workers' National Committee, 1914-20', in Asa Briggs and John Saville (eds.), *Essays in Labour History, 1886-1923*, London, 1971, pp. 211-59.

Conference; through Henderson, they directed Head Office. The inclusion of the parliamentary party in the formulation of electoral policy at all came only in a late amendment, inspired in large measure by the belief that it, too, would be union-dominated. Finally, the policy adopted in the party constitution, including a socialist commitment, directly reflected the corporate forms of collectivism now espoused by the unions. The party constitution in 1918 represented a series of defeats for the socialist ILP at the hands of the trade unions. It was a struggle between two visions of 'low politics', the utopian and the industrial. The small body of fifty-seven Labour MPs who survived the holocaust of the 'coupon election' in December 1918 were truly 'handmaids to the party' as H. C. Raikes had once termed the Conservatives' National Union. Within the 'people's party', roles were reversed. Indeed, the fact that forty-nine of these fifty-seven MPs were trade-union nominees (and twenty-five of them miners) underlined the subordinate status accorded to the parliamentary party.

The years that followed the rise and collapse of the Lloyd George peacetime coalition, and Labour's advance to 191 seats in 1923, enabling the party to take office as a minority government in January 1924, strongly emphasized the extramural character of the Labour party in these early years. In major respects, its behaviour was the precise opposite of that postulated in Mr Cowling's model. It is certainly the case, as Ross McKibbin has shown, that the authority of Head Office under Henderson over various organs within the party—the Research Department; the Policy Advisory Committees; the national newspaper, the *Daily Herald*—increased steadily from 1919 onwards.[9] It is also true that the party's parliamentary ineffectiveness was unnaturally exaggerated by the jingoism of the 1918 election, and that in 1922 and 1923 the party's parliamentary representation significantly increased. The return to the House of such major figures as MacDonald, Henderson, and Snowden greatly increased the national impact of the party and assisted in Labour's self-imposed task of supplanting the Liberals as the leading voice of the British

[9] Ross McKibbin, *The Evolution of the Labour Party, 1910–1924*, Oxford, 1975, chs. 7 and 9.

left. Yet, down to 1924 Labour was still in essence Hardie's 'Labour alliance', with power diffused through a variety of institutions, with the ILP, especially in Glasgow, constantly emphasizing the impact on policy of constituency activists, and above all with the trade unions still only partly reconciled to political action. The Miners' Federation's handling of the problems of the coal industry from 1918 to 'Black Friday' in April 1921 was totally indifferent to political considerations. Not only spokesmen of the industrial left, such as A. J. Cook amongst the miners, or militants such as Purcell, Hicks, or Alonso Swales, but even such mainstream figures as Ernest Bevin within the newly-formed Transport and General Workers or Herbert Smith of the Miners, saw the unions as detached from the political wing of the party. Labour was still in its pressure-group, defensive phase, with its policy-making processes still obscure. Churchill in a famous jibe in 1920 had described Labour as 'unfit to govern'.[10] Whatever his rhetorical excesses as he moved from Lloyd George Liberalism to 'constitutionalist' anti-Bolshevism, his view that the Labour coalition was differently constructed from the other parties was basically correct.

II

A new phase was launched by MacDonald's taking office as Labour's first prime minister in January 1924. The short-lived first Labour government that ensued seems to provide unassailable evidence of Labour as wedded to the 'high politics' approach. To the fury of the left, MacDonald took office without consulting the party nationally. He selected his Cabinet—which included Liberals like Haldane and even recent Tories like Chelmsford and Parmoor—entirely on his own initiative, as Liberal and Conservative party leaders had done in the past.[11] Throughout the ten months of Labour government, the influence of the constituencies, conference, and unions upon the thinking and policy of the government

---

[10] Speech at Dundee: *The Times*, 14 Feb. 1920.

[11] David Marquand, *Ramsay MacDonald*, London, 1977, pp. 299 ff. 'It was taken for granted that MacDonald . . . would enjoy as much freedom in appointing the rest of his government as his predecessors had done.'

was negligible. The new Executive Committee of the PLP was very far from being a left-wing 'Junta'. In foreign affairs above all, MacDonald assumed authoritative command in his handling of disarmament, reparations, and diplomatic relations with the Soviet Union. Not merely did the left in the constituencies bring little influence to bear. Even the Union of Democratic Control, which prided itself on voicing the international idealism of the left after the 'betrayals' of Versailles and other peace treaties, was largely impotent; its main propagandist, E. D. Morel, died a disappointed man.[12] In domestic policy, the party's commitment to a capital levy— the one remotely Socialist element in the manifesto—was calmly dropped by MacDonald during the debate on the King's Speech. Nothing resembling nationalization was advocated for any industry or public utility. Even a rare left-wing minister like John Wheatley, the Minister of Health, pursued a policy on housing and the poor law far removed from the expectations of the left.[13]

But the Government soon fell and did so in the chaotic circumstances of the Campbell case fiasco, followed by the Zinoviev letter affair, which posed serious questions about MacDonald's traditional and high-handed methods of leadership. Moreover, the politics of 1924 were soon swept away by the recurrent troubles of the coal-mining industry, with the collapse of the export trade, the eventual abandonment of the government subsidy and a massive programme of wage cuts leading to a national miners' lock-out and to the General Strike of May 1926. The events of 1926, however unsuccessful the general strike itself, served to re-emphasize the distinction between the Labour party and the other parties. MacDonald was little more than an outside observer or go-between. Further, the collapse of the general strike, and the national miners' strike that dragged on for some months afterwards, did not necessarily persuade the unions of the folly of elevating industrial action above political. It pointed rather to the need for a more sophisticated strategy and for a far stronger organization within a workforce ravaged by mass

[12] Keith Robbins, *The Abolition of War*, Cardiff, 1976, p. 202.
[13] Cf. J. S. Rowett, 'The Labour Party and Local Government: Theory and Practice, 1918–39' (unpublished Oxford University D.Phil. thesis, 1979), ch. IV.

unemployment in the staple industries. It was poverty, industrial defeat, and declining membership and funds that forced the unions into a more quiescent role in the later twenties, not the conviction that their view of the relationship to the political wing of the Labour movement required a reinterpretation. Ernest Bevin's outlook was industrial rather than orientated towards parliamentarism.

MacDonald's second government of June 1929 to August 1931, even more than his first, illustrated his traditional, authoritarian style of leadership. Yet, even more cataclysmically than the first Labour administration, it fell amidst clear evidence that extra-parliamentary pressure within the party could be decisive in a crisis in a way inconceivable for either the Conservative or Liberal parties. MacDonald's early months as premier set the tone, with policy moulded in traditional terms. Snowden embodied the old dominance of the Treasury over domestic policy. Henderson's conduct of the Foreign Office did not differ greatly in method from that of his predecessor, Austen Chamberlain, though his policies, notably on disarmament and Anglo-French relations, were certainly distinctive. Other ministers such as Thomas, Clynes, or Margaret Bondfield were largely in the hands of the civil servants. The government had been constructed so as largely to exclude the left. The one significant rebel, Sir Oswald Mosley, resigned in dramatic fashion in June 1930 in protest over the government's failure to accept his proposals on unemployment and monetary policy. But other potentially rebellious ministers, Tom Johnston and George Lansbury, also associated with unemployment policies, did not join him. MacDonald was able to dominate the party conference in 1930 as usual. Otherwise, there seemed to be few internal constraints upon the Labour government. Back-bench rebellions were rare and ineffective. The ILP was now lapsing into impotence, and indeed in 1932 was finally to disaffiliate from the Labour party, leaving only a small rump of Clydeside MPs as a remnant of its former glory. The trade unions found themselves excluded from key decisions upon social and economic policy, including the decision to set up a Royal Commission on Unemployment Insurance in early 1931. Even a trade-unionist like Vernon Hartshorn, now a member of the

Cabinet, condemned TUC suggestions that they should help shape government policy.[14] He asked Citrine rhetorically: 'As a trade union leader, what notice do you expect from the government?' MacDonald's second government, like his first, was apparently the apotheosis of high politics.

But the manner of its fall (virtually ignored in R. T. McKenzie's account) is highly instructive. There is no need to recapitulate the well-known details of the financial crisis of July–August 1931, the report of the May Committee, the deep rifts in the Cabinet, and the resignation of the Government of 23 August, to be followed by the unexpected formation of a National government, with MacDonald still premier, the next day. What is clear is that the role of the TUC, isolated though it was from the main deliberations of the Government on economies in social expenditure, was none the less decisive. Arthur Henderson, the key figure, was but one minister who first accepted the principle of a cut even in unemployment benefit in order to protect the pound, but who changed his mind as a result of TUC pressure. Eight of the nine Cabinet Ministers who opposed MacDonald and Snowden over the economies proposed (the ex-Liberal doctor, Addison, was the ninth) were trade-unionists, responding to the call of class and to the inherent pressure that the TUC exercised within the Labour party.[15] If the course of events down to 20 August 1931 suggests how a charismatic leader could steer Labour into the traditional 'high politics' approach, the crucial deployment of power by the unions on 20–3 August underlines how, in a supreme crisis, pressures from outside the charmed circle of Westminster could operate within the Labour party in a different manner from those of its opponents. As a result, whatever their private convictions and, in some cases, their close attachment to MacDonald himself, the overwhelming majority of the Cabinet, even such right-wing figures as Clynes, Morrison, and Alexander, and all save a handful of the parliamentary party, broke with their leadership. Nor did the shattering defeat of the Labour party at the polls in October 1931, with its parliamentary representation

---

[14] Robert Skidelsky, *Politicians and the Slump*, London, 1969, pp. 263–7.
[15] Alan Bullock, *The Life and Times of Ernest Bevin*, vol. 1, London, 1960, pp. 489–91; Marquand, *MacDonald*, pp. 623–6.

reduced from over 280 to a mere 46, lead to any significant change. There were no defections to 'National Labour' after the election, nothing comparable to the drift to the SDP after 1979. Indeed, the relationship between the parliamentary party and grass-roots activists, political and industrial, became far more intimate, reinforced by ties of legend and sentiment, as a result of the shared traumatic experiences of August–October 1931. Since that time, the vision of Labour as high politics under the cloth cap façade has never been the same.

III

For the rest of the thirties, Labour was in opposition. Not until the advent of world war in 1939 did new prospects of power beckon to a party still to some degree reeling from the impact of 1931. By the end of the thirties, under the pragmatic leadership of Attlee, backed up by professional politicians such as Dalton, Morrison, and Greenwood, the parliamentary party appeared to be firmly in command. The left, after some flourishes in the party conferences of 1932–3, gradually subsided. The Socialist League, always a small body in terms of membership, collapsed after the Southport party conference in 1934. Movements for a Popular or Unity Front with the Communists or other anti-government groups always fell through. Sir Stafford Cripps, the tribune of Popular Front coalitions in the mid-thirties, was in early 1939 expelled from the parliamentary party, along with Bevan and Strauss, with barely a murmur. Within the unions, the solidly right-wing domination of the General Council, founded on the axis of Bevin and Citrine, powerfully reinforced the elements upholding the party's official leadership. As Labour refashioned its ideals, embracing a kind of reformist quasi-Keynesian management as the basis of its home policies, and abandoning its old semi-pacifist opposition to armaments, it was the right and its parliamentary spokesmen, rather than the militant left, that played the major part. Compared with the intellectual fertility of the XYZ group and young economists such as Jay, Gaitskell, and Durbin who clustered round Hugh Dalton, the left was relatively barren. The Socialist League petered out, the ILP was impotent and sectarian, while the Popular

Front fiascos discredited left-wing leaders such as Cripps. The new left-wing weekly, *Tribune*, founded in 1937, barely scraped through its early years and owed everything to financial aid from Cripps himself.[16]

For all that, pressure from below upon the party leadership had something to show in this period. The thirties were a period of redefinition in the relations between the left and the Labour party, and the outcome was perhaps less barren than Ben Pimlott's interesting book has argued. The annual party conference underwent a revival in the thirties. This left a permanent imprint upon the party machinery with the creation of the constituency section of the National Executive, elected during a party conference, that was agreed upon in 1937. The first seven elected in 1937 included three left wingers, Cripps, Laski, and D. N. Pritt. A good many of the more radical innovations in policy emanated directly from constituency pressures. In particular, Labour's specific and precise commitment to the nationalization of basic industries and services, spelt out in *For Socialism and Peace* in 1934 and *Labour's Immediate Programme* in 1937, was originated by conference resolutions in the early thirties, following the crisis of 1931. On the social side, the influence of the Socialist Medical Association, led by doctors such as Somerville Hastings, resulted in Labour's programme for health and welfare acquiring a much sharper and more socialist image, notably with the adoption of the idea of a National Health Service as a formal item on the party's programme in 1934.[17] Here, a major feature of Labour's welfare policies, and a clear breach with the old contributory insurance principle, emerged from below. The myriad policy committees that the party spawned in the later thirties afforded new opportunities for activists in the constituencies and intellectuals in mobilized pressure-groups to introduce new radical initiatives. The New Fabian Research Bureau, run by the Coles with Addison as an early chairman, was part of the same process. In fact, the precision of Labour's election programme in 1945, commonly attributed by historians to the experience of the wartime

---

[16] Ben Pimlott, *Labour and the Left in the Thirties*, Cambridge, 1977, *passim*.
[17] Harry Eckstein, *The English Health Service*, Cambridge, Mass., 1959, pp. 106–8. Also see D. Stark Murray, *Why a National Health Service?*, London, 1971.

coalition and the cross-party blueprints published during the war years, probably owes more in reality to the new vitality within the party during the middle and later thirties. Socialist critics after 1945 were disarmed because their programmes had been adopted a decade earlier. If Labour was hardly democratized in its internal processes in the thirties, such opportunities as existed for party members to help remodel party policy were used more vigorously and effectively than ever before.

During the years of the Churchill coalition, following Labour's acceptance of office on 11 May 1940, the party's dual role as both a part of the 'high politics' structure of government and an external agency of pressure and protest survived in full. Indeed, the way by which Attlee and his colleagues entered the Churchill government is highly instructive. The parliamentary leadership based its decision specifically on agreement (by an 18 to 1 vote) by the national executive, a majority of which consisted of trade union members.[18] Thereafter, Labour seemed almost to be serving in government and in opposition at the same time. Attlee, Morrison, Greenwood, Dalton, and Alexander became major figures within the administration. Indeed, Labour largely dominated the Government's domestic programme, especially the Cabinet Reconstruction Committee in 1943–4. Bevin, brought in as Minister of Labour, symbolized the direct involvement of the unions with the management of the war economy. So, to a scarcely lesser degree, did Citrine, the secretary of the TUC general council, who played a vital part in a myriad of bodies concerned with planning, production, investment, and man-power.

Yet the differences between Labour and the other parties were surely heightened rather than obliterated by the events of the war years. More clearly than in the other parties, Labour's party machinery remained actively in being. It was this, far more than the alleged political indoctrination of members of the armed services or the political activism of the unions, that underlay Labour electoral triumph in 1945. The constituency parties remained alive and vigorous between 1940 and 1945, reinforced by a surge of party membership

[18] Labour Party, National Executive Committee minutes, 11–12 May 1940 (Labour Party archives).

amongst those who remained on the home front. The annual party conference attained new heights of influence. In 1942 it was the party conference, reaching its view months before the publication of the Beveridge Report, which committed Labour to a specific centrally financed system of social security, including immediate family allowances. Interestingly, a union potentate like Arthur Deakin of the TGWU was over-borne. The commitment to a national health service, including a state-salaried medical service and the nationalization of hos-pitals—far more radical than the Government's Willink scheme—was confirmed.[19] In 1944, the national executive's wish to modify a resolution on nationalization and economic planning was swept aside by a motion from Ian Mikardo, the prospective parliamentary candidate for Reading, which specified the need for public ownership of the major sources of distribution and exchange.[20] The most precise result of this was the eventual adoption by the Policy committee on 11 April 1945 of the nationalization of iron and steel as items on Labour's programme for the next general election, along with coal, gas, electricity, transport, aviation, the Bank of England, and cable and wireless. This was much to the dis-may of Herbert Morrison, a consistent opponent of steel nationalization, and chairman of the Home Policy committee. In this case, grass-roots pressure forced a radical measure upon the leadership and had it enshrined in the next election manifesto, a manifesto to which party leaders clearly felt themselves bound. Again, the immense accretion of strength for the trade unions was a double-edged weapon for Labour's leadership. It became all the harder to co-ordinate the indus-trial workforce on behalf of a common economic strategy, or to view the Labour party as in some sense a national party transcending class, sectional, and regional divisions. Industrial troubles during the war years were far more widespread than concentration upon a few well-known episodes like the 1942 Betteshanger coal dispute in Kent has suggested.[21]

[19] *Report of the 41st Annual Conference of the Labour Party*, Westminster, 25–8 May 1942, pp. 110 ff.
[20] *Report of the 43rd Annual Conference of the Labour Party*, 11–15 Dec. 1944, pp. 160 ff.
[21] See, for example, Stuart Broomfield, 'The Apprentice Boys' Strike of the Second World War', *Llafur*, 3, No. 2 (Spring 1981), 53–67.

The rising tide of popular enthusiasm and growing party membership stirred the democratic processes within the party anew in the summer of 1945 as the war and the Churchill coalition came to their close. There was no question of the party leadership being permitted to remain within the coalition until the ending of the war with Japan, as Churchill had suggested to Attlee—and as some Labour ministers, including Bevin, secretly preferred. The new mood was clearly indicated at the Labour party conference at the end of May 1945, just before the launching of the formal election campaign. During the campaign, Churchill made much play with the statement by Professor Laski, chairman of the national executive for that year, that Attlee as party leader was subject to the dictates of the party executive, especially in relation to foreign policy, and that he should attend the Potsdam conference basically as an observer only. Attlee brushed Churchill's attacks aside. The Laski demonology could be dismissed as yet another Tory election 'stunt', spiced with anti-Semitism.[22] Certainly, the merits of the case were obscured by Laski's voluble and erratic presentation of his case. Nevertheless, it is clear that Churchill's point had much substance. Under the 1918 party constitution it was indeed the case that policy was formed by the national executive, the interpreter and custodian of resolutions passed at annual conference. This had been shown by the decision to leave the coalition in 1918, to take office in 1924, and to join a coalition in 1940. It had never been the theoretical position that a Labour leader could proceed on his own volition to ignore manifesto pledges or conference policy commitments, without reference to the national executive. There was the appalling historical precedent of Ramsay MacDonald as a warning of what could arise if a leader acted in so high-handed and irresponsible a fashion. Attlee's own writings in the thirties had consistently condemned the precedent of MacDonald and emphasized the internal democratization that uniquely characterized the Labour party.[23] Accountability and democracy were precious

[22] The exchange between Churchill and Attlee is contained in Public Record Office, PREM 4/65/4.

[23] e.g. C. R. Attlee, *The Labour Party in Perspective*, London, 1937, especially ch. 4.

concepts within the world-view of Labour and its leaders. Attlee's reply to Churchill, while no doubt electorally effective and reassuring to lovers of parliamentary tradition and folklore, merely fudged the issue.

IV

The Attlee government of 1945–51 is the paradigm instance of the 'high politics' view of Labour as a political party. Most of the academic analyses focus upon the main features of the period—the total dominance of Attlee, Morrison, Cripps, and other parliamentary leaders; the ineffectiveness of the party conference; the deferential loyalism of the national executive and Head Office; the disciplining of trade-union dissidents with the aid of union general secretaries; the inability of the left to make any consistent impact upon government policy until Aneurin Bevan's unexpected resignation from the government over national health service charges in April 1951. That this was generally the picture cannot reasonably be disputed. The Labour government was a powerful and disciplined one, usually in harmony within itself. Unlike the experiences of MacDonald in 1931, or of Wilson in 1969, the threats it faced were almost entirely external—outside economic or overseas constraints upon its programmes— rather than deriving from internal pressures upon the Government.

On the other hand, it is important to examine precisely why the Attlee government should be so secure and why it should conform so faithfully to the 'high politics' model. If the foundations are examined, it emerges that the Attlee years, impressive and creative in so many ways, are really untypical of the overall history of the Labour party. After 1945, there were several unique factors which imposed a rare unity upon the movement as a whole. The egalitarian climate of opinion was unprecedented. The Cabinet consisted of experienced political figures like Attlee, Dalton, Greenwood, and Morrison, reinforced by the now loyalist and centrist personality of Cripps who had re-emerged from the wilderness after his expulsion from the party in 1939. These men had not only been central figures in the wartime Churchill coalition.

They had also led Labour through the wilderness in the thirties, and had been as vital in the drafting of the Interim Programme of 1937 as in the manifesto, *Let us Face the Future*, in 1945. Ernest Bevin, the dominant Cabinet minister in 1945–50, was even more crucial. Apart from his major role as foreign secretary, he was the unique voice of the unions at the summit of power—masking the fact that other trade-union representatives such as Isaacs, Shinwell, Hall, or Lawson were less influential. Bevin's massive presence ensured a degree of co-ordination between the trade unions and the parliamentary party unique in Labour's history. It made it all the easier to negotiate such difficult passages as the implementation of a wage freeze in 1948, or the acceptance of a huge rearmament programme in 1950. At the other extreme, Aneurin Bevan, the most brilliant and persuasive of the left wing, sat in the Cabinet as Minister of Health, followed by a brief period as Minister of Labour. Quite apart from his central task of launching the National Health Service, he proved to be willing enough to accept the Government's policy of wage restraint at home, and a strongly anti-Communist foreign policy, including alliance with the United States, overseas. With Bevan and Shinwell firmly loyalist within the Cabinet (as also was the former Marxist ideologue, Strachey, now Minister of Food), there was no significant leader for the Labour left either in the constituencies or on the back-benches.

At all levels, the Attlee government firmly maintained its ascendancy. At each stage the movement was impelled, as never before or since, by the unifying memories of the sufferings of the thirties and the new social comradeship forged during a 'people's war', which, unlike its predecessor of 1914–18, was overwhelmingly popular amongst the British working class. In Parliament, there were spasmodic back-bench rebellions, notably over foreign policy and defence. The 'keep left' resolution of December 1946;[24] the revolt against conscription in April–May 1947 which forced A. V. Alexander, the Minister of Defence, to cut the period of national service from eighteen months to twelve, 'solely from

[24] *The Times*, 19–20 Nov. 1946. About 70 Labour MPs abstained in a foreign affairs debate in which Crossman and others attacked the government for 'the drift towards an armed camp' and for its hostility towards the Soviet Union.

political considerations' as Montgomery complained;[25] the row over the dispatch of the Nenni telegram in April 1948[26] —all produced their troubles. But Crossman, Silverman, and other rebels were easily contained by the Government. The expulsion of a small fellow-travelling fringe of MPs headed by Platts-Mills and Zilliacus in 1948–9 was supported by all shades of opinion from Ernest Bevin to the columns of *Tribune*, edited by Jennie Lee and Michael Foot.[27] The dominant figures within the trade-union world, the troika of Arthur Deakin, Will Lawther, and Tom Williamson, all fiercely anti-Communist, were able to draw on vast reserves of loyalty and goodwill in pushing through an acceptance of wage restraint, public investment cuts, or devaluation. They enforced this view on the national executive. In any event, a government so strongly committed to a trade-union-backed policy of nationalization, social welfare, economic planning, and full employment could rely on quite unusual support throughout the movement, not least because, for once, the priorities of a Labour government were crystal-clear and unambiguous.

The party conference was largely quiescent. Bevin's foreign policy aroused some protests for its anti-Soviet tone. Zionists were incensed by his handling of the troubles in Palestine. In 1947 Bevin stormed to the conference to complain of a 'stab in the back' by the Keep Left group while he was representing his country abroad in summit diplomacy. At that same party conference, Aneurin Bevan, the darling of the constituencies, was rebuffed over the issue of tied cottages. A year later at Scarborough, he had to proclaim his independence from party conference resolutions.[28] He managed to get away with this declaration in a manner inconceivable in the 1930s—or the 1970s. In any case, subsequent party conferences in 1948–50 were remarkably docile and easily stage-managed by Herbert Morrison. After the general election of

[25] *The Times*, 2 Apr. 1947; Montgomery to Alexander, 9 Apr. 1947, annexed to Cabinet Conclusions, 3 Apr. 1947 (CAB 128/9).

[26] *The Times*, 21–9 Apr. 1948.

[27] See *Tribune*, 21, 30 Apr. 1948; Labour Party NEC minutes, 27 Apr., 17 May 1949. Bevan and Foot protested mildly over Zilliacus, but only on procedural grounds. Bevan firmly supported his expulsion.

[28] *Report of the 46th Annual Conference of the Labour Party*, Margate, 26–30 May 1947; *Report of the 47th Annual Conference*, Scarborough, 17–21 May 1948, p. 214.

February 1950, the Government's small majority was in itself a guarantee that loyalty and good fellowship would prevail.

For all that, the potential outside pressures were still there, and the unusual and euphoric circumstances of 1945-51 should not obscure the fact. Key aspects of the Government's policy even then owed much to grass-roots pressure, usually in a leftward direction. In the difficult cabinet debates over the nationalization of iron and steel in the summer of 1947, the decisive factor for such ministers as Dalton and Bevan was not so much the positive economic advantages for taking steel into public ownership: these were hard to argue, so thriving did the steel industry now appear to be, even after the hybrid of the Iron and Steel Federation was formed in 1946. A crucial element was always that steel had a symbolic importance. It was regarded by the Labour left as a touchstone of the party's socialist commitment, and its intention of moulding a new social order.[29] Morale, not management; men, not measures: these were the priorities. There were certainly many forces within the party at the local level which could have been far more troublesome. The party archives for 1945-51 contain shoals of protests from party workers against the course of Bevin's foreign policy in Greece, Palestine, Spain, and elsewhere; against the operation of the wage freeze policy and the disciplining of unofficial strikers; the failures to push on with more nationalization schemes in 1948-9, the disciplining of Zilliacus, and so on.[30] Morgan Phillips, the party's resourceful secretary, swept them all aside. Equally, adroit management of the annual party conference by the manœuvres of the party rules committee made these assemblies deceptively harmonious. There were always potential rumblings in the constituency section of the national executive. Michael Foot's presence on the executive in 1948-50, like that of Mikardo in 1950 and Driberg in 1951, heralded a demand for more full-blooded socialist policies, long before the breakthrough of the Bevanite left at Morecambe in 1952.

Above all, it is clear that trade-union acceptance of the government's policies in many industries was skin-deep only,

[29] Cabinet Minutes, 24, 31 July 1947 (PRO, CAB 128/10).
[30] Labour Party Archives, General Secretary's files, GS 13/15-17, GS 14/4-13, GS 17/1, GS 23/7, etc.

and required the maximum of heavy-handed suppression from
Arthur Deakin of the Transport Workers and other union
paternalists. There was an ominous sequence of 'unofficial'
disputes in the London and other docks in 1947, 1948, and
1949, amongst gas workers, London busmen, Smithfield
lorry drivers, and in the power industry amongst electricity
supply workers in 1950-1. The Government's willingness
(shared fully by left-wingers like Bevan and Shinwell) to use
the maximum of coercion under the 1920 Emergency Powers
Act, including royal proclamation, the use of troops, and
even the legal prosecution of Communist agitators supposedly
at the root of these rank-and-file activities, is indicative of
their strength of feeling.[31] In spite of it all, the unofficial
movements continued to mount. In the end, the Government's strategy rested on persuading the unions to accept the
policy of wage restraint reluctantly agreed in early 1948. By
late 1950 it was clear that the unions, notably the railwaymen and electricians, were in revolt. At the TUC of that year,
it emerged that wage-freeze policies no longer had majority
support, and the result was a 9 per cent rise in the weekly
wage rate in 1951 for adult males employed in manufacturing.
By 1951, trade-union disaffection was expressing itself in a
range of protests at the government's economic policies, and
perhaps its foreign and defence policy as well: 'go-slow'
workings, absenteeism, and loss of production in the South
Wales coalfield in 1951 provided one indication.[32] This mood
flowed into local constituency parties as membership soared
ever upwards in the period from 1947 when the repeal of the
Trades Disputes Act, which restored the 'contracting out' by
unionists from the political levy, had its impact. There was
a mounting grass-roots protest now which could not easily be
contained, however feeble, at Westminster. What was needed
was a focus and a leader. The resignation of Aneurin Bevan in

[31] Cabinet Minutes, 14 Sept., 16 Oct. 1950 (CAB 128/18); Cabinet Emergen-
cies Committee (CAB 134/175, 176); files on 1948-9 dock strikes (PREM 8/1081,
1085-6), and industrial disputes, 1950 (PREM 8/1290 and Lab 10/940).
[32] National Coal Board: *Annual Report* and Statement of Accounts for the
Year ended 31st December 1951 (Parl. Papers, 1951-2, VIII, 675). The loss of
production in the South-Western division in 1951 was 276,000 tons, the largest
in any division since nationalization in 1947. Of course, the high and rising
average age of the working miners should also be borne in mind.

April 1951 over the scale of rearmament and health service
charges provided both. But the significance of this event
heavily coloured by personal rivalry between Bevan and the
new Chancellor, Gaitskell, is not to be seen merely in debates
over the finances of the health service, or even perhaps defence postures adopted during the Korean war in response to
American pressure. The roots of Bevanism lay in industrial
and political disaffection mounting up against the Attlee
government from 1947 onwards, though concealed under a
façade of party solidarity elaborately constructed by Morrison, Morgan Phillips, and Arthur Deakin, in their different
fashions.[33] The age-old debate about the relationship between
a gradualist parliamentary leadership and radical activist pressure, between high and low politics, Labour-style, was about
to resume and to take on a more ominous form. We are still
living in the new political world created in April 1951.

V

The turmoil that engulfed the Labour party in the fifties was
a new and powerful commentary on the dissensions and tensions inherent in the structure of the party. For much of the
time, the trade-union hierarchy was able to shore up the
leadership, first of Attlee, then Gaitskell, but it was a pyrrhic
victory. The obvious artifice adopted over the endorsement
of German rearmament in 1954–5 underlined dissatisfaction
with the character of trade-union leadership. The succession
of Frank Cousins to Arthur Deakin as general secretary of the
Transport Workers in 1956 emphasized the new climate
Henceforth, the movement towards the left within the party
rank and file was remorseless. Of course, some of this was
artificial, and owed much to the accident of Cousins's succession as head of the largest trade-union block vote in the
Labour movement. Nor should the effect be exaggerated
Cousins's prestige was dented by an unsuccessful strike by
London busmen in 1958. In addition, between 1955 and
1959, Gaitskell was able to reaffirm the primacy and the
autonomy of the parliamentary party. He was much assisted

[33] See Mark Jenkins, *Bevanism: Labour's High Tide*, London, 1979, for an
interesting discussion of this theme.

by the apparent reconciliation he underwent with Bevan in
1957, and the Welshman's subsequent break with his followers
over defence policy, and elevation first to the role of shadow
foreign affairs spokesman and then deputy-leader of the party.

Nevertheless, there is a clear continuity between the mass
trade-union support for the Bevanites in the early fifties, and
the growing pressures against the domestic and international
policies of the leadership towards the end of that troubled
decade. After Labour's electoral defeat, the third in a row, in
1959, Gaitskell discovered that the limits to a party's leader's
power were clearly demarcated. With open revolt in the constituencies and the Young Socialists, and widespread hostility
at the Blackpool party conference and within the major
unions, he had no hope of enforcing the remodelling of the
1918 party constitution that he had sought, including the
abolition of Clause IV and the party's historic commitment
to socialism. In 1960, the defeat of the party leadership over
unilateral nuclear disarmament—emotional, parochial, and
muddled though the debate was—underlined the way in
which a Labour leader could be routed by external pressures
within his party in a manner inconceivable for a Conservative
leader, save only in the very special circumstances of October
1922. Crossman's rebuttal of Gaitskell's naïve view that 'Historically, in our Party, the leadership has always been in
Parliament', was proved to be correct.[34] The narrow victory
that Gaitskell gained over the CND and unilateralist wing of
the party at the 1961 conference should not mask the em-
phatic nature of his defeat in 1960.

Indeed, the victory of the Gaitskellite right in 1961 owed
much, not to the power of the party leader or the ascendancy
of the parliamentary wing, but rather to right-wing activists
enlisted in the Campaign for Democratic Socialism, under the
intellectual inspiration of Anthony Crosland and the tactical
direction of its chairman, William Rodgers. It adopted the
same techniques of grass-roots entryism and mobilization
traditionally exploited by the left.[35] Union branches, the

[34] Janet Morgan (ed.), *The Backbench Diaries of Richard Crossman*, London,
1981, p. 884, citing entry for 18 Oct. 1960.
[35] See Stephen Haseler, *The Gaitskellites*, London, 1969, ch. 10; information
from the late Rita Hinden.

co-operative movement, the Young Socialists, above all the constituency parties—were successfully penetrated. In 1961, 63 per cent of the constituency party vote was cast in favour of Gaitskell and the official arms policy. The reversal of Labour's posture on defence and nuclear weapons in 1961 was really a testimony to the power of low politics rather than high within the Labour movement. So, too, perhaps was Gaitskell's final endorsement of an opposition to entry into the European Common Market in the 1962 conference. Gaitskell himself, like others on the right, had been wavering. Hampstead pulled him one way, Transport House the other.[36] In the end, as much as his unquestioned emotional commitment to the Commonwealth, it was the realization that, in a centrifugal, disparate party, he would not carry his followers with him if he endorsed the EEC. Even the Gaitskellite Campaign for Democratic Socialism was divided. In the face of the Anti-Common Market Committee, headed by such varied figures as Douglas Jay on the right and Barbara Castle on the left, even Gaitskell could not fight and fight all the time.

The position was papered over when Gaitskell was succeeded as party leader in early 1963 by Harold Wilson who had supposedly left-wing credentials since his resignation from the Attlee government in April 1951. His election, so claimed Michael Foot, showed that 'the incredible had happened' and that the left had won after all.[37] Old Bevanites such as Richard Crossman, Barbara Castle, and George Wigg felt justified in joining Wilson's Cabinet in October 1964, and proved to be vigorous and capable ministers. Mrs Castle's *In Place of Strife* document made her the whipping-girl of the unions. Another minister, a less happy selection, was Frank Cousins of the Transport Workers, also a voice of the rank-and-file left, and now made Minister of Technology. Michael Foot did not join the Government but he re-entered the parliamentary party and began a flirtation with power

[36] Philip Williams, *Hugh Gaitskell*, London 1979. There were, of course, other matters that helped to sway Gaitskell including the terms of entry proposed, his deteriorating relations with Monnet and other spokesmen of the 'Six', and the problem of Commonwealth preferences. But a governing factor was that the 'party should not become divided on this issue', as it had been over unilateralism (Williams, p. 707).

[37] *The Backbench Diaries of Richard Crossman*, p. 973, entry of 8 Feb. 1963.

and official politics that led to his entering the Shadow Cabinet in 1970 and to being elected party leader in November 1979. Ian Mikardo was busy with his Nationalized Industries Committee from 1966 onwards. Poachers everywhere seemed to be turning gamekeeper. The high and the low roads to socialism were merging into a somewhat muddy middle way.

VI

Events since Harold Wilson's taking office in 1964 raise issues that range far beyond this brief survey. The slump in party membership was relentless, furthered by the decline in the economy which cut away employment in staple industries such as coal, steel, and shipbuilding where Labour's strength had traditionally lain. Even amongst working-class electors (especially the low paid), free welfare benefits, nationalization, and high social expenditure proved less attractive. The growing gulf between the political and industrial wings of the movement, heralded by the split over the white paper, *In Place of Strife* in 1969, a gulf confirmed later by the unions' campaign against pay restraint in the winter of 1978-9 which brought down the Callaghan government, was another factor. Leading figures within the trade-union world in the early eighties, men like Len Murray, Moss Evans of the Transport Workers, Arthur Scargill of the Miners, or Clive Jenkins of ASTMS, scarcely thought in political terms at all. The distance between the union leadership and parliamentary party, widening all the time since the disappearance of Deakin and Williamson in the fifties, seemed almost unbridgeable at times. The party secretary in 1972-82, Ron Hayward, unlike Morgan Phillips or Arthur Henderson before him, often identified openly with Bennite dissidents rather than with the leadership. With the Labour movement more incoherent and rootless than ever before in its history, what was required was one powerful symbol to provide charisma and credibility for grass-roots pressure on behalf of greater socialism, resistance to incomes policy, opposition to the Common Market and to nuclear weapons. Such a symbol emerged through the talents, eloquence, and ambitions of Tony Benn (under his previous incarnation of Anthony Wedgwood Benn, a centrist

pro-European technocrat within the Wilson Cabinet). Under
his determined leadership, the left won victory after victory
—over an electoral college to choose the party's leader and
deputy leaders; over the re-selection of candidates (a novel
demand in the 1970s); and soon, it was hoped, over the writing of the party's manifesto.[38] Despite a narrow defeat over
the deputy leadership in October 1981, at the hands of Denis
Healey, the eventual leadership of Benn, or his disciples, over
a vastly changed, truncated, broad-left style of Labour party
remained entirely possible. How significant was the swing to
the right in the NEC elections in the October 1982 party conference remained unclear. It owed everything to the artificial
operations of the trade-union block vote. Constituency parties
throughout England (though much less so in Wales or Scotland) were increasingly falling under left-wing, even Trotsky-
ite, control, as the growth of Militant Tendency, '*l'affaire*
Tatchell' in Bermondsey, and the opinions of grass-roots activists as voiced in the press and at party conferences clearly
indicated.

But Benn's influence and the recent transformation of the
party become intelligible only if viewed against the wider
history of Labour since the foundation years at the start of
the century. It is clear that the parliamentary party, and its
leaders, from Hardie to Foot, wished to pursue a 'high
politics' approach, one which established the primacy and
autonomy of the parliamentary party. They were generally
successful in so doing, especially when MacDonald arrogated
for the chairman of the PLP the title of 'leader' as well in
1922. The classic phase was the Attlee government of 1945-
51, but 'high politics' were predominant also during the
administrations of 1924, 1929-31, and (in its early phase) of
1964-70. In times of opposition, too, such as in 1926-9,
1935-9, or the early fifties, the parliamentary leadership
generally retained command in the face of pressures for a
popular front or other diversions.

Nevertheless, the influence of other sections within the
party—not always in a leftward direction—remained extraordinarily buoyant. At times, as in the TUC opposition to
cuts in social welfare in August 1931 or the CND victory at

[38] See Tony Benn, *Arguments for Democracy*, London, 1981, *passim*.

Scarborough in October 1960, they could overwhelm the
leadership and carry the party with them. After 1970, the
trend appeared permanent and irreversible. Undoubtedly there
is a difference between Labour's national party, political and
industrial, and the genteel grass-roots pressures exerted upon
successive Conservative leaders from Law to Thatcher, or the
formal mechanism of the National Liberal Federation once it
had been captured by the official Gladstonians in 1886 after
its early Chamberlainite phase. The history of the Labour
party is a story throughout the century, even in muffled form
in 1945–51, of tension between a gradualist, moderate parliamentary party and leadership, and political constituency activists and trade-union rank-and-file militants usually attempting
to goad the party in a more explicitly socialist direction. They
have frequently failed, in part because the British working
class has so seldom displayed radical or revolutionary inclinations, and has preferred affluence, employment, home ownership, and a quiet life. At times, trade-union pressure upon the
parliamentary party has served to defeat the left as well, as
the ILP were crushed by the 1918 party constitution. The
tension within the party has always been there and was recognized by leaders from Hardie to Attlee. 'There must be free
play between the sections,' declared Hardie in 1907, 'otherwise they were in for a spill.'[39] Michael Foot expressed an
identical view seventy-five years later. When the priorities
were clear or the economic omens reasonably favourable,
that free play was preserved, but always with difficulty. In
the later 1970s, when Labour's objectives became less distinct,
its morale enfeebled, and the economic pressures overwhelming, the latent stresses over the procedures of policy-
making spread to the new area of the choice of personnel,
with new procedures to try to control MPs through re-selection processes, and attempts to have parliamentary front-
bench spokesmen and their leader made rigidly accountable
to the rank and file in constituency management committees.
Labour, then, fits with difficulty into the 'high politics' pattern. It has always been a coalition, with uncertainty and

[39] *Report of the Seventh Annual Conference of the Labour Party*, Belfast,
1907, pp. 49–50, for Hardie's speech; cf. Michael Foot, *My Kind of Socialism* (reprinted from *The Observer*, Jan. 1982), p. 7.

ambiguity surrounding the ultimate source of power. The populism inherent in the 1918 party constitution has been both an inspiration and a curse. It is democracy rather than socialism that has plagued Labour throughout its singularly unfraternal history. The problem confronting Tony Benn and his generation, as it confronted Keir Hardie and his, seventy years earlier, is whether the imperatives of 'high politics' will, or can, permit democracy in our time.

Notes on Contributors

MICHAEL BENTLEY lectures in history at the University of Sheffield. His book *The Liberal Mind 1914-1929* was published by Cambridge University Press in 1977, and a volume for the Fontana History of England, *Politics Without Democracy 1815-1918*, will appear in 1984.

PETER CLARKE is University Lecturer in History and Fellow of St. John's College, Cambridge. He is author of *Lancashire and the New Liberalism* (Cambridge, 1971) and *Liberals and Social Democrats* (Cambridge, 1978). His current research interest lies in the interface between politics and the history of ideas and he intends to write further on Keynes.

JOSÉ HARRIS is Fellow and Tutor in Modern History, St. Catherine's College, Oxford. She has written *Unemployment and Politics* (Oxford, 1972) and her biography of William Beveridge was published by Oxford University Press in 1977. She is currently preparing a volume for the Pelican Social History of Britain.

BRIAN HARRISON is Fellow and Tutor in Modern History and Politics, Corpus Christi College, Oxford. He is author of *Drink and the Victorians* (1971), *Separate Spheres* (1978), and *Peaceable Kingdom: stability and change in Modern Britain* (Oxford, 1982).

BOYD HILTON is Fellow and Tutor in History, Trinity College, Cambridge and author of *Corn, Cash, Commerce: the economic policies of the Tory governments 1815-30* (Oxford, 1977). He is currently writing *The Age of Atonement: the impact of evangelicalism on social and economic thought, c.1795-1870* and preparing a volume for the New Oxford History of England.

OLIVER MACDONAGH is W. K. Hancock Professor of History in the Institute of Advanced Studies of the Australian

314 Notes on Contributors

National University. His books include *The Pattern of Government Growth 1800–1860* (1961), *Ireland: the Union and its Aftermath* (1968), *Early Victorian Government* (1977), and *The Inspector General: Sir Jeremiah Fitzpatrick* (1981). He is currently preparing a biography of Daniel O'Connell and a study of the novels of Jane Austen.

KENNETH O. MORGAN is Fellow and Praelector, The Queen's College, Oxford. His previous works include *Wales in British Politics* (1963), *The Age of Lloyd George* (1971), *Keir Hardie* (1975), *Consensus and Disunity* (Oxford, 1979), and *Rebirth of a Nation* (Oxford, 1981). He is currently writing a history of the Labour governments of 1945–51 to be published by Oxford University Press in 1984.

HENRY PELLING is a Fellow of St. John's College, Cambridge, and Emeritus Reader in Recent British History. He has written many studies of British and American labour movements and more recently a biography of Sir Winston Churchill. He is at present completing a study of the Attlee governments and contemplating research on Britain and the Marshall Plan.

JOHN STEVENSON is Senior Lecturer in History at the University of Sheffield. His previous books include *Social Conditions in Britain between the Wars* (1977), *Popular Disturbances in England, 1700–1870* (1979), and *British Society 1914–1945* (1983). He is currently writing a study of William Cobbett and preparing a social history of Britain.

D. CAMERON WATT is Stevenson Professor of International History in the University of London. He is the author of *Personalities and Policies* (1965) and *Too Serious a Business* (1975). He is currently working on Anglo-American relations since 1900, a study of the coming of war in 1939, and a history of the organization of British defence since 1945.

Index

The editors have supplied thematic and cross-referenced entries in order to help readers locate material of interest to them. Students wishing to examine the central theme of communication within the political structure are especially directed to entries under 'Cabinet', 'Civil Service', 'Democracy', 'Elections', 'Franchise', 'High Politics', 'House of Commons', 'Ideology', 'Party', 'Policy formation', and 'Rhetoric'.